SECURED
TRANSACTIONS

SECOND EDITION

Frederick M. Hart
Nathalie Martin
University of New Mexico School of Law

The *Emanuel Law Outlines* Series

Wolters Kluwer
Law & Business

AUSTIN   BOSTON   CHICAGO   NEW YORK   THE NETHERLANDS

Aspen Publishers
Attn: Permissions Department
76 Ninth Avenue, 7th Floor
New York, NY 10011-5201

To contact Customer Care, e-mail customer.service@aspenpublishers.com, call 1-800-234-1660, fax 1-800-901-9075, or mail correspondence to:

Aspen Publishers
Attn: Order Department
PO Box 990
Frederick, MD 21705

Printed in the United States of America.

2 3 4 5 6 7 8 9 0

ISBN 978-0-7355-9463-0

Library of Congress Cataloging-in-Publication Data

Hart, Frederick M.
  Secured transactions / Frederick M. Hart, Nathalie Martin. — 2nd ed.
    p. cm. — (The Emanuel law outlines series)
  Includes index.
  ISBN 978-0-7355-9463-0
  1. Security (Law)—United States—Outlines, syllabi, etc. I. Martin, Nathalie, 1961- II. Title.

KF1050.Z9H37 2010
346.7307′4—dc22

                                                                    2010044904

This book is intended as a general review of a legal subject. It is not intended as a source for advice for the solution of legal matters or problems. For advice on legal matters, the reader should consult an attorney.

About Wolters Kluwer Law & Business

Wolters Kluwer Law & Business is a leading provider of research information and workflow solutions in key specialty areas. The strength of the individual brands of Aspen Publishers, CCH, Kluwer Law International and Loislaw are aligned within Wolters Kluwer Law & Business to provide comprehensive, in-depth solutions and expert-authored content for the legal, professional and education markets.

CCH was founded in 1913 and has served more than four generations of business professionals and their clients. The CCH products in the Wolters Kluwer Law & Business group are highly regarded electronic and print resources for legal, securities, antitrust and trade regulation, government contracting, banking, pension, payroll, employment and labor, and healthcare reimbursement and compliance professionals.

Aspen Publishers is a leading information provider for attorneys, business professionals and law students. Written by preeminent authorities, Aspen products offer analytical and practical information in a range of specialty practice areas from securities law and intellectual property to mergers and acquisitions and pension/benefits. Aspen's trusted legal education resources provide professors and students with high-quality, up-to-date and effective resources for successful instruction and study in all areas of the law.

Kluwer Law International supplies the global business community with comprehensive English-language international legal information. Legal practitioners, corporate counsel and business executives around the world rely on the Kluwer Law International journals, loose-leafs, books and electronic products for authoritative information in many areas of international legal practice.

Loislaw is a premier provider of digitized legal content to small law firm practitioners of various specializations. Loislaw provides attorneys with the ability to quickly and efficiently find the necessary legal information they need, when and where they need it, by facilitating access to primary law as well as state-specific law, records, forms and treatises.

Wolters Kluwer Law & Business, a unit of Wolters Kluwer, is headquartered in New York and Riverwoods, Illinois. Wolters Kluwer is a leading multinational publisher and information services company.

Summary of Contents

Table of Contents

CHAPTER 1

INTRODUCTION TO SECURED TRANSACTIONS: COLLECTION OF DEBTS AND LIENS

CHAPTER 2

SCOPE OF ARTICLE 9 AND TYPES OF COLLATERAL

CHAPTER 3

REMEDIES: THE SECURED PARTY'S RIGHTS AGAINST THE DEBTOR

CHAPTER 4

CREATION OF A SECURITY INTEREST

CHAPTER 5

PERFECTION OF SECURITY INTERESTS

CHAPTER 6

PRIORITIES

Chapter 7

SOME BASIC BANKRUPTCY CONCEPTS

Preface

Introduction to Second Edition

Secured Transactions is about a great American tradition, as deeply engrained in our culture as baseball and apple pie: CREDIT. It is vital to the economy of this country. The laws that affect it are as important as the Bill of Rights and the Criminal Code. Everyone borrows money: governments, large corporations like Intel and General Electric, small businesses, and consumers, to name a few.

Shakespeare may say, "Neither a borrower nor a lender be," but think for a moment about what our society would be like if there came a sudden edict prohibiting borrowing. No more new schools, no more new roads, no more new factories. Businesses of all sizes would fail: there would be no commercial growth.

And what about us? With no access to consumer credit, most people would be unable to purchase new cars, build new houses, or enjoy the latest electronic gadget. There would be no credit cards! No student loans!

Why is the ability to secure a debt by pledging personal property important? How is it accomplished? What are its advantages to the creditor who takes the security interest? These are the questions we attempt to answer in the Secured Transactions class. The class involves an in-depth study of Article 9 of the Uniform Commercial Code (UCC).

This is the second edition of this *Emanuel Law Outline*. While not a great deal of law has changed since the first edition, this version is more user-friendly and takes into account many useful comments we have received from students regarding how to improve this *Outline*.

Reading a Statute

Article 9 is a statute. Students frequently believe that statutory courses are more difficult than those in which the law has been developed through cases. Why this is true is not altogether clear. Statutes, including the UCC, give you the rule of law without much effort. Each section is a rule, stripped of the facts of a particular controversy and without the rationalizations of a judge. It organizes the law; it tells you what you have to know in straightforward language. In many ways, reading statutes is a bit like reading poetry. It is often difficult, particularly on first reading, to know what the poet is trying to convey. The language is succinct, and the words subject to different interpretations. Naturally, when you study poetry, you must first read the poem, and then read it again, and again, and again.

Although it is no substitute for reading Article 9, this *Outline* can help you learn to read and interpret statutes. The *Outline* explains—in clear, understandable language—what you need to know about secured transactions to understand the law of secured transactions. We try to define all the pertinent terms and to explain all the applicable rules in the simplest way we can. Throughout, we have included summaries of the law and numerous examples to help make even the most abstract terms and concepts more concrete. We also tell you what we test on, and what we think most professors test on. We hope the examples, Quiz Yourself Questions and Answers, and the practice essay, true/false, and short-answer exams will help you successfully attack any exam question.

The best way to use your *Emanuel Law Outline* is to read the relevant portions of the Capsule Summary first and then read the class assignment in your casebook. This will give you a feel for the concepts and issues you will encounter. Then study portions of the *Outline* that cover the topic of your assignment. This book is not intended to substitute for your statutory or casebook reading, but used as a study guide, it will be a great help as you prepare for class and exams.

Sequence of This *Outline*

As is true in many courses, teachers differ in the order or sequence in which they teach these materials. For this outline, we have adopted the sequence that we use and that is used by many others. However, the order of the chapters may differ from that of your professor. For example, some start with the scope of Article 9. We cover that in Chapter 2. Some professors place default at the end of the course. We cover it in Chapter 3. We believe that you can either follow our approach, or else change the order in which you study using this outline. A Casebook Correlation Chart is provided for those who wish to study chapters in the order of the casebook being used in their class.

A Word of Thanks

Finally, we would like to express our sincere appreciation and thanks to research assistant Leigh Haynes and administrative assistant Sunne Spicer for their invaluable assistance in preparing this book for press. We also would like to thank our indispensable editor, Barbara Lasoff.

Professor Fred Hart
Professor Nathalie Martin
University of New Mexico School of Law
November 2010

Casebook Correlation Chart

(Note: General sections of the outline are omitted for this chart. NC = not directly covered by this casebook. For updates to the correlation chart, visit *www.AspenLaw.com*.)

Emanuel's Secured Transactions Law Outline *(by chapter and section heading)*	LoPucki & Warren: *Secured Credit: A Systems Approach* (6th Ed., 2009)	Picker: *Security Interests in Personal Property: Cases, Problems, and Materials* (4th Ed., 2009)	Warren & Walt: *Secured Transactions in Personal Property* (7th Ed., 2007)	Whaley: *Problems and Materials on Secured Transactions* (8th Ed., 2010)	White: *Secured Transactions: Teaching Materials* (3rd Ed., 2006)
CHAPTER 1 INTRODUCTION TO SECURED TRANSACTIONS: COLLECTION OF DEBTS AND LIENS					
I. Putting Secured Transactions in Context	xxxi-xxxii	1-2, 20-22	2-3, 19-22	1-3	2-3
II. Definitions	21-22	2-4, 22-28, 38	20-22	2-3	NC
III. Collection of Unsecured Debts	3-12, 17-20, 23-26	2-20, 23	3-6	NC	NC
IV. Priority Among Creditors	275-277	27-32	5-9, 117	3	NC
V. Bankruptcy	93-95	38	6	3-5	71-72
VI. A Short History Lesson: Pre-Code Security Devices	NC	20-21, 24-25	18-20	5-13	NC
CHAPTER 2 SCOPE OF ARTICLE 9 AND TYPES OF COLLATERAL					
I. Which Transactions Are Covered by Article 9 and Why Do We Care?	657-660	25-26	8-9, 19-20	15-17	NC
II. Scope of Article 9: What Transactions Are Governed by Article 9's Rules?	28-30, 572-573, 605-614	24-25, 452-477, 497	19-20	17-40	NC
III. Types of Collateral					
CHAPTER 3 REMEDIES: THE SECURED PARTY's RIGHTS AGAINST THE DEBTOR					
I. Introduction	217	358	5-6, 266-268	NC	NC
II. Default	217-221	359-366	248-251	281-292	NC
III. Acceleration	221-226	361	249-250	287	NC
IV. Obtaining Possession of the Collateral	38-57	366-384	269-280	292-337	67-70, 363-392
V. Disposing of the Collateral	78-92	384-399	280-289, 295-296	304-337	68

Emanuel's Secured Transactions Law Outline *(by chapter and section heading)*	LoPucki & Warren: *Secured Credit: A Systems Approach* (6th Ed., 2009)	Picker: *Security Interests in Personal Property: Cases, Problems, and Materials* (4th Ed., 2009)	Warren & Walt: *Secured Transactions in Personal Property* (7th Ed., 2007)	Whaley: *Problems and Materials on Secured Transactions* (8th Ed., 2010)	White: *Secured Transactions: Teaching Materials* (3rd Ed., 2006)
CHAPTER 3 continued					
VI. Application of the Proceeds of the Sale	87, 423-426, 433	384-385	309-310	334-336	3, 68, 184
VII. Secured Party's Right to a Deficiency Judgment: What Happens if the Secured Party Fails to Hold a Commercially Reasonable Sale?	34, 71-73, 80	384, 388, 397	296-302	304-337	68-70
VIII. Calculation and Explanation of Deficiency or Surplus in Consumer Transactions	34, 80-81	384	299	304, 339	NC
IX. Collection When the Collateral Is Accounts, Chattel Paper, or General Intangibles (Including Payment Intangibles) and Deposit Accounts	367-368, 370	477-493	311-321	49-53, 108-109	268-270, 309-332
X. Rights of a Transferee of the Collateral Taking From a Repossession Sale	80	NC	309	158-164	254-270, 358-360
XI. XI. Acceptance of the Collateral in Satisfaction of the Debt	78-79	399-403	305-311	339-341	NC
XII. Right to Redeem the Collateral	71, 226-228	402-403, 472	321-322	337-341	NC
XIII. Debtor's Waiver of Rights	NC	NC	260-266	324	NC
XIV. Debtor's Remedies for a Secured Party's Failure to Fulfill Its Obligations on a Debtor's Default	223-226	399	308-310	325-337	68
XV. Real Estate Foreclosures	34	NC	305-306	38-39	NC
XVI. Bankruptcy and the Automatic Stay	93	526	469-470	237, 304-305	84
CHAPTER 4 CREATION OF A SECURITY INTEREST					
I. Introduction	149-150	39-41	22-23	54, 71-72	2-3
II. Function of a Security Interest	149-150	71-87	5-6	15-17, 41-53	3
III. Methods of Creating a Personal Property Security Interest Under Article 9	150-153	40-47	22-23	53-55, 64-69, 83	2-3
IV. The Security Agreement	134-150	47-71, 89-98	22-44	53-71	4-18
V. Enforceability of a Security Interest: Attachment	131-134	39-98	21-50	71-82	41-43

Emanuel's Secured Transactions Law Outline *(by chapter and section heading)*	LoPucki & Warren: *Secured Credit: A Systems Approach* (6th Ed., 2009)	Picker: *Security Interests in Personal Property: Cases, Problems, and Materials* (4th Ed., 2009)	Warren & Walt: *Secured Transactions in Personal Property* (7th Ed., 2007)	Whaley: *Problems and Materials on Secured Transactions* (8th Ed., 2010)	White: *Secured Transactions: Teaching Materials* (3rd Ed., 2006)
CHAPTER 5 **PERFECTION OF SECURITY INTERESTS**					
I. Introduction	327	99-100	51-53	83	18
II. Methods of Perfection Under Article 9	327	26-28, 100-109	51-52	83	19
III. Perfection by Filing	373-413	27-28, 32-37, 109-156, 202-206, 291-315	53-88	110-113	18-41, 204-229, 271-273, 347-351
IV. Perfection by Secured Party Taking Possession of the Collateral	327-333	157-169	95-99, 542	84-86	NC
V. Automatic Perfection	334-337	157	103-105	86-109	232, 344-347
VI. Perfection by Taking Control	331-333	169-186	100-101	113	NC
VII. Continuous Perfection	379-385	202-206	91	111-112	232-235
VIII. Perfection of Security Interests in Proceeds	165-168	264-283	66-67	261-268	229-235
IX. Perfection of Security Interests in Fixtures	347-356	517-518	445-447	201-216	333-335
X. Perfection of Agricultural Liens	601-603, 610-614	497	118	53	NC
XI. Assignment of Security Interests	NC	181-186	91-92	111	NC
CHAPTER 6 **PRIORITIES**					
I. An Introduction to Priority Problems	433	192-194	117	127	41
II. Priorities Involving Parties Each Claiming a Security Interest in the Collateral: Secured Party Versus Secured Party	433-436	195-223, 237-262	118-119, 126-146	127-155	43-46
III. Priorities Between a Secured Party and a Transferee (or Buyer) from the Debtor	585-600	283-290	148-151	158-188	254-255
IV. Priorities Between a Secured Party and a Lien Creditor	463-473, 605-656	496-515	146-147	200-201, 216-235	NC
V. Future Advances and Priorities	474-476, 480-488	323-326	147-148	235-236	201-204
VI. Fixtures	340-349, 542-544	515-523	447-453	201-216	336-343
VII. Crops	NC	289-290	NC	175-188	266-267
VIII. Accessions and Commingled Goods	NC	NC	NC	216	231
IX. Miscellaneous Priority Rules	NC	NC	181-196	189-190	NC

Capsule Summary

This capsule summary is intended for review at the end of the course. Reading it is not a substitute for mastering the material in the main Outline. Some of the exceptions to general rules are not contained in this summary. Also, these explanations are short. If something is confusing to you or does not make sense, go back and reread the longer Outline.

CHAPTER 1

INTRODUCTION TO SECURED TRANSACTIONS: COLLECTION OF DEBTS AND LIENS

I. PUTTING SECURED TRANSACTIONS IN CONTEXT

A. What's secured transactions all about?: A secured transaction is a transaction involving a security interest in *personal*, as opposed to *real*, property. Secured transactions (or secured credit) is the study of these types of interest, which secure obligations. [1]

Usually the obligation is a promise to pay back a loan. Security interests are property interests in assets of a business or person that are *not real estate*, assets like cars, inventory, equipment, accounts receivable, household goods, etc.

B. A brief introduction: Secured transactions fall within the broad category of debtor-creditor law. The law of secured transactions is contained in Article 9 of the Uniform Commercial Code (UCC), which is a set of uniform laws written to make interstate trade more predictable and the laws more uniform.

Not everyone who finances a business gets a security interest. Nonfinancial institutions, like suppliers of business inventory, e.g., the produce in a grocery store, often lack the leverage to obtain a security interest under Article 9. Thus, many creditors are unsecured rather than secured creditors, meaning that they do not have any security for the obligations owed to them.

Secured creditors have the right to repossess their collateral through self-help repossession. Unsecured creditors do not.

C. Types of secured transactions questions: If you are facing an exam of all or part essay questions, there are two basic types of questions that can be asked: (1) questions involving a dispute between the secured party and the debtor, and (2) questions involving who as among two or more creditors have superior rights to money obtained from the sale of the property in which a security agreement has been given (the collateral).

The first type of question requires knowledge and understanding of Chapters 3 and 4 of this outline. For example, your professor may pose a fact situation that requires you to know whether the secured party has made a peaceful repossession, has given the proper notice before a sale of the property, or whether the secured party has made a commercially reasonable sale. More complicated is the issue of when a secured party is entitled to a deficiency judgment, but these questions tend to be more straightforward, and there are probably fewer of them on law school examinations. Indeed, in some of the casebooks, the rights of the secured party and the debtor are at the end of the book and sometimes not covered in the Secured Transactions class. If you are in one of those courses, you can pretty much ignore this type of question.

The second type of question involves the rights of a secured party against others claiming an interest in the collateral. We call these "priorities" problems. Thus, for example, the conflict may be with another person to whom the debtor has given a security interest, a person who claims a lien through the execution process, or perhaps one who has purchased goods from the debtor not knowing that the debtor has given a security interest on it.

Priorities problems tend to be complicated and demand a knowledge of many parts of Article 9. You have to know whether the secured party has a valid security interest (Chapter 4), the type of collateral (Chapter 2), whether the security interest has been perfected (Chapter 5) and the numerous priorities rules (Chapter 6).

But don't despair. Thousands of others have mastered these materials and done well in examinations. Article 9 is logical, and as you learn more about it you will become more comfortable with it. We will give you approaches to Article 9 questions, and don't hesitate to reread provisions or to make you own "Capsule Summary" or outline.

Although it is important in answering essay questions to know the details of Article 9, it is much more important if you are facing a short-answer examination. You must know the "little rules" because you are likely to face questions requiring you to apply them.

II. DEFINITIONS

A. **Lien:** A *lien* is an interest in property that gives the holder of the lien a right to possession of some of a debtor's property in the event that the debtor fails to perform its obligations, e.g., fails to repay money when it is due. One holding a lien has the further right to sell the property and to use the proceeds of the sale to satisfy all or part of the debt.

A failure to pay is called a *default*. A lien is a limited property interest in that it is a right to possession of the property contingent on default.

Liens are divided into three categories: (1) judicial or execution liens, (2) statutory and common law liens, and (3) consensual liens. [3]

Liens are always *in specific property,* never just existing in the abstract.

1. **Judicial liens:** A judicial lien is one that arises from judicial proceedings, i.e., lawsuits. A judgment is not an order to the defendant to pay; it is simply a recognition by the juridical system that the defendant owes the plaintiff money. The plaintiff must then enforce the judgment by obtaining a writ of execution. [4]

A writ of execution is an order by the court directing the sheriff to seize property of the defendant necessary to satisfy the judgment. The writ of execution gives rise to a lien on the property that the sheriff seizes. The plaintiff will get paid only by executing on the judgment, *unless* the defendant voluntarily pays the judgment.

The mere granting of a judgment by a court does not result in a lien on any of the debtor's property because a judgment is not a lien.

If the creditor is executing on real property, the judgment creditor normally need only docket (file) its judgment in the proper place, usually the county recorder of deeds, to get a lien on the real property.

2. **Statutory and common law liens:** The law, usually by statute but sometimes by court decision, grants to certain creditors a lien in certain property of the debtor. See UCC § 9-333(a). [4]

Most states grant statutory liens to contractors and subcontractors who work on real property, for work and materials used to improve the property. Those who repair cars or other personal property usually are given liens on the car or other property that is improved.

One feature common to many statutory and common law liens on personal property is the requirement that the lienholder have possession of the property. In these instances, the lien is lost if the lienholder gives possession to the debtor or to someone else.

Agricultural liens are treated specially by Article 9. Although they are created by a statute outside of the code, there "perfection" is governed by Article 9 as is the priority they are given vis-à-vis security interests.

3. **Consensual liens—Mortgages and security interests:** A consensual lien arises from the agreement of the owner of property to grant a lien. In real property, one who purchases a house frequently gives a "mortgage" to the person lending the money to enable the buyer to purchase it. The mortgages give the lender a lien on the house. When a consensual lien is given on personal property it is called a "security interest," and Article 9 of the UCC applies to the transaction. UCC § 1-201(a)(35). [5]

B. **General or unsecured creditors:** *General* or *unsecured creditors* are those to whom an obligation is owed but who have no lien on any property of the obligor. UCC § 9-201(a)(13). They have an unsecured claim or debt. [5]

C. **Security interest:** Article 9 of the UCC defines a security interest very broadly to include *every interest* in personal property or fixtures that *secures* payment or performance of an obligation. UCC § 9-201(a)(35). [5]

These include chattel mortgages, trust receipts, conditional sales, and other concepts. Some of these words are relics from pre-Code practice that are still used today but to a lesser extent.

A security interest also includes outright sales of certain kinds of assets, like accounts, chattel paper, payment intangibles, and promissory notes, mostly because it can be hard to tell the difference between a security interest in these things and an outright sale of them.

D. **Security agreement:** A *security agreement* is a contract between a debtor and a secured party that grants or gives the secured party a security interest in certain assets. Security agreements are discussed in Chapter 3. UCC § 9-102(a)(73).

E. **Secured party:** A *secured party* is the lender, seller, or other person who has been given an Article 9 security interest in the collateral. UCC § 9-102(a)(72).

F. **Collateral:** The specific assets in which the secured party holds a security interest are called *collateral*. [6]

G. **Debtors and obligors:** Technically, a "debtor" is a person who has an ownership interest in the collateral, UCC § 9-102(a)(28), and an "obligor" is a person who owes the debt that is secured by the security interest. UCC § 9-102(a)(59). In most cases this is the same person: a retail store that owns inventory borrows money giving back a security interest in the inventory. The retail store is both an obligor and a debtor. [6]

III. COLLECTION OF UNSECURED DEBTS

A. **Obtaining a judgment:** The substantive law courses in law school teach you what law you need to know to prove that a debt or obligation is owed, e.g., to prove a contract right, it is necessary to prove agreement, consideration, and breach. Each of these courses teaches you how to *obtain* a judgment, which is a recognition by the state, through one of its courts, that a debt is owed. These courses do not, however, teach you how to *collect* a judgment. [7]

A judgment is not money, nor does it magically transform itself into money at some certain point in time. Rather, the judgment is a mere piece of paper stating that the defendant is indebted to the plaintiff for a certain amount of money. Sometimes the defendant will send a check to the plaintiff in payment of the judgment, but at other times the plaintiff has to obtain the money by enforcing the judgment.

B. Enforcing a judgment: Judgments are enforced by the execution process. Once a judgment is obtained, the plaintiff becomes a "judgment creditor," and is entitled to a "writ of execution."

    1. Writ of execution: The writ of execution is an order from the court to the sheriff to seize enough property of the defendant to satisfy the judgment. [7]

    2. Levy: In most cases, levy involves asking the sheriff to take possession of (or control over) personal property. When the property is real property, the sheriff will file a notice in the real property records stating that the sheriff has levied on the property. [7]

        When the property is personal property, the sheriff will physically take possession of the property if this is practical. [8]

        If the property is large equipment, the sheriff will tag it with a notice that there has been a levy, and if it is goods in a warehouse, the sheriff may place a lock on the building and post a notice that a levy has been made.

    3. Opportunity to discover assets of the defendant: A judgment creditor may examine the debtor-defendant under oath after the judgment is entered to determine what property the defendant owns. [8]

    4. Sheriff's instructions: Executing creditors must use the discovery they have gained to give detailed instructions to the sheriff about how and where to execute on the available assets. If other creditors are also executing on the same assets, the first to actually levy on the assets, through the sheriff, often gets priority in any proceeds realized on the sale. [9]

    5. Details of the execution process and legal ramifications of timing of execution: Once an unsecured creditor has obtained a judgment, he or she is called a *judgment creditor*. Again, a judgment creditor does not obtain a lien by getting the judgment and is not a secured creditor. Once a judgment creditor has executed on the judgment, then the creditor becomes a secured creditor, albeit an involuntary secured creditor. This means the executing creditor, like a voluntary secured creditor who has been granted an Article 9 security interest, has a property interest in whatever particular property the sheriff has executed on through the writ execution (or levy) process. [9]

    6. Sale of the property: The sheriff will be directed in the instructions to sell the property on which the levy was made. Usually, the sale is by auction, often held on the courthouse steps. The price obtained is unlikely to equal what might be considered the fair market value of the property because there are no warranties of title or quality given by the sheriff, and the title of the purchaser may be subject to encumbrances on the property. If the sale does not bring enough money to satisfy the debt, the judgment creditor may have another writ issued. If the sale brings more money than is necessary to satisfy the judgment, the surplus is given to the debtor/defendant. [9]

7. **Garnishment:** In seeking to satisfy a debt, the judgment creditor has the right to reach intangible property as well as tangible property. The simplest example of intangible property is a bank account, which is essentially a debt owned by the bank to the account holder. Intangible property is normally reached by what is called *garnishment.* The garnishment proceedings involve serving a writ on the bank, which orders the bank to pay the judgment creditor rather than the debtor who has the account. [10]

C. **Enforcement of a secured party's rights:** One of the main purposes of a security interest is to make it easier for a creditor to collect a debt that is secured. Article 9 gives to a secured party the right to avoid the execution process. A secured party may obtain possession of the collateral, i.e., the property in which the debtor has given a security interest, either by taking possession of it peacefully or by obtaining possession by a writ of replevin. UCC § 9-609. [10]

After obtaining possession, the secured creditor may sell the property itself, using the proceeds to satisfy the debt. UCC § 9-610. Thus, collection of a debt by a secured party can be much easier than collection by a general creditor who must invoke the execution process.

D. **State exemption law:** Most states have laws that protect some property from the claims of executing creditors. Exemption laws often prevent executing creditors from obtaining payment from many of the most valuable and easy-to-find assets. [10] The exemption statutes do not protect the debtor's property if a security interest has been given on it.

E. **Sheriff's sale rules:** Before personal property is sold at a sheriff's sale, the sale is advertised. Despite this, these sales often bring very low prices. The debtor himself can bid on the property for cash, as can anyone else who shows up. [11]

Only creditors that have executed on their claims can be paid from the proceeds of the sale. Creditors who have executed are paid in order of their priority, and the rest of any net proceeds are returned to the debtor. This is true even if there are numerous judgment creditors who have not yet completed the execution process. They receive none of the proceeds of the sheriff's sale.

F. **Special rules for involuntary liens on real property:** It is easier for a judgment creditor to obtain a judicial lien on real property as compared to personal property. No writ of execution is needed. All the judgment creditor must do is record his or her judgment in the county recorder of deeds office in which the debtor owns property. This will create a lien on the property that must be satisfied on the sale of the property. [11]

The judgment lien creditor can also force the sale of real property through a sheriff's sale, as is discussed previously for personal property sheriff's sales.

IV. PRIORITY AMONG CREDITORS

To collect money owed a general creditor, the creditor must bring a lawsuit and go through the execution process. Frequently, the debtor will have a number of creditors. Determining the order in which to pay judicial liens from the assets is called determining the creditors' priority. [11]

U.S. law takes the position that priority is given to the creditor who first obtained a lien on an item of the debtor's property.

When the judgment creditor obtains a lien on specific property of the debtor, the judgment creditor's debt will be satisfied first out of that piece of property. If other creditors obtain liens later on the same property, they will share only in any money obtained from the sale that is in excess of the amount necessary to pay the creditor with the first lien.

This priority system, first to get a lien is the first to be paid, gives rise to the second purpose of taking a security interest. Because a security interest is a lien, a creditor can ensure that certain property of the debtor, the property in which the security interest is given, will be available for the satisfaction of the secured party's debt provided the secured party takes the steps necessary to protect its security interest before there is any execution on the property. This explains the importance of getting a security interest in the debtor's property. Obtaining a security interest in some of the debtor's property gives the secured party the right to possession of that property and the right to sell it. Thus, a big advantage to being a secured party should be obvious.

V. BANKRUPTCY

When a debtor files a petition in bankruptcy, the rights of both secured and unsecured creditors are determined by the Bankruptcy Code, a federal statute found in the U.S. Code. [12]

Chapter 7 of the Bankruptcy Code covers liquidation of the debtor's estate, i.e., the trustee collects all of the debtor's nonexempt property, sells it, and distributes the proceeds to creditors. Chapters 11 and 13 of the Bankruptcy Code are quite different. In each, the debtor usually keeps his or her or its property, and pays some claims through a repayment plan over a period of time, with some adjustment of the rights of individual creditors.

In each of the three types of bankruptcy, the Bankruptcy Code provides for a "stay" of all attempts by creditors to collect from the debtor. 11 U.S.C. § 362(a). If a case is in trial, the trial must stop. If a creditor has started the execution process, it must stop. If a secured creditor is attempting to take possession of the collateral, the secured creditor must stop. All collection efforts must cease, and the creditors are forbidden to even send a letter to debtors trying to collect.

Secured creditors fare better in bankruptcy than unsecured creditors.

VI. A SHORT HISTORY LESSON: PRE-CODE SECURITY DEVICES

A. **Article 9's beginning:** Article 9 is part of the UCC, a set of uniform laws drafted by lawyers and academics to make commercial law more uniform around the country and thus to make it easier to do business across state lines. All states have adopted Article 9, generally with few changes.

B. **Old English law on security interests in personal property:** In 1570 England, the "Statute of Elizabeth" made it fraudulent and void for a debtor to grant a lender a security interest in property and then keep possession of the property.

This was thought to mislead the debtor's other creditors into believing that since the debtor was still in possession of the assets, the assets were available to satisfy general unsecured claims (claims for which there was *no* collateral).

C. **Possession of collateral:** Old English law did not preclude security interests in personal property; however, it did require the secured party to take possession of the collateral.

Possession was also called a "pledge" or "hypothecation" and constituted notice to all others that the party in possession had an interest in the assets.

1. **Chattel mortgages:** In the early nineteenth century, creditors' lawyers borrowed from real property mortgage law to create chattel mortgages. These were consensual liens on

personal property. By the 1820s, many states had enacted statutes governing them (Chattel Mortgage Acts), generally requiring filing of the chattel mortgages in a central office. [14]

2. **Conditional sales:** In a conditional sale, the secured party is the seller in the deal and the debtor is the buyer. When the transaction is the sale of goods on an installment payment plan, conditional sales contracts are used.

   The idea was that the seller retained title to the goods until the buyer paid the entire purchase price. Because title had not passed, the seller-creditor was protected from other creditors of buyer who might attempt to obtain a lien on the goods and from those who might purchase the goods from the buyer. [14]

3. **Trust receipts:** This legal fiction was created based on trust law. The idea was that when financing something that turns over, like inventory (think cereal at your grocery store), the lender could retain title to the inventory while the debtor remained in possession of it. The debtor in essence held the collateral in "trust" for the lender. [14]

4. **Field warehousing:** This term describes a process in which working assets like inventory (and sometimes equipment) are left in the debtor's place of business, but the secured party tries to remain in physical possession of it (despite the debtor's ongoing use), by physically segregating the goods from the debtor's other assets.

   The secured party appoints an agent to supervise the separately stored inventory. When an item is sold, the agent releases the goods to the debtor, perhaps in return of an immediate payment of part of the credit. Field warehousing is still used, but is now governed by Article 9.

5. **Assignment of accounts receivable:** Pre-Code, the debtor would often assign outright its accounts receivable (those amounts others owe it for goods or services) to its lender, without telling the account debtors. The creditor would allow the debtor to continue to collect these accounts until there was a default on the loan between the debtor and the creditor. Current Article 9 also governs the assignment of accounts and requires the secured party to file a financing statement to protect itself against subsequent creditors. [15]

D. **This history and Article 9's current notice requirements:** No matter what pre-Code lenders and lawyers did to avoid the filing requirement, it was always re-imposed, for the benefit of those who required notice of the debtor's true financial condition and the status of the debtor's assets (encumbered or not). Article 9's primary theme is notice, which is served by the filing requirement.

CHAPTER 2
SCOPE OF ARTICLE 9 AND TYPES OF COLLATERAL

I. WHICH TRANSACTIONS ARE COVERED BY ARTICLE 9 AND WHY DO WE CARE?

Whenever a transaction is covered by Article 9 of the UCC, the secured party (with the debtor's help) will be required to comply with Article 9. Most of these technical requirements deal with giving notice of the secured party's security interest. [19]

II. SCOPE OF ARTICLE 9: WHAT TRANSACTIONS ARE GOVERNED BY ARTICLE 9'S RULES?

Article 9 covers security interests in personal property, but transactions don't have to be called "security interests" to be covered by Article 9. As with most areas of the law, substance prevails over form so if it looks and acts like a security interest, it is covered by Article 9, regardless of name and purported form. UCC § 9-102(a)(73).

The Article applies to all transactions that create a *security interest* in *personal property*. UCC § 9-109(a). [20] A security interest in *personal property* is defined broadly by the Code to include every "interest in personal property or fixtures that secures payment or performance of an obligation." UCC § 1-201(a)(35).

A *security interest* is an interest in personal property that secures an obligation, giving to the secured party the right to possession of the property if the obligor defaults. Although a security interest can secure any type of obligation, in most cases it secures a debt arising either from a loan of money or from the sale of goods.

Article 9 also governs agricultural liens, consignments, and some security interests created under the Article on Sales, Article 2; the Article on Bank Deposits and Collection, Article 4; and the Article on Letters of Credit, Article 5. In addition, Article 9 governs the *sale* of certain intangibles because the sale of these intangibles raises the same problems as the granting of a security interest in them.

A. **Sales of certain intangibles:** A person who needs money may sell certain types of intangible personal property instead of borrowing money and giving a security interest in them. These transactions are within the scope of Article 9.

Thus, Article 9 applies to the *sale* of accounts, chattel paper, payment intangibles, and promissory notes, but not to the sale of a business's customer lists. [20]

B. **Consignments:** If a retail business wishes to increase the inventory that it has for sale, it may buy new inventory on credit, giving back to the seller a security interest to secure payment of the price. This is clearly a secured transaction under Article 9.

Alternatively, a retailer and a supplier of inventory, a wholesaler or manufacturer, may enter into a "consignment agreement." In a consignment, the agreement between the supplier and the retailer is that title to the new inventory will remain in the supplier and the retailer will act as the supplier's agent for the purpose of selling the goods.

Because a consignment could be used to circumvent Article 9, and because a consignment transaction raises similar problems to those when the transaction is a secured transaction, Article 9 governs consignment transactions. UCC § 9-109(a)(4). [21]. The consignor becomes a "secured party" having an Article 9 security interest in the good; the consignee gets title to the good and becomes a "debtor."

C. **Conditional sales contracts:** When a seller is financing a sale and the buyer is to pay back the loan over a period of time, the transactions can be set up as a sale on credit with the buyer giving a security interest in the goods that are sold to secure the promise to pay.

Another way of designing the transaction is to have the seller retain title to the goods until the final payment is made.

As the intent of the transaction is that the buyer's obligation to pay for the goods is secured by the goods, even though the contract provides that the seller will retain title, the transaction is a secured transaction within Article 9. 11 U.S.C. § 2-102, UCC § 9-109(a)(4). The seller becomes a "secured party" and the buyer becomes a "debtor."

D. Leases of goods: When a person wishes to obtain possession of property that will be used over an extended period of time, such as office equipment or a motor vehicle, the person may buy it or lease it. If the transaction is really a lease (what we call a *true lease*), then Article 9 does not apply. [22]

If the lessee can acquire ownership of the property for a nominal payment at the end of the lease, the transaction is treated as a secured transaction and Article 9 applies.

Whether a lease is a true lease or a disguised security interest actually involves other considerations as well, although what the debtor has to pay at the end of the "lease" is the most important consideration. Section 1-201(37) and the cases interpreting it look at a long list of considerations, which include the following:

- whether the purchase price at the end of the lease is nominal;

- whether the lessee obtains any equity in the property being leased during the leased term;

- whether the lessee bears the risk of loss;

- whether the lessee pays the tax, licensing, and registration fee for the leased property;

- whether the lessor can accelerate payment on default; and

- whether the lease contains a disclaimer of warranties.

E. Agricultural liens: Lessors of farms and sellers of seed and other farm supplies are given liens on crops, animals, and other personal property in many states. These are called agricultural liens and are created not under Article 9 but by other statutes. They are not consensual security interests because they are not voluntarily granted by the debtor. To determine whether they exist and the extent of the lien, it is necessary to consult the statute creating them.

Article 9 governs how the creditor protects the lien against third parties and the priority of agricultural liens when others have rights in the goods in which the lien arises. UCC § 9-109(a)(2). [22]

F. Security interests arising under other Articles of the UCC: Articles 2 (Sales), 4 (Bank Deposits and Collection), and 5 (Letters of Credit) provide for security interests in certain cases. These security interests are within Article 9 to a limited extent. UCC §§ 9-109(a)(5), 9-110.

G. Transactions excluded from Article 9: A number of transactions that could be included within Article 9 have been excluded. For these transactions, one must consult other statutory or case law to determine the rights and obligations of the parties. [23]

1. **Landlords' liens:** Most landlords' liens are created by statute, but in some jurisdictions they come from the common law. However, when the lessor of a farm has a lien on crops or other property of the lessee, the lien is treated as an agricultural lien and is subject to Article 9. UCC § 9-109(d)(1).

2. **Real property transactions:** Most real estate transactions are excluded from Article 9. A mortgage given on real property is outside the scope of the Article. However, a security interest in rights that a mortgagee has under a mortgage is subject to the Article. UCC § 9-109(d)(11).

   Additionally, fixtures, which are items of personal property attached to real property, are governed by Article 9. UCC § 9-109(d)(3).

3. **Liens for services:** State statutory law frequently provides that those who supply certain services can obtain a lien for the value of those services if they are not paid for. For example, contractors and subcontractors are usually given a lien on the building being constructed or improved, and those who repair automobiles, jewelry, and other items of personal property often have a lien on the goods in the amount of the repair bill. [23]

Article 9 does not govern the creation of these liens, but it does provide priorities rules when these certain types of lienholders and a secured party claim an interest in the goods. See UCC § 9-333.

4. **Assignment of wages:** Assignments of claims for wages, salary, or other employee compensation, such as bonuses, are not within Article 9.

5. **Some sales and assignments of intangible property:** Although Article 9 governs the sale or assignment of intangible property, as well as the creation of security interests in them, some transactions involving intangible property are excluded from Article 9. Sales of accounts, chattel paper, payment intangibles, and promissory notes *in connection with the sale of a business* are not covered, UCC § 9-109(d)(4), and outright assignments of these types of collateral for the purpose of collection are also excluded. UCC § 9-109(d)(5).

When a contract is assigned and the assignee undertakes performance of the assignor's duties under the contract, the transaction is not covered under Article 9. UCC § 9-109(d)(6). Article 9 also does not apply to the assignment of a single account in satisfaction of a debt. UCC § 9-109(d)(7).

6. **Tort claims:** Claims arising from a tort are generally not within Article 9, except that commercial torts, such as claims for interference with contractual relations, are covered by the Article when a security interest is given in them. UCC § 9-109(d)(12).

7. **Insurance claims:** The assignment of claims against an insurance company is not within Article 9, except for claims based on health-care insurance by or to a health-care provider, which *are* within the Article. UCC § 9-109(d)(8).

8. **Rights of set-off:** If two persons each owe one another money, the law sometimes allows them to set off their mutual debts against each other. For example, a bank that lent money to the debtor might be able to set off that debt against the debtor's checking account. With two limited exceptions, rights to set-offs are not covered by Article 9. UCC § 9-109(d)(10).

III. TYPES OF COLLATERAL

Collateral generally falls into one of two categories: *goods* or *intangible collateral*.

A. **Goods:** Goods are all things movable, including such tangible property as automobiles, tables, televisions, etc. UCC § 9-102(a)(44). [26]

1. **Consumer goods:** Consumer goods are goods that are either used or bought for use primarily for personal, family, or household purposes. UCC § 9-102(a)(23). This category includes furniture in one's house, automobiles used for pleasure or family transportation, including driving to and from work, watches and other jewelry, etc.

2. **Equipment:** The definition of equipment is goods other than consumer goods, inventory, or farm products. UCC § 9-102(a)(33). Thus it is the catchall category, and goods are equipment if they do not fit into any of the other types. In the vast number of cases, equipment is goods used in a business that are not normally sold or consumed by the business. For example, an automobile owned by a business and used by a salesperson would be equipment as would be the business's trucks, cash registers, tools, bulldozers, cranes, etc.

3. **Inventory:** Basically, inventory is goods held for sale (or short-term use) by a business. UCC § 9-102(a)(48). The refrigerators, dishwashers, trash compactors, etc. that an appliance store has for sale are included. Inventory also includes, however, consumables used by a business (other than a farming business), such as the copier paper held by a lawyer, toilet paper in the bathroom of a car dealership, and raw materials held by a manufacturer. Inventory also includes property held for lease, such as the automobiles owned by a car rental company.

4. **Farm products:** Farm products are goods unique to farming operations. Businesses that are not involved in farming will not have farm products. Farm products include:

   • crops, whether they have grown, are growing, or are to be grown, including crops grown on trees, vines, and bushes;

   • fish that are grown in a fish-farming business;

   • livestock, whether born or unborn;

   • supplies used in farming operations, such as feed or seed; and

   • products of crops or livestock so long as they are in an unmanufactured state.

5. **Fixtures:** Fixtures are in that never-never land between personal property and real property. They are personal property that has been affixed to a building so that a real property interest exists in them. UCC § 9-102(a)(41). [27]

6. **Accessions:** Accessions are goods that are affixed to other goods in such a way that they do not lose their identity. UCC § 9-102(a)(1). Thus, a new engine installed in a used automobile or boat is an accession.

7. **Timber to be cut:** There is no definition of timber to be cut in Article 9, but the term refers to standing timber that is under a contract to be cut. UCC § 9-102(a)(44)(ii). Thus, if an owner of land has entered into a contract to allow someone to cut timber from the land, the timber becomes "timber to be cut."

8. **Manufactured homes:** The definition of manufactured homes is very detailed, UCC § 9-102(a)(53), but the category basically refers to a dwelling that is produced offsite and taken to the site to be erected. What are generally called "mobile homes" are manufactured homes if they are intended to be placed on a pad and used as a permanent home. Recreational vehicles used only for vacations are not manufactured homes.

9. **As-extracted collateral:** Oil, gas, coal, and other minerals are treated as real property and are outside the scope of Article 9 so long as they remain in the ground. On extraction, however, they become goods, and can be collateral under Article 9.

10. Changes in goods used for more than one purpose: When goods are used for more than one purpose, the primary use of the goods determines the category. For example, an automobile may be used part of the time in a business and part for the owner's personal use. Whichever is the primary use will determine whether it is consumer goods or equipment. The amount of miles driven and the number of hours driven for each purpose are considerations taken into account to determine the proper category, as would be the manner in which the car was depreciated for tax purposes. [28]

B. Intangibles as collateral: Intangible property is property you cannot see or touch. Intangible assets are created when one person owes an obligation to another. The right of payment is an asset of the person who has it and is property that can be reached for the satisfaction of debts. With few exceptions, for example, rights arising from a tort that is not a commercial tort (see UCC § 9-109(d)(12)), intangible property is property in which a security interest can be given. [28]

Because these are *assets* of a debtor that are being pledged as collateral to a secured party, they are generally obligations that a third party owes to a debtor.

1. Accounts: Accounts are unsecured obligations owed to a person for goods supplied or services rendered, but the definition of account in Article 9 is very broad. UCC § 9-102(a)(2). For example, if a retail merchant sells 20 ovens to a contractor in return for the contractor's unsecured promise to pay in 60 days, the obligation of the contractor is an account and the retailer can grant a security interest in it. [29]

Under the definition of "account," the obligation can arise from a large variety of transactions. If personal property is sold, leased, licensed, assigned, or otherwise disposed of, the obligation to pay is an account. If services have been rendered or are to be rendered, the obligation to pay for them is an account. If the obligation is incurred in return for an insurance policy issued or to be issued for the hiring of a vessel, or an obligation to a credit card issuer resulting from the use of a credit card, the obligation to pay is an account. Even a right against a state obtained by purchasing a winning lottery ticket is an account.

Health-care insurance receivables are obligations to health-care providers from insurance companies. This category includes payments from government social-service providers, such as Medicare and Medicaid. Although these are accounts, they are a subtype of accounts separately defined in Article 9. UCC § 9-102(a)(46).

2. Chattel paper: Chattel paper is an obligation that is itself secured. UCC § 9-102(a)(11). In general, the chattel paper consists of documents that a debtor has rights in. Those documents are then pledged as collateral for a loan the debtor takes out. The debtor is actually in the role of creditor as to some third party, but is also a debtor to a secured party. The documents themselves, the chattel paper, is the collateral for the secured loan. The chattel paper can be viewed as a package of two rights that the debtor has: the right to payment plus the right to possession if the person owing the obligation defaults. [29–30]

Chattel paper is divided into "tangible" chattel paper and "electronic" chattel paper. Tangible chattel paper is represented by a tangible medium—usually paper documents. UCC § 9-102(a)(78). Electronic tangible paper consists of information that is stored in an electronic medium. UCC § 9-102(a)(31).

3. General intangibles: A *general intangible* is any intangible property that is not otherwise defined as a separate category. UCC § 9-102(a)(42). Perhaps it is most helpful to list some of the property that would fall within this category. General intangibles include patents, trademarks, the goodwill of a business, and architectural drawings, for example. [30]

"Payment intangibles" is a separately defined subcategory of general intangibles. *Payment intangibles* are general intangibles in which the right is a right to the payment of money. An example of a payment intangible would be rents due from the lease of a building or payments due on a loan.

Payment intangibles are similar to accounts, but if the payment obligation arises from the sale of goods or from providing services, the collateral is an account and not a payment intangible. If the promise to pay is in the form of an instrument, including a promissory note (see paragraph 4, below), the obligation is not a payment intangible because it fits into that category. An example of a payment intangible is the obligation to repay a loan that is not in the form of a promissory note or an instrument.

4. **Instruments:** *Instruments* are negotiable instruments as defined in Article 3 of the UCC and any other right to the payment of money that, in the ordinary course of business, is transferred by delivery and endorsement or assignment. UCC § 9-102(a)(47). A subcategory of instrument is "*promissory notes*," promises to pay that meet the requirements of an instrument. UCC § 9-102(a)(65). Checks are also instruments.

5. **Deposit accounts:** *Deposit accounts* are accounts in a bank, including savings accounts and checking accounts. UCC § 9-102(a)(29).

6. **Commercial tort claims:** *Commercial tort claims* are rights arising from torts committed against a business organization or against an individual while engaged in operating a business or as a professional. UCC § 9-102(a)(13). For example, a cause of action for trade disparagement would be a commercial tort, as would be a claim for damages caused to a business vehicle through the negligence of another. As mentioned previously, noncommercial tort claims are not covered by Article 9 and cannot be taken as collateral under Article 9.

7. **Documents:** Documents are *documents of title* such as bills of lading and warehouse receipts. UCC § 9-102(a)(30). These documents represent the right to possession of the goods described in them and entitle the possessor of the documents to title to the goods, thus their name. They are a very formal type of paper, and as we say, title to the goods is locked up in the documents.

8. **Letter-of-credit rights:** *Letter-of-credit rights* are rights arising from a letter-of-credit transaction. UCC § 9-102(a)(51). Generally, these are rights of the beneficiary of a letter of credit whether or not the beneficiary has earned rights under the letter of credit.

9. **Investment property:** *Investment property* is stocks, bonds, and similar types of property traded on a securities exchange. UCC § 9-102(a)(51).

10. **Commodity accounts and commodity contracts:** A *commodity account* is an account carried by a commodity intermediate for one of its customers when the commodity customer is under an indirect holding system of the securities market. UCC § 9-102(a)(14). A *commodity contract* is a commodity futures contract or other option trade on a board of trade. UCC § 9-102(15).

CHAPTER 3

REMEDIES: THE SECURED PARTY'S RIGHTS AGAINST THE DEBTOR

I. INTRODUCTION

A. **Secured versus unsecured creditor remedies:** One purpose of a secured transaction is to make it easier for the secured party to collect the debt owed to it, compared to the rights of an unsecured creditor. A critical step in the collection process is obtaining a lien on some of the debtor's property, because a creditor cannot take any of the debtor's property in satisfaction of its debt unless and until it has created a lien. [42]

   Secured parties have voluntary liens and can repossess collateral without going to court, but only if the debtor has defaulted on the obligations to the secured party.

B. **The remedies are not dependent on perfection:** Do not confuse perfection of a security interest with a secured party's right to exercise its remedies. If a secured party has created a security interest pursuant to the rules set out in Chapter 4, then the secured party is entitled to all the remedies we are about to tell you about. Perfection is irrelevant to these remedies.

II. DEFAULT

A. **Importance of default:** "Default" is important because the secured party generally can do very little until the debtor defaults. Particularly, the secured party cannot take possession of the collateral or sell it. Essentially, the secured party's right arises only on default. [43]

B. **Defining a default in the security agreement:** The secured party's remedies arise only when there is a *default* by the debtor. The UCC does not define default, but a default can be and usually is defined in the security agreement. If there is no provision defining default in the security agreement, probably the only default is a failure by the debtor to make a payment when it becomes due. In most agreements, however, there are many default provisions. [43]

   Default clauses commonly provide that a breach by the debtor of any of its obligations under the agreement or any false statement by the debtor in the agreement or the negotiations leading up to the loan constitute a default. Because the debtor usually promises to insure the property, keep it in good repair and at a designated location, use it only for specific purposes, pay any applicable taxes, etc., a breach of any of these promises will typically constitute a default under the typical default clause found in the security agreement.

C. **Insecurity clauses:** A provision common to many security agreements allows the secured party to declare a default whenever the secured party "deems itself insecure," or "at will." These provisions are valid, but to be enforceable, the secured party must in good faith believe "that the prospect of payment or performance is impaired." [43]

D. **Waiver of default by the secured party:** The secured party can waive a default. If, for example, the debtor is late in making a payment but the secured party accepts the payment, the default would be waived. Frequently, the security agreement contains a "no waiver" clause, stating that the failure to enforce an obligation of the debtor does not estop the secured party from requiring strict performance in the future. However, sometimes courts refuse to enforce these clauses. [44]

E. **Default for agricultural liens:** The time of default for agricultural liens is the time that the lienholder has the right to enforce the lien under the non-UCC law creating it. [44]

III. ACCELERATION

An acceleration clause is a provision in an agreement between a debtor and a creditor providing that if the debtor breaches or defaults, by missing a payment or otherwise, the entire debt becomes due. Acceleration is most important when the debt is to be paid in installments.

IV. OBTAINING POSSESSION OF THE COLLATERAL

A. **In general:** Upon default, a secured party has the right to possession of the collateral. Sometimes the debtor will voluntarily turn over possession. In other cases, however, the debtor will refuse. When the collateral is goods, Article 9 gives the creditor two ways of obtaining possession: (1) by simply taking the collateral if this can be done without a breach of the peace, or (2) by bringing a court action. [44–48]

B. **Peaceful repossession:** To be effective, self-help repossession has to be peaceful or, as we say, done without breaching the peace. Many cases hold that whether a repossession is peaceful depends on whether there is potential for violence or whether there is unauthorized entry on the land of the debtor, and the nature of the premises intruded upon. A simple trespass on the debtor's land during the repossession does not constitute a breach of the peace, but if a person tries to stop the repossession the likelihood of violence goes up. [44]

C. **Right to disable collateral:** When it is impossible or difficult to obtain physical possession of the collateral, the secured party has the right to disable the collateral.

D. **Debtor's obligation to assemble the collateral:** The security agreement may provide that the debtor has an obligation to assemble the collateral on default and make it available to the secured party at a place designated by the secured party. The security agreement can even provide that the obligation to assemble exists even before default, presumably to allow the secured party to examine the collateral.

E. **Obtaining possession by use of the judicial process:** The secured party may also obtain possession by bringing an action for possession. Under the common law, and under the law of many states, the action is for *replevin*, but some states simply label it an *action for possession*. [47]

   To obtain a writ of replevin, the secured party must furnish a bond insuring that the debtor will be reimbursed for any damages if the writ was improperly granted, and the debtor is entitled to a hearing soon after the seizure. After seizing the property, the sheriff turns it over to the secured party who then can proceed to sell it in satisfaction of the debt.

F. **Secured party's obligations as to repossessed collateral:** A secured party that has obtained possession of collateral has an obligation to use reasonable care in its custody and preservation. The cost of preserving the collateral can be added to the debt owed by the debtor, and the risk of loss remains on the debtor absent negligence by the secured party.

V. DISPOSING OF THE COLLATERAL

A. **In general:** The secured party has wide discretion in selling collateral. The collateral may be sold by private or public sale, altogether or in parts, for cash or on credit, and at any reasonable time or place. UCC § 9-610(b). The secured party may also lease it, license it, or otherwise dispose of the collateral. The disposition, however, must be commercially reasonable in every aspect, including the method, manner, time, place, and terms. The frequently litigated *commercially reasonable* test is heavily fact-based. The fact that a greater price could have been obtained by a different disposition does not, by itself, make the disposition commercially unreasonable, UCC § 9-627(a), but a low price may indicate that the sale was not properly conducted. [48]

   Three methods of disposition are *per se* reasonable: (1) sale on a recognized market, (2) sale at a price current in a recognized market, and (3) sale in conformity with reasonable commercial practice of dealers in the type of property being disposed of. UCC § 9-627(b). Also, a sale approved in a judicial proceeding or by a creditors' committee, representative of creditors, or an assignee for the benefit of creditors is *per se* commercially reasonable. The secured party has a duty to preserve the collateral once it has repossessed it and to take reasonable steps to lessen its depreciation. UCC § 9-207(a).

   The secured party can prepare or process the collateral before sale if it would be commercially reasonable to do so. The secured party has a *duty* to repair or prepare the collateral before it is sold, if it would be commercially unreasonable *not* to do so. Official Comment 4 to UCC § 9-610.

   The timing of the sale is important. The sale must take place within a reasonable time after repossession. If the property is perishable or subject to rapid depletion, the sale should be made immediately. However, if the collateral is highly valuable and not easy to sell, or if the custom is to provide an extended period of inspection, the sale should not be too soon.

B. **Public sales:** Public sales, usually auctions, are generally commercially reasonable if properly held. For a sale to be considered *public,* the public must be invited and told the time and place of the sale and the sale must be made at the time and place stated in the advertisement. [49]

   In a public sale, sufficient advertising is necessary to ensure that there will be a suitable number of bidders. The sale also must be honest and aboveboard. Additionally, as a general rule, the property being sold must be available for inspection by potential bidders.

   All in all, whether a public sale is commercially reasonable depends on whether the secured party proceeded to sale in a reasonable way and tried to get a fair price for the collateral.

   The secured party may bid and purchase at a public sale. UCC § 9-610(c)(1).

C. **Private sales:** In some cases it may make more sense, and be more commercially reasonable, for the secured party to sell the collateral at a private sale rather than a public one. Indeed, holding an auction sale might be commercially unreasonable under some circumstances. When a sale is private, whether it is commercially reasonable will depend on the efforts made by the secured party to obtain potential buyers and to obtain the best price. Depending on the nature of the collateral, a longer period of time may be required to consummate a reasonable private sale; a hasty sale might be commercially unreasonable. [49]

   The secured party may purchase its collateral at a private sale but only if the collateral is of a kind that is customarily sold on a recognized market or is the subject of widely circulated standard price quotations. This is because private sales do not involve bidding wars and it is hard to tell if they result in a fair price.

D. Notice of disposition

1. **Notice of sale in general:** Whether the sale is public or private, the secured party must give notice of the sale to the debtor and to others claiming an interest in the collateral. The notice must be in the form of a record that is authenticated. Thus oral notification is insufficient. Article 9 does not require that the notice be received, only that it be sent, but the method of sending it must be reasonably calculated to reach the recipient. Notice need not be sent if the goods are perishable or are likely to decline quickly in value. Nor need the notice be given if the goods are to be sold on a recognized market. UCC § 9-611(d). [50]

2. **To whom must notice be sent?** If the goods are consumer goods, notice must be sent only to the debtor and other secondary obligors. Secondary obligors are those who undertook liability on the debt, basically as sureties or guarantors. If the collateral is of another type of goods, e.g., equipment, the notice also must be sent to anyone who has notified the secured party that it has a claim in the goods and to other secured parties who have filed a financing statement or had their security interest noted on a certificate of title for a vehicle at least ten days before the notice is sent. UCC § 9-611(c).

3. **Time within which notice must be given:** The notice must be sent within a reasonable time before the disposition is to occur. What constitutes a reasonable time is a question of fact (we know this is getting a bit repetitive), but in nonconsumer transactions, notice sent ten or more days before disposition is *per se* reasonable. UCC § 9-612.

4. **Contents of notice:** In nonconsumer transactions, the notice must (1) describe the debtor, the secured party, and the collateral; (2) state the method of disposition and that the debtor is entitled to an accounting; (3) provide the time and place of disposition if the sale is public or, if the sale is private, the time after which the private disposition will be made. UCC § 9-613.

   The following additional information must be given in consumer transactions: (1) a description of the debtor's liability for a deficiency judgment, (2) a telephone number from which the debtor can obtain information about the cost to redeem the collateral, and (3) a telephone number or mailing address from which the debtor can obtain additional information about the disposition. UCC § 9-614.

5. **Waiver of the right to notice:** The debtor and secondary obligors may not waive the right to notice of the disposition before default. UCC § 9-602(7). However, they may waive the right to notice after default by an authenticated record. UCC § 9-624(a).

VI. APPLICATION OF THE PROCEEDS OF THE SALE

Article 9 specifies how proceeds of a sale of collateral are to be distributed, UCC § 9-615(a). The proceeds must be distributed first to pay the costs of sale, next to pay the claim of the secured party who is holding the sale, and then to any subordinate or junior lienholders who have met certain guidelines discussed below. Only if there is money left over after all this does the debtor get anything back. Unsecured creditors and secured parties with superior security interests do not get paid out of secured creditor's sale. A buyer at the sale will, however, take subject to superior security interests. [51]

VII. SECURED PARTY'S RIGHT TO A DEFICIENCY JUDGMENT: WHAT HAPPENS IF THE SECURED PARTY FAILS TO HOLD A COMMERCIALLY REASONABLE SALE?

If insufficient funds result from the sale of the property, the secured party is entitled to a deficiency judgment in the amount of the difference. UCC § 9-615(d). Article 9 does not provide for the automatic issuance of a deficiency judgment; rather, the secured party must bring an action in the appropriate court to obtain a deficiency judgment. [53]

If the secured party fails to abide by the requirements of Article 9 by properly taking possession of the collateral, by failing to give notice of its disposition, or by failing to hold a commercially reasonable disposition of the collateral, the secured party risks losing its right to a deficiency.

A. Deficiencies in nonconsumer sales: In the action for a deficiency, for business collateral, the secured party need not prove compliance with Article 9 unless the debtor raises it in a defense or counterclaim. If the debtor does raise it, the burden of proof is on the secured party to prove compliance. [53]

If the secured party fails to prove compliance as set out previously, a presumption arises that the debtor is damaged by the amount claimed in the action for deficiency. To recover a deficiency, the secured party must rebut the presumption by showing that the damages suffered by the debtor do not equal the amount of the deficiency.

B. Deficiencies in consumer sales: In consumer transactions, some courts have held that failure to follow the Article 9 rules on disposition results in the secured party forfeiting its rights to a deficiency. [53]

VIII. CALCULATION AND EXPLANATION OF DEFICIENCY OR SURPLUS IN CONSUMER TRANSACTIONS

A. Definition of deficiency or surplus: If the sale does not bring the exact amount necessary to pay the costs and the amount owing to the secured party who sells after repossessing, there will be either a surplus that must be paid to someone or the secured party will be entitled to a deficiency judgment.

B. Explanation of calculation: Article 9 describes how the surplus or deficiency is to be calculated, and requires that the secured party provide an explanation of the surplus or deficiency to the debtor in a consumer transaction. UCC § 9-616. This explanation is obligatory and must be given whether the debtor requests it or not. Article 9, unlike in most other situations in which a "record" suffices, requires that the explanation be in writing, but there is no requirement that it be signed. It must be given before or when the secured party makes any distribution of a surplus or demands that the debtor pay a deficiency. The specific things that must be contained in this statement are highly technical. The explanation must contain the following information, in this order: (1) the aggregate amount of obligations secured by the security interest under which the disposition was made; (2) the amount of proceeds of the disposition; (3) the amount of the obligations after deducting the amount of proceeds; (4) the amount and types of expenses; (5) the amount of credits; and (6) the amount of the surplus or deficiency. UCC § 9-616(c).

The explanation must be given after the disposition and before or when the secured party makes any distribution of a surplus or makes a demand that the debtor pay a deficiency.

CAPSULE SUMMARY

Because the secured party may delay distribution or seeking a deficiency, Article 9 allows the secured party to make a demand for one. The request must be an authenticated record and can be sent any time after the collateral is sold or otherwise disposed of. When requested, an explanation must be given by the secured party within 14 days after the request is received. UCC § 9-616(b)(2).

If the secured party fails to fulfill its responsibility to either send an explanation or waive its right to a deficiency when one is due, the debtor is entitled to statutory damages in the amount of $500, in addition to any losses suffered by the debtor as a result of the secured party's inaction. UCC § 9-625(e)(5)(6).

IX. COLLECTION WHEN THE COLLATERAL IS ACCOUNTS, CHATTEL PAPER, OR GENERAL INTANGIBLES (INCLUDING PAYMENT INTANGIBLES) AND DEPOSIT ACCOUNTS

A. **Remedies on outright sale of the accounts, chattel paper, or instruments compared to merely obtaining a security interest in these assets:** A person wanting to raise money using its accounts, chattel paper, or payment intangibles can either give a creditor a security interest in them or sell them outright. Either approach gives rise to a secured transaction under Article 9. There is a difference in the remedy, however, when the debtor defaults. [55]

If the transaction is one in which the debtor gives a security interest in the accounts, chattel paper, or payment intangibles, the distribution of the proceeds that are collected from the account debtors is basically the same as when the collateral is goods. The secured party first pays expenses, then pays itself, then pays any subordinate secured parties who have given the required notice, and finally, gives anything left to the debtor. UCC § 9-608(a). If the transaction is an outright sale of the accounts, chattel paper, promissory notes, or payment intangibles, the debtor is not entitled to any surplus, nor can the secured party recover any deficiency, unless the agreement provides for payment of a surplus or the obtaining of a deficiency judgment. UCC § 9-608(b).

B. **Secured party's contact with account debtors:** Article 9 allows the secured party to contact the account debtors only after default, but the secured party and debtor may agree, in the security agreement or otherwise, that the secured party can contact the account debtors directly, even before a default. When the collateral is deposit accounts, e.g., savings or checking accounts in a bank, the secured party will perfect (a concept discussed in Chapter 5) by taking *control* of the account. This is often done by making the bank account a joint account between the debtor and the secured party. In effect, this means that both debtor and the secured party will be able to make withdrawals from the account. Upon default, the secured party's remedy is simple: to withdraw the money in the deposit account and apply it to the debt.

X. RIGHTS OF A TRANSFEREE OF THE COLLATERAL TAKING FROM A REPOSSESSION SALE

A person who purchases or otherwise obtains collateral at foreclosure sale obtains all of the rights of the debtor in the collateral. Usually, the purchaser takes free of the security interest of the secured party conducting the sale and of all subordinate security interests and liens. The transferee, however, always takes subject to any security interests or liens that have priority over those of the foreclosing secured party. UCC § 9-617. [57]

A. **Sales made to a purchaser in good faith:** If a transferee takes in good faith, it takes free of junior or subordinate liens that others have on the collateral, even if the secured party does not conduct the sale in accordance with the requirements of Article 9, e.g., fails to give notice of the sale or holds a sale that is not commercially reasonable. UCC § 9-617(b).

B. **Sales without good faith:** If the transferee does *not* act in good faith, it takes subject to the rights of the debtor, the security interest of the person selling the collateral, and of all subordinate liens. UCC § 9-617(c). In other words, the purchaser who *is not* in good faith does not take free and clear of these liens.

C. **The implied warranty of good title:** When an Article 9 secured party sells collateral under the Code, it gives the purchaser an implied warranty of good title by law. Thus, the purchaser may have rights against the secured party if the property was encumbered or the debtor did not have title to it. UCC § 9-610(d). The warranty provides protection to one purchasing at a sale made by a junior secured party, who fails to disclose the existence of the superior security interest.

XI. ACCEPTANCE OF COLLATERAL IN SATISFACTION OF THE DEBT

A. **Introduction:** Another remedy the secured party may pursue when the debtor defaults is to accept the collateral in full or partial satisfaction of the debt. This is sometimes called *strict foreclosure*. Except where the goods are consumer goods, acceptance of the collateral may be in full or partial satisfaction of the debt. UCC § 9-620(a). If the goods are consumer goods, the remedy of acceptance is only available if the secured party agrees to discharge the debtor from all of the obligations secured. UCC § 9-620(g). This remedy requires the consent of the debtor and of others interested in the collateral (such as people who have guaranteed the debt). [57]

B. **Technical requirements for acceptance in satisfaction:** There are four requirements when the secured party wishes to accept the goods in satisfaction of the debt: (1) the debtor must consent, (2) there must be no objection (by the debtor on another interested party), (3) the debtor cannot be in possession of the collateral if it is consumer goods, and finally, (4) the debtor must *not* have paid 60 percent or more of the debt if the collateral is consumer goods.

C. **Effect of acceptance:** An acceptance in satisfaction transfers all of the debtor's right in the collateral to the secured party. The acceptance also terminates the security interest of the person accepting, as well as all subordinate security interests and liens. It does not terminate prior security interests, and to keep the collateral the secured party will have to pay prior secured parties. The acceptance in satisfaction terminates the debtor's obligations—all of them if it is a full satisfaction, or that part of them specified in the proposal and consent if it is a partial satisfaction. Thus, if it is a full satisfaction, the secured party no longer has a right to a deficiency judgment, and the debtor has no right to any surplus if one would have resulted from a sale.

XII. RIGHT TO REDEEM THE COLLATERAL

The debtor has the right to redeem the collateral until it is sold, accepted in full or partial satisfaction of the debt, or until the secured party has collected payment from the debtor's accounts, chattel paper, general intangibles, or promissory notes. To redeem, all obligations the debtor owes to the secured party must be paid, including expenses the secured party incurred in retaking possession, preparing to dispose of the collateral, storing the collateral, processing the collateral, and, to the extent provided for in the agreement, attorneys' fees. When the debt is to be paid in installments, once the debt has been *accelerated,* the debtor must pay all of it. [59]

XIII. DEBTOR'S WAIVER OF RIGHTS

The rights of the debtor that cannot be waived prior to default include:

1. the obligations of the secured party to care for collateral in its possession;
2. the right of the debtor to an accounting of the collateral and the amount of the debt, and to an explanation of how a deficiency or surplus was calculated;
3. the provisions dictating how the proceeds of a repossession sale shall be paid;
4. the methods of collecting a debt from an account debtor;
5. the duty to repossess by self-help only without breaching the peace;
6. the provisions on the disposition of the collateral, including the requirement of giving notice; and
7. the provisions regarding acceptance of the collateral in satisfaction of the debt.

UCC § 9-602.

XIV. DEBTOR'S REMEDIES FOR A SECURED PARTY'S FAILURE TO FULFILL ITS OBLIGATIONS ON A DEBTOR'S DEFAULT

A. Court orders: If the secured party is not proceeding in accordance with the provisions of Article 9 on foreclosure, a court may restrain a secured party's action or order the secured party to take action "on appropriate terms or conditions." UCC § 9-625(a). [60]

B. Debtor's general right to recover damages: The secured party can lose its deficiency judgment in the situations noted previously. Article 9 also has a general provision allowing damages for any loss caused by the failure to comply with this article. Recoverable losses include those resulting from the debtor's inability to obtain credit or the increase in the cost of credit. UCC § 9-625(b).

XV. REAL ESTATE FORECLOSURES

When there is a default in an obligation secured by a mortgage on real property, the secured party has a right to foreclose. A mortgage foreclosure, however, is quite different from foreclosure (or sale) under Article 9. The mortgagor is entitled to retain possession of the real property until it is actually sold. Half of the states require a judicial sale of the property, and in others, a public sale is mandated. Frequently, even in the states allowing a public sale, a judicial sale is required unless the mortgage contains a "power of sale" provision allowing a private sale.

In most states, the debtor can redeem the collateral after the sale, sometimes for as long as a year. In some states, deficiency judgments on mortgage debts are prohibited when the land is farm or residential property.

XVI. BANKRUPTCY AND THE AUTOMATIC STAY

A description of Article 9 is incomplete and misleading without some reference to the automatic stay imposed upon the borrower's bankruptcy. If a borrower goes into bankruptcy, all of a secured party's collection efforts must cease. The secured party must stop any act to repossess property, stop all collection letters and calls, and stop selling any collateral it already has in its possession. A failure to halt collection efforts can result in actual and punitive damages against the creditor in the borrower's bankruptcy.

For example, if the repo person is on the sidewalk ready to take the debtor's car, he or she must stop. If a secured party has repossessed and is in the middle of a sale, the sale must stop. In sum, *all* attempts to collect a debt or to obtain or perfect a security interest must stop upon the filing of a bankruptcy.

CHAPTER 4

CREATION OF A SECURITY INTEREST

I. INTRODUCTION

A. **Creation versus perfection:** Creation is different from perfection of a security interest. First comes creation, then comes perfection in most cases. Do not confuse the two, as they each have their own requirements. [72]

B. **The elements or requirements for attachment:** To be enforceable, a security interest must attach, which means become enforceable. The requirements for attachment of a security interest are value, agreement, and rights:

• **Value:** The creditor must have given value such as a loan or a binding commitment to lend.

• **Agreement:** The debtor must agree to grant the secured party a security interest.

• **Rights:** The debtor must have rights in the collateral, usually ownership but sometimes something short of ownership. [73]

Many find it easier to remember this by the acronym "VAR."

II. FUNCTION OF A SECURITY INTEREST

A. **How does a security interest affect a creditor's rights?** On receipt of a security interest, the creditor becomes a secured party. This serves two important purposes: (1) it makes the debt easier to collect for the creditor, and (2) it is more likely that the creditor-secured party will be one of the first to get paid out of a sale of the collateral when there are many creditors and the debtor has insufficient assets to pay them all.

B. What is an Article 9 security interest? The security interest is a "consensual" lien, created by the debtor by giving an interest in some or all of the debtor's property. This gives the secured party the right to possession of the collateral if the debtor fails to perform on its obligations, which may be of any kind, most, however, arising out of a contract.

C. Real property and personal property security interests

    1. Creation of personal property security interests versus real property: Since the adoption of the UCC, there is only one type of personal property interest, which we call a *security interest.* Security interests are governed by Article 9 of the UCC. They are created when a debtor grants a security interest to the secured party in collateral in which the debtor has rights, and the secured party has given value in return.

    2. Different types of security interests in real property: Security interests in real property are created in a very different way. Several types of security interests can be created in real property. The most common is the *mortgage*, but in some states a security interest in real estate can be affected by a *deed of trust.* Other states allow the creation of a security interest by the use of a *real estate contract or an installment sales contract.* Each of these real property security interests is governed by state law outside of the UCC, which varies from state to state and between the types of security interests.

    3. Formalism in real estate law: Mortgages are much more formalistic than Article 9 security interests in personal property. States have various requirements for the creation of a mortgage. Usually, the property has to be defined in the mortgage document by its legal description to create a valid security interest in real estate. Also, some states require that the document be notarized or witnessed, and others require that it be executed "under seal." Furthermore, under real property law, the amount of the debt being secured must often be included in the mortgage.

III. METHODS OF CREATING A PERSONAL PROPERTY SECURITY INTEREST UNDER ARTICLE 9

A. Intent: To create a security interest, the debtor must have an intent to grant the creditor a security interest in some personal property with the additional intent that the creditor be entitled to sell the collateral in the event that the debtor defaults on its obligations. The intent, objectively manifested, may be either explicit or implicit and in most cases is manifested in a *security agreement,* which contains "granting language." A security interest is always *in* something in particular and will only be in the property in which the debtor intends to give the security interest. This may be a single item or a wide variety of property. [75]

B. Disguised security interests: Parties may try to disguise a secured transaction as an outright sale. Some of these transactions are still security interests even though the documents involved do not contain the granting language. The parties also may set up a transaction as a lease or consignment, or as a conditional sale. Article 9 treats these types of agreements as security interests if that was the intent of the parties. This is true even if the granting language is missing. [75]

C. Intent alone isn't enough—The requirement of possession, control, or a written security agreement: In addition to requiring that the debtor intend to grant a security interest, Article 9 requires that the secured party have one of three things: (1) possession of the collateral, (2) control over the collateral, or (3) a written security agreement executed by the debtor documenting the transaction.

1. **Creating a security interest through possession of the collateral:** Creating a security interest through possession of the collateral is the primary alternative to a written security agreement. This occurs when the creditor takes physical possession of the collateral with the debtor's understanding that the creditor is entitled to keep possession until the debt is repaid *and* that if the debt is not repaid, the creditor may dispose of the property and use the proceeds of the disposition to discharge the debt. *Field warehousing*, another form of possession, is a method of financing inventory by which the inventory is held in custody for the lender by an agent of the lender, to be released to the debtor as the lender indicates to its agent. When the lender has possession of the collateral there needn't be a written agreement, but if there is no written agreement, the creditor loses its security interest if it returns possession of the collateral to the debtor. [76]

2. **Creating a security interest by exercising control over the collateral:** A security interest can also be created by exercising control over certain collateral, meaning a secured party can engage in transactions regarding the collateral. How the secured party gains control depends on the type of the collateral, which will fall into one of the following categories: (1) deposit accounts, (2) electronic chattel paper, (3) investment property, (4) letter-of-credit rights, or (5) electronic documents. [77]

3. **A written security agreement:** If the secured party has neither possession nor control of the collateral, a security interest can be created only if the secured party has obtained an authenticated record called a security agreement. This is by far the most common way to create a security interest in the modern world. [77]

IV. THE SECURITY AGREEMENT

A. **The elements of a security agreement**

1. **Intent to grant a security interest and other requirements:** The security agreement must evidence the debtor's intent to grant a security interest to the secured party as shown by UCC sections defining the security agreement. UCC § 9-102(a)(73) says that a security agreement is "an agreement that creates a security interest." Agreement is defined as "the bargain of the parties in fact as found in their language" and in the surrounding circumstances in UCC § 1-201(3) [UCC § 1-201(b)(3) of the revised version], while UCC § 1-201(a)(37) [UCC § 1-102(a)(35) of the revised version] defines *security interest* as "an interest in personal property or fixtures which secures payment or performance of an obligation." Additional requirements of the security agreement, more concretely set out in UCC § 9-203, are that the agreement must be (1) a record (2) authenticated by the debtor that (3) contains a description of the collateral. [77]

2. **Form over substance:** The substance of the document determines whether it is a security agreement, not the name, so long as it contains the necessary requirements and shows that the intent of the debtor was to give the creditor a security interest in its property. A typical security agreement will have (1) representations made by the debtor, (2) obligations of the debtor, and (3) other details of the transaction. Although these provisions are not necessary to create a security interest, they serve to specify the rights and obligations of the parties, the same as the provisions of any contract. It is not necessary that the security agreement (1) be authenticated by the *secured party*,

(2) include any addresses, (3) be witnessed or sealed, or (4) contain any information about the terms of the loan. Neither are misspellings fatal.

3. **The security agreement versus the financing statement:** It is important to know the difference between the *security agreement* and the *financing statement*. The security agreement is the contract granting the creditor a security interest, while the financing statement is the document that a creditor files to give notice (to third parties) that the creditor has a security interest in some of the debtor's property. The financing statement must contain (1) the names of both the debtor and secured party, and (2) an indication of the collateral. UCC § 9-502. It need not be signed or otherwise authenticated nor have any language indicating the debtor's intent to grant a security interest. Filing a financing statement alone will not grant to the creditor a security interest in the property described in the financing statement, however, under the "composite document" rule some courts have found that several documents, read together, may suffice as a security agreement. [81]

B. **Requirement of a record:** Article 9 provides that the security agreement must be a "record." A *writing* is always a record, UCC § 9-102(a)(69), and almost all of today's security agreements meet the record requirement by being in writing. If the document is in electronic form, it meets the requirement if it is stored on a tangible medium, such as a hard drive or disk.

C. **Authenticated by the debtor:** Although a security agreement must be authenticated by the debtor, there is no requirement that the secured party sign or otherwise authenticate the security agreement. A written security agreement may be authenticated using a signature or other mark, and an electronically prepared and stored agreement may be authenticated by using an electronic symbol or encryption instead of a signature. UCC § 9-102(a)(7). Most important, the authentication, regardless of how it is made, must be made with the present intention that it constitutes an authentication. To determine if a document was authenticated, cases discussing the question of whether a writing is signed for the purposes of the Statute of Frauds are relevant. For example, the signature or authentication need not be at the end of the document but could be the debtor's name contained within the document so long as the debtor intended that the inclusion of his name operate as a signature.

D. **Description of the collateral**

1. **General requirement that collateral be described:** A security agreement must include a description of the property in which the security interest is given (the collateral). The test to determine whether words of description fulfill this requirement is whether the language "reasonably identifies" the property. UCC § 9-108(a). The requirement is also flexible, emphasized by the statutory language of "any . . . method if the identity of the collateral is objectively determinable." UCC § 9-108(b)(6). However, there are limitations on the language that may be used in certain situations. [85]

2. **Methods of describing the collateral:** Collateral may be described by specific listing, category, type, quantity, or use of a formula. A specific description may be very simple, however, it must not be misleading. Also, it is important to note that the less information given about the collateral, the more likely the description will be insufficient. Listing the collateral may be on an attachment to the security agreement, and that list can contain an unlimited number of items. Although it may seem unclear, a description by category means that you can describe collateral using language such as "all *goods*" or "all *intangibles*" of the debtor or describe the collateral by the kind (such as, "all automobiles"). To describe collateral by type, use of one or more the types of collateral defined by Article 9 will suffice (e.g., "inventory" or "chattel paper"), but there must be a reference to exactly

which collateral is covered, e.g., "All of the debtor's inventory." However, consumer goods, commercial tort claims, security entitlements, security accounts, or commodity accounts cannot be described by type and must be defined specifically. The last method of describing collateral, by quantity or use of a formula, also requires that the description contain a specific listing or that a type or category be named.

3. **After-acquired property:** In most, but not all, cases, a security interest can be taken in property to be acquired by the debtor in the future, i.e., after-acquired property. A security interest may be taken in after-acquired consumer goods, but only in those that the debtor acquires within ten days after the secured party gives value. Some courts have held that the security interest extends to after-acquired accounts even when there is no reference to such in the security agreement. On the other hand, after-acquired clauses are prohibited when the collateral is commercial torts, and courts have consistently held that when the collateral is equipment or another type of collateral, the security interest does not extend to after-acquired property unless explicitly stated by the agreement. [89]

4. **Proceeds:** When the debtor sells or otherwise transfers collateral, the secured party obtains a security interest in the proceeds—whatever is received in exchange for the collateral; this arises automatically and need not be included in the security agreement. A secured party does not automatically obtain a security interest in accessions (goods that are united with other goods in such a way that the added goods lose their identity) or products (property produced by the collateral such as the young of animals) as they are not proceeds. But depending on the description included in the security agreement, a secured party may acquire a security interest in products. [89]

5. **Accessions and products:** *Accessions* are goods that are united with other goods in such a way that the added goods do not lose their identity. UCC § 9-102(a)(1). For example, if a secured party has a security interest in a tractor and the owner-debtor has a new engine installed, the engine is an accession. Priority problems arise when one person has a security interest in the tractor and another in the engine. UCC § 9-335.

6. **The debt secured:** A security agreement can secure any obligation, whether it be one or many, and need not include a reference to the obligation secured by the security interest, but in most cases it includes a statement of what debt is secured by the collateral or a reference to some other document that states the obligation. The security agreement may also secure present, past, or future obligations with language known as a *dragnet clause* or a *future advances clause*. If additional advances are to be made, the inclusion of a future advances clause is essential or the later advances will not be secured. [90]

V. ENFORCEABILITY OF A SECURITY INTEREST: ATTACHMENT

A. **Introduction to attachment:** In addition to the requirements that the debtor intend to create a security interest and that the secured party have possession, control, or an authenticated security agreement, two additional requirements must be met for the security interest to be enforceable: (1) value must have been given by the secured party, and (2) the debtor must have rights in the collateral or the power to transfer rights in the collateral to the secured party.

When all four requirements are met, the security interest *attaches* to the collateral. In many if not most transactions, value is given and the debtor has rights in the collateral when the security agreement is signed or around that time. [91]

B. Value: Article 9 gives no separate definition of value; however, Article 1, UCC § 1-201(44) [UCC § 1-204 of the revised version], provides that a secured party can give value (1) in return for any consideration sufficient to support a simple contract, (2) as security for a preexisting claim, (3) in full or partial satisfaction of a preexisting claim, or (4) in return for a binding commitment to extend credit whether or not the credit has actually been given. This is a very broad definition of value, and there has been little litigation questioning whether a secured party has given value. [92]

C. Debtor's rights in the collateral: The requirement that the debtor have rights in the collateral is more complicated. The issue most often arises when a security agreement covers both present and after-acquired property. Attachment can also be delayed if the debtor gives a security interest in property in which it does not yet have rights; for example, collateral that it is in the process of buying—the general rule is that the debtor obtains rights in the property as soon as it is determined to be the subject of the contract between the retailer and the debtor. Additionally, the debtor may have less than all of the rights in the collateral and still pledge it as collateral. A debtor may also grant a security interest in collateral it does not own if the owner gives permission. Usually, the extension of credit goes to the person giving the security interest, but if the extension of credit goes to another person, the person giving the security interest is called the *debtor,* UCC § 9-102(a)(28), while the person to whom credit is extended is called the *obligor,* UCC § 9-102(a)(59). [92–93]

CHAPTER 5

PERFECTION OF SECURITY INTERESTS

I. INTRODUCTION

Perfection is the general process of providing notice to the world of one's security interest in collateral. Perfection by filing is constructive notice because the notice is given by sending notices to a particular place so that people who are interested can come and find them. Notice is sometimes also given by having the creditor retain possession of the collateral. [100]

The theory behind this kind of notice is that creditors who wish to take collateral for an obligation can and should ask the debtor to see the collateral. Article 9 provides four ways in which a security interest can be perfected: (1) by filing, (2) by the secured party taking possession of the collateral, (3) by the secured party taking control of the collateral, and (4) automatically (the security interest is perfected even though the secured party does nothing to perfect it). In some cases, the secured party has a choice of how to perfect. For example, if the collateral is equipment, the secured party may perfect either by filing or by taking possession.

However, sometimes only one method of perfection is available. For example, if the collateral is accounts, the only way to perfect is by filing.

A. Real property recording systems: If you want to purchase real estate, you, your lawyer, or a title company will do a "title search" to make certain the seller has title and that there are no liens on the farm.

There will be a file containing the documents (deed, mortgage, etc.) that represent every transaction involving that particular piece of property. The process of selling property or encumbering it with a mortgage is initially a secret one because only the parties to the transaction know about it. It becomes public by the recording of the transaction.

The essence of a recording system is that it provides a method of discovering interests in property that would otherwise be unknown to third parties. It protects parties who purchase the property or loan money against the property from interests that would otherwise be unknown and undiscoverable.

B. Perfection under Article 9: The rationale of perfection of an Article 9 security interest is the same as that of recording real property transactions. Perfection is merely a method of giving third parties notice that property is encumbered by a security interest. The details of the process, however, are quite different. To start with, personal property is moveable, whereas real property is not. A refrigerator may go from one town to another, from one county to another, from one state to another. Secondly, as you have seen, personal property falls into various types or categories, some tangible and some intangible. Finally, Article 9 governs a number of different types of transactions, running the gamut from a security interest in a television that a consumer purchases to a complicated transaction in which a business borrows money and gives a security interest in its inventory, accounts, equipment, etc. Collateral also can change forms or turn into something else, which creates other perfection issues. [103]

II. METHODS OF PERFECTION UNDER ARTICLE 9

A security interest cannot be perfected until it has attached, UCC § 9-308(a), and, in most cases, something more than attachment must occur.

III. PERFECTION BY FILING

A. Introduction: Filing is the most common way to perfect and will work for all collateral except deposit accounts, letter-of-credit rights, or money. UCC § 9-312(a). However, in some cases the secured party may obtain better rights, and thus be better protected against third parties, by perfecting in some way other than by filing. [104]

Unlike the real estate recording system in which the actual contract between the parties (the deed or mortgage) is filed, Article 9 adopts what is commonly called a "notice" filing system. The document filed, called a *financing statement*, provides little information and is designed to simply put third parties on notice that the debtor may have given a security interest in the described property.

The determination of whether a security interest is perfected involves a two-step process: (1) where the filing must be made, and (2) what actually must be filed.

B. Where to file a financing statement
   1. Introduction: In determining where to file a financing statement, two inquiries must be made: (1) In which jurisdiction or state must the filing be made, and (2) in which office should it be filed within that jurisdiction? The question of which state or jurisdiction is the proper one is the more complicated question. [105]

2. **The proper state in which to file**

    a. **Baseline rule—Location of debtor:** In most cases the rule is simple: Filing must be in the state where the debtor is located. UCC § 9-301(1). Article 9 provides where a debtor is located in UCC § 9-307. That, of course, raises the question of where the debtor is a resident.

        i. **Registered organizations:** If an organization is registered in a state, the organization is located in that state for legal purposes and that state is the proper place to file. Corporations, limited partnerships, and limited liability companies come within this rule. UCC § 9-307(e).

        ii. **Individuals:** Filing as to individuals must be done in the state of the individual's principal residence. UCC § 9-307(b)(1).

        iii. **Sole proprietorships:** Because sole proprietorships have no legal existence, filing must be done where the owner has his or her principal residence.

        iv. **Organizations that are not registered:** Some organizations are generally considered to be entities, although not necessarily legal entities, even though they are not registered with a state. These include partnerships, unincorporated associations, business trusts, governments and governmental subdivisions. See UCC § 1-201(25) [2001 version]. The proper state to file for these types of organizations is as follows:

            • if the organization has only one place where it conducts its affairs, in that state, UCC § 9-307(b)(2);

            • if the organization conducts its affairs in more than one state, in the state where it has its executive offices. UCC § 9-307(3).

    b. **Exceptions to baseline rule**

        i. **Goods covered by a certificate of title:** When goods are governed by a certificate of title—motor vehicles in all states and boats in some states—the location of the debtor does not determine the proper state in which to file. Rather, it is the state that issued the certificate of title. UCC § 9-303.

        ii. **Fixture filings; timber to be cut and as-extracted collateral:** To obtain maximum protection for a security interest in fixtures, the secured party must file a "fixture filing." Fixture filings are discussed in more detail below, but for now, just know that a fixture filing must be filed in the state where the real property to which the goods are affixed is located. UCC § 9-301(3)(A).

           When the collateral is timber to be cut or as-extracted minerals, the law where the timber to be cut or minerals are located controls. UCC §§ 9-301(B), 9-301(4).

        iii. **Agricultural liens:** Agricultural liens must be filed under Article 9. The proper state in which to file is the state in which the real property is located. UCC § 9-302.

3. **The proper office in which to file**

    a. **Statewide office for most transactions:** For most transactions, the office in which to file is a statewide office established for that purpose. UCC § 9-501(a)(2). In most states, one files financing statements in the Secretary of State's office. [104–105]

   b. Exceptions

      i. Goods for which a certificate of title has been issued.

      ii. Property subject to federal perfection rules.

      iii. Fixture filings.

      iv. Timber to be cut and as-extracted minerals.

      v. Transmitting utilities.

C. What must be filed

1. **Introduction:** Unlike real property recording systems that require filing of the actual document, e.g., the deed or mortgage, Article 9 requires only that a "financing statement" be filed. There is a form of financing statement in Article 9 at § 9-521 and Chapter 5 of this Outline. The financing statement contains only enough information to alert one searching the files that a debtor has, or at least may have, given a security interest in the described property. UCC § 9-502. To be *sufficient*, a financing statement must: (1) provide the debtor's name, (2) provide the name of the secured party or the name of a representative of the secured party, and (3) indicate the collateral covered by the financing statement. [107–110]

   These minimal requirements for the *sufficiency* of a financing statement do not tell the whole story. Section 9-516, which provides grounds for a filing officer's refusal to file a financing statement, includes several provisions that go to the contents of the financing statement. A filing officer is authorized, and indeed is required, to refuse to accept a financing statement if it does not contain: (1) the address of the secured party, (2) a mailing address for the debtor, (3) an indication of whether the debtor is an individual or an organization, and (4) the organizational number if there is one. UCC § 9-520.

   The requirements for determining whether a financing statement should be *filed* by the filing officer do not go to the *sufficiency* of the financing statement. If the financing statement is not sufficient, i.e., lacks debtor's name, the secured party's name or an indication of the collateral, it cannot result in an effective filing even if filing officer in fact does file it. However, if the financing statement lacks some of the other additional bits of information, such as the organization's organizational number, it is effective if the filing officer files it.

2. **Name of the debtor:** The name of the debtor must be correctly stated on the financing statement because the statement will be filed under the debtor's name and those searching will search by the debtor's name. Any mistake in naming the debtor is almost certain to render the filing ineffective. The only exception is if a search of the record under the incorrect name used on the financing statement would in fact disclose the financing statement. UCC § 9-506(c). [112]

   Section 9-503 has directions on how a name must be stated:

   a. Individuals: As you would expect, you state the name of the individual in the appropriate boxes.

   b. Sole proprietorships: The name of the owner of the business must be listed. If the person uses a trade name it may be listed, but this is not required, and listing only the trade name is insufficient.

    c. Registered organizations: If the debtor is a corporation, limited partnership, or limited liability company, the name must be the official registered name of the organization. Again, if the organization uses a trade name, it may be included but need not be. Using only the trade name makes the financing statement insufficient.

    d. Other organizations: When the debtor is an unregistered organization or partnership, the name of the organization or partnership must be used in the financing statement. If the organization or partnership does not have a name, the name of the members of the organization or the names of the partners must be used. As you can imagine, this vague rule causes plenty of confusion.

3. Indication of the collateral: The requirement that the collateral be "indicated" in the financing statement is similar to the requirement that a security agreement contain a "description" of the collateral. Any description of collateral that is sufficient for a security agreement is sufficient as the indication of the collateral for the financing statement as well. UCC § 9-504(1). Thus, the collateral may be described by specific listing, by category, by type, by quantity, by formula, or by any other method if the identity of the collateral is objectively determinable. [112]

    However, because the financing statement need merely "indicate" the collateral whereas the security agreement must "describe" it, the test of what is sufficient for a financing statement is more liberal. When the security agreement grants a security interest in after-acquired property, the financing statement need not contain any reference to after-acquired property to perfect the security interest in after-acquired property. Official Comment 7 to UCC § 9-204. Although a generic description of the collateral such as "all of the debtor's assets," or "all of the debtor's personal property" is insufficient in a security agreement, it is permitted in a financing statement. UCC § 9-504(2).

D. Effect of mistakes or omissions

1. Introduction: Because Article 9 has adopted a "notice" theory of filing, some errors in a financing statement will not invalidate a filing. A financing statement may be effective even though it contains minor errors or omissions, as long as (a) it substantially satisfies the requirement of Article 9, and (b) the error or omission does not make it seriously misleading.

    The basic test is whether the filing actually puts someone who searches the database on notice that a particular person, the debtor, gave or might have given a security interest in particular property. [113]

2. Debtor's name: As previously noted, an error of any kind in the debtor's name is fatal unless a search under the improperly stated name would disclose the financing statement. Searches for financing statements are now done by computer, and most search systems will not disclose the financing statement if there is any mistake in the name of the debtor.

3. Indication of collateral: A small error in the description of the collateral will not invalidate the filing. For example, a mistake in a product's serial number or a simple misspelling is not fatal so long as it would not seriously mislead someone reading the financing statement.

4. Name of the secured party and addresses: Mistakes in the name of the secured party are less critical, and, unless they make the filing seriously misleading, they will not render the filing ineffective. The same is true of the addresses of the debtor and secured party.

E. Subsequent changes: A number of events may occur after the filing that will affect the likelihood that one searching the filings will discover the financing statement. Although there are some exceptions, the starting point is that changes will not invalidate the filing. UCC § 507(b). [114]

1. **Change in the location of the debtor:** If a debtor changes its location within the state in which the financing statement is filed, the financing statement will become *inaccurate* because it no longer contains the correct address of the debtor. However, the financing statement does not become *ineffective,* and there is no need to file a new financing statement. UCC § 9-507(b). [115]

   If the debtor moves to a different jurisdiction, the secured party will need to file a new financing statement subsequent to the debtor's move in the new state. However, filing in the old state remains effective for four months after the move. It then becomes ineffective and the security interest becomes unperfected, unless the secured party files in the new state. UCC § 9-316(a).

2. **Change in the name of the debtor:** Searches are done by the debtor's name, thus the name is the most critical part of the financing statement. The secured party has four months from the time the name changes to file its new financing statement. Thus, if the name of the debtor changes and, as a result, the financing statement becomes seriously misleading, the filing remains effective but only as to collateral that was obtained before the change in name or within the four months after the change in name, unless an amendment to the financing statement is filed to show the name change. UCC § 9-507(c). The filing remains effective as to all collateral acquired by the debtor before the name change, so the danger of losing perfection because of a change in name only applies when there is an after-acquired property clause and where the security interest is secured by collateral obtained by the debtor more than four months after the change in name. [115]

   a. **How does a secured party best protect against losses resulting from name changes**

      i. **For searchers:** Inquire to the extent possible (based on the size of the loan) into the names the debtor has used during the past four months, or perhaps to be safe, the past six months. Search under those names too.

      ii. **For filers:** Require notification of changes and stay alert to changes through the debtor's documents, and for big loans, a periodic (at least every four months) search of public documents.

3. **Changes affecting the description of collateral—When bad things happen to good collateral:** Sometimes, a debtor grants a security interest in certain collateral and then changes the way it uses that collateral. In other cases, the debtor trades or barters pieces of collateral for other kinds of assets, or simply sells collateral and buys something else with the money. In all of these situations, the new assets acquired, or the old asset being used differently, are proceeds of the secured party's collateral and thus remain part of the collateral. The question is whether the security interest in these new or transformed items remains *perfected.* [117]

   a. **Changes in use:** In some cases the person who gave the security interest in the collateral will keep it but use it in a way that changes its characterization. For example, a business selling copiers may take one of the copiers out of its inventory and use it in its business, thereby changing it from inventory to equipment. If the financing statement describes the collateral as "all of debtor's inventory," the financing statement is now misleading, probably seriously misleading, as to the copier that has become equipment. However, the secured party's filing remains effective. UCC § 9-507(b).

b. **Changes in collateral through barter, sale, or proceeds:** Sometimes collateral changes from one form to another, say from inventory to equipment, because the debtor trades inventory for a piece of equipment. These kinds of transactions are called *barters* and do not involve any cash changing hands, just a trade. In these situations, the secured party obtains a security interest in the property received by the debtor as a result of the trade under the proceeds provisions of Article 9. UCC § 9-315.

c. **Changes in the collateral description resulting from cash sales or involving proceeds of proceeds:** Let's say that the debtor sells a hammer and uses the resulting cash to buy equipment. When cash proceeds are involved, the rule changes. Now the secured party must file an amended financing statement to reflect the transformation of inventory to equipment, even though it's all proceeds, unless the financing filed as to the inventory also included equipment as collateral. UCC § 9-315(d). The new filing must take place within 20 days of the debtor obtaining the new collateral, purchased with the cash proceeds. UCC § 9-315(d)(2).

Finally, any time collateral changes its form from something that is filed in one office to something that is perfected by filing in another office, a new financing statement must be filed in the new office.

4. **Change in form of business:** A person operating a business as a sole proprietor may incorporate or form a limited liability company or partnership. When this occurs, the filing may be in the "wrong place." For example, if the sole proprietor is located in Illinois and incorporates in Delaware, filing of financing statements after the incorporation would be in Delaware rather than Illinois. [119]

If the person has granted security interests before the incorporation, the financing statements will be filed in Illinois; after the incorporation the correct state is Delaware. In effect, the debtor has "moved" from Illinois to Delaware. Any financing statements filed in Illinois are effective for only four months after the move. UCC § 9-316(a).

5. **The so-called "new debtor" problem:** When there is a change in the form of a business, frequently there is a transfer of the assets to the new business form and the new form assumes the debts of the original entity. For example, if a sole proprietorship or general partnership incorporates, the assets of the business will be transferred to the new corporation that will also assume all of the debts of the prior business. The security interest in goods existing at the time of incorporation will not be cut off as a result of the transfer of the assets, UCC § 9-315. A problem arises, however, if the security interest is in after-acquired property.

F. **When to file:** A security interest cannot be perfected until it has attached (UCC § 9-308(a)), i.e., until there is an agreement that it attach, value has been given by the secured party, and the debtor has rights in the collateral. However, the secured party can file its financing statement before perfection, and in any event should file as soon as possible because priority often depends on the time of filing. Searching before filing is important in determining whether other parties have taken a security interest in the collateral, but searching after filing is also important. [117] To be safe, a lender should obtain permission from a potential debtor to file. The lender should then file and then, after a few days, search to make sure that its financing statement is the only one that is filed. Only then should the lender lend the money,

Timely filing is also important if the debtor subsequently files a petition in bankruptcy. If the filing is made significantly after the credit is extended, the security interest may be avoidable by the trustee in bankruptcy as a preferential transfer. 11 U.S.C. § 547. The possibility of a preferential transfer owes to two rules: (1) under the Bankruptcy Code the granting of a security interest is a transfer, and (2) the transfer does not occur until the security interest is perfected. 11 U.S.C. § 347(e)(1).

G. Authority to file: The secured party must have authority to file. UCC §§ 9-509 and 9-510(a). If the debtor signs a security agreement, its signature constitutes authority to file a financing statement, but only as to the collateral that is described in the security agreement. UCC § 9-509(b). Thus, if the security agreement only creates a security interest in inventory, the secured party has no authority to file as to equipment. If a secured party files a financing statement without the authority to do so, it is liable for any loss resulting, including the debtor's inability to obtain other financing or to obtain it only at an increased cost. In addition, the secured party is liable for statutory damages in the amount of $500. UCC § 9-625(e). [121]

H. Duration of filing, continuation statements, and termination statements

1. **Lapse after five years:** Financing statements must be refiled or extended every 5 years, assuming the loan in question is still outstanding. A financing statement that has not been refiled or extended will lapse five years after it is filed. UCC § 9-515(a). [121]

   Thus, a financing statement remains on record and effective for 5 years after it is filed unless it is extended by a continuation statement or earlier terminated by a termination statement. UCC § 9-515(a). The five-year period runs from the date of filing, not the date of attachment. Hence, if a filing statement is filed on February 1, but the loan is not finalized until March 1, the filing would still terminate five years after February 1.

2. **More on continuation statements:** The life of a financing statement may be extended beyond the five-year period by the filing of a continuation statement, but there is a short window of time during which a continuation statement can be filed. UCC § 9-515. The statement must be filed no earlier than six months before the expiration date and no later than the expiration date of the original financing statement. UCC § 9-515(d).

3. **More on termination statements:** When the debt secured has been paid and the secured party has no obligation to extend additional credit, the debtor is entitled to have a termination statement filed to show that there is no longer a security interest on the collateral. When the collateral is other than consumer goods, the secured party must give the termination statement to the debtor and the debtor will file it. However, if the collateral is consumer goods, the secured party must file it. If the secured party fails to file the termination statement (also called a loan satisfaction) and the debtor is injured by the failure to satisfy, the debtor can recover actual damages as well as a civil penalty of $500. See UCC § 9-625(b), (e)(4). [122]

IV. PERFECTION BY SECURED PARTY TAKING POSSESSION OF THE COLLATERAL

A. Introduction: Originally, taking possession of collateral was the only way to perfect. Called a *pledge*, this method of "perfection" greatly limited the availability of secured credit because frequently the purpose of a secured transaction was to allow the debtor to retain possession of assets it needed to run its business. For example, if the debtor is financing its equipment, it needs the equipment to run its business and to make money to repay the loan. [123–126]

The rationale for allowing the creditor to perfect by taking possession of the collateral is that one dealing with property should be suspicious if the person with whom he or she is dealing does not have possession.

B. Types of collateral subject to perfection by possession: Although filing is the most common method of perfection under Article 9, the Article allows perfection by possession for many types of collateral. Perfection by possession is allowed when the collateral is:

1. goods,
2. instruments,
3. tangible negotiable documents of title,
4. money,
5. tangible chattel paper, and
6. certificated securities.

UCC § 9-313.

As to other types of collateral, there is nothing to possess that would give the "possessor" dominion over the collateral. Consider accounts. Although accounts usually will be represented by a writing that can be possessed, possession of the writing is not possession of the account; it is possession only of evidence of the account. Thus, generally, a security interest in intangibles cannot be perfected by filing.

Some intangibles, however, are so integrated into a writing that possession of the writing is tantamount to possession of the intangible. Consider negotiable notes, which are instruments under Article 9. Security interests in them can be perfected by filing, because possession of the instrument is usually necessary to its enforcement (UCC § 9-310), but they can also be perfected by possession (UCC § 9-313). Indeed, perfection by possession provides better protection to the secured party with instruments.

The same is true of tangible negotiable documents of title. If the owner of goods stores the goods with a warehouse, the warehouse will issue a "warehouse receipt." If the owner of goods ships the goods by a common carrier, the carrier will issue a "bill of lading." Both are documents of title under Article 9. UCC § 1-201(a)(16). [123]

C. What constitutes possession: Possession by an agent of the secured party is also sufficient so long as the agent is holding the collateral solely as agent of the secured party. Official Comment 3 to UCC § 9-313. However, if the goods are given to an escrow agent with instructions to return them to either the secured party or the debtor, depending upon the happening of some event, the secured party would not have possession because the escrow agent has obligations running to both the debtor and the secured party. Official Comment 3 to UCC § 9-313. [128]

"Field warehousing" is a method of securing loans secured by inventory. Primarily to obtain better control over the collateral, the secured party sets up a warehouse near the debtor, perhaps on the same premises where the debtor operates its business, and the inventory is kept in that warehouse. Sometimes the so-called warehouse is just an area of the debtor's premises that is cordoned off in some way from the rest of the premises.

D. Possession as substitute for security agreement—Necessity of attachment: No *written* security agreement is necessary when the secured party takes possession of the collateral. Hence, possession has a twofold use: (1) it substitutes for the writing usually required to create a security interest, and (2) it may operate to perfect the security interest.

V. AUTOMATIC PERFECTION

Article 9 provides that perfection occurs automatically as soon as the security interest attaches in a few very narrow situations. UCC § 9-309. In other words, the secured party need do nothing to perfect its security interest; it need neither file nor take possession of the collateral. The most important situation in which perfection is automatic is when the collateral is consumer goods *and* the security interest is a purchase-money security interest (PMSI). UCC § 9-309(1). [129]

Even though a PMSI in consumer goods is automatically perfected, the secured party can file. By filing, the secured party obtains greater protection. If the secured party relies on its automatic perfection and does not file, a casual buyer takes free of the security interest. UCC § 9-320(b).

Sales of promissory notes, a subclass of instruments, are secured transactions. They are perfected automatically, UCC § 9-309(4), but buyers of a promissory note in the ordinary course take free of the security interest.

Security interests in an account created by an assignment of the account are automatically perfected if the assignment "does not by itself or in conjunction with other assignments to the same assignee, transfer a significant part of the assignor's account." UCC § 9-309(2).

VI. PERFECTION BY TAKING CONTROL

Control, as used in Article 9 as a means of perfection, is a technical term. Perfection by control is possible only when the collateral is:

1. investment property,
2. deposit accounts,
3. letter-of-credit rights,
4. electronic chattel paper, or
5. electronic documents.

UCC § 9-314.

As to deposit accounts and letter-of-credit rights, control is the *only* way in which perfection can be accomplished. How a secured party obtains control depends on the type of collateral. UCC §§ 9-104, 9-105, 9-106, and 9-107. The secured party need not necessarily have exclusive control. For example, if the collateral is a deposit account, an agreement with the bank giving both the secured party and the debtor access to the account constitutes sufficient control. UCC § 9-104.

VII. CONTINUOUS PERFECTION

If a financing statement is filed after the security interest has attached, perfection remains continuous from the time of filing, which is the moment when the financing statement is given to the clerk, until the filing terminates either by the passage of time (five years if no continuation statement is filed), or by the filing of a termination statement.

When perfection is by possession, questions may arise regarding whether the perfection is continuous from the time that the secured party obtains possession. If the secured party returns the property to the debtor, perfection will cease, and if the debtor subsequently gives possession back to the secured party, the date of perfection becomes the time that the property is returned.

When there is a change in the method of perfection, e.g., the secured party takes possession and some time later files a financing statement, the perfection is continuous so long as there is no time during which there was no perfection by one or the other method. UCC § 9-308(c).

VIII. PERFECTION OF SECURITY INTERESTS IN PROCEEDS

As is discussed in Chapter 4, a secured party automatically obtains a security interest in identifiable proceeds. UCC § 9-315(a)(2). The security interest in the proceeds is perfected automatically for 20 days. UCC § 9-315(c)(d). If the proceeds are cash proceeds, perfection continues automatically after the 20 days. UCC § 9-315(d)(2). Perfection in the proceeds also continues if the secured party perfects the security interest in the proceeds by taking possession or by filing within the 20-day period. UCC § 9-315(3). [131]

Perfection as to proceeds may also occur under the "same office" rule. If there is perfection by filing as to the original collateral and the proceeds are collateral that can be perfected in the same office, there is perfection as to the new collateral of the proceeds. For example, if the original collateral is inventory and the proceeds are accounts, because both can be perfected by filing in the Secretary of State's office, there is perfection as to the accounts.

IX. PERFECTION OF SECURITY INTERESTS IN FIXTURES

A security interest can be perfected in fixtures by filing a regular UCC financing statement, as with other goods, but the perfection obtained by simply filing in the central office does not provide much protection. It is totally ineffective as to purchasers of the real property and mortgagees. To obtain protection against those who have an interest in the real property, the secured party must file a "fixture filing." Both the contents of the fixture filing and the location in which it is filed are different from filings as to other collateral. [132]

A *fixture filing* is a financing statement that contains additional information. In addition to the requirements of an ordinary financing statement it must:

1. state that the goods are fixtures;
2. state that the financing statement is to be filed in the real property recording system;
3. contain a description of the real property to which the fixture is or will be affixed; and
4. contain the name of the record owner of the real property if the debtor does not have an interest in the real property.

UCC § 9-502(b).

The description of the real property is sufficient if it complies with the requirements of the real property filing rules of the jurisdiction. Official Comment 5 to UCC § 9-502. A fixture filing must comply with the real property recording rules of the jurisdiction. In most states, this means filing with the county clerk or some other office in the county where the real property is located. The fixture filing must be filed in the filing system for real property. In most cases this will be in the county clerk's office in the country where the real property is located.

X. PERFECTION OF AGRICULTURAL LIENS

Agricultural liens can be perfected only by filing. UCC § 9-308(b). Perfection becomes effective when the financing statement has been filed and the lien has become attached under the state law creating it.

XI. ASSIGNMENT OF SECURITY INTERESTS

If a perfected security interest is assigned by the secured party, no new filing is required to continue the perfection. UCC § 9-310(c).

CHAPTER 6

PRIORITIES

I. AN INTRODUCTION TO PRIORITIES PROBLEMS

A. **What is a "priorities problem"?** Priorities problems under Article 9 involve situations in which a security interest has been created in certain personal property, the collateral, and someone other than the secured party also claims an interest in this property. [144]

B. **The three types of priorities problems:** Article 9 governs three basic types of priorities problems:

   1. Disputes between the secured party and persons to whom the collateral has been sold or otherwise transferred by the debtor;
   2. Disputes arising when the debtor has given a security interest in the same collateral to two or more persons; and
   3. Disputes in which a secured party and a creditor with a judicial, statutory, or common law lien (other than an agricultural lien) are contesting who has better rights in the collateral.

C. **An approach to priorities problems:** In analyzing priorities problems, the first step is to determine the status of the parties. At least one of the parties will be claiming a security interest under Article 9. The other party may also be a secured party, or might instead be a transferee of the collateral from the debtor, or a lien creditor. [145]

   Each time you analyze a priorities problem, we suggest you answer four questions about the secured party:

   1. Is the claimed security interest valid?
   2. What is the type of collateral?
   3. Is the security interest a purchase-money security interest (PMSI)?
   4. Is the security interest perfected, and, if so, when and how was it perfected?

   1. **Validity of the security interest:** There are four requirements for creation of a security interest: (1) there must be an agreement by the debtor that the creditor is to have a security interest; (2) unless the secured party has possession, the agreement must be a record that is authenticated by the debtor; (3) the agreement must contain a description of the collateral; and (4) the agreement must contain language indicating that the purpose of the transaction is to create a security interest. See Chapter 4.

2. **Type of collateral—Goods versus intangible personal property:** Goods are subdivided into consumer goods, equipment, inventory, and farm products (including livestock and crops). Also to be considered separately in the context of priorities are a few tangible categories of collateral that are special kinds of goods, namely fixtures, accessions, and commingled goods. Intangible collateral includes accounts, chattel paper, commercial tort claims, deposit accounts, electronic chattel paper, general intangibles, health-care insurance receivables, instruments, letter-of-credit rights, payment intangibles, software, and tangible chattel paper. See Chapter 3.

3. **PMSIs:** A PMSI is one in which the credit was extended to allow the debtor to obtain the collateral. When the debtor is buying goods and is to pay for them in the future, perhaps in installments, and gives back to the seller a security interest in the goods, the seller-secured party has a PMSI. Also, if a third party extends credit to allow the debtor to obtain the goods in which a security interest is granted to the creditor, the creditor has a PMSI.

4. **Perfection:** Perfection usually occurs through the filing of a financing statement, but may be accomplished by the creditor taking possession of the collateral if the collateral is of a certain type. Also, in a few cases, perfection occurs automatically. In still other types of cases, perfection occurs by the creditor taking "control" of the collateral. The time that perfection occurs is often critical in determining priority problems. However, a secured party often gets the earlier date of filing or perfection when perfection occurs at a time different from the time of filing. See Chapter 5.

    The final step is to apply the priorities rules. A starting point, but only a starting point, is the "first in time–first in right" rule, which means that the first person to acquire a right will have priority over parties whose rights arise later. This rule does not, however, apply to all priority competitions.

5. **Apply the priorities rules:** The final step is to apply the priorities rules. Article 9 contains a significant number of rules governing priority, and they cannot be condensed into a "general rule" that applies to all transactions.

6. **Agricultural lien:** Analysis of the status of one holding an agricultural lien is somewhat simpler. Whether it exists (has been created) will depend on state law outside the Uniform Commercial Code (UCC). Whether the collateral falls within the scope of agricultural lien and how it should be characterized and described, also will depend on the non-Code statute.

II. PRIORITIES INVOLVING PARTIES EACH CLAIMING A SECURITY INTEREST IN THE COLLATERAL: SECURED PARTY VERSUS SECURED PARTY

A. **Introduction:** Priority competitions only occur when the debtor has granted a security interest to more than one creditor in the same collateral. The time that a secured party perfects or files is the most important event in determining priority between two secured parties. However, PMSIs are given preferential treatment in some instances. [147]

B. **When none of the secured parties has a PMSI:** If the debtor has given a security interest to two or more parties, and none of the secured parties has a PMSI, three rules determine priority.

1. **Perfected versus unperfected:** If only one of the secured parties has perfected its security interest, the perfected security interest has priority over the other unperfected security interests.

   2. Unperfected versus unperfected: When none of the parties has perfected, the first security interest to attach prevails. UCC § 9-322(3). Attachment requires (1) that there be an agreement that the security interest attach (the security agreement), (2) that the secured party has given value, and (3) that the debtor has rights in the collateral. See Chapter 3.

   3. Perfected versus perfected: When all of the security interests are perfected, the first to either perfect or file has priority if neither party has a PMSI. UCC § 9-322(1). The rule is NOT that the first to *perfect* prevails, but that the first to *either* file or perfect prevails. Thus, a secured party gets the benefit of the earlier of the time of perfection or the time of filing.

C. When one of the secured parties has a PMSI

   1. Introduction: Only when the collateral is goods (other than crops) or software can there be a PMSI. Article 9 gives special priority treatment to PMSIs under several different rules. Distinctions among the various types of goods are important in the consideration of these rules. The rules for software and livestock are also distinct. [150]

   2. PMSIs in goods other than inventory and livestock: A PMSI in goods other than inventory or livestock has priority over all other security interests in the same collateral if it is perfected within 20 days of the date on which the debtor obtains possession of the goods. UCC § 9-324(a).

   3. PMSIs in inventory: When the collateral is inventory, the preferred treatment given to a PMSI is narrower. A PMSI in inventory prevails over another security interest in the same inventory only if (1) the PMSI is perfected *before* the debtor obtains possession of it; and (2) notice was given to the conflicting secured party.

   4. Consignments: A consignment is a secured transaction (see UCC §§ 9-109(a)(4), 9-102(a)(20)), and a consignor's security interest in the goods consigned is a PMSI (UCC § 9-103(d)). Because the goods are held by the consignee for the purpose of sale, the collateral is inventory and the PMSI rules for inventory apply. Official Comment 7 to UCC § 9-324. [153]

   5. PMSIs in livestock: A PMSI in livestock, a subcategory of farm products, is treated similarly to a PMSI in inventory. To gain priority, the purchase money secured party must perfect before the debtor obtains possession of the livestock. Also, the purchase money secured party must give notice, this time within the six years preceding the time that the debtor received possession of the livestock in which the purchase money secured party claims a security interest. The notice must state that the purchase money secured party has or intends to take a security interest in the livestock and must describe the livestock.

D. Conflicting security interests in proceeds

   1. Introduction: A secured party obtains a security interest not only in the collateral described in the security agreement but also in any proceeds. UCC § 9-315(a)(2). A security interest in proceeds is perfected automatically for 20 days and remains perfected if the proceeds are (1) identifiable cash, (2) there is a new filing as to the proceeds, or (3) the proceeds are of a type that can be perfected by filing in the same manner as the original collateral, as long as there was a filing as to the original collateral. UCC § 9-315(d). [153]

   Conflicts may arise between the secured party who has a security interest in the collateral as proceeds and a secured party who specifically took a security interest in the collateral that constitutes the proceeds. The most common conflicts arise when the debtor has given a security interest in inventory to one person and a security interest in accounts to a second person. When inventory is sold and generates accounts, both secured parties will have a security interest in the accounts, and the question may arise as to who has priority. If neither is a PMSI, priority goes to the first to file or perfect.

2. **Priorities in proceeds when there is no PMSI:** If neither the secured party with the security interest in the collateral as proceeds nor the secured party who took a security interest in the proceeds as original collateral has a PMSI, the first in time–first in right rule is applied to conflicts between security interests in the same collateral. UCC § 9-322(a). This rule applies even though one of the parties took a security interest in the collateral as original collateral and the other obtained its security interest as proceeds. [154]

   Thus, if both security interests are perfected, the secured party who is first to file or perfect prevails. In making the determination as to which secured party has filed or perfected first, the secured party who has the security interest in the property as proceeds of the original collateral gets the date when it perfected or filed as to the original collateral. UCC § 9-322(b)(1).

3. **Priorities in proceeds when the security interest in the original collateral is a PMSI:** A PMSI in the original collateral retains its preferred status as a PMSI in all proceeds if the original collateral is anything other than inventory. UCC § 9-324(a). Thus, as to the proceeds, a secured party who has perfected its security interest in the original collateral within 20 days of the delivery of the original collateral prevails over all other secured parties who have a security interest in the proceeds of the original collateral. [155]

   When the original collateral is inventory, the PMSI preference given to proceeds is much narrower than in equipment and other collateral. Although in some cases the special treatment given to PMSI lenders extends to instruments and chattel paper, it basically extends only to cash proceeds that are received by the debtor on or before the inventory is delivered to the debtor. UCC § 9-324(b). Thus, in most cases, the first in time rule applies to priority disputes in the proceeds of inventory.

III. PRIORITIES BETWEEN A SECURED PARTY AND A TRANSFEREE (OR BUYER) FROM THE DEBTOR

A. **Introduction:** After a debtor has granted a security interest to a secured party, the debtor may transfer the collateral to a third person. Also, a debtor whose property is subject to an agricultural lien may transfer it. The transfer raises the question of whether the secured party's security interest or the agricultural lienholder's lien continues in the collateral after the transfer or whether it is cut off as a result of the transfer. [156]

   A security interest or agricultural lien continues in the collateral and the secured party or lienholder can repossess the collateral from the transferee *unless* there is a provision in Article 9 giving the transferee better rights. UCC § 9-315(a)(1). The resolution of a dispute requires an inspection of situations in which Article 9 protects the transferee by providing that the security interest does not continue in the collateral.

   Ask the same four questions about the secured party: (1) Is the security interest properly created? (2) What kind of property is the collateral? (3) Is the security interest a PMSI? (4) Is the security interest perfected, and, if so, when and how?

   Now classify the transferee. Is the transferee a purchaser with value who has taken delivery without knowledge of the security interest or agricultural lien? UCC § 9-317(b). Or is the transferee a buyer in ordinary course (BIOC) of business? UCC § 1-201(a)(9), § 9-320(a).

Or is the transferee a casual buyer? UCC § 9-320(b). Once the status of the secured party and the transferee are established, the applicable priorities rules determine who has priority.

B. Transferees who are donees or who take with knowledge of the security interest: Between a secured party and a transferee who does not give value to the debtor-transferor (a donee), the secured party prevails and its security interest can be asserted against the donee. The secured party wins even though the secured party has failed to perfect its security interest.

With one exception for BIOCs, the same is true of transferees who take with knowledge of the security interest. Security interests, even though unperfected, beat out transferees who had knowledge of the security interest at the time that they purchased the collateral.

C. Transferees who give value without knowledge of the security interest and receive delivery of the collateral

1. **When the security interest is not a PMSI:** One type of transferee protected under Article 9 is a purchaser who gives value, and takes delivery, without knowledge of an existing security interest, or a "P/V w/o K." The priorities rule applied is first in time–first in right. The critical times are the time that the buyer meets all of the requirements of a P/V w/o K (value and delivery without knowledge of an existing security interest) and the time that the secured party perfected. UCC § 9-317(b). Knowledge is actual knowledge, not simply notice. Value is broadly defined to include any consideration, including a preexisting debt. See UCC § 1-202. [157]

2. **When the security interest is a PMSI:** If the security interest is a PMSI, and the secured party files within 20 days of the time that the buyer receives delivery of the goods, see UCC § 9-317(e), the PMSI secured lender has 20 days in which to file, and the 20 days starts when the buyer receives delivery. If this filing is done during the 20 days, the secured party's rights are superior to those of the buyer. [158]

D. Casual buyers: Casual buyers, sometimes called "consumer buyers" or "garage sale buyers," are buyers who (1) buy the goods for their own personal, family, or household use *and* (2) purchase the goods from a seller who is holding the goods as consumer goods. UCC § 9-320(b). Casual buyers take free of all security interests that are not perfected by filing, but take subject to security interests that are perfected by filing. The protection for casual buyers applies most frequently when the secured party had a PMSI that was perfected automatically because the debtor purchased the goods as consumer goods, and the debtor then sells the goods to someone who also intends to use the goods as consumer goods. [159]

A secured party who has perfected by possession and is still in possession of the collateral also can enforce its security interest against a casual buyer even if there is no filing. See UCC § 9-320(e).

E. Buyers in ordinary course (BIOCs)

1. **Who is a BIOC?** BIOCs usually, but not always, take free of a security interest on the goods purchased. A BIOC is a buyer: (1) who buys goods (2) in good faith (3) without knowledge that the sale violates the rights of another person (4) in the ordinary course of business (5) from someone selling goods of the kind purchased, and (6) who takes possession, or who has the right to possession from the seller. UCC § 1-201(a)(9). [160–161]

The requirement that the person be a "buyer" excludes a donee. The definition also excludes persons who acquire goods as security for, or in total or partial satisfaction of, a debt. Good faith requires acting honestly and observing reasonable commercial standards of fair dealing. The definition does not prevent one from knowing of the existence of a security interest; rather, it requires knowledge that the sale is in violation of another's rights. Thus, a buyer may know that the seller has given a security interest and still be a BIOC, but if the buyer knows that the security agreement or some other agreement prohibits the sale of the goods without the secured party's permission, the buyer is not a BIOC unless permission is given.

The sale must be in the ordinary course of business. The test is whether the sale comports with usual or customary practices. In most cases, a BIOC purchases from a retailer, but a sale from a wholesaler or manufacturer to a retailer can be in the ordinary course. Purchasers at sales where the price is reduced can be BIOCs, as can be purchasers who buy on credit.

Connected with the requirement that the sale be in the ordinary course is the requirement that the seller be in the business of selling goods of that kind. Manufacturers, wholesalers, and retailers clearly meet this test as to goods they normally sell. However, a retailing clothing store would not be a seller of goods of the kind if it sold its computer. A sale by a pawnbroker is excluded from this exception, so a buyer who purchases from a pawnbroker cannot be a BIOC.

The buyer must either take possession of the goods or have a right to possession as against the seller. A buyer who has paid for the goods has a right to possession of them under Article 2, and a sale to a buyer who directs that the goods be delivered to someone else as a gift also meets the possession test.

2. Rights of a BIOC: A BIOC takes free of all security interests *created by the seller,* even if the security interest is perfected. Thus, if a retail appliance store has given a security interest in all of its inventory, a purchaser of inventory takes free of the security interest and the secured party may not repossess the goods from the purchaser. However, the security interest of a secured party in possession of the goods is not cut off by a sale to a BIOC. Thus, the security interest can be enforced against the buyer. [161]

F. Transferee's derivative rights: A transferee of goods gets all of the title and rights of its transferor, and if the transferor took free of an existing security interest, so does the transferee. This is true even though the transferee is a donee or took with knowledge of the security interest.

IV. PRIORITIES BETWEEN A SECURED PARTY AND A LIEN CREDITOR

A. Introduction: A security interest itself is a type of lien, called a consensual lien because it arises by agreement of the debtor, but Article 9 calls the interest a *security interest* instead of a lien. UCC § 9-102(a)(52). When Article 9 uses the term "lien" by itself, the reference is only to these types of liens. [162]

Judicial liens usually arise as a result of a creditor obtaining a judgment and then executing on the debtor's property. Liens may also arise as a result of statutes or the common law. For example, a landlord usually has a lien on all of the tenant's property that is on the leased premises. Article 9 calls these "possessory liens" and treats them separately from judicial liens. UCC § 9-333.

Agricultural liens are another separate type of lien defined under Article 9. UCC § 9-102(a)(5). For most purposes, agricultural liens are treated the same as security interests, and the priorities rules for them are generally the same as for security interests.

B. Priorities between security interests and judicial liens: The basic rule is first in time–first in right. The critical time for the lienholder is the time that the lien arose or attached to the property. The critical time for the secured party is a little more complicated. In most cases, it is the time of perfection. However, if the secured party has filed earlier, and there is a later security agreement granting the secured party a security interest in the property, the secured party is given the benefit of the earlier filing. UCC § 9-317(a). [163]

A secured party with a PMSI has 20 days in which to perfect to retain its preferred PMSI status. If the purchase money secured party files during that period, the secured party has priority over intervening lien creditors, meaning those who obtain their liens during the 20-day period. UCC § 9-317(e). As you can see, this makes the PMSI security interest a secret lien during the 20 days.

V. FUTURE ADVANCES AND PRIORITIES

A. **Introduction:** In addition to securing obligations owed to the secured party at the time that the security interest is given, a security interest may also secure advances made in the future. UCC § 9-204(c). If the secured party is required to extend credit in the future, these promises to lend are made, in the words of Article 9, "pursuant to commitment." UCC § 9-102(a)(68). A secured party who makes a future advance pursuant to commitment may have better rights than one who makes an advance without any obligation to do so. In most cases, the secured party who makes future advances gets the earlier of the time of either perfection or filing in determining priority. [164]

B. **Future advances in competitions between two or more secured parties:** When the debtor has given a security interest to two parties and one of them is claiming that its security interest secures a future advance, the first to perfect or file rule applies in most cases. In effect, the time that the advance is made is immaterial. See Official Comment 3 to UCC § 9-323. Whether the future advance is made "pursuant to commitment" is immaterial in determining the priority between two or more voluntary secured parties with interests in the same collateral. [165]

C. **When the competing party is a transferee (buyer) or lessee of the collateral from the debtor:** When the competing parties are a secured party and a transferee or buyer, the rules are more complex. Assume that after a debtor has given a security interest in collateral, the debtor sells or leases the collateral and that the transfer does not cut off the security interest. Clearly, the secured party may repossess the collateral and take from the sale enough money to satisfy the debt incurred before the sale. However, if the secured party makes an advance to the debtor subsequent to the sale, the question arises as to whether the amount of that advance also has priority as to the buyer or lessee. In other words, when the collateral is repossessed, and sold by the secured party, can the secured party take enough money out of the proceeds of the sale to satisfy both the debt incurred before the sale and also the debt incurred by the advance made after the sale? UCC § 9-323(d), (f). [164–165]

If the future advance is not made "pursuant to commitment," Article 9 provides that the priority of the secured party extends to future advances made less than 45 days after the purchase or lease, which becomes enforceable if they are made by the secured party without knowledge of the security interest. UCC § 9-323(c), (g). Thus, the secured party will lose its priority over the transferee as to any future advance made after 45 days from the time of the transfer *or* after having knowledge of the transfer.

D. **When the competing party has a lien:** When the competition is between a secured party and a lienholder, the rules regarding future advances are even more complex. The priorities rule between a secured party making an advance and a lienholder uses a 45-day period, but in a very different way than the time period is used in relation to buyers. The rule is much more favorable to the secured party. During the 45 days after the transfer, an advance by the secured party has priority even if the secured party knows of the transfer. After the 45 days has run, the secured party still has priority if it made the advance either: (1) without knowledge of the lien, *or* (2) in fulfillment of a commitment. UCC § 9-323(b). [167]

VI. FIXTURES

A. **Introduction to fixtures:** Fixtures are goods that have been attached to real property in a way that gives them some of the characteristics of realty and in a way that causes an interest in them to arise under real property law. UCC § 9-102(a)(41). They retain sufficient aspects of personal property to allow a creditor to take an Article 9 security interest in them. UCC § 9-334(a). However, an Article 9 security interest cannot be created in ordinary building materials that become a part of the structure. [169]

If the goods that are fixtures were not attached to the realty they would be classified under Article 9 as either equipment or consumer goods. Thus, if a heating unit is attached to an office building and becomes a fixture, it would also be equipment; if attached to a home, it would be consumer goods. So long as no person claiming an interest in a fixture has an interest in the real property to which it is attached, the normal rules of perfection and priority apply. Perfection is by filing a financing statement with the Secretary of State, and the rules discussed previously apply.

If one of the parties has an interest in the fixture because it has an interest in the real property to which the fixture is affixed, different rules on both perfection and priority apply. These rules apply when the dispute:

1. is between a creditor with a security interest in the fixture and a purchaser of the building in which the fixture is installed; or
2. is between a secured party and someone claiming a consensual lien on the building, for example a mortgagee, or between a secured party and a person claiming a judicial lien on the real property.

UCC § 9-334.

Perfection of the security interest must be different if the secured party is to have any rights against these persons, as discussed in Chapter 5. The secured party must file a "fixture filing," and the filing must be with the real property records.

B. **Priority when a security interest in fixtures is not a PMSI:** As between a secured party and the person having an interest in the real property, the first to file or record rule applies. In most cases, for the secured party to prevail, (1) it must have filed a fixture filing before a recording of the real property interest, i.e., the mortgage or deed, and (2) the debtor must have been in possession of the real property or have an interest in it when the security interest was given. UCC § 9-334(e)(1). The debtor will have an interest in the property as long as it is the owner or has a lease that is recorded. A secured party also must have priority over the predecessor in title to the one claiming a real property interest. *Id.* [170]

C. **Priority when a security interest in fixtures is a PMSI:** A PMSI in fixtures takes priority over a conflicting interest of a mortgagee or owner of the property if:

1. the interest of the mortgagor or owner arose before the goods became fixtures, and
2. the secured party filed a fixture filing within 20 days of the time the goods became fixtures.

UCC § 9-334(d). [171]

VII. CROPS

Crops, a subtype of farm products (see UCC § 9-102(a)(34)(A)), are not fixtures but bear a similarity to them in that crops are a part of the real property, and a person having an interest in the realty has an interest in the crops. Crops can, however, be collateral for an Article 9 security interest.

When the dispute is between a security interest in crops and a second security interest in the same crops, or a creditor with a lien on the crops, the default priority provisions apply. The same applies when there is a dispute between a secured party and one having an agricultural lien, because agricultural liens are treated as security interests. As between a secured party and one having a judicial lien, the rule is that the lien creditor prevails if the lien attached before the time at which the secured party perfected.

Article 9 does not give the usual protection given to BIOCs if the collateral is crops. UCC § 9-320(a). Thus, a buyer of crops prevails only over unperfected security interests. UCC § 9-317(b). However, BIOCs of crops will take free of security interests under the Federal Farm Security Act unless there is compliance with the notice or filing requirements of that Act. The special preferences given to purchase money secured parties do not apply, because it is impossible to have a PMSI in crops. As between a security interest in crops and those having an interest in the real property, the security interest has priority so long as the security interest is perfected and the debtor has possession of the land or has a recorded interest in it. The time of perfection is immaterial.

VIII. ACCESSIONS AND COMMINGLED GOODS

A. **Accessions:** An *accession* is a good that is physically united with another good without losing its identity. UCC § 9-102(a)(1). For example, if an engine is installed in an automobile, the engine is an accession. A security interest may be created in an accession and will continue in the accession after it becomes part of the other goods. Perfection of the accession also continues after it is united with the other goods. [173]

The regular priorities rules apply to any conflict between the person having a security interest in the accession and the person who has a security interest in the goods of which the accession becomes a part. Thus, if the party having the security interest in the accession filed before the person who has the security interest in the goods of which the accession becomes a part, the accession secured party has priority. A secured party in accessions also gains the preference given to PMSIs.

B. **Commingled goods:** *Commingled goods* are goods that are united with other goods in a way that causes them to lose their identity. UCC § 9-336(a). For example, if a farmer stores grain in a commercial silo with the grain of other farmers, the grain loses its identity. Article 9 provides that there can be no security interest in goods that are commingled with other goods (UCC § 9-336(b)), but that a security interest in the goods before they are commingled becomes a security interest in the whole of goods. UCC § 9-336(c).

If the secured party has perfected its security interest in the goods before they are commingled, its security interest in the whole is also perfected. If more than one secured party has a security interest in the whole, perfected security interests have priority over unperfected security interests. If more than one security interest is perfected, the security interests rank in proportion to the value of the collateral at the time it was commingled. UCC § 9-336(f).

IX. MISCELLANEOUS PRIORITIES RULES

A. Licensee of general intangibles: A person who obtains a licensee of general intangibles in good faith, without knowledge that the license violates the rights of another and in the ordinary course of business is called a *licensee in the ordinary course of business.* A licensee in the ordinary course of a nonexclusive license takes free of all security interests created by the licensor even if they are perfected and the lessee knows of their existence. UCC § 9-321(a).

B. Lessee in ordinary course of business: A lessee in the ordinary course of business of goods takes free of all security interests created by the lessor even if they are perfected and the lessee knows of their existence. UCC § 9-321(b).

C. Priority of security interests in deposit accounts: A security interest in deposit accounts (which are bank accounts, and should not be confused with accounts), can be perfected only by the secured party taking control of the deposit account. UCC § 9-312(b)(1). When the secured party has taken control of the account, and thus perfected its security interest, the security interest takes priority over all unperfected security interests and security interests that were perfected later. UCC § 9-327.

    Transferees of money from a deposit account take free of any security interests in the account, even if perfected, unless the transferee acts in collusion with the debtor in violating the rights of the secured party. UCC § 9-332.

D. Purchasers of chattel paper

    1. When the secured party claims an interest in the chattel paper as proceeds: A purchaser of chattel paper (as opposed to a person who takes a security interest in chattel paper to secure a loan) has priority over a security interest in chattel paper if the security interest arises solely because it is proceeds of collateral in which the secured party has a security interest when the purchaser (1) is in good faith, (2) buys in the ordinary course of the purchaser's business, (3) gives new value, (4) and either takes possession of the chattel paper or obtains control of it, provided that the chattel paper does not contain a legend on it that indicates that it has been assigned to someone other than the purchaser. UCC § 9-330(a). New value is defined as "(i) money, (ii) money's worth in property, services or new credit, or (iii) release by a transferee of any interest in property previously transferred to the transferee." UCC § 9-103(a)(57). New value does not include an obligation substituted for another obligation. *Id.* When the secured party's security interest in the chattel paper exists because the chattel paper is proceeds, a purchaser who meets these requirements takes free of the security interest even if the purchaser knows that the sale violates the rights of the secured party. [175]

    2. When the security interest in chattel paper does not arise as proceeds: A secured party may take a security interest directly in chattel paper as the collateral securing a loan. In these cases, a purchaser takes free of the security interest only if meets the requirement noted previously (the purchaser (1) takes for new value, (2) takes possession or control of the chattel paper, (3) takes in the ordinary course of the purchaser's business, (4) takes in good faith, and (5) also takes without knowledge that the sale violates the rights of the secured party). UCC § 9-330(b). "Knowledge" is actual knowledge, and there is no obligation on the purchaser to check the filing records or otherwise attempt to obtain knowledge that the sale violates the secured party's rights. Even if the purchaser knows that a security interest has been given in the chattel paper, this does not mean that it knows (i.e., has actual knowledge) that the sale violates the rights of the secured party. Again, this is similar to the rule protecting BIOCs.

E. Purchasers protected under other Articles of the Code: Certain bona fide purchasers are protected under other Articles of the Code. In Article 3, a "holder in due course" is given significant rights against ownership claims to a negotiable instrument by another person. Similarly, under Article 7, persons who take a negotiable document of title by "due negotiation," and "protected persons" under Article 8, generally take free of adverse claims.

Because negotiable instruments, documents of title, and investment securities can be collateral under Article 9, the person protected in Articles 3, 7, and 8 are given the same protection against secured parties as they are as against another person who deals with the documents. UCC § 9-302. In other words, a holder in due course's rights are not impaired by any priorities rule in Article 9, and a holder in due course takes free of all security interests in the transferred instrument. UCC § 9-302.

CHAPTER 7

SOME BASIC BANKRUPTCY CONCEPTS

I. INTRODUCTION

Most textbooks we have reviewed address the topic of bankruptcy at the end of the course, just as this Outline will do. Bankruptcy topics can be interspersed throughout a course, but for a more cohesive approach, we choose to address them at the end of the text here. Some Secured Transactions courses follow this approach as well; however, we suspect that most barely touch on the information we have included in this chapter. We therefore assume that you'll learn most of this in another law school course, and discuss only the basic types of bankruptcy here: the automatic stay, the treatment of secured claims in bankruptcy, and certain of the bankruptcy avoidance powers. We will also tell you here if the bankruptcy topic discussed below is substantively connected in some way to something we covered already in another chapter of this Outline.

II. THE DIFFERENT TYPES OF BANKRUPTCY

Bankruptcy cases in the United States fall into either of two categories: (1) "sell-out" or liquidation style, in which the assets available for creditors are sold and distributed to creditors, and (2) "pay-out" cases in which the debtor promises in a repayment plan to pay some or all creditors from future income over time. Just as under state law, secured creditors have superior rights in bankruptcy when compared to creditors who do not have any collateral. [183–186]

A. Chapter 7

1. General theme: A Chapter 7 case is called a liquidation, or sell-out, case and is quickly resolved. In each case, a trustee, who serves as a fiduciary for all unsecured creditors and is charged with maximizing value for estate creditors, is appointed to gather all assets available to pay creditors and sell them, distributing the proceeds according to a structured priority scheme. [186]

2. **Exemptions and discharge:** Just as under state law, some property is exempt in a bankruptcy. Generally none of the debtor's exempt property is liquidated. In exchange for a complete and full disclosure of all financial information, the debtor receives a discharge of most debts within 90 days of filing the case. However, secured debts are not discharged.

3. **Simplicity:** Most of the time, Chapter 7 cases are simple and uneventful. They are administered by the Chapter 7 trustee within 90 days of the filing, involve no court hearings, and the debtor obtains a discharge of most debts after 90 days.

4. **Possible issues:** Occasionally issues come up in simple Chapter 7 cases. These include partial disclosure by the debtor; disagreement between the trustee and the debtor about which property is exempt or the values of the debtor's property; or objection, by the trustee or an individual creditor, to the debtor's discharge due to wrongdoing by the debtor right before or during the case. The Bankruptcy Code also imposes a means test, which can cause the trustee to question whether the debtor has appropriately filed the case under Chapter 7 or should have filed a repayment plan case under Chapter 13.

B. Chapter 13

1. **General theme:** Chapter 13 is most often used for the purpose of curing past due amounts on secured debts. These are payout-style cases. [186]

2. **Exemptions:** The Chapter 13 debtor is allowed to keep all of his or her property, both exempt and nonexempt, as long as the debtor is paying at least the value of these nonexempt assets to creditors under the repayment plan.

3. **The repayment plan:** The debtor proposes a repayment plan and will make the proposed payments for three to five years during which time all secured claims and priority claims will be paid in full. A distribution is paid to unsecured creditors as well if the debtor has sufficient disposable income.

4. **The Chapter 13 trustee:** The case is administered by a Chapter 13 trustee who is a fiduciary for creditors and charged with creating the best possible recoveries for the debtor's creditors. The Chapter 13 trustee plays a large role in the success of a Chapter 13 case and is often the one to object to the repayment plan and otherwise ensure that it complies with the Code.

5. **Possible issues:** Common issues arising in Chapter 13 include: (1) the value of the allowed secured claims, (2) the priority treatment of certain claims, (3) whether the debtor has contributed all of his disposable income to the plan, which is required under Chapter 13, and (4) the value of exempt property, as that bears on the minimum distributions the debtor must pay under the plan.

C. Chapter 12

1. **General theme:** Chapter 12 is a bankruptcy scheme for family farmers and family fishermen. A family farmer or fisherman is a person who receives more than 80 percent of his or her gross income from farming or fishing and who (with his or her family) owns a large part of the business that generates that income. [187]

2. **The repayment plan and debt limits:** Chapter 12 is very similar to Chapter 13 but has slightly easier repayment rules and higher debt limits. The debt limits for a family farmer is

$3,237,000, and for a family fisherman, $1,500,000, meaning a person can file a Chapter 12 if his or her debts are at this level or lower.

D. Chapter 11

1. **General theme:** Chapter 11 is a payout-style case almost always used by business entities like corporations, although available to individuals. Most individuals prefer Chapter 13 to restructure their debts because Chapter 13 is much easier and cheaper than Chapter 11 and only file a Chapter 11 case if they are over the Chapter 13 debt limits. [187]

2. **The repayment plan:** Just as in Chapter 13 cases, the Chapter 11 debtor will repay a portion of its debts over time from its future operations. Its plan will need to pay its allowed secured claims in full, its priority claims in full, and will usually pay a distribution to its unsecured creditors as well. The plan approval process is different, however, in that the debtor will solicit votes from classes of creditors. If all classes of creditors vote to go along with the plan, the court generally approves the plan. If there are "no" votes, the court can sometimes force creditors to accept the plan if various tests are met by the plan and the debtor.

3. **The management of the business:** In Chapter 11, the company continues to be run by management—either the same as before the filing or newly appointed. There is no trustee. The debtor continues to run the company but is now called the "debtor-in-possession," or the "DIP." Under the bankruptcy code, the debtor-in-possession has all of the duties and powers of a trustee as a fiduciary with the charge of creating the best possible distribution for creditors.

III. THE AUTOMATIC STAY

A. The automatic stay is an injunction against collection: A bankruptcy petition acts as an immediate injunction order, directing creditors to cease all collection activity. This is accomplished through the automatic stay, and as soon as the debtor files his bankruptcy petition, all creditors must stop any and all collection efforts against the debtor or the debtor's property. The automatic stay continues in place until the bankruptcy case is over or until a creditor gets the stay lifted or removed to pursue its own particular debt. [188]

B. The automatic stay and secured creditors: Secured creditors should not try to repossess or foreclose on property once a debtor has filed for bankruptcy and, in most cases, are forbidden from perfecting a security interest after a bankruptcy. Also, a secured creditor cannot sell property in its possession that it has repossessed but not sold as of the filing of the debtor's bankruptcy petition since the debtor still has an interest in the property. The type of bankruptcy case filed is irrelevant, and if a creditor continues to try to collect from a debtor after filing, the creditor can be held liable for actual and pecuniary damages. [188]

IV. RELIEF FROM THE AUTOMATIC STAY FOR SECURED CREDITORS

A. The basic philosophy behind lifting the stay: Sometimes secured creditors are able to have the automatic stay removed or lifted so that they can continue trying to collect the debt, just as if there was no bankruptcy. In a Chapter 7 bankruptcy, the most common situation in which the stay will be lifted is when a secured creditor is *undersecured* or *upside-down*, meaning that the debt is larger than the value of the collateral. Although this seems counterproductive, the rationale is that there is no value in the property for the estate, the debtor's other creditors. The debtor has no equity in the property and, being behind on his obligations, will find very little relief under a Chapter 7 case.

B. Two common ways to get the stay lifted: There are two common ways for a secured creditor to get the stay lifted in order to pursue its rights under state law, which are found in § 362(d)(1) and (2) of the Bankruptcy Code.

1. Cause including a lack of adequate protection: Under § 362(d)(1), the stay shall be lifted if the court finds that there is "cause, including a lack of adequate protection of an interest in property of the moving party," requiring that the creditor's interest in its collateral be safe and steady. The creditor is not adequately protected if its position might be worsened through the debtor's use of the collateral, often meaning that the debtor has no significant equity in the property, the property also is depreciating, and as a result of this combined condition the creditor is not protected against loss resulting from the debtor's continuing possession and use of the collateral. A lack of adequate protection may also be found if the creditor is already undersecured or if the equity cushion is not large enough to cover any diminution in the value of the collateral resulting from the debtor's use.

2. The debtor has no equity in the property and the property is not necessary to an effective reorganization: Under § 362(d)(2), obtaining relief from the automatic stay involves looking only at the position of the moving party and whether there is equity in the property over and above that secured party's claim. The creditor must prove two things: (1) that the debtor has no equity in the property and (2) that the property is not necessary to an effective reorganization of the debtor. The equity referred to in the first part of the test refers to total equity in the property requiring that one add up all the secured claims against the property and determine if the debtor has any equity over and above all of those secured claims. For the second prong, the court must first determine if it is the kind of property that the debtor needs for its reorganization and then determine whether an effective reorganization is likely.

After a certain amount of time has passed, the court may grant relief from the stay when there is no equity because even if this property would be necessary in an effective reorganization of this debtor, an effective reorganization looks unlikely given all the time that has passed.

V. THE TREATMENT OF SECURED CLAIMS IN BANKRUPTCY

A. Undersecured and oversecured creditors: The undersecured creditor, whose claim is bigger than the value of its collateral, and the oversecured creditor, whose collateral value more than covers the amount due on their loan to the debtor, are treated very differently in bankruptcy. [192]

The oversecured creditor receives extra benefits not available to unsecured or undersecured creditors. These include interest that continues to accrue at the contract rate after the bankruptcy case has been filed, as well as allowed fees for the creditor if the creditor must go to court to enforce its right to be paid. Thus, the oversecured creditor's claim can grow during the case while the unsecured and undersecured claim stays the same. See 11 U.S.C. § 506(b).

If a secured claim is undersecured, the claim is split into two parts for bankruptcy treatment purposes. This is called *bifurcation of the claim.* 11 U.S.C. § 506(a). The part that is covered by the collateral is treated as secured, and the part that is not covered is treated as unsecured. The secured creditor's claim is for the most part allowed in the amount of the value of the collateral for the purposes of payment in bankruptcy. Whatever is left over of the claim is an unsecured claim.

B. Practicing the calculations: As you will soon see, it is always good from the creditor's perspective to have more collateral than one needs. Sometimes cases can drag on for some time. This is particularly true in a Chapter 11 case. We noted previously that the secured creditor's claim continues to accrue interest and attorneys' fees at the contract rate, if it is oversecured. Section 506(b) makes it clear, however, that such postpetition interest and fees can accrue only for as long as there is still value left in the collateral over and above the secured party's claim.

C. Secured creditor treatment under a Chapter 11 plan: A Chapter 11 debtor can drastically reduce the amount that he or she pays on undersecured loans, paying just the value of the secured property, along with interest, over the life of the plan.

   1. Bifurcation and "stripdown": Chapter 13 is very beneficial because the debtor can reduce the debt to the amount of the value of the collateral. Section 506(a) defines a secured debt as secured "to the extent of the value of such creditor's interest . . . in such property." This process is called the "stripdown" or "cramdown," and is one of the biggest benefits of Chapter 13 and Chapter 11. Congress limited stripdown in Chapter 13 cases in its 2005 amendments to the Bankruptcy Code.

   2. Valuation: Value is the most important determination with respect to whether a debtor will be able to afford to pay the crammed down or stripped down value of the more expensive items under the repayment plan. Stripdown requires determining the value of the collateral. In large business cases and in some consumer cases, valuation is often accomplished through an appraisal of the property in question. Smaller items of personal property are rarely appraised due to the cost of an appraisal, and if the property is vehicles or mobile homes, most parties use the Kelley Blue Book or a similar resource. The proper measure of value for stripdown purposes is not the wholesale or retail value but rather the replacement value—namely, the price at which the debtor could purchase a comparable used item.

   3. The present value interest rate: The other variable in determining the cost of paying off the debt on the property that has been stripped down is the present value interest rate that the debtor will be required to pay. Section 1129 requires that to strip down a secured creditor class, the secured party must receive "fair and equitable" treatment. Courts have determined fair and equitable treatment to be payment to the secured party of the present value of its claim over the life of the collateral and also to allow the secured party to retain its liens during the payment period. This has been interpreted to mean that the creditor is entitled to the value of that claim as if it were being paid all at once on confirmation. Because the Code allows payment over time, the debtor must compensate the creditor for the time value of money.

VI. THE AVOIDING POWERS

Avoiding powers are the powers that trustees and debtors-in-possession have to bring certain property that has been transferred away prior to a debtor's bankruptcy back into the debtor's estate. The three most commonly avoided types of transfers are preferential transfers, fraudulent transfers, and transfers of security interests that are never perfected. [195]

A. Preferential transfers: Section 547(b) contains the elements of an avoidable preferential transfer, requiring that there be (a) a transfer of property (b) for or on account of an antecedent debt (c) made within 90 days before the filing (one year for transfers to insiders such as family members), (d) while the debtor was insolvent, (e) that allowed the creditor to receive more than it would have received in a Chapter 7 case. [195]

   1. When the transfer is a security interest: If the property transferred is a security interest, collateralizing an old or antecedent debt rather than a new one, it is an avoidable preferential transfer as long as the debtor was insolvent at the time the transfer was made, or as long as no one proved otherwise. If the transfer of a security interest is made in connection with a new loan it is not a preference because one element, that the transfer be "for or on account of an antecedent debt," is not met. [196]

   2. When the transfers are payments made to secured creditors during the preference period: No payment made to fully secured creditors during the preference period is a preference. Because in Chapter 7, fully secured creditors get their debts paid in full, they do not meet the element needed in order to get the transfer back from the creditor because the creditor does not receive more than the creditor would get in a Chapter 7. If the creditor receiving the payments is not fully secured, some of the payments may be preferential transfers.

B. Avoidance of unperfected security interests under the trustee's strong-arm powers contained in § 544(a): Unperfected security interests can be avoided in bankruptcy, turning the previously secured creditor into an unsecured creditor. The security interest is returned to the estate and the value of the property can be distributed to unsecured creditors. The priority themes found in Article 9 are continued in the Bankruptcy Code, but the avoidance powers go further and allow the trustee to dispose of unperfected security interests entirely rather than letting it remain in its low-priority state. The Code gives the trustee rights akin to those of a judgment lien creditor, and the trustee can beat out an unperfected security interest. These are called the trustee's strong-arm powers. [197]

CHAPTER 1

INTRODUCTION TO SECURED TRANSACTIONS: COLLECTION OF DEBTS AND LIENS

ChapterScope

This chapter is an introduction to the concept of an Article 9 security interest and describes the collection process for unsecured creditors, and then briefly compares these collection rights to those of secured creditors. The chapter also briefly discusses the role of state exemption law in collections rights, describes sheriff sale rules, and then very briefly introduces the concept of priority under Article 9 of the Uniform Commercial Code (UCC). It then introduces you to the concept of bankruptcy and describes a few pre-Code security devices. The key points in this chapter are as follows:

- **Securing a loan:** Secured transactions is the law of securing a loan with personal property, as opposed to real estate.

- **Debt collection:** Secured transactions is a systematic part of the overall law of debt collection.

- **Loan collateral:** When obtaining a loan, a borrower may give a lien on particular assets or collateral, which the lender may keep or sell if the borrower fails to meet his or her loan obligations.

- **Collecting on claims:** This chapter shows you how a creditor without collateral gets paid on his or her claim, compared to how a creditor with collateral gets paid.

- **State exemption law:** The state exemption law allows debtors to keep some property, even if they owe creditors money.

- **Notice requirements under UCC Article 9:** Pre-Code security devices, such as conditional sales contracts, chattel mortgages, and trust receipts led to today's UCC Article 9 notice requirements.

I. PUTTING SECURED TRANSACTIONS IN CONTEXT

A. **What's secured transactions all about?** Think of a mortgage on a house. Assume the owner borrowed money, probably to buy the house, and has promised to repay the loan. In addition, the owner has given a "mortgage" on the house. If the owner, the mortgagor, does not pay, the one holding the mortgage (the mortgagee) can take the house, sell it, and use the proceeds to pay the amount owed. What the lender has is a "security interest" in the house.

Note: We use this real estate example as an analogy to the secured lending on personal property this course teaches, because most people are more familiar with the concept of a home mortgage than with a security interest on personal property.

As we just said, this course is about security interests in *personal*, as opposed to *real*, property. Secured transactions (or secured credit) is the study of these types of interests, which secure obligations. Usually the obligation is a promise to pay back a loan. Security interests are property interests in assets of a business or person that are *not real estate* assets like cars, inventory, equipment, accounts receivable, household goods, etc.

Think of buying an automobile. Most people don't pay cash. Instead, they borrow at least part of the purchase price from the dealer or a bank. The lender will almost certainly require the buyer-borrower to give a security interest in the car. This transaction is perhaps the most common one involving Article 9 security interests. If we didn't have Article 9, or some similar law allowing security interests, it would be difficult to buy cars unless we saved enough to pay cash.

You may be thinking that this seems rather narrow and irrelevant, a lot like the law of socks. In reality though, billions of dollars are lent in our economy, secured by personal property. And, irrelevant as it all may seem, this area of the law frequently touches on many other areas and is the subject of one of the most elaborate and cohesive systems of law there is.

Let's say you want to start a retail business selling large appliances. Where do you get the money? You may have saved some money, or won a lottery, but it's unlikely that you will have enough to buy all the washers, dryers, trash compactors, etc. that you will need to fill your sales-room and your warehouse. Also, you will have to buy some equipment: delivery trucks, computers, etc. You'll have to borrow the money, and the lender will want a security interest in the inventory and equipment. The lender may also want a security interest in your business name and your goodwill. If you sell goods on credit, the lender may take a security interest in your right to payment from those who purchase from you on the installment plan. As you can see, Article 9 is important in providing capital to businesses because it is unlikely that you could get the loans without giving a security interest. And, as you can imagine, the transactions can become quite complicated.

Students who take this course often report that they had "no idea" all this was out there. They are glad to discover this area of law because it is a system that, for the most part, makes sense, and also accomplishes its goals. In other words, this course can be both useful and interesting.

B.   A brief introduction: The law of secured transactions falls within the broad category of debtor-creditor law. The law of secured transactions is contained in Article 9 of the UCC, a set of uniform laws written to make interstate trade more predictable and uniform. The legal concepts of *debtor* and *creditor* are themselves much broader than one would think. One typically thinks of the secured party or secured creditor as someone (typically a bank) who has lent money to someone else (the debtor) and taken a security interest in some of the debtor's property to secure the loan. While this is commonly the way in which a security interest arises, anyone to whom a legal obligation is owed can obtain a security interest (collateral) to secure the obligation, whether it is a typical commercial or consumer debt, a contractual obligation of another kind, or even a tort claim. Other creditors who might receive a security interest to secure an obligation include any plaintiff who has recovered a judgment or the beneficiary of future child support payments.[1]

The security interests in which the most money is at stake are granted in the context of business financing. In a sense, these are the most important security interests. Not everyone who finances a business gets a security interest, however. Nonfinancial institutions, like suppliers of business inventory, e.g., the produce in a grocery store, often lack the leverage to obtain a security interest under Article 9. They also may lack the knowledge to obtain a security interest. Thus, many creditors are unsecured rather than secured creditors, meaning they do not have any security for the obligations owed to them.

---

1. Although debtor-creditor law can involve the process of collecting any judgment, e.g., a judgment awarded to a plaintiff who has been negligently injured by the defendant, in cases involving secured transactions, credit has normally been voluntarily given to another. One person, the creditor, has lent money to another, the debtor, or the debtor has purchased goods giving the seller a promise to pay in the future, and the debtor has failed to repay the creditor.

While secured creditors have the right to repossess their collateral through self-help repossession (see Chapter 3), an unsecured creditor who attempts to take some of the debtor's property in satisfaction of his or her claim can be found liable for the *tort* of conversion, the wrongful exercise of dominion and control over another's property. Such a creditor also can be found guilty of the *crime* of conversion. Collecting unsecured creditors also must be careful not to engage in wrongful collection practices and can only coerce payment through narrowly constructed judicial processes.

C. **Types of secured transactions questions:** If you are facing an exam of all or part essay questions, there are two basic types of questions that can be asked: (1) questions involving a dispute between the secured party and the debtor, and (2) questions involving who as among two or more creditors have superior rights to money obtained from the sale of the property in which a security agreement has been given (the collateral).

The first type of question requires knowledge and understanding of Chapters 3 and 4 of this outline. For example, your professor may pose a fact situation that requires you to know whether the secured party has made a peaceful repossession, has given the proper notice before a sale of the property, or whether the secured party has made a commercially reasonable sale. More complicated is the issue of when a secured party is entitled to a deficiency judgment, but these questions tend to be more straightforward, and there are probably fewer of them on law school examinations. Indeed, in some of the casebooks, the rights of the secured party and the debtor are at the end of the book and sometimes not covered in the secured transactions class. If you are in one of those courses, you can pretty much ignore this type of question.

The second type of question involves the rights of a secured party against others claiming an interest in the collateral. We call these "priority" problems, Thus, for example, the conflict may be with another person to whom the debtor has given a security interest, a person who claims a lien through the execution process, or perhaps one who has purchased goods from the debtor not knowing that the debtor has given a security interest on it.

Priority problems tend to be complicated and demand a knowledge of many parts of Article 9. You have to know whether the secured party has a valid security interest (Chapter 4), the type of collateral (Chapter 2), whether the security interest has been perfected (Chapter 5), and the numerous priority rules (Chapter 6).

But don't despair. Thousands of others have mastered these materials and done well in examinations. Article 9 is logical, and as you learn more about it you will become more comfortable with it. We will give you approaches to Article 9 questions, and don't hesitate to reread provisions or to make your own "Capsule Summary" or outline.

Although it is important in answering essay questions to know the details of Article 9, it is much more important if you are facing a short answer examination. You must know the "little rules" because you are likely to face questions requiring you to apply them.

II. DEFINITIONS

Before we move on, we need to define some terms that are basic to an understanding of secured transactions and the collection of debts. Other words and phrases will be defined later in this outline.

A. **Lien:** The concept of a "lien" is something that is very simple once you understand it, but the road to understanding can be difficult. A *lien* is an interest in property that gives the holder of the lien a right to possession of some of a debtor's property in the event that the debtor fails to perform its obligations, e.g., fails to repay money when it is due. Generally, the failure to pay is called a "default." A lien is a limited property interest in that it is a right to possession of the property contingent on default. Liens are usually divided into three categories: (1) judicial or execution liens, (2) statutory and common law liens, and (3) consensual liens.

Note: Liens are always *in specific property*, never just existing in the abstract. If you cannot figure out what the lien you are working with *is in*, chances are there is no lien. Perhaps the creditor just has a judgment which, as you'll see below, is *not* a lien.

When the word "lien" is used by itself, it is often necessary to figure out what type of lien is being described. For example, when the word "lien" is used in Article 9 of the UCC, it refers only to a *judicial lien*, and not to a statutory lien, a common law lien, or a voluntary security interest under Article 9.[2] See UCC § 9-102(a)(52). On the other hand, when the word "lien" is used in the Bankruptcy Code, it refers to all types of liens, voluntary security interests, judicial liens, statutory liens, etc. See 11 U.S.C. § 101(37). When a provision of the Bankruptcy Code applies only to judicial liens, the Bankruptcy Code uses the term "judicial lien" to mean a lien that arises through the judicial process. 11 U.S.C. § 101(36).

Three types of liens are described in the following paragraphs.

1. **Judicial liens:** A judicial lien is one that arises from judicial proceedings, i.e., lawsuits. The plaintiff files a complaint, and if the defendant files an answer, there are motions, perhaps a trial, and, when the plaintiff prevails, there is a judgment. A judgment is not an order to the defendant to pay; it is simply recognition by the judicial system that the defendant owes the plaintiff money. The plaintiff must then enforce the judgment by obtaining a writ of execution which, as far as personal property of the debtor is concerned, is an order by the court to the sheriff to seize so much of the defendant's property as is necessary to produce sufficient money from a sale of that property to satisfy the judgment. The plaintiff will get paid only by executing on the judgment, unless the defendant voluntarily pays the judgment.

    The *mere* granting of a judgment by a court does not result in a lien on any of the debtor's personal property. Again, a judgment is not a lien. Instead, the creditor who obtained the judgment, the judgment creditor, must execute on the judgment to obtain a lien. As to the debtor's real property, this usually means that the judgment creditor need only docket (file) its judgment in the proper place, usually the county recorder of deeds. As to personal property, the judgment creditor must "execute" on the property through a writ delivered to the sheriff. The execution process is explained below. UCC § 9-102(a)(52).

2. **Statutory and common law liens:** The law, usually by statute but sometimes by court decision, grants to certain creditors a lien in certain property of the debtor. See UCC § 9-333(a). Most states grant statutory liens to contractors and subcontractors who work on real property, for work and materials used to improve the property. Those who repair cars or other personal property usually are given liens on the car or other property that is improved. In many states, hotels and motels are given liens on property brought into a sleeping room or suite, and landlords usually have liens on the personal property brought onto the leased premises, to secure amounts due under the lease. The statutes and cases establishing these liens have many features in common, but there is significant variance from state to state and from lien to lien. One feature common to many statutory and common law liens on personal property is the requirement that the lienholder have possession of the property. In these instances, the lien is lost if the lienholder gives possession to the debtor or someone else.

---

2. The definition of a lien creditor does include the trustee in bankruptcy, however. UCC § 9-102 (a)(52)(C). We will discuss this more later.

Many states give liens on personal property to those who extend credit to farmers. These liens are not created under Article 9; they are created by separate statutes and are a form of statutory lien. However, they are defined as Agricultural Liens by Article 9. As we will see, how the holder of an agricultural lien protects itself from other creditors—how it perfects its lien—is covered by Article 9, and Article 9 also governs priorities when a party has an agricultural lien.

3. **Consensual liens—Mortgages and security interests:** A consensual lien arises from the agreement of the owner of property to grant a lien. In real property, one who purchases a house frequently gives a "mortgage" to the person lending the money to enable the buyer to purchase it. A mortgage is basically a lien, giving the mortgagee the right to take possession of the property and to sell it if the mortgagor fails to make payments on the loan. When a lien is given on personal property it is called a "security interest," and Article 9 of the UCC applies to the transaction. UCC § 1-201(a)(35).

A Brief Review of Liens

- **A lien is a property interest.** Think about one of those estates in land that you learned about in property: the life estate. A life estate in a house gives you the right to possession of the property during your life. Although someone else is the owner fee, the law treats the holder of the life estate as having an interest in the property.
- **A lien "secures" an obligation**, e.g., a loan, and it gives the holder of the lien the right to possession of the property if the loan is not repaid. Someone else is the owner of the property, but the lienholder has an interest in it. Once the lienholder gets possession, he or she can sell the property (or have the sheriff sell it) and you can take the proceeds of the sale to pay off the loan.
- **The lien is in specific property**, a house, an automobile, a bank account. If you have a lien in someone's boat, it doesn't mean that you have a lien in their automobile.
- **Liens are divided into three types:** (1) **judicial**, obtained through the execution of and levy under a judgment, (2) **statutory or common law**, which result automatically because of a statute or case law, and (3) **consensual, mortgages, and Article 9 security interests**. In this outline we are most interested in consensual liens, which are governed by Article 9.

For the most part, this outline does not discuss real property security interests but confines itself to security interests created under Article 9. Still, you now know the names of the two most common forms of consensual liens: mortgages and security interests.

Note: Many teachers do not refer to Article 9 security interests in personal property as liens, because Article 9 uses the word *lien* only to describe judicial or statutory liens, not voluntary security interests. On the other hand, in bankruptcy, Article 9 security interests are one of the categories of liens. To us, conceptually, all these categories are interests in property and in that sense are liens.

B. **General or unsecured creditors:** The plight of the general or unsecured creditor (the one with no lien) is not pretty. *General or unsecured creditors* (the words "general" and "unsecured" are used here interchangeably) are those to whom an obligation is owed but who have no lien on any property of the obligor. UCC § 9-201(a)(13). They have an unsecured claim or debt. You'll see shortly what is so undesirable about being unsecured.

C. **Security interest:** A *security interest* is the interest in personal property (property that is not real estate) that a secured party takes to secure the repayment of the debt or obligation owed by the debtor.

Article 9 of the UCC defines a security interest very broadly, however, to include *every interest* in personal property or fixtures that secures payment or performance of an obligation. UCC § 9-201(a)(35). These include the typical grants of a security interest that we'll be working with throughout this outline as well as some other things like chattel mortgages, trust receipts, conditional sales, and other concepts about which you will learn more later. Some of these words are relics from pre-Code practice that are still used today but to a lesser extent. Suffice it to say that Article 9 defines a security interest very broadly and thus subjects all these transactions to the provisions of Article 9. A security interest also includes outright sales of certain kinds of assets, like accounts, chattel paper, payment intangibles, and promissory notes, mostly because it can be hard to tell the difference between a security interest in these things and an outright sale of them. The scope of Article 9 is discussed in Chapter 2.

D. **Security agreement:** A *security agreement* is a contract between a debtor and a secured party that grants or gives the secured party a security interest in certain personal property. Security agreements are discussed in Chapter 3. UCC § 9-102(a)(73).

E. **Secured party:** A *secured party* is the lender, seller, or other person who has been given a security interest in the collateral. UCC § 9-102(a)(72).

F. **Collateral:** The specific assets in which the secured party holds a security interest are called *collateral*. The collateral will be described in the contract between the debtor and the secured party, known as the *security agreement*. Remember, security interests (and all other liens) *must be in* specific property. UCC § 9-102(a)(12). The various types of collateral are described in Chapter 2.

G. **Debtors and obligors:** Technically, under Article 9, a "debtor" is a person who has an ownership interest in the collateral, UCC § 9-102(a)(28), and an "obligor" is a person who owes the debt that is secured by the security interest. UCC § 9-102(a)(59). In most cases this is the same person: a retail store that owns inventory borrows money giving back a security interest in the inventory. The retail store is both an obligor and a debtor.

In this outline, we will use the term "debtor" to mean the person who both owes the debt and owns the collateral unless there is a need to talk of debtors and obligors separately.

Note: Please do not move on until you understand this basic terminology. These few definitions are fundamental vocabulary words that we'll use to define new concepts as they arise. One thing that makes this course and other technical business law courses difficult is that students do not take the time to make sure they know the basic vocabulary. Before long, as new concepts are added, it starts to sound like the course is being taught in a foreign language.

III. COLLECTION OF UNSECURED DEBTS

To help you understand the purposes and function of a voluntary security interest, we'll explore the collection process that takes place when a creditor does not have a security interest. The purpose of getting a security interest is to make a debt easier to collect and to make it more likely that the creditor, the secured party, will be paid. As a point of comparison, the following paragraphs discuss the collection of debts in cases in which no security interest has been given to the creditor.

Understanding the impediments faced by unsecured creditors in the collection process is critical to understanding the enhanced collection remedies that secured creditors have, as well as to an understanding of the whole purpose of Article 9.

A. Obtaining a judgment: The substantive law courses in law school, e.g., contracts, torts, property, etc., teach you what law you need to know to prove that a debt or obligation is owed, e.g., to prove a contract right, it is necessary to prove agreement, consideration, and breach. Each of these courses teaches you how to *obtain* a judgment, which is recognition by the state, through one of its courts, that a debt is owed. These courses do not, however, teach you how to *collect* a judgment. A judgment is not money, nor does it magically transform itself into money at some certain point in time. Rather, the judgment is a mere piece of paper stating that the defendant is indebted to the plaintiff for a certain amount of money. Sometimes the defendant will send a check to the plaintiff in payment of the judgment, but at other times, the plaintiff has to obtain the money by enforcing the judgment.

Example 1: Seller sells an expensive television to Buyer. Buyer agrees to pay $200 a month over the next 3 years. Buyer misses several payments. Although Seller is a creditor of Buyer, Seller can do nothing until it sues Buyer and obtains a judgment. Even obtaining the judgment does not ensure that Seller will be paid as Seller still has to enforce that judgment.

Warning: The Seller has *no special rights* in the television sold to Buyer. Seller is a general creditor and does not have any rights in the television just because he or she sold it to Buyer and does not have a lien until he or she obtains one through the execution process. As we will see, however, Seller could have taken an Article 9 security interest in the television and become a consensual lien creditor.

Collection Remedies for Unsecured Creditors

Unsecured debt, meaning debt for which there is no collateral, can be very hard to collect involuntarily. Unsecured creditors faced with an unwilling debtor must complete the following steps to collect:

- Get a judgment, which may be contested and thus may take time, as with any lawsuit;
- Do discovery about what assets the debtor has and how a sheriff could gain possession of these assets, which can again be time-consuming;
- Prepare detailed paperwork for the sheriff, describing the creditor's right to be paid and a description and location of the assets to be seized;
- Get the sheriff to seize, execute, or levy on these property items; and
- Finally, have the sheriff sell the items at a sheriff's sale.

B. Enforcing a judgment: Judgments are enforced by the execution process. Once a judgment is obtained, the plaintiff becomes a "judgment creditor," and is entitled to a "writ of execution."

    1. Writ of execution: The writ of execution is an order from the court to the sheriff to seize enough property of the defendant to satisfy the judgment. It is usually issued by a clerk of the court. When the sheriff takes possession of property of the defendant this is called a "levy."

2. **Levy:** The concept of a levy is pretty simple. When the property is personal property, the sheriff will physically take possession of the property if this is practical. (Just picture, if you will, the sheriff throwing the goods into the back of his or her pickup and driving off.) If the property is large equipment, the sheriff will tag it with a notice that there has been a levy, and if it is goods in a warehouse, the sheriff may place a lock on the building and post a notice that a levy has been made. Although having the sheriff levy on goods under a writ of execution seems straightforward, it is fraught with difficulties and frustrating gray areas. The sheriff will not search for the property. The judgment creditor must instruct the sheriff as to the property to be seized and tell the sheriff where it is located. And, before the sheriff can levy on it, the property may be moved by the defendant or trashed.

There is some question about whether an executing sheriff must take actual possession of the goods, though it is always safest to do so. When a sheriff executes on a writ, he is required by law to exercise "dominion and control" over the property being executed upon. Remember your property course! Most courts have interpreted this to mean taking actual possession of moveable items and placing sheriff execution notices or stickers on bigger or heavier items that cannot be moved and taken to the sheriff's office. Generally, then, it is not sufficient for the sheriff to merely go to the place where an asset is located and announce that he is executing on the property but then leave the property there. If this type of behavior could constitute valid execution, and thus create a valid executing lien in the property, other potential creditors could not see the lien and thus would not be on notice of the lien. Nevertheless, this issue has caused courts some confusion, and some have even found such announcements of execution to constitute valid executions. *See Credit Bureau of Broken Bow v. Moninger*, 204 Neb. 679, 284 N.W. 2d 855 (1979).

When the property is real property, the sheriff will file a notice in the real property records stating that the sheriff has levied on the property.

3. **Opportunity to discover assets of the defendant:** A judgment creditor may examine the debtor/defendant under oath after the judgment is entered to determine what property the defendant owns.

Typical ways to learn about which assets are available for execution include performing depositions in aid of execution and hiring private investigators, if the creditor thinks assets are being hidden.

When doing a deposition in aid of execution, try to ask the most specific questions you can think of.

Example of important question not asked: Debtor is asked in deposition for the location of every bank account and every stock account in which he holds assets but is not asked whether he is carrying any cash on his person.

Some Sample *Deposition in Aid of Execution* Questions

1. Do you own any automobiles, real estate, household goods?
2. Do you have or own any interest in any investment accounts?
3. Do you have or own any interest in any retirement accounts?
4. Does anyone owe you money?
5. Have you prepaid for any contracts or services?
6. Are you a plaintiff in any lawsuits?
7. Do you have any causes of actions or rights to bring lawsuits against anyone?
8. Are you owed a tax return?
9. Do you have any bank accounts?
10. Have you given any money to anyone to hold? Any other property?
11. How much money do you have on you today?
12. Do you own any interests in any partnerships? Limited liability companies? Corporations?

Of course, in a deposition in aid of execution, you must follow up on the answers you receive.

4. **Sheriff's instructions:** Sheriffs are busy people and do not get paid extra for being innovative in the execution process. Executing creditors must use the discovery they have gained to give exacting details to the sheriff about how and where to execute on the available assets. Tell the sheriff exactly what the assets are and where they should be. This is done in the *writ of execution*, which is part of the *writ package*. Each state and the counties within have their own writ package, which is often simple, but time consuming, to fill out. The execution process itself is also exacting. Little mistakes can mean redoing the entire execution. If other creditors are also executing on the same assets, the first to actually levy on the assets, through the sheriff, usually gets first priority in any proceeds realized on the sale. Thus, careful preparation of the writ package can make the difference between payment and nonpayment.

5. **Details of the execution process and legal ramifications of timing of execution:** Once an unsecured creditor has obtained a judgment, he or she is called a *judgment creditor*. Again, a judgment creditor does not obtain a lien by getting the judgment and is not a secured creditor. Once a judgment creditor has executed on the judgment, then the creditor becomes a secured creditor, albeit an involuntary secured creditor. This means the executing creditor, like a voluntary secured creditor who has been granted an Article 9 security interest, has a property interest in whatever particular property the sheriff has executed on through the writ execution (or levy) process.

State law determines which executing creditor has priority over other executing creditors, if there are any. States generally follow one of two rules regarding which creditor has priority. The majority of state execution laws provide that the actual time of execution of the writ by the sheriff determines priority. This means that if the sheriff chooses to execute on one writ before another that is already in his office, the writ first executed upon will create the involuntary lien that has the first priority. Other state statutes provide that priority is determined by the date on which the writ is delivered to the sheriff and that if the actual levy occurs later, the execution will relate back to the date the writ was delivered. This eliminates the favoritism issues but creates the possibility of secret or invisible liens.

6. **Sale of the property:** The sheriff will sell the property on which the levy was made. Usually, the sale is by auction, often held on the courthouse steps. The price obtained is unlikely to equal what might be considered the fair market value of the property because there are no warranties of title or quality given by the sheriff, and the title of the purchaser may be subject to encumbrances on the property. If the sale does not bring enough money to satisfy the debt, the judgment creditor may have another writ issued. If it brings more money than is necessary to satisfy the judgment, the surplus is given to the debtor/defendant.

Example 2: Seller in Example 1 issues a judgment against Buyer. It may be that Buyer fails to answer the complaint and a default judgment is obtained, but Buyer may also contest the complaint based on defenses that are covered in substantive law courses. If Seller prevails in the action, the court will award judgment to Seller. Assuming no appeal, Seller can now obtain a writ of execution from the clerk of the court. To get paid, Seller will have to identify property of Buyer and tell the Sheriff to execute on it.

7. **Garnishment:** In seeking to satisfy a debt, the judgment creditor has the right to reach intangible property as well as tangible property. The simplest example of intangible property is a bank account, which is essentially a debt owed by the bank to the account holder. The execution process described above is limited to tangible property. Intangible property is normally reached by what is called *garnishment*. The garnishment proceeding involves serving a writ on the bank, which orders the bank to pay the judgment creditor rather than the debtor who has the account.

C. **Enforcement of a secured party's rights:** One of the main purposes of a security interest is to make it easier for the creditor to collect the debt that is secured. Article 9 gives to a secured party the right to avoid the execution process. A secured party may obtain possession of the collateral, i.e., the property in which the debtor has given a security interest, either by taking possession of it peacefully or by obtaining possession by a writ of replevin. UCC § 9-609. After obtaining possession, the secured creditor may sell the property itself, using the proceeds to satisfy the debt. UCC § 9-610. Thus, collection of a debt by a secured party can be much easier than collection by a general creditor who must invoke the execution process. These rights of the secured party are covered in Chapter 3.

Example 3: If Seller in Examples 1 and 2 had taken a security interest in the television that it sold to Buyer, Seller would have a consensual lien called, in Article 9 parlance, a "security interest" in the television. As a secured creditor, Seller does not have to obtain a judgment or go through the execution process. Instead, Seller could repossess the television, sell it, and use the proceeds to satisfy the obligation that Buyer owed Seller.

D. **State exemption law:** Most states have laws that protect some property from the claims of executing creditors. The theory is that everyone needs at least basic assets to survive and that executing creditors should not be able to collect from these basic assets.

The exemptions vary from state to state but can be quite rich. Both Texas and Florida protect a home of any value from the claims of executing creditors. Normally, a variety of different property is exempt under state law: a home, cars, furniture, clothing, retirement funds, usually up to a certain dollar value. Every writ package asks the executing creditor to provide the debtor with an opportunity to list all property that is exempt from the claims of executing creditors. Another important advantage of having a security interest: the exemption statutes do not protect the debtor's property if a security interest has been given on it. Thus, if a debtor has an automobile that is exempt under the state's exemption statutes, but the debtor has given a security interest to a creditor, the creditor may repossess the vehicle in spite of the exemption statutes.

E. Sheriff's sale rules: Before personal property is sold at a sheriff's sale, the sale is advertised. Despite this, these sales often bring very low prices. The debtor himself can bid on the property for cash, as can anyone else who shows up. Creditors can bid with their claims, which is known as *credit bidding*. If they do this, they receive the property in satisfaction of their claims, or whatever portion of the claim was bid.

For example, assume that a creditor has received a judgment of $1,000 and that the sheriff has levied on the debtor's nonexempt television worth $2,000. At the sale, the creditor can bid up to $1,000 without laying out any cash. If the creditor had bid $1,000 and that was the highest bid, he would have to pay the sheriff $1,000, the amount of his or her bid, and then the sheriff would turn around and give the money back because the creditor is entitled to the proceeds of the sale. Obviously, this exchange is unnecessary; the sheriff will just give the television to the creditor and the duty to pay will be extinguished. The creditor's right to payment from the debtor would be decreased by $1,000, and the creditor would own the $2,000 television set.

Only creditors who have executed on their claims can be paid from the proceeds of the sale. Creditors who have executed are paid in order of their priority, and the rest of any net proceeds realized are returned to the debtor. This is true even if there are numerous judgment creditors who have not yet completed the execution process. They receive none of the proceeds of the sheriff's sale.

F. Special rules for involuntary liens on real property: As mentioned previously, it is much easier for a judgment creditor to obtain a judicial lien on real property as compared to personal property. No execution is needed. All the judgment creditor must do is record his or her judgment in the county recorder of deeds office in which the debtor owns property. This will create a lien on the property that must be satisfied on the sale of the property. The judgment lien creditor can also force the sale of the property through a sheriff's sale, as discussed previously, for personal property sheriff's sales.

IV. PRIORITY AMONG CREDITORS

To collect the money owed a general creditor, the creditor must bring a lawsuit and go through the execution process. Frequently, the debtor will have a number of creditors, all of whom are pursuing their rights. Determining the order in which those with judicial liens are to be paid from the assets is called *determining the creditors' priorities*. In deciding which of the many creditors will be paid if the debtor does not have sufficient reachable property to satisfy all of the debts, the law could take any one of several approaches. For example, the ranking of who should be paid and in what order could be based on whose cause of action accrued first or on who obtained a judgment first.

American law, however, takes the position that priority is given to the creditor who first obtained a lien on an item of the debtor's property. Thus, when the judgment creditor obtains a lien in specific property of the debtor, the judgment creditor's debt will be satisfied first out of that piece of property. If others obtain liens later, they will share only in any money obtained from the sale that is in excess of the amount necessary to pay the creditor with the first lien.

This priority system, first to get a lien is the first to be paid, gives rise to the second purpose of taking security interests. Because a security interest is a lien, a creditor can ensure that certain property of the debtor, the property in which the security interest is given, will be available for the satisfaction of the secured party's debt provided the secured party takes the steps necessary to protect its security interest before there is any execution on the property. Because the secured party has obtained a lien on the property first, the secured party will be paid first when the property is sold. See, e.g., UCC § 9-317.

Example 4: If on July 6, *A* obtained a judgment, got a writ of execution, delivered it to the sheriff, and the sheriff levied on the defendant's automobile, *A*'s date for determining priority, which will be based on the first to obtain a lien rule, would be July 6. *A* would prevail over *B* if *B* did not obtain a writ of execution until July 10 because *B* would not obtain a lien any earlier than July 10. However, if *S* had taking a security interest in the automobile and "perfected" her security interest on June 15, *S* would have priority over *A*. The method of obtaining a security interest, how it is protected against creditors and other parties, and some more complicated rules of priority are the subject of a later chapter of this outline.

Now you should see how important it is for a creditor to get a lien on the debtor's property. A creditor will never be paid if the debtor does not voluntarily come across with the cash unless the creditor gets a lien. A judgment is not enough—the judgment must be enforced.

Because obtaining a security interest in some of the debtor's property gives you the right to possession of that property and the right to sell it, the advantage of being a secured party should be obvious. You should also see how important it is to get a lien quickly, because of the first-in-time rule. Again, getting a security interest becomes important because it will put the secured party ahead of all other creditors who get a lien by the judicial process later in time.

V. BANKRUPTCY

Chapter 7 of this outline covers the interplay between bankruptcy and secured transactions in some detail. At this point, we simply want to warn you of the effect of bankruptcy on a creditor's collection efforts, both by the execution process and by repossession under Article 9. Chapter 7 discusses bankruptcy in more detail.

When a debtor files a petition in bankruptcy, the rights of both secured and unsecured creditors are determined by the Bankruptcy Code, a federal statute found in the U.S. Code. Chapter 7 of the Bankruptcy Code covers liquidations of the debtor's estate, i.e., the trustee collects all of the debtor's nonexempt property, sells it, and distributes the proceeds to the creditors. Chapters 11 and 13 of the Bankruptcy Code are quite different. In each, the debtor usually keeps his or her or its property, and pays some claims through a repayment plan over a period of time, with some adjustment of the rights of individual creditors.

In each of the three types of bankruptcy, the Bankruptcy Code provides for a "stay" of all attempts by creditors to collect from the debtor. 11 U.S.C. § 362(a). If a case is in trial, the trial must stop. If a creditor has started the execution process, it must stop. If a secured creditor is attempting to take possession of the collateral, the secured creditor must stop. All collection efforts must cease, and the creditors are forbidden to even send a letter to debtors trying to collect.

Although any generalization of the rights of secured creditors is dangerous, it is safe to say that security interests are recognized in each type of bankruptcy and that a secured creditor will be paid up to the extent of the value of the collateral securing the debt.

Example 5: Manny purchases a machine from Lucy, promising to pay her $100,000 in 6 months. When the debt becomes due, Manny fails to pay. (a) To recover the $100,000 from Manny, Lucy must get a judgment by suing Manny. She must then obtain a writ of execution, deliver it to a sheriff, have the sheriff execute on some of Manny's property, and have the sheriff sell the executed property, giving the proceeds of the sale to her. (b) Manny has no lien in the machine by virtue of the sale. (c) Lucy will not have a lien on the machine or any other personal property of Manny until, depending on state law, the writ of execution is delivered to the sheriff or there is an actual levy on the machine or some of Manny's other property. Once Manny files for bankruptcy, assuming Lucy has not yet levied by the filing, the sheriff can no longer levy on any of Manny's property. It is too late. Moreover, Lucy will be a general (unsecured) creditor and likely get very little from the proceeding.

Example 6: When Lucy sold the property to Manny, she took a security interest in the machine under Article 9 of the UCC. In this case, Lucy has a lien on the machine, and she has the right to possession of the machine when Manny defaults. On obtaining possession, Lucy can sell the machine and apply the proceeds of the sale to the debt. If Lucy took the proper steps to protect her security interest from third parties, even if another of Manny's creditors got a judgment and had the sheriff levy on the machine, the sheriff would have to sell the machine subject to Lucy's security interest. Lucy could then take possession of the machine from the buyer at the sale unless the buyer paid her what she was owed by Manny. In bankruptcy, Lucy will be a secured creditor and, assuming she has taken the proper steps to perfect her security interest, she will receive the value of her collateral in the bankruptcy proceeding. If that is insufficient to discharge her debt, she will have claim for the deficiency as a general creditor.

VI. A SHORT HISTORY LESSON: PRE-CODE SECURITY DEVICES

We will now diverge into a bit of history to better understand the current law of secured transactions.

A. **Article 9's beginning:** Article 9 is part of the UCC, a set of uniform laws drafted by lawyers and academics to make commercial law more uniform around the country and thus to make it easier to do business across state lines. The first version of the UCC was drafted in 1951 (a long time ago for most of you, I'm sure), but even before that time, American businesspeople figured out many ways to obtain security interests in personal property.

B. **Old English law on security interests in personal property:** Initially, back in 1570 England, the "Statute of Elizabeth" made it fraudulent and void for a debtor to grant a lender a security interest in property and then keep possession of the property. This was thought to mislead the debtor's other creditors into believing that because the debtor was still in possession of the assets, they were available to satisfy general unsecured claims (claims for which there was *no* collateral).

One of the motives of the Statute of Elizabeth was to prevent "Papist recusants" from holding false sales of their assets before fleeing the country, thereby defrauding creditors. In fact, one of the themes of lending law throughout the ages has been deciding what to do about debtors who defraud their creditors.

C. **Possession of collateral:** Thus, while old English law did not preclude security interests in personal property, it did require the secured party to take possession of the collateral. Interestingly, possession is still one of the main ways that a secured party can obtain superior rights in collateral (over other parties), though it is not too practical for working assets that the debtor needs to use in its business.

Possession was also called a "pledge" or "hypothecation," and it constituted notice to all others that the party in possession had an interest in the assets. This is still true. Today, lawyers also often use the word "pledge" simply to mean to grant a security interest, which is obviously a totally different use of that term. (More on that later.)

1. **Chattel mortgages:** In the early nineteenth century, creditors' lawyers borrowed from real property mortgage law to create chattel mortgages. Although states varied as to how they conceptualized chattel mortgages, basically they were consensual liens on personal property. By the 1820s, many states had enacted statutes governing them (Chattel Mortgage Acts), generally requiring filing of the chattel mortgages in a central office. The filing gave "constructive notice" that the creditor had a lien on the property. Chattel mortgages were limited in that in most states the lien could not be given on property acquired by the debtor after the lien was established, and they generally could not be used to obtain a lien on property that was obtained by the debtor in the future.

2. **Conditional sales:** Back in the pre-Code days, secured parties looked for ways around the Chattel Mortgage Acts, which required a public filing.

    In a conditional sale, the secured party would be, in essence, the seller in the deal, and the debtor would be the buyer. When the transaction was the sale of goods on an installment plan, the conditional sales contract was often used. The idea of this device was that the seller retained title to the goods until the buyer paid the entire purchase price. Because title had not passed, the seller-creditor was protected from other creditors of the buyer who might attempt to obtain a lien on the goods and from those who might purchase the goods from the buyer.

    Some courts found this structure legitimate, but others invalidated conditional sales because they created secret liens that failed to give notice of an interest in the property. A number of states adopted statutes governing conditional sales, and ultimately the Uniform Conditional Sales Act was promulgated and adopted by a minority of the states. The Uniform Act required a notice filing, as did its predecessors.

    Article 9 as it is now structured places no significance whatsoever in whomever holds title in the collateral. Filing or possession by the secured party is required no matter what, so a conditional sale is covered by the Article 9 filing requirements. We'll discuss this in more detail in Chapter 4.

3. **Trust receipts:** This nifty legal fiction was created based on trust law. The idea was that when financing something that turns over, like inventory (think cereal at your grocery store), the lender could retain title to the inventory while the debtor remained in possession of it. The debtor in essence held the collateral in "trust" for the lender. Once this practice became popular, another statute was enacted to require (you guessed it) a notice filing describing this transaction. This law was called the Uniform Trust Receipts Act. This was drafted by Karl Llewellyn in 1932. At the time, he called the law the best-conceived and the worst-drafted statute in history.

    The notice system created under the Uniform Trust Receipts Act was fraught with technicalities, and was thus hard to comply with. Moreover, although it was designed for rolling collateral (that which turns over), it was really not appropriate for numerous smaller items because the notice document had to be excruciatingly specific. Modern Article 9 takes care of all these problems, as you will see.

4. **Field warehousing:** Another term you'll hear kicked around at times, *field warehousing*, describes a process in which working assets like inventory (and sometimes equipment) are left in the debtor's place of business, but the secured party tries to remain in physical

possession of it (despite the debtor's ongoing use) by physically segregating the goods from the debtor's other assets. The secured party appoints an agent to supervise the separately stored inventory. When an item is sold, the agent releases the goods to the debtor, perhaps in return of an immediate payment of part of the credit. Field warehousing is still used, but now it is governed by Article 9.

5. **Assignment of accounts receivable:** Pre-Code, the debtor would often assign outright its accounts receivable (those amounts others owe it for goods or services) to its lender, without telling the account debtors (the people who owed the money to the debtor). Why would the debtor want to assign these accounts? The point was to use them as a way to obtain financing; a way to generate cash.

   The creditor would allow the debtor to continue to collect these accounts until there was a default on the loan between the debtor and the creditor. At that time the creditor would simply notify the account debtors to pay the lender directly. Sometimes, however, the debtor would assign the same account more than once, creating questions about who was entitled to collect the account. Eventually, some states enacted a statute requiring a notice filing for assignments of accounts to put future creditors on notice of the assignment. Current Article 9 governs the assignment of accounts and requires the secured party to file a financing statement to protect itself against subsequent creditors.

D. **This history and Article 9's current notice requirements:** That completes our historical discussion, as well as this introductory chapter. In writing this, we are not trying to belabor boring facts from the past, but only to show you how important the notice concept is in current Article 9 law. No matter what pre-Code lenders and lawyers did to avoid the filing requirement, it was always re-imposed, for the benefit of those who required notice of the debtor's true financial condition and the status of the debtor's assets (encumbered or not).

   Having endured this history lesson, you now know what these former security devices were called and what they essentially tried to do. You are also familiar with Article 9's primary goal, the notion of giving *notice* to third parties of existing security interests. This notion is so embedded in the history of Article 9 that knowing this history will help you remember the rules.

   One of the most innovative aspects of Article 9 is that it abolished the distinctions between the methods of securing a debt that previously existed. Hence, chattel mortgages, condition sales contracts, trust receipt transactions, and assignments of accounts are all now simply secured transactions. Even if the paperwork looks like the transaction is a chattel mortgage or conditional sales contract, it is a security interest governed by Article 9.

Quiz Yourself on
INTRODUCTION TO SECURED TRANSACTIONS: COLLECTION OF DEBTS AND LIENS

1. What is the difference between a secured and an unsecured creditor? _____

2. What is an Article 9 security interest? _____

3. Why would a creditor want to get a security interest? _____

4. What law governs the creation of security interests? _____

5. What is a lien? _____

6. What are the three kinds of liens and how is each type created? _____

7. Define each of the following:

    a. security party _____

    b. collateral _____

    c. debtor _____

    d. obligor _____

8. What is a judgment? _____

9. What is the difference between a judgment and an involuntary lien? _____

10. What is a levy and how is one typically accomplished? _____

11. How does an unsecured party find assets to execute upon? _____

12. What is the difference between execution and garnishment? _____

13. Does a secured party need to worry about the state law exemptions? _____

14. If you had to describe Article 9's primary theme or goal in one word, what would the one word be? _____

Answers

1. A secured creditor gets the debtor to give it collateral or property to secure the debt. This means the secured party can collect its debt from this property granted to the secured party without going through the execution process.

2. A security interest is an interest in personal property given to a secured party (often a lender) to secure repayment of an obligation.

3. A security interest allows a secured party to avoid the execution process and to simply repossess the collateral pledged. Getting a security interest also encourages repayment of the loan because the threat of repossession causes the debtor to repay this obligation over other obligations. Finally, a person with a security interest will usually take priority over creditors who do not have a security interest and over the trustee in bankruptcy.

4. Article 9 of the UCC is a uniform statute, which all states have adopted. Each state was allowed to tinker with the model laws, however, so they can differ a bit from state to state. The state's own statute governs.

5. A lien is an interest in property which gives the holder of the lien the right to have its debt repaid out of the proceeds when the property is sold.

6. A lien can be created (1) consensually, as in the case of an Article 9 security interest or a mortgage, (2) by statute, or (3) through the execution process (an involuntary lien).

7. a. Secured party: one holding a voluntary Article 9 security interest.

b. Collateral: the property pledged to the secured party to secure or collateralize the obligation.

c. Debtor: person who has an ownership interest in the collateral, although we often use the term more broadly in this outline, to include the one who owes the debt.

d. Obligor: the person who owes the debt that is secured by the security interest.

8. A judgment is an order of a court recognizing that a debt is owed.

9. Many people think that obtaining a judgment makes an unsecured debt turn into a secured debt. This is not true. A judgment is really just a piece of paper recognizing the debt. To turn this into a lien and obtain the right to collect a debt from particular property, the judgment creditor (the one holding the judgment) must execute on property of the debtor.

10. A levy is the process of executing on the judgment, which is accomplished by taking possession of personal property that is small enough to haul away, or posting notices on personal property that is too big to haul away. This is done by the sheriff. The technical requirement of a levy is that the sheriff exercise control over the property.

11. Through discovery in the lawsuit in which the creditor is getting its judgment on the debt. The information is obtained during a deposition in aid of execution.

12. Garnishment is a specific kind of execution, used for reaching the debtor's intangible property. Often it involves serving notice on a third party (e.g., a bank, the debtor's employer) that the executing creditor is claiming an interest in the intangible asset held by another.

13. No, this is a concern for only unsecured creditors, who may not execute on an asset that is protected by the state law exemptions. Secure creditors can always repossess their collateral without regard to the exemptions.

14. Notice.

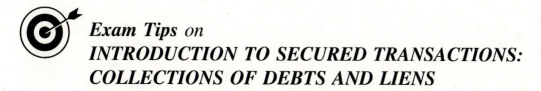

Exam Tips on
INTRODUCTION TO SECURED TRANSACTIONS: COLLECTIONS OF DEBTS AND LIENS

Here are a few things to keep in mind in connection with any secured transactions exam.

☛ First determine whether each party is a *general creditor* or a *lien creditor*. In doing so, remember these points:

☞ There are *three ways to create a lien*: by judicial execution, by statute, or voluntarily by giving an Article 9 security interest or a mortgage. All of these create a property interest in specific property.

☞ *Execution:* A judgment does not in and of itself give rise to a lien—the judgment creditor must execute on the judgment to have a lien.

☞ *Security interest:* A creditor will have a lien if the debtor has given it a security interest in some of its property.

☞ *Property:* A lien can only exist in specific property. If the creditor has a lien on an automobile, that does not give it a lien on the debtor's computer.

☛ If the question asks you about the *creditor's rights against the debtor*, distinguish between lien creditors and general creditors. In doing so, remember these points:

☞ *Rights of a general creditor:* A general creditor has no right to any of the debtor's property.

☞ *Rights of a judicial lien creditor:* A judicial lien creditor can have the sheriff sell the property and give the proceeds to the creditor.

☞ *Rights of an Article 9 secured party:* A secured party can repossess the goods given as collateral itself and sell the goods taking the proceeds in satisfaction of the debt.

☛ If the question asks you about the *creditor's rights against third parties*, the creditor will almost certainly lose if it is a general creditor, and will win if it is a lien creditor. It will probably win if its lien is the first to arise. In doing this analysis, remember these points:

☞ *Secured interest:* The lien of an Article 9 secured party usually arises when the secured party gives notice either by taking possession of the collateral or by filing.

☞ *Judicial lien:* The lien of a judicial lien creditor arises either when the writ of execution is delivered to the sheriff or when the sheriff levies on the goods depending on the jurisdiction.

CHAPTER 2

SCOPE OF ARTICLE 9 AND TYPES OF COLLATERAL

ChapterScope

This chapter describes which transactions are covered by Article 9 and which are not. It also describes the different categories of collateral that are recognized and covered by Article 9. The chapter ends with an interactive game that you can use to test your knowledge of the Article 9 categories of collateral. The key points in this chapter are as follows:

- **Article 9 mandates:** When a transaction is covered by Article 9, the secured party is often required to comply with a number of technical provisions of Article 9.

- **Security interest in personal property:** Any transaction that creates a security interest in personal property falls within Article 9, regardless of what it is called, including consignments, leases, and some sales of assets.

- **Other secured interests:** Article 9 covers agricultural liens, leases intended as security devices, conditional sales, and sales of certain intangible assets.

- **Interests not covered:** Article 9 does not cover real estate transactions, landlords' liens, other statutory liens, wage assignments, the pledge of personal tort claims, insurance claims, set-off rights, and certain other transactions.

- **Collateral categories:** Article 9 classifies collateral or property pledged as security for a loan. Knowing these categories of collateral is critical to understanding the rest of this course and to practicing commercial law.

- **General collateral categories:** Collateral falls into two general categories, tangible property (goods), and intangibles. Within these broad categories are many other categories.

  - **Tangible goods:** Tangible property or goods are subdivided into consumer goods, equipment, inventory, farm products, fixtures, and a few others of less importance.

  - **Intangible assets:** Intangible assets include accounts receivable, chattel paper, general intangibles, instruments, deposit accounts, commercial tort claims, investment accounts, and some others of less importance.

I. WHICH TRANSACTIONS ARE COVERED BY ARTICLE 9 AND WHY DO WE CARE?

Whenever a transaction is covered by Article 9 of the Uniform Commercial Code (UCC), the secured party (with the debtor's help) will be required to comply with a number of requirements to fully protect its position. Most of these technical requirements deal with giving notice of the secured party's security interest.

Note: Article 9 is part of the UCC, a uniform law that the states were encouraged to enact. The real law of secured transactions differs a bit state by state because states adopted the uniform version with some variations. When you are in practice, make sure you read the actual statute in your state in which Article 9 appears.

Article 9 covers security interests in personal property, but transactions don't have to be called "security interests" to be covered by Article 9. As with most areas of the law, substance prevails over form so if it looks and acts like a security interest, it is covered regardless of name and purported form. UCC § 9-102(a)(73).

In Chapter 1 we learned how pre-Code lenders tried to avoid the notice requirements by devising intricate systems that claimed to be not security interests but sales, trusts, conditional sales, sales and leasebacks, field warehousing, and so on. Remembering those failed attempts will help you see that the scope of Article 9 is broad and that Article 9 covers transactions that constitute security interests in personal property regardless of what they are called. Sometimes these transactions are outright "sales" but because of the problems they raise, they operate no differently than a security interest would and are within Article 9. Sometimes they are called "assignments," but they are covered by Article 9 nevertheless, if they create a security interest in personal property.

Quick note: The UCC defines *purchaser* to refer both to actual buyers of assets, as well as a person who takes a security interest in assets. See UCC § 1-201 (29) and (30). Thus, the word "purchaser" covers transfers for value of security interests and recipients of security interests.

Example: UCC § 9-330 protects a *purchaser* who takes possession of chattel paper or instruments from those perfected by filing. This means the secured party who takes possession is protected against those who perfect by filing.

II. SCOPE OF ARTICLE 9: WHAT TRANSACTIONS ARE GOVERNED BY ARTICLE 9'S RULES?

To start, then, Article 9 applies to all transactions that create a *security interest* in *personal property*. UCC § 9-109(a). An interest in personal property is defined broadly by the Code to include every "interest in personal property or fixtures that secures payment or performance of an obligation." UCC § 1-201(a)(35).

Although the statutory definition of *security interest* is complicated, it is basically an interest in personal property that gives to the secured party the right to possession of the property if the obligor defaults. It gives the secured party the further right to sell the property and to apply the proceeds to the obligation to satisfy the debt or part of the debt. Although a security interest can secure any type of obligation, in almost all cases it secures a money obligation arising either from a loan of money or from the sale of goods. Subsequent chapters discuss how a security interest is created and the rights that it gives to the secured party. Article 9 also governs agricultural liens, consignments, and some security interests created under the Article on Sales, Article 2; the Article on Bank Deposits and Collection, Article 4; and the Article on Letters of Credit, Article 5. In addition, Article 9 governs the *sale* of certain intangibles because the sale of these intangibles raises the same problems as the granting of a security interest in them.

A. Sales of certain intangibles: A person who needs money may sell certain types of intangible personal property (which is discussed in greater detail below) instead of borrowing money and giving a security interest in them. Because the sale of these intangibles may be difficult to actually distinguish from a grant of a security interest in such collateral, and also because a sale of these may result in the same type of litigation that would arise if the seller borrowed the money and gave a security interest in them, the sale of certain intangibles is within the scope of Article 9. UCC § 9-109(a)(3).

Article 9 applies only to the sale of accounts, chattel paper, payment intangibles, and promissory notes. It does not apply, for example, to the sale of a business's customer lists.

Example 1: ABC, Inc., a retail large-appliance business, is in need of working capital. One of its assets is the money owed to it by customers who purchased goods on credit. ABC, Inc. could go to a bank and borrow money, giving to the bank a security interest in this asset, called "accounts" by Article 9. Instead, ABC, Inc. sells the accounts to Frank Factor who purchases them outright (he is not merely granted a security interest) at somewhat below their face value.

Although the parties speak of a "sale" of the accounts, and there is no mention that a security interest is created, the transaction falls under Article 9, and the sale amounts to the creation of a security interest. Thus, a "sale" of accounts is treated as the creation of a "security interest" in the account. It's sort of like those statutes that say "for the purpose of this statute all horses are cows." The transaction between ABC, Inc. and Frank Factor is a secured transaction governed by Article 9. ABC is a "debtor," and Frank is a "secured party."

B. Consignments: If a retail business wishes to increase the inventory that it has for sale, it may buy new inventory on credit, giving back to the seller a security interest to secure payment of the price. This is clearly a secured transaction under Article 9. Alternatively, the retailer and the supplier of the inventory, a wholesaler or manufacturer, may enter into a "consignment agreement." In a consignment, the agreement between the supplier and the retailer is that title to the new inventory will remain in the supplier and the retailer will act as the supplier's agent for the purpose of selling the goods. Since the consignment could be used to circumvent Article 9, and because a consignment transaction raises similar problems to those when the transaction is a secured transaction, Article 9 governs consignment transactions. UCC § 9-109(a)(4).

Example 2: A wholesaler of jewelry and a retailer enter into a contract providing that the retailer will be given possession of diamonds with the understanding that the retailer will sell them and account to the wholesaler, giving the wholesaler a part of the price paid by the consumer who purchased them. The agreement may designate the debtor as the creditor's agent, and may contain numerous other provisions, for example, that the price to be sold at retail may be set by the wholesaler. Still, the transaction is treated as a secured transaction, and what the wholesaler has is a security interest in the goods with the buyer as a debtor having the title.

C. Conditional sales contracts: When a seller is financing a sale and the buyer is to pay back the loan over a period of time, the transactions can be set up as a sale on credit with the buyer giving a security interest in the goods that are sold to secure the promise to pay. Another way of designing the transaction is to have the seller retain title to the goods until the final payment is made. Because the intent of the transaction is that the buyer's obligation to pay for the goods is secured by the goods, even though the contract provides that the seller will retain title, the transaction is a secured transaction within Article 9. 11 U.S.C. § 2-102, UCC § 9-109(a)(4).

Example 3: Betty enters into a contract to purchase a car from Sam, agreeing to pay in installments over the next year. The contract provides that Sam will retain title to the car until Betty makes all of the required payments. Article 9 applies to the transaction; Sam has a security interest in the car and Betty has title.

D. Leases of goods: When a person wishes to obtain possession of property that will be used over an extended period of time, such as office equipment or a motor vehicle, the person may buy it or lease it. If the transaction is really a lease (what we call a *true lease*), then Article 9 does not apply. Questions arise, however, when the lessee has the right to become owner of the property at the end of the lease period. If the lessee can acquire ownership of the property for a nominal payment, the transaction is treated as a secured transaction and Article 9 applies. If the lessee must make more than a nominal payment to obtain title, whether it will be treated as a lease or a secured transaction generally depends on the amount of the payment and the useful life of the property at the end of the lease. UCC § 1-201(37).

Example 4: Larry wishes to acquire a tractor for use in his contracting business. He enters into a contract with Sally that is entitled "Lease," and which provides that he is to pay a rental fee each month for 2 years. At the end of the 2 years, he has an option to purchase the tractor for $5,000. Whether this is a lease, and not covered by Article 9, or a secured transaction depends on how much the tractor is worth at the end of the lease period. If it is worth about $5,000, it will be treated as a lease. If it is worth $75,000, it will most likely be treated as a secured transaction and Sally will have only a security interest in the tractor and Larry will have title.

Whether a lease is a true lease or a disguised security interest actually involves other considerations as well, although what the debtor has to pay at the end of the "lease" is the most important consideration. Section 1-201(37) and the cases interpreting it look at a long list of considerations, which include the following:

1. whether the purchase price at the end of the lease is nominal;
2. whether the lessee obtains any equity in the property being leased during the leased term;
3. whether the lessee bears the risk of loss;
4. whether the lessee pays the tax, licensing, and registration fee for the leased property;
5. whether the lessor can accelerate payment on default; and
6. whether the lease contains a disclaimer of warranties.

E. Agricultural liens: Lessors of farms and sellers of seed and other farm supplies are given agricultural liens in many states. These agricultural liens are created by statute and are not consensual security interests because they are not voluntarily granted by the debtor. To determine whether they exist and the extent of the lien, it is necessary to consult the statute creating them. However, Article 9 governs how the creditor protects the lien against third parties and the priority of agricultural liens when others have rights in the goods in which the lien arises. UCC § 9-109(a)(2).

Example 5: The law of the state of West Dakota provides that a supplier of seeds has a lien on all of the crops grown from the seeds. Supplier sells seeds to a farmer on credit and does not take an Article 9 security interest in them. Bank loans money to the farmer and takes an Article 9 security interest in the crops. Article 9 does not govern the creation of Supplier's lien or its extent. Article 9 does, however, govern how Supplier perfects its security interest and the priority between Bank and Supplier.

F. Security interests arising under other articles of the UCC: Articles 2 (Sales), 4 (Bank Deposits and Collection), and 5 (Letters of Credit) provide for security interests in certain cases. These security interests are within Article 9 to a limited extent. UCC §§ 9-109(a)(5); 9-110.

G. Transactions excluded from Article 9: A number of transactions that could be included within Article 9 have been excluded. For these transactions, one must consult other statutory or case law to determine the rights and obligations of the parties.

1. **Landlords' liens:** Most landlords' liens are created by statute, but in some jurisdictions they come from the common law. Note that when the lessor of a farm has a lien on crops or other property of the lessee, the lien is treated as an agricultural lien and is subject to Article 9. UCC § 9-109(d)(1).

   Helpful Hint: It is sometimes difficult to remember the difference between the "ors" and the "ees": the lessor and lessee, the mortgagor and mortgagee, the transferor and transferee. Normally the "ors" give something to the "ees" or do something to the "ees." Thus, a lessor leases property to the lessee, a mortgagor gives a mortgage to the mortgagee, and a transferor transfers something to a transferee.

2. **Real property transactions:** Most real estate transactions are excluded from Article 9; a mortgage given on real property is clearly outside the scope of the Article. However, a security interest in rights that a mortgagee has under a mortgage is subject to the Article. UCC § 9-109(d)(11).

   Example 6: Peggy purchases a house and gives a mortgage to Bank One to secure her promise to pay money advanced to her. The mortgage is not governed by Article 9. Bank One subsequently borrows money from Bank Two, giving to Bank Two a security interest in Bank One's rights under the mortgage against Peggy. The transaction between Bank One and Bank Two is a security interest within the scope of Article 9. UCC § 9-203(g).

   Note that fixtures, which are personal property attached to real property, are governed by Article 9. UCC § 9-109(d)(3).

3. **Liens for services:** State statutory law frequently provides that those who supply certain services can obtain a lien for the value of those services if they are not paid for. For example, contractors and subcontractors are usually given a lien on the building being constructed or improved, and those who repair automobiles, jewelry, and other items of personal property often have a lien on the goods in the amount of the repair bill. Article 9 does not govern these liens except that it does provide priority rules when the certain types of lienholders and a secured party both claim an interest in the goods. See UCC § 9-333.

4. **Assignment of wages:** Assignments of claims for wages, salary, or other employee compensation, such as bonuses, are not within Article 9.

5. **Some sales and assignments of intangible property:** Although Article 9 governs the sale or assignment of intangible property, as well as the creation of security interests in them, some transactions involving intangible property are excluded from the Article. Sales of accounts, chattel paper, payment intangibles, and promissory notes *in connection with the sale of a business* are not covered (UCC § 9-109(d)(4)), and outright assignments of these types of collateral for the purpose of collection are excluded (UCC § 9-109(d)(5)).

   When a contract is assigned and the assignee undertakes performance of the assignor's duties under the contract, the transaction is not covered under Article 9. UCC § 9-109(d)(6). Article 9 also does not apply to the assignment of a single account in satisfaction of a debt. UCC § 9-109(d)(7).

Example 7:

a. Ron, the owner of Ron's Retail, sells the business to Paula. Included in the sale is an assignment of all of the business's accounts, chattel paper, payment intangibles, and promissory notes. The transaction is not within Article 9.

b. Doris, a dentist, is owed money by a number of her patients. After trying to collect the debts herself, she assigns them to the Crul Collection Agency for collection. The transaction is not within Article 9.

c. Andy, a builder, contracts with Patrick to build a garage next to Patrick's house. Andy discovers that he has more work than he can do and agrees with Brigid that she will build the garage and that Patrick will pay her. The assignment of Andy's rights against Patrick are not within Article 9.

d. George owes Ellen $100, and Carlton owes George $100. To satisfy the debt that he owes Ellen, George assigns to her the right he has against Carlton. The transaction is not covered by Article 9.

6. **Tort claims:** Claims arising from a tort are generally not within Article 9, except that commercial torts, such as claims for interference with contractual relations, are covered by the Article when a security interest is given in them. UCC § 9-109(d)(12).

7. **Insurance claims:** The assignment of claims against an insurance company is not within Article 9, except that claims based on health-care insurance by or to a health-care provider are within the Article. UCC § 9-109(d)(8).

Example 8: Joan, a physician, has a number of claims against the insurers of her patients for care given to them. She assigns these claims to a company whose business it is to purchase claims and process them with the insurer. The transaction is covered by Article 9.

8. **Rights of set-off:** If two persons each owe one another money, the law sometimes allows them to set off their mutual debts against each other. For example, a bank that lent money to the debtor might be able to set off that debt against the debtor's checking account. With two limited exceptions, rights to set-offs are not covered by Article 9. UCC § 9-109(d)(10).

Summary of the Scope of Article 9[*]

I: Transactions Covered

1. Transactions explicitly granting a security interest in personal property
2. Consignments
3. "Sales" or "assignments" of accounts, chattel paper, payment intangibles, and promissory notes
4. Some transactions set up as a lease of personal property
5. Agricultural liens when the question involves perfection or priority

II: Transactions *NOT* Covered by Article 9

1. Landlords' liens
2. Real property security interests and other transactions
3. Statutory and common law liens, except as to their priority
4. Assignments of wages
5. Sales or assignments of intangibles in connection with the sale of a business
6. Sales or assignments of intangibles for collection
7. Sales or assignments of intangibles when transferee is to perform the contract
8. Personal tort claims, but commercial tort claims are covered
9. Insurance except health-care insurance obligations to a health-care provider
10. Rights of set-off

_____

[*] Like all summaries, the details that are omitted are important, and you should carefully study the materials that precede this summary.

III. TYPES OF COLLATERAL

Article 9 applies to a great many transactions which, from a practical point of view, are quite different and require different treatment. For example, if a consumer gives a security interest to a retailer to secure a promise to pay for a home entertainment system over 3 or 4 years, the transaction is covered by Article 9. Compare that transaction to one in which the retailer borrows money from a bank, giving back a security interest in its inventory and accounts. Again, Article 9 applies, but the transaction is quite different from the consumer transaction. Although the concept of a "security interest" is unitary—there is only one kind—different rules do apply to different types of transactions. Which set of rules applies usually depends on the type or *classification* of the collateral.

It is difficult to overstate how important it is to be able to accurately classify collateral. Later it will make a huge difference in your legal practice, as incorrectly characterizing collateral can invalidate a security interest. Even now, if you misclassify it in answering an exam question, it gives the impression that you don't know much about the course. More importantly, it may lead you to make other mistakes in your answer. For example, a purchase-money security interest is perfected automatically in consumer goods, but only in consumer goods. If you started off calling something consumer goods when it wasn't, you could easily mistakenly say that the security interest was perfected when it was not.

Somewhat frustratingly, the Code sometimes defines categories of collateral in the negative, e.g., is not in category *x*, is not in category *y*, and so on. Even so, classification of collateral can be fun if you think of it as a game of sorts. At the end of this chapter, we have included a game that you can use to test your mastery of these categories. In the abstract, it may not seem to matter much which category a piece of collateral falls into, but you'll see that learning these well now will make a tremendous difference later, particularly when you study the materials on perfection and priorities found in Chapters 5 and 6 of this Outline.

The same item of property may be categorized differently depending on who is holding it and what it is being used for.

Example 9: A television is inventory when it is held for sale by an appliance store. If it is sold to a dentist who installs it in her office, it becomes equipment. If the dentist decides that her patients do not like it and she takes it home for use in her home, it becomes a consumer good. You must look to the time at which the transaction occurred to determine the correct classification of the television. If, for example, the appliance store gave a security interest in the television while it was in its warehouse, the security interest would be in inventory; if the dentist gave a security interest in it while it was in her office, she gave a security interest in equipment; and if she gave a security interest in it while she had the television in her home, the secured party will take a security interest in consumer goods.

The fact that this same television can be so many different types of collateral is what makes this part of the course interesting and challenging. You may still be having trouble seeing why this matters, but trust us, it will soon become clear.

Article 9 makes an initial distinction between *tangible personal property (goods)* and *intangible property*. Each of the categories is then subdivided into more specific types. Correctly pigeonholing the type of collateral securing a debt is the first step in analyzing problems under Article 9.

A. **Goods:** Goods are all things movable, including such tangible property as automobiles, tables, televisions, etc. UCC § 9-102(a)(44). Note that these are also *things* in the most commonsensical sense. They are things you can see and touch. Article 9 defines four principal types of goods and five other less significant categories of goods in some instances.

   1. **Consumer goods:** Consumer goods are goods that are either used or bought for use primarily for personal, family, or household purposes. UCC § 9-102(a)(23). This category includes furniture in one's house; automobiles used for pleasure or family transportation, including driving to and from work; watches and other jewelry; etc. The *used* or *bought* language means that something that was originally bought for consumer use but was later used in a business would still be categorized as consumer goods for transactions entered into while the property was being held as consumer goods.

   2. **Equipment:** The definition of "equipment" is goods other than consumer goods, inventory, or farm products. UCC § 9-102(a)(33). Thus, equipment is the catch-all category. If the goods do not fit into any other category, the goods are equipment. A more meaningful definition of equipment is goods used in a business that are not normally sold or consumed by the business. For example, an automobile owned by a business and used by a salesperson would be equipment as would be the business's trucks, cash registers, tools, bulldozers, cranes, etc.

Inventory is the other type of tangible property used in a typical business. Sometimes a question arises about whether a piece of business collateral is equipment or inventory. Equipment, however, is goods used long term in a business, whereas inventory is goods held for sale or lease or used in the short term.

3. **Inventory:** Basically, inventory is goods held for sale (or short-term use) by a business. UCC § 9-102(a)(48). The refrigerators, dishwashers, trash compactors, etc. that an appliance store has for sale are inventory. Consumables used by a business (other than a farming business), such as the copier paper held by a lawyer, toilet paper in the bathroom of a car dealership, and raw materials held by a manufacturer are also included. Finally, inventory includes property held for lease, such as the automobiles owned by a car rental company.

   Thus, inventory includes all goods *sold, used*, or *consumed* by a business on a short-term basis. It also includes things not sold at all, but things used on a short-term basis (compared to equipment, which includes only long-term business assets). Thus, plastic wrap used in the deli of the supermarket is inventory even though it is not being sold there. The plastic wrap for sale in Aisle 8 is inventory too, but the stuff being given away for free with the meat also qualifies.

4. **Farm products:** This fourth category of goods is unique to farming operations. Businesses that are not involved in farming will not have farm products. Several types of goods connected with farming operations are classified as farm products (UCC § 9-102(a)(34)):

   > i. Crops, whether they have grown, are growing or are to be grown, including crops grown on trees, vines and bushes,
   > ii. Fish that are grown in a fish farming business,
   > iii. Livestock, whether born or unborn,
   > iv. Also included are supplies used in farming operations, such as feed or seed, which would be inventory if not used in farming operations,
   > v. Products of crops or livestock so long as they are in an unmanufactured state.

   Thus, milk would be a farm product, but if the farmer made cheese from the milk and held it for sale, it would no longer be a farm product but instead would be inventory.

   To be *farm products*, the goods must be held by one engaged in farming, including an individual farmer or a farming corporation. Once they are transferred (for example, to a broker), the goods are no longer farm products. Usually they would become inventory.

5. **Fixtures:** Fixtures are property that fall in "never-never land" between personal property and real property. They are personal property that has been affixed to a building so that a real property interest exists in them. UCC § 9-102(a)(41). They are property that is covered by a mortgage of the real property or passed to a buyer if the real property is sold.

   Whether property is a fixture is largely left to non-Code state law. It is generally said that whether something is a fixture depends on the intent of the parties, but that it is the objectively discernable intent that is important. Consideration will be given to the extent that the goods become a part of the building, the amount of integration into the building, the difficulty of removing the goods after they have been affixed, and the type of goods.

   Building materials such as lumber and bricks are personal property when they are delivered to a building site, but once they are used to construct the building they become part of the building and are no longer personal property (nor are they fixtures). Easily moveable personal property, such as free-standing refrigerators or stoves, never takes on any of the aspects of real property and continues to be personal property. When an oven or dishwasher is incorporated into the kitchen cabinetry or an air conditioner is built into a window, they may become fixtures. The same is true of furnaces and other heating units.

6. **Accessions:** Accessions are goods that are affixed to other goods in such a way that they do not lose their identity. UCC § 9-102(a)(1). Thus, a new engine installed in a used automobile is an accession. Accessions are distinguished from "commingled goods," which describes goods that lose their identity when combined—for example, wheat that is put into a silo with other wheat.

7. **Timber to be cut:** There is no definition of "timber to be cut" in Article 9, but the term refers to standing timber that is under a contract to be cut. UCC § 9-102 (a)(44)(ii). Thus, if the owner of land has entered into a contract to allow someone to cut timber from the land, the timber becomes "timber to be cut."

8. **Manufactured homes:** The definition of "manufactured homes" is highly detailed, UCC § 9-102(a)(53), but the category basically refers to a dwelling that is produced offsite and taken to the site to be erected. What are generally called "mobile homes" are manufactured homes if they are intended to be placed on a pad and used as a permanent home. Recreational vehicles used only for vacations are not manufactured homes.

9. **As-extracted collateral:** Oil, gas, coal, and other minerals are treated as real property and are outside the scope of Article 9 so long as they remain in the ground. On extraction, however, they become goods, and can be collateral under the Article.

10. **Changes in goods used for more than one purpose:** When goods are used for more than one purpose, the primary use of the goods determines the category. For example, an automobile may be used partly in the operation of a business and partly for the owner's personal activities. Whichever is the primary use will determine whether it is consumer goods or equipment. The amount of miles driven and the number of hours a week driven for each purpose would be considerations taken into account to determine the proper category, as would be the extent to which the car was depreciated for tax purposes.

B. **Intangibles as collateral:** Intangible property is the property that you cannot see or touch. These categories are often hard to master because many of the types of intangible property are unfamiliar. They are things with which most people will have no experience. They require learning new vocabulary.

Intangible assets are created when one person owes an obligation to another. The right of payment is an asset of the person who has it and is property that can be reached for the satisfaction of debts. With few exceptions, intangible property is property in which a security interest can be given.

Because these are *assets* of a debtor that are being given[1] as collateral to a secured party, they are obligations that a third party owes to the debtor. These obligations can be just plain old debts someone owes the debtor, like the right to payment for services provided by a plumber that arose out of an oral contract, or they can be memorialized in some very formal legal document, such as a promissory note or even a promissory note accompanied by a security interest.

---

1. Here we do not mean "pledge" in the sense of giving someone possession of collateral, but in the sense of granting or giving a security interest.

Article 9 divides intangible property into more than a dozen types. We cover them in the following paragraphs in the order of the frequency with which they arise and their general importance.

1. **Accounts:** Although basically accounts are unsecured obligations owing to a person for goods supplied or services rendered, the definition of "account" in Article 9 is very broad. UCC § 9-102(a)(2). For example, if a retail merchant sells 20 ovens to a contractor in return for the contractor's unsecured promise to pay in 60 days, the obligation of the contractor is an account and the retailer can grant a security interest in it. Typically, a business will issue an invoice for such services, with payment to be made by the person owing the debtor the money within a certain number of days. You can picture something like this when you think of an account. There is no fancy legal document, just a piece of paper telling the debtor's customer (account debtor) how much and when to pay the bill. Indeed, there may be no writing evidencing the accounts.

   Under the definition of "account," however, the obligation can arise from a large variety of transactions. If personal property is sold, leased, licensed, assigned, or otherwise disposed of, the obligation to pay is an account. If services have been rendered or are to be rendered, the obligation to pay for them is an account. If the obligation is incurred in return for an insurance policy issued or to be issued for the hiring of a vessel, or an obligation to a credit card issuer resulting from the use of a credit card, the obligation to pay is an account. Even a right against a state obtained by purchasing a winning lottery ticket is an account.

   A very important form of account for many businesses is a credit card receipt. Credit card receipts are obligations owed by the issuer of the credit cards to the retail businesses that accepted the card for payment.

   "Accounts receivable" or "receivables" are names often used by the business community for money owed to a business for goods supplied or services rendered, but neither of these terms are used in Article 9. These phrases usually mean what the Code calls "accounts." "Health-care insurance receivables" are obligations to health-care providers from insurance companies. This category includes payments from government social-service providers, such as Medicare and Medicaid. Although these are accounts, they are a subtype of accounts separately defined in Article 9. UCC § 9-102(a)(46).

   It is helpful to recognize that certain types of obligations that could be within the definition of accounts are not: chattel paper, payment intangibles, commercial tort claims, deposit accounts, instruments, and letter of credit rights are not accounts. Each of these types of collateral is discussed below. Most involve more formal pieces of paper memorializing the debt but some do not.

2. **Chattel paper:** Chattel paper is an obligation that is itself secured. UCC § 9-102(a)(11). It can be viewed as a package of two rights that the debtor has: the right to payment plus the right to possession of personal property owned by the person who owes money to the debtor if the person owing the obligation defaults.

   Chattel paper is best understood by considering an example of it. Assume that a retailer sells goods on the installment plan to a consumer who intends to use the goods for household purposes. The retailer takes back the consumer's obligation to pay for the goods over time and a security interest in the goods sold to secure the obligation to pay. As between the retailer and the buyer of the goods, the retailer has a security interest in the goods sold, which would be classified as consumer goods. Now assume that the retailer borrows money from a bank and gives as collateral the obligation of the consumer. The bank has a security interest in chattel paper, not in an account, because the consumer's obligation was itself secured. Chattel paper, then, frequently takes the form of a promissory note and security agreement, much like the ones depicted below.

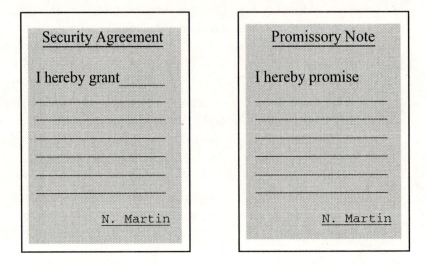

Chattel paper is divided into "tangible chattel paper" and "electronic chattel paper." Tangible chattel paper is represented by a tangible medium, usually paper documents. UCC § 9-102(a)(78). Electronic tangible paper consists of information that is stored in an electronic medium. UCC § 9-102(a)(31).

3. **General intangibles:** A *general intangible* is any intangible property that is not otherwise defined as a separate category. UCC § 9-102(a)(42). Perhaps it is most helpful to list some of the property that would fall within this category. General intangibles include patents, trademarks, the goodwill of a business, and architectural drawings, for example.

"Payment intangibles" is a separately defined subcategory of general intangibles. *Payment intangibles* are general intangibles in which the right is a right to the payment of money. An example of a payment intangible would be rents due from the lease of a building, or payments due on a loan.

Payment intangibles are similar to accounts, but if the payment obligation arises from the sale of goods or from providing services, the collateral is an account and not a payment intangible. If the promise to pay is in the form of an instrument, including a promissory note (see below), the obligation is not a payment intangible because it fits into the category of instruments. An example of a payment intangible is the right to repay a loan that is not in the form of a promissory note or an instrument.

4. **Instruments:** Instruments are negotiable instruments as defined in Article 3 of the UCC and any other right to the payment of money that, in the ordinary course of business, is transferred by delivery and endorsement or assignment. UCC § 9-102(a)(47). A subcategory of instruments is "promissory notes," which are promises to pay that meet the requirements of an instrument. UCC § 9-102(a)(65). Checks are also negotiable instruments and thus instruments under Article 9.

5. **Deposit accounts:** Deposit accounts are accounts in a bank, including savings accounts and checking accounts. UCC § 9-102(a)(29).

6. **Commercial tort claims:** Commercial tort claims are rights arising from torts committed against a business organization or against an individual while engaged in operating a business or as a professional. UCC § 9-102(a)(13). For example, a cause of action for trade disparagement would be a commercial tort, as would a claim for damages caused to a business vehicle through the negligence of another. As mentioned previously, noncommercial torts are not covered by Article 9 and cannot be taken as collateral.

7. **Documents:** Documents are documents of title such as bills of lading and warehouse receipts. UCC § 9-102(a)(30). These documents represent the right to possession of the goods described in them and entitle the possessor of the documents to title to the goods, thus the name "documents of title." They are a very formal type of paper, and as we say, title to the goods is locked up in the documents.

8. **Letter-of-credit rights:** Letter-of-credit rights are rights arising from a letter of credit transaction. UCC § 9-102(a)(51). Generally, these are rights of the beneficiary of a letter of credit whether or not the beneficiary has earned the rights under the letter of credit.

9. **Investment property:** Investment property are stocks, bonds, and similar types of property traded on a securities exchange. UCC § 9-102(a)(51).

10. **Commodity accounts and commodity contracts:** A commodity account is an account carried by a commodity intermediate for one of its customers when the commodity customer is under an indirect-holding system of the securities market. UCC § 9-102(a)(14). A commodity contract is a commodity futures contract or other option trade on a board of trade. UCC § 9-102(15).

11. **Summary and collateral identification game:** Practice your collateral identification skills using the summary chart below and the game that follows it.

Summary of Possible Collateral Categories

Category	Description
Goods	
Inventory	Goods held for sale or short-term use by a business
Equipment	Assets held by a business for long-term use
Farm Products	Inventory of a farm, crops, livestock, supplies used in farming, products of farm in unmanufactured state
Consumer Goods	Goods used or bought for use primarily for personal, family, or household purposes
Fixtures	Personal property affixed to a building
Non-Goods	
Accounts	Usually debts owing to the debtor by third parties for goods or services
General Intangibles	Patents, trademarks, goodwill, architectural drawings
Chattel Paper	Obligation owed to the debtor that is accompanied by a security interest. An example is a note and security agreement
Instruments	Negotiable instruments under Article 3 of the UCC, including promissory notes and checks
Deposit Accounts	Bank accounts of the debtor
Commercial Tort Claims	Rights arising from tort held by a business
Health-Care Receivables	Accounts arising from a health-care business
Other	
Real Estate	Real property

Collateral Jeopardy: Next to each of the following, specify what Article 9 category of collateral you think the item falls into. If two are possible, list them both. Good luck! The answers follow the game.

Questions

Business: Rowland's Nursery

a. Plants held for sale in greenhouse   _____
b. Toilet paper in the bathroom   _____
c. Dollies and carts   _____
d. Seeds held for sale   _____
e. Seeds to be planted by Rowland's next year   _____
f. Amounts corporate customers owe for plant maintenance contracts   _____
g. The name "Rowland's"   _____
h. Promissory notes owed to Rowland's by other nurseries Rowland's sells as a wholesaler   _____

Business: Perfection Honda

a. Cars in showroom   _____
b. Cars used to lend to customers getting their own serviced   _____
c. Notes and security agreements issued by people who bought cars on credit   _____
d. Screwdrivers   _____
e. Lifts   _____
f. Auto parts   _____
g. Coffee in the waiting room   _____
h. The telephone   _____
i. The speaker system   _____
j. Television in the waiting room   _____

Business: Dairy and Tree Farm

a. Fencing in the fields   _____
b. Cows   _____
c. Trees growing in the ground   _____
d. Milking machines   _____
e. Food for the staff   _____
f. Pens and pencils in the office   _____
g. Cattle feed   _____
h. Plant food   _____
i. Trees in containers on their way to Rowland's   _____
j. Television in the employee lounge   _____
k. Magazines in the employee lounge   _____
l. Owner's truck   _____

Assets owned by Nathalie and Fred
(the authors of this Outline)

a. Computer in Nathalie's living room   _____
b. Fred's car   _____
c. Fred's refrigerator   _____
d. The refrigerator in Nathalie's office   _____

Business: Raley's Supermarket

a. Milk   _____
b. Cash register   _____
c. Money people owe for corporate parties   _____
d. Bank accounts   _____
e. Meat cutters   _____
f. Soap in restroom   _____
g. Soap dispenser in restroom   _____
h. Cheese and meat in dairy case   _____
i. Soap dispensers for sale on Aisle 12   _____
j. Frozen food cases   _____
k. Shopping carts   _____
l. Floor mats in doorways to store   _____
m. Credit card receipts   _____
n. Discount coupons issued by manufacturers   _____

Business: P&S Fireplace Logs: Sales and Service

a. Truck   _____
b. Sand and fireplace logs   _____
c. Grates   _____
d. Carbon monoxide testers used by the service department _____
e. Unpaid invoices for service   _____
f. Notes and security agreements for new setups   _____
g. Forklifts   _____
h. Toolboxes   _____

Business: Enron

a. Energy contracts   _____
b. Copyrights and trademarks   _____
c. Stock owned by investors   _____
d. Chairs in office   _____
e. Office buildings   _____
f. Blueprint for unfinished office space   _____
g. Blueprint for unfinished Web page   _____

Business: Sprint PCS

a. Contracts with customers   _____
b. Phones   _____
c. Phone repair kits   _____
d. Testers   _____
e. Billing clerk's computer   _____
f. Phone systems in office   _____
g. Lighting in stores   _____
h. Customer lists   _____

Business: Hyatt Tamaya Resort and Spa

a. Checks in cash register   _____
b. Credit card invoices   _____
c. Spa massage tables   _____
d. Invoices for room service   _____
e. Art in lobby   _____
f. Computers at front desk   _____
g. Computers in business-class rooms   _____
h. Shower heads   _____
i. Towels   _____
j. Soaps in rooms   _____
k. Landscaping machinery   _____
l. Kiva fireplaces near pool   _____
m. Big slide   _____
n. Statues in front of resort   _____
o. Lamps on roadside   _____

Answers

Business: Rowland's Nursery

a. Plants in greenhouse: *inventory or farm products*
b. Toilet paper in the bathroom: *inventory*
c. Dollies and carts: *equipment*
d. Seeds held for sale: *inventory*
e. Seeds to be planted next year: *inventory*
f. Amounts corporate customers owe for plant maintenance contracts: *accounts*
g. The name "Rowland's": *general intangibles*
h. Promissory notes owed to Rowland's by other nurseries Rowland's sells to wholesale: *instruments*

Business: Perfection Honda

a. Cars in showroom: *inventory*
b. Cars used to lend to customers getting their own serviced: *equipment*
c. Notes and security agreements issued by people who bought cars on credit: *chattel papers*
d. Screwdrivers: *equipment*
e. Lifts: *equipment*
f. Auto parts: *inventory*
g. Coffee in the waiting room: *inventory*
h. The telephone: *equipment*
i. The speaker system: *equipment*
j. Television in the waiting room: *equipment*

Business: Dairy and Tree Farm

a. Fencing: *equipment or fixtures*
b. Cows: *farm products*
c. Trees growing in the ground: *farm products*
d. Milking machines: *equipment*
e. Food for the staff: *inventory*
f. Pens and pencils in the office: *inventory or equipment*
g. Cattle feed: *farm products*
h. Plant food: *farm products*

i. Trees in containers on their way to Rowland's: *inventory*

j. Television in the employee lounge: *equipment*

k. Magazines in the employee lounge: *inventory*

l. Owner's truck: *equipment or consumer goods*

Assets owned by Nathalie and Fred

a. Computer in Nathalie's living room: *consumer goods or equipment*

b. Fred's car: *consumer goods*

c. Fred's refrigerator: *consumer goods*

d. The refrigerator in Nathalie's office: *consumer goods or equipment*

Business: Raley's Supermarket

a. Milk: *inventory*

b. Cash register: *equipment*

c. Money people owe for corporate parties: *accounts*

d. Bank accounts: *deposit accounts*

e. Meat cutters: *equipment*

f. Soap in restroom: *inventory*

g. Soap dispenser in restroom: *equipment*

h. Cheese and meat in dairy case: *inventory*

i. Soap dispensers for sale on Aisle 12: *inventory*

j. Frozen food cases: *fixtures or equipment*

k. Shopping carts: *equipment*

l. Floor mats in doorways to store: *equipment*

m. Credit card receipts: *accounts*

n. Discount coupons issued by manufacturers: *general intangibles or accounts*

Business: P&S Fireplace Logs: Sales and Service

a. Truck: *equipment*

b. Sand and fireplace logs: *inventory*

c. Grates: *inventory*

d. Carbon monoxide testers: *equipment or inventory*

e. Unpaid invoices for service: *accounts*

f. Notes and security agreements for new setups: *chattel paper*

g. Forklifts: *equipment*

h. Toolboxes: *equipment*

Business: Enron

a. Energy contracts: *general intangibles*

b. Copyrights and trademarks: *general intangibles*

c. Stock owned by investors: *NOT AN ASSET OF ENRON*

d. Chairs in office: *equipment*

e. Office buildings: *real estate*

f. Blueprint for unfinished office space: *general intangible*

g. Blueprint for unfinished Web page: *general intangible*

Business: Sprint PCS

a. Contracts with customers: *general intangibles*

b. Phones: *inventory or equipment*

c. Phone repair kits: *equipment*

d. Testers: *equipment*

e. Billing clerk's computer: *equipment*

f. Phone systems in office: *equipment*

g. Lighting in stores: *equipment or fixtures*

h. Customer lists: *general intangibles*

Business: Hyatt Tamaya Resort and Spa

a. Checks in cash register: *instruments*

b. Credit card invoices: *accounts*

c. Spa massage tables: *equipment*

d. Invoices for room service: *accounts*

e. Art in lobby: *equipment*

f. Computers at front desk: *equipment*

g. Computers in business-class rooms: *equipment*

h. Shower heads: *equipment*

i. Towels: *equipment*

j. Soaps in rooms: *inventory*

k. Landscaping machinery: *equipment*

l. Kiva fireplaces near pool: *equipment or fixtures or real estate*

m. Big slide: *equipment or fixtures*

n. Statues in front of resort: *fixtures or equipment*

o. Lamps on roadside: *fixtures or equipment*

Quiz Yourself on
SCOPE OF ARTICLE 9 AND TYPES OF COLLATERAL

15. What is the test for whether a transaction falls within Article 9? _____

16. Name some transactions that constitute security interests under Article 9, but that have names that suggest they are *not* security interests. _____

17. Why do parties name these transactions in a way that suggests they are not Article 9 secured transactions? _____

18. Name some transactions that are outside Article 9. _____

19. Name as many categories of collateral as you can. _____

20. Can you define each type of collateral, in just a few words?

   a. inventory _____

   b. equipment _____

   c. farm products _____

    d. consumer goods   _____

    e. fixtures   _____

    f. accounts   _____

    g. general intangibles   _____

    h. chattel paper   _____

    i. instruments   _____

    j. deposit accounts   _____

    k. commercial tort claims   _____

21. Can you name some examples of assets that will change their categorization based on who owns them or other facts?   _____

Answers

15. The test for whether a transaction falls within Article 9 is whether the transaction creates a security interest in personal property.

16. Assignments of accounts, consignments, conditional sales contracts, some personal property leases.

17. Parties often use these other names to avoid the technical rules and notice requirements of Article 9. Article 9 is drafted to include these transactions, however, so that its goals are not thwarted by clever lawyers.

18. Some of the things that are outside Article 9 are landlords' liens, real property mortgages, personal tort claims, and set-off rights.

19. There are four big categories that most businesses of all kinds have: inventory, accounts, equipment, general intangibles. Another way of learning these has to do with whether the asset is tangible or intangible, or put another way, goods or non-goods. Goods are inventory, equipment, farm products, consumer goods, and fixtures. Non-goods are accounts, general intangibles, chattel paper, instruments, deposit accounts, and commercial tort claims. There is also real estate, though it is outside the scope of Article 9.

20. **a.** Inventory: goods held for sale or short-term use by a business.

    b. Equipment: assets held by a business for long-term use.

    c. Farm products: the inventory of a farm: crops, livestock, supplies used in farming, products of farm in unmanufactured state.

    d. Consumer goods: goods used or bought for use primarily for personal, family, or household purposes.

    e. Fixtures: personal property affixed to a building.

    f. Accounts: amounts owing to the debtor by third parties for goods or services.

g. General intangibles: patents, trademarks, goodwill, architectural drawings.

h. Chattel paper: an obligation owed to the debtor that is accompanied by a security agreement. An example is a note and security agreement.

i. Instruments: negotiable instruments under Article 3 of the UCC, including promissory notes and checks.

j. Deposit accounts: bank accounts of the debtor.

k. Commercial tort claims: rights arising from tort held by a business.

21. Milk in the hands of the dairy farmer would be farm products, at least before pasteurization. In the hands of convenience store 7-Eleven, it's inventory. An unattached fence is equipment, but if the farmer attaches it to the land, it is a fixture. A computer is held as inventory by Best Buy; equipment for a printing business; and a consumer good to a 12-year-old using it to play computer games.

Exam Tips on
SCOPE OF ARTICLE 9 AND TYPES OF COLLATERAL

Here are some important issues to keep in mind when taking your secured transactions exam:

☛ A transaction is covered by Article 9 (with all its rules), regardless of the way the transaction is named, any time the intent of the transaction is to grant a security interest to a creditor in personal (as opposed to real) property.

☛ The distinction between a true lease and one that operates as a security interest is important. A *lease* is a security device and thus covered by Article 9 if the debtor owns the property under the lease by the end of the lease term, or can buy the property for a nominal amount. Other facts suggesting that a lease is a security device include that the lender has a right to accelerate the amounts due under the lease upon a default; that the debtor bears the risk of loss; that the debtor pays for registration, taxes, and licensing; and that the lease contains a disclaimer of warranties.

☛ You need to know how to characterize various types of collateral recognized by Article 9. When determining the proper character of collateral, consider the use of the asset in the context of how it is used at the time a secured interest is given. If you don't understand this concept, you will not know how to successfully create and perfect your client's security interests and thus make them valid and enforceable.

☛ Collateral falls into two general categories: tangible (goods) and intangible. These general categories are then split into several smaller categories. The distinction is sometimes important to understand what is required to perfect the security interest.

☞ Here are a few tricky things to keep in mind:

    ☞ Inventory is sometimes confused with equipment. Inventory is goods held for sale, lease, or short-term use in a business, whereas equipment is goods held and used in business for long-term use.

    ☞ Farm products include growing crops, all supplies used in a farming operation, and the products of crops or livestock in their unmanufactured state.

    ☞ Feed, which would certainly seem to be inventory, will be a farm product if it is used to feed farm animals. Moreover, milk from a cow is a farm product until it is "manufactured" at which point it becomes inventory.

    ☞ How one categorizes collateral depends in large part upon who is holding it. Heavy-duty equipment being held for sale by a John Deere dealer is not equipment, but inventory. This can be quite tricky, so practice with the game.

CHAPTER 3

REMEDIES: THE SECURED PARTY'S RIGHTS AGAINST THE DEBTOR

ChapterScope _____

In this chapter, you will learn about the secured creditor's remedies. The key points in this chapter are as follows:

- **Remedy differences:** In this chapter, you will learn the differences between the remedies of secured creditors under the Uniform Commercial Code (UCC) and unsecured creditors pursuant to state law.

- **Default:** Although there is no specific definition for default under the UCC, this chapter explains what constitutes a default by a debtor under a security agreement and why you care.

- **Acceleration:** Acceleration is a legal mechanism established by contract that causes the entire debt to become due.

- **Acceleration clause:** An acceleration clause is a contract provision that accelerates the debt upon default, and this chapter teaches you why a secured creditor should include such a clause in its security agreement.

- **Collateral possession:** This chapter describes how a secured party obtains possession of its collateral on default, either through self-help repossession or through judicial action.

- **Property sale:** This chapter explains how a secured party goes about selling its collateral and getting paid from the proceeds of the sale.

- **Application of proceeds:** Article 9 defines how the secured party must apply the proceeds of sale, meaning who it must pay and in what order, as well as what it must do with any surplus or excess proceeds.

- **Deficiency judgment:** When the proceeds of the sale are insufficient to satisfy the debt, the secured party is entitled to a deficiency judgment and this chapter explains how the deficiency judgment is obtained and how it is calculated. It also describes what happens to the deficiency if the secured party fails to follow the requirements of Article 9 in repossessing or selling the collateral.

- **Collection on intangibles:** You will learn how the secured party collects its claim when its collateral is accounts and other intangible collateral.

- **Strict foreclosure:** A secured party can keep its collateral in full or partial satisfaction of its claim under certain conditions.

- **Redemption:** Under Article 9, a debtor has a right to redeem its collateral under certain circumstances discussed in this chapter.

- **Violation of Article 9:** A debtor can recover damages from the secured party as a result of the secured party's violation of Article 9, and this chapter explains when those provisions apply.

- **Bankruptcy filing:** A debtor's bankruptcy affects the secured party's right to recover from its collateral, and this chapter describes and explains those effects.

I. INTRODUCTION

A. **Secured versus unsecured creditor remedies:** As you know, one of the purposes of a secured transaction is to make it easier for the secured party to collect the debt owed to it. Remember the difficulty that an unsecured creditor might have in collecting: The creditor must obtain a judgment and then find some property of the debtor and obtain a lien on it by following the execution process.

   A critical step in the collection process is obtaining a lien on some of the debtor's property. A creditor cannot take any of the debtor's property in satisfaction of its debt unless and until it has created a lien, and a lien is generally not created until the sheriff levies under a writ of execution. To top it off, much of an individual debtor's property will be exempt in many states.

   Now consider the situation of a secured creditor. By giving the secured party a security interest in the property, the debtor creates a lien in whatever property was described in the security agreement. Thus, the secured party starts off by having a lien and does not have to get one through the execution process. That lien gives the secured party the right to possession of the debtor's property if the debtor doesn't pay—defaults—and the further right to sell that property and to apply the money obtained from the sale to the debt.

   If that were all there was to it, this chapter would be unnecessary, but problems can arise. For starters, the secured party's right to possession is contingent upon a default by the debtor. But what is a "default," you might ask? Assuming a default, how does the secured party obtain possession? And then, assuming that the debtor has possession, what kind of sale must it conduct? The questions continue. What happens when there isn't enough money generated by the sale to satisfy the debt? What if the sale produces more than enough? What happens to the surplus? Then there is the possibility of "strict foreclosure," meaning that the secured party can keep the goods in full or partial satisfaction of the debt. Also, the debtor may have a right to redeem the property.

   Although in most cases the secured party will take possession of the collateral after default and either sell it or keep it in satisfaction of the debt, Article 9 allows other remedies as well. The secured party may sue on the debt—bring an action in contract for breach or bring an appropriate judicial proceeding to enforce its rights. The secured party's rights are cumulative and can be exercised simultaneously. For example, the secured party might repossess the goods and at the same time commence an action on the debt.

   These and other problems will be addressed in this chapter. This chapter is about Article 9 security interests in personal property, but also briefly discusses the rights of creditors holding consensual liens in real property, e.g., mortgagees.

   In many places in this chapter, we emphasize that Article 9 requires the secured party to act in a commercially reasonable way in exercising its remedies. We repeatedly tell you here that what is commercially reasonable depends on the facts of a particular case. As a result, Article 9 is filled with tests that are fact-based and sound entirely too vague for the rule-seeking student. This is particularly true in the 9-600 series, which covers the remedies of the secured party. We understand that this is frustrating, particularly for students with no business experience. We try to present you with many hypothetical situations to help you predict answers under changing facts.

   Note: Before we get started, please take a breath and make a mental note of one thing: In Chapter 5 you will soon learn all about *perfection* of security interests, often through the filing of a financing statement. The filing of this little paper will soon occupy many cavities of your brain and become your paramount concern. Don't let that happen!

B. The remedies are not dependent on perfection: If a secured party has created a security interest pursuant to the rules set out in Chapter 4, then the secured party is entitled to all the remedies we are about to tell you about. Perfection is irrelevant to these remedies. Thus, a failure to file a financing statement (to perfect a security interest) does not affect a secured party's rights against the debtor to pursue collateral, but only the creditor's priority vis-à-vis other parties. This is something students frequently forget, so try not to!

II. DEFAULT

A. Importance of Default: ''Default'' is important because the secured party generally can do very little until the debtor defaults. Particularly, the secured party cannot take possession of the collateral or sell it. Essentially, the secured party's right arises only on default.

B. Defining a default in the security agreement: The UCC does not define ''default,'' but a default can be and usually is defined in the security agreement. The security agreement is the contract in which the debtor grants the secured party a security agreement. This is the subject of Chapter 4. If there is no provision defining default in the security agreement, probably the only default is a failure by the debtor to make a payment when it becomes due.

Note: Because the security agreement is a contract between the debtor and the secured party, the security agreement can define a default in whatever way the parties choose.

Default clauses commonly provide that a breach by the debtor of any of its obligations under the agreement or any false statement by the debtor in the agreement or the negotiations leading up to the loan constitutes a default. Because the debtor usually promises to insure the property, keep it in good repair and at a designated location, use it only for specific purposes, pay any applicable taxes, etc., a breach of any of these promises will constitute a default under the typical default clause.

Misstatements in the security agreement or the loan application of the debtor's financial resources, the type of entity it is, addresses, etc. will also constitute a default if the security agreement provides that it is a default. The security agreement also often makes it a default if any other lien attaches to the collateral, the debtor dies or otherwise ceases to exist, or if the collateral is lost or stolen.

Frequently, the secured party is entitled to inspect the books of the debtor and the collateral, and, if these rights are refused by the debtor, the agreement usually makes the refusal an event of default.

C. Insecurity clauses: A provision common to many security agreements allows the secured party to declare a default whenever the secured party ''deems itself insecure'' or ''at will.'' These provisions are valid, but to enforce them, the secured party must in good faith believe ''that the prospect of payment or performance is impaired.'' UCC § 1-208 [UCC § 1-309 of Revised Article 1]; *J.R. Hale Contracting Co. v. United New Mexico Bank at Albuquerque*, 799 P.2d 581 (N.M. 1990). *Good faith* means ''honesty in fact and the observance of reasonable commercial standards of fair dealing.'' UCC § 9-102(a)(20).

Under a clause allowing the secured party to call or declare a default when it deems itself insecure, there must be an event directly affecting the debtor that occurs *after* the loan has been made.

For example, if the secured party believes in retrospect that it should never have made the loan, this is insufficient to constitute a good faith belief of insecurity. Also, a general downturn in the economy would not allow the secured party to call a default. On the other hand, if the secured party discovers that the debtor is failing to meet its other obligations, e.g., its obligation to pay rent on its store or to pay its suppliers, the secured party would have reason to call a default under its insecurity clause. The test is whether the lender in good faith believes that its ability to collect its debt is impaired owing to circumstances arising after the loan was made.

D. Waiver of default by the secured party: The secured party can waive a default. If, for example, the debtor is late in making a payment but the secured party accepts the payment, the default would be waived. In fact, the secured party may even be estopped from enforcing a future default when the debtor subsequently makes another late payment. *Dunn v. General Equities of Iowa, Ltd.*, 319 N.W.2d 515 (Iowa 1982).

For example, if the debtor has made payment five days late for a few months and the secured party accepted the late payment each time, the secured party could not refuse to accept a payment that was a few days late and call a default unless the secured party had served notice on the debtor that in the future it intended to require payment on time. See *J.R. Hale Contracting Co. v. United New Mexico Bank at Albuquerque*, 799 P.2d 581 (N.M. 1990).

Frequently, the security agreement contains a "no waiver" clause, stating that the failure to enforce an obligation of the debtor does not operate to estop the secured party from requiring strict performance in the future. However, sometimes courts refuse to enforce these clauses. See *Cobb v. Midwest Recovery Bureau*, 295 N.W.2d 232 (Minn. 1980).

A note about material defaults versus minor defaults: Under the prevailing cases, a slight breach by the debtor will constitute a default, but some courts require that the breach be material. *Sahadi v. Continental Illinois National Bank & Trust Co.*, 706 F.2d 193 (7th Cir. 1983). If the breach is minor (obviously a question of fact), declaring a default may be inconsistent with the secured party's obligation to exercise its remedies in good faith. UCC § 1-203 [UCC § 1-304 of the revised version of Article 1].

E. Default for agricultural liens: The time of default for agricultural liens (which are covered by Article 9 and described in Chapter 1 of this Outline, as well as in UCC § 9-109(a)(2)) is the time that the lienholder has the right to enforce the lien under the law creating it. UCC § 9-606. State and federal statutes, not Article 9, create these agricultural liens.

III. ACCELERATION

An *acceleration clause* is simply a provision in an agreement between a debtor and a creditor providing that if the debtor breaches or defaults, by missing a payment or otherwise, the entire debt becomes due. Acceleration is most important when the debt is to be paid in installments. The failure of the debtor to pay one installment is a breach only as to that installment, unless the agreement between the parties contains an acceleration clause. Without the clause, the creditor can sue only for that installment, and if the debtor *cures* by making payment of that installment, the secured party cannot repossess the collateral.

If the agreement contains an acceleration clause, the secured party may accelerate the whole debt, making the full amount payable immediately. If the debt is not paid, the creditor can proceed to repossess the collateral.

IV. OBTAINING POSSESSION OF THE COLLATERAL

A. In general: Upon default, the secured party has a right to possession of the collateral. Sometimes the debtor will voluntarily turn over possession. In other cases, however, the debtor(s) will refuse. When the collateral is goods, Article 9 gives to the debtor two ways of obtaining possession: (1) by simply taking the collateral if this can be done without a breach of the peace, or (2) by bringing a court action. This is usually called *replevin,* or simply, an action for possession. When the collateral is intangibles, for example accounts, a different procedure is used.

B. Peaceful repossession: To be effective, self-help repossession has to be peaceful or, as we say, done without breaching the peace. The Code does not elaborate on what constitutes a peaceful repossession. As a result, many cases have addressed this question, some of which are funny and others sad, but all intensely fact-based.

Many cases turn on the potential for violence when there is an unauthorized entry on the land of the debtor. See *Salisbury Livestock Co. v. Colorado Central Credit Union,* 793 P.2d 470 (Wyo. 1990). The cases do not present a clear picture of what constitutes a peaceful repossession, because the facts of each case are the key to the outcomes. However, a number of general observations can be made.

1. Potential for violence: If there is the likelihood, or perhaps only the possibility, of violence, the party repossessing should desist even if no violence actually results. A continuation of the repossession constitutes a breach of the peace. The question is not whether violence actually occurred but the extent to which there is the potential for violence.

Thus, if the debtor is present and threatens to hit the person repossessing the collateral with a baseball bat, continuation of the repossession would constitute a breach of the peace. However, if the debtor is present but does nothing and says nothing, the repossession can continue and there is no breach of the peace. Even if the debtor protests the taking, it must be done in a manner that suggests that violence will result if the repossession is not stopped. *Williams v. Ford Motor Credit Co.,* 674 F.2d 717 (8th Cir. 1982). For example, if the debtor sees the repossession and simply says something like, "Please don't take my car, I need it for work," without any indication that the debtor will intervene, the repossession is likely peaceful. *See Chrysler Credit Company v. Kroontz,* 661 N.E.2d 1171 (Ill. App. 1996).

The debtor must object at the time of the repossession; once the collateral is in the possession of those repossessing it, an objection will not result in a breach of the peace. *Clark v. Auto Recovery Bureau Conn., Inc.,* 889 F. Supp. 543 (D. Conn. 1994). A confrontation at the time of repossession, even a threat to shoot anyone attempting to repossess, does not carry over to a second attempt to repossess that is done without any confrontation. *Wade v. Ford Motor Credit Co.,* 668 P.2d 183 (Kan. App. 1983).

2. Trespass not necessarily a breach of the peace: Repossession of a vehicle that is parked on a public street when the debtor is absent clearly does not constitute a breach of the peace, even though it may be noisy and disruptive to others. *Giles v. First Virginia Credit Services, Inc.,* 560 S.E.2d 557 (N.C. App. 2002).

In fact, even trespass on the debtor's land during the repossession does not constitute necessarily a breach of the peace. For example, if the debtor's car is in the driveway and the "repo" person goes on the debtor's land without permission to get it, there is no breach of the peace as a result of the trespass. If the car is in an attached garage with the door open, the result may be different because the repo person would have to enter the abode of the debtor. If the door is closed, it is more likely to constitute a breach of the peace, and if the door is locked and the creditor's agent breaks the lock, it is almost certainly a breach of the peace. *Davenport v. Chrysler Credit Corp.,* 818 S.W.2d 23 (Tenn. App. 1991).

Caveat: If the security agreement allows the secured party to enter the premises without liability, breaking the locks may not result in a breach of the peace. *Wombles Charters, Inc. v. Orix Credit Alliance, Inc.*, 39 UCC Rep. Serv. 2d (Callaghan) 599 (S.D.N.Y. 1999). If a car is located on the land of a house that is in a remote location, where it is likely that the owner will shoot at intruders, it is more likely that coming on the land will result in violence and make the repossession a breach of the peace. *Salisbury Livestock Co. v. Colorado Central Credit Union*, 793 P.2d 470 (Wyo. 1990).

3. **Law officer in attendance:** If the secured party has a sheriff or other officer of the law attend the repossession, it is a breach of the peace if the officer is in uniform and in any way participated in the repossession. *Stone Machinery Company v. Kessler*, 463 P.2d 651 (Wash. App. 1976). If, on the other hand, the officer remains hidden, there is no breach of the peace.

4. **Trickery or fraud:** The use of trickery, or even fraud, usually will not result in a breach of the peace. For example, if the secured party induces the debtor to drive to its office under the pretext of "working things out," the fact that the car is blocked so that the debtor cannot drive it away would not make the repossession improper. *K.B. Oil Co. v. Ford Motor Credit Co., Inc.*, 811 F.2d 310 (6th Cir. 1987).

   Trickery, however, can go too far. For example, if the person repossessing brings a friend dressed as a police officer, who tells the debtor that he must give up possession, there probably is a breach of the peace.

5. **Personal property taken during repossession:** If personal property that is not collateral is taken, the secured party has committed conversion of that property. For example, if an automobile is repossessed and it contains property of the debtor in the trunk or glove compartment that is not covered by the security agreement, there is a conversion of that property, and the debtor will be entitled to compensatory damages. However, if the property is returned promptly, there may be no damages. *Clark v. Auto Recovery Bureau Conn., Inc.*, 889 F. Supp. 543 (D. Conn. 1994).

6. **Secured party liable for agent's breach of the peace:** If the secured party hires someone to repossess the property and the person doing the repossession is liable for conversion or otherwise, the secured party will be liable because the duty not to breach the peace cannot be delegated. *Robinson v. Citicorp Nat'l Servs., Inc.*, 921 S.W.2d 52 (Mo. Ct. App. 1996).

Example 1: FMCC hired an independent contractor who attempted to repossess a vehicle but was threatened by the debtor. The contractor aborted the repossession effort. FMCC then filed an application for a writ of replevin to have the sheriff take possession of the vehicle. Prior to securing this writ, the independent contractor again attempted to repossess the vehicle. The contractor entered the debtor's private property and traveled nearly a quarter of a mile, where he found one of two vehicles that were to be repossessed. The contractor entered the vehicle and, once inside, began fleeing the property. The debtor, noticing all the action, ran from his home and attempted to stop the repossession by entering the pathway of the fleeing contractor. The contractor feared a fight, so he continued to drive the vehicle off the property. During his getaway, the contractor ran over the debtor and killed him. The duty to repossess without a breach of the peace is nondelegable and therefore FMCC is liable.

7. Waiver right to peaceful repossession not allowed: The debtor cannot waive the right to a peaceful repossession, UCC § 9-602(6), nor may the parties agree to what constitutes the standard for peaceful possession. UCC § 9-603(b).

If there has been a wrongful repossession, the debtor can proceed under the Article 9 provision allowing damages, UCC § 9-625(b) discussed in Section XIV, *infra*, or sue for conversion, or, as the suit is sometimes called, an action for wrongful possession. In a suit in conversion, punitive damages may be awarded. *Stone Machinery v. Kessler*, 463 P.2d 651 (Wash. Ct. App. 1970).

8. Louisiana law: Louisiana does not even allow self-help repossession, under the theory that self-help is too conducive to violence. Rather, in Louisiana, a secured party must proceed by judicial process, described below. All other states allow self-help repossession.

C. Right to disable collateral: When it is impossible or difficult to obtain physical possession of the collateral, the secured party has the right to disable the collateral instead. UCC § 9-609(a)(2). Thus, if the collateral is large earth-moving equipment, the secured party might remove an essential part of the machinery, making it impossible to operate. When the collateral is disabled, the secured party may sell it where it is located.

As an example, a student told about a cousin who failed to pay her car loan. The finance company installed a device that would not allow the car to be started until the loan was paid.

D. Debtor's obligation to assemble the collateral: The security agreement may provide that the debtor has an obligation to assemble the collateral on default and make it available to the secured party at a place designated by the secured party. The security agreement can even provide that the obligation to assemble exists even before default, presumably to allow the secured party to examine the collateral.

E. Obtaining possession by use of the judicial process: The secured party may also obtain possession by bringing an action for possession. Under the common law, and under the law of many states, the action is for replevin, but some states simply label it an *action for possession*.

Note: Why would a secured creditor ever proceed with judicial action rather than just taking possession of the collateral? Normally the creditor will get a court order if it cannot repossess peacefully or if it is selling an entire business and thinks it would be more orderly to proceed through a court order. Your instincts are correct, though. If a creditor can repossess without going to court, it usually will do so.

Prior to the 1970s, the required legal action for replevin was simple: The secured party filed an action and, without notice or an opportunity for the debtor to be heard, the sheriff would seize the collateral and turn it over to the secured party. Ending with *North Georgia Finishing Corp. v. Di-Chem, Inc.*, 419 U.S. 601 (1975), the Supreme Court considered several cases and imposed limits on the writ of replevin based on the Due Process Clause of the U.S. Constitution. Initially, it seemed as though the Court was requiring that there be notice and a hearing before the seizure by the sheriff, *Fuentes v. Shevin*, 407 U.S. 67 (1972).

In later cases, however, the Court appeared to modify its ruling to allow a seizure if: (1) there was an allegation that the property would become unavailable or be wasted if the writ was not immediately issued, (2) the writ were issued by a judge, and (3) there was a right to prompt hearing after the seizure. See *Del's Big Saver Foods, Inc. v. Carpenter Cook, Inc.*, 603 F.Supp. 1071 (W.D. Wis. 1985).

Most states have amended their replevin statutes to comply with the Supreme Court opinions. Today replevin actions are usually started with a petition accompanied by an affidavit that the collateral is likely to be destroyed or made available. The writ, without any preseizure notice or hearing, is issued by a judge ordering a sheriff to seize the property.

To obtain the writ, the secured party must furnish a bond insuring that the debtor will be reimbursed for any damages if the writ was improperly granted, and the debtor is entitled to a hearing soon after the seizure. After seizing the property the sheriff turns it over to the secured party who then can proceed to sell it in satisfaction of the debt.

F. **Secured party's obligations as to repossessed collateral:** A secured party that has obtained possession of the collateral has an obligation to use reasonable care in its custody and preservation. UCC § 9-207(a). *City National Bank v. Unique Structures, Inc.*, 49 F.3d 1330 (8th Cir. 1995). The costs of preserving it can be added to the debt owed by the debtor. The risk of loss remains on the debtor absent negligence by the secured party. UCC § 9-207(b).

V. DISPOSING OF THE COLLATERAL

A. **In general:** The goal of the Code provisions on the disposition of the collateral after it has been repossessed is to make it convenient for the secured party to dispose of the collateral. A countervailing goal is to assure that the collateral will be sold for a fair price.

Note: Unlike sales resulting from the execution process, when the sheriff has seized property under a writ of replevin, the sheriff will turn the property over to the secured party, and the secured party will hold its own sale.

The secured party has wide discretion in selling the collateral. The collateral may be sold by private or public sale, altogether or in parts, for cash or on credit, and at any time or place. UCC § 9-610(b). The secured party also may lease it, license it, or otherwise dispose of it. The disposition, however, must be commercially reasonable in every aspect, including the method, manner, time, place, and terms. *Id.*

The frequently litigated *commercially reasonable* requirement is a murky one. It is heavily fact-based. Article 9 gives few indications of when a disposition is commercially reasonable. The fact that a greater price could have been obtained by a different disposition does not, by itself, make the disposition commercially unreasonable, UCC § 9-627(a), but a low price may indicate that the sale was not properly conducted. *Hall v. Owen County State Bank*, 370 N.E.2d 918 (Ind. App. 1977).

Three methods of disposition are *per se* reasonable: (1) a sale in a recognized market, (2) a sale at a price current in a recognized market, and (3) a sale in conformity with reasonable commercial practice of dealers in the type of property being disposed of. UCC § 9-627(b). Also, a sale approved in a judicial proceeding or by a creditors' committee, representative of the creditors or an assignee for the benefit of creditors, is *per se* commercially reasonable.

A sale on a *recognized market* is a very narrow concept with a specific meaning. The phrase refers only to sales in markets like the stock exchange or commodities market.

The requirement that a sale be made in conformity with reasonable business practices embodies a much broader and more flexible standard.

Example 2: A credit union repossesses an automobile and sells it at an auction of used cars held weekly. The sale is not a sale on a recognized market. However, if all or at least many of the financial institutions in the community sell repossessed vehicles in that market, it would be a sale in conformity with the reasonable practices and be a commercially reasonable sale.

The secured party has a duty to preserve the collateral once it has repossessed it and to take reasonable steps to lessen its depreciation. UCC § 9-207(a). *City National Bank v. Unique Structures, Inc.*, 49 F.3d 1330 (8th Cir. 1995). The secured party can prepare or process the collateral before sale if it would be commercially reasonable to do so, and the secured party has a duty to repair or prepare the collateral before it is sold, if it would be commercially unreasonable *not* to do so. Official Comment 4 to UCC § 9-610.

The timing of the sale is important. The sale must take place within a reasonable time after repossession. If the property is perishable or subject to rapid depletion, the sale should be made immediately. However, if the collateral is highly valuable and not easy to sell, or if the custom is to provide an extended period of inspection, the sale should not be too soon. *In re Frazier*, 93 B.R. 366 (Bankr. M.D. Tenn. 1989). Again, the cases are intensely fact based.

B. Public sales: Public sales, usually auctions, are generally commercially reasonable if properly held. For a sale to be considered public, the public must be invited and told the time and place of the sale and the sale must be made at the time and place stated in the advertisements.

A sale open only to dealers is probably a public sale if there is a sufficient number of dealers in the locale to provide a significant number of bidders. For example, even though only registered retailers can bid at some auction sales of automobiles, the sale would be a public sale if a large number of retailers attended the auction.

In a public sale, sufficient advertising is necessary to ensure that there will be a suitable number of bidders. The sale also must be honest and aboveboard. Additionally, as a general rule, the property being sold must be available for inspection by potential bidders.

All in all, whether a public sale is commercially reasonable depends on whether the secured party proceeded in a reasonable way and tried to get a fair price for the collateral.

The secured party may bid and purchase at a public sale. UCC § 9-610(c)(1).

C. Private sales: In some cases it may make more sense, and be more commercially reasonable, for the secured party to make a private sale rather than a public one. Indeed, holding an auction sale might be commercially unreasonable under some circumstances.

Example 3: If the collateral is expensive equipment that is used only by a limited number of businesses, an auction would predictably yield few or no bidders. A better price would be obtained by contacting those who use this type of equipment and negotiating a sale. To simply hold an auction would probably result in a commercially unreasonable sale.

When a sale is private, whether it is commercially reasonable will depend on the efforts made by the secured party to obtain potential buyers and to obtain the best price. Depending on the nature of the collateral, a longer period of time may be required to consummate a reasonable sale, and a hasty sale might not be commercially reasonable. *In re Frazier*, 93 B.R. 366 (Bankr. M.D. Tenn. 1989).

Example 4: Sally has a security interest in an airplane owned by David securing a debt of $1 million. David defaults and Sally repossesses. The airplane is located in Fairview, a small geographically remote city of 35,000 people. To hold an auction in Fairview would be commercially unreasonable. To hold an auction in a large city, or to put the airplane up for sale with a company that is in the business of auctioning airplanes, would probably constitute a commercially reasonable sale. To sell the airplane privately by contacting a significant number of private airplane rental companies in the state, offering them the opportunity to inspect the airplane, and solicit bids from them within three months, would also probably be commercially reasonable.

The secured party may purchase its collateral at a private sale, but only if the collateral is of a kind that is customarily sold on a recognized market or is the subject of widely circulated standard price quotations. UCC § 9-610. *Munao v. Lagattuta*, 691 N.E.2d 818 (Ill. App. 1998). It's easy to see why: Private sales do not involve bidding wars, and it is hard to tell if they result in a fair price.

D. Notice of disposition

1. **Notice of sale in general:** Whether the sale is public or private, the secured party must give notice of the sale to the debtor and to others claiming an interest in the collateral. The notice is important because it gives the debtor and other persons who have an interest in the collateral an opportunity to redeem the collateral and gives all of the parties a chance to spread the word about the sale and thus to increase the number of potential purchasers.

    The notice must be in the form of an authenticated record. Thus, oral notification is insufficient. Article 9 does not require that the notice be received, only that it be sent, but the method of sending it must be reasonably calculated to reach the recipient. If notice is given of a public sale and the secured party later decides to have a private sale (or vice versa), new notification must be given. *First National Bank of Belen v. Jiron*, 106 N.M. 261 (1987); 741 P.2d 1382.

    A notice stating that the sale would be *either* public *or* private has been found to be sufficient. *Federal Deposit Insurance Corp. v. Lanier*, 926 F.2d 462 (5th Cir. 1991). If more than one disposition is to be made, notice must be given of each sale. *Spillers v. First National Bank of Arenzville*, 400 N.E.2d 1057 (Ill. App. 1980).

    Notice need not be sent if the goods are perishable or are likely to decline quickly in value, nor need the notice be given if the goods are to be sold on a recognized market. UCC § 9-611(d).

2. **To whom must notice be sent?** If the goods are consumer goods, notice must be sent to the debtor and other secondary obligors. *Secondary obligors* are those who undertook liability on the debt, basically as sureties or guarantors. If the collateral is of another type of goods, e.g., equipment, the notice also must be sent to anyone who has told the secured party that it has a claim in the goods and to other secured parties who have either filed a financing statement or had their security interest noted on a certificate of title for a vehicle at least ten days before the notice is sent. UCC § 9-611(c).

3. **Time within which notice must be given:** The notice must be sent within a reasonable time before the disposition is to occur. What constitutes a reasonable time is a question of fact (we know this is getting a bit repetitive), but in nonconsumer transactions, notice sent ten days or more before the disposition is *per se* reasonable. UCC § 9-612. In some non-consumer transactions, less than ten days is a sufficient notice period. The secured party and debtor can agree in the security agreement on what constitutes a reasonable time, provided that the time frame chosen is not manifestly unreasonable. UCC § 1-204 [UCC § 1-205 of revised Article 1].

4. **Contents of notice:** In nonconsumer transactions, the notice must (1) describe the debtor, the secured party, and the collateral; (2) state the method of disposition and that the debtor is entitled to an accounting; and (3) provide the time and place of disposition if the sale is public or, if the sale is private, the time after which the private disposition will be made. UCC § 9-613.

    The following additional information must be given in consumer transactions: (1) a description of the debtor's liability for a deficiency judgment, (2) a telephone number from which the debtor can obtain information about the cost to redeem the collateral, and (3) a telephone number or mailing address from which the debtor can obtain additional information about the disposition. UCC § 9-614.

5. **Waiver of the right to notice:** The debtor and secondary obligors may not waive the right to notice of the disposition before default. UCC § 9-602(7). However, they may waive the right to notice after default by an authenticated record. UCC § 9-624(a).

VI. APPLICATION OF THE PROCEEDS OF THE SALE

Article 9 specifies how the proceeds of a sale of collateral are to be distributed (UCC § 9-615(a)). The proceeds must be distributed first to pay the costs of sale, next to pay the claim of the secured party who is holding the sale, and then to any subordinate or junior lienholders who have met certain guidelines, as discussed below. Only if there is money left over after all this does the debtor receive anything back. Note that unsecured creditors never get paid out of a secured creditor's sale.

A. **Reasonable expenses:** The proceeds of sale are first distributed to pay the reasonable expenses of retaking, holding, preparing for disposition, processing, and disposing of the collateral. If the security agreement provides for them (and you can bet it will), the secured party can also recover its reasonable attorneys' fees and legal expenses.

B. **The debt of the secured party who is *selling* the collateral:** Next to be paid is the secured party who disposed of the collateral to the extent of the debt secured, including interest, late fees, etc.

C. **Subordinate liens:** In Chapter 6 we will discuss priorities. For now, please take as a given that there are subordinate and superior secured parties. If a *subordinate* (lower in priority) secured party or other lienholder has made a demand for payment from the sale in an authenticated record to the secured party disposing of the collateral, the net proceeds go next to subordinate secured parties, to the extent their debts are secured by the collateral. Note that a subordinate secured party must give notice to the disposing secured creditor to be eligible for payment.

    How does a subordinate lienholder know there is a sale pending? Recall that the secured party does a UCC search before the sale. The selling secured party must then notify other persons who have filed financing statements of the pending sale.

    Note also that only *subordinate* secured parties are entitled to payment. The reason is that subordinate security interests are discharged as a result of the sale.

Note: Superior lienholders are not entitled to participate in the distribution because their security interests will remain in the collateral after the sale and, hence, their rights are not disturbed. Students miss this repeatedly, so it is a common area for testing.

D. To the debtor: If there is money remaining, it goes to the debtor. Students often assume unsecured creditors are next in line, but this is not true. If they do not have a lien, they are not entitled to any of the proceeds.

Example 5: On May 1, Dave gives a security interest in his inventory to Sally to secure a loan of $15,000. On June 1, Dave gives a security interest in the same inventory to Susan to secure a debt of $10,000. On July 1, he gives another security interest in the same inventory to Sarah to secure a debt of $5,000. Assuming all have perfected by filing, the priority is Sally, Susan, and Sarah, in that order.

On August 1, Dave is in default as to all three secured parties. Susan repossesses the collateral and sells it to Paul on September 1 for $21,000. Her costs are $1,000.

In distributing the proceeds of the sale, the first $1,000 will go to the costs, leaving $20,000. Then, Susan pays herself the $10,000 owing to her, leaving $10,000.

If Sarah, who has a subordinate security interest, has made a demand in an authenticated record before Susan has made a distribution, Sarah receives $5,000, leaving $5,000. That $5,000 then goes to Dave. If Sarah has not made a demand, Dave gets all of the remaining $10,000. In either event, Sally, who has a superior security interest, receives nothing, but her lien remains on the collateral after the sale.

The following implications flow from this simple example.

> Since Sally's security interest is not discharged by the sale, Paul takes the inventory subject to her security interest and he will have to pay Sally the $15,000 owed to her or Sally will repossess. That means that unless the inventory is worth more than $36,000 ($21,000 he paid for it + $15,000 he must pay Sally), he has not made a good bargain in purchasing it.

If Sally wishes, she can disrupt the sale by Susan, in effect by repossessing the inventory from Susan. Sally can then sell the property free of the security interests of both Susan and Sarah, and will have to pay them out of the proceeds only if they made a demand on her for payment. If they do not make a demand, then any surplus after costs and payment to Sally will go to Dave, but the security interests of Susan and Sarah will be discharged as a result of Sally's sale. This rule is confusing to students and teachers alike. The bottom line is that senior secured parties can hold their own sale if they do not wish to subject themselves to a junior secured party's sale.

Remember, as previously noted, a secured party disposing of collateral may sell it to someone else on credit. This raises the issue of when the sale price is to be distributed. In the next example, the secured party repossesses an RV and sells it on credit at a properly conducted private sale after giving notice to the debtor. If the purchaser is to pay in installments a certain amount each month, when, and to what extent, must the debtor, and others entitled to share in the distribution, be paid? As you may have guessed by now, Article 9 simply requires that the secured party apply the sale price in a commercially reasonable manner. UCC § 9-615(c).

Example 6: Debtor owes Secured Party $5,000 secured by a security interest in an RV. Secured Party repossesses the RV and at a private sale sells it for $10,000. The purchaser pays $1,000 down and is to pay the additional $9,000 over three years. Secured Party is under no obligation to distribute the $5,000 surplus to the debtor immediately, but may pro-rate it over the term of the credit extended to the purchaser, or perhaps even pay it to the debtor at the end of the three years.

VII. SECURED PARTY'S RIGHT TO A DEFICIENCY JUDGMENT: WHAT HAPPENS IF THE SECURED PARTY FAILS TO HOLD A COMMERCIALLY REASONABLE SALE?

If insufficient funds result from the sale of the property, the secured party is entitled to a deficiency judgment in the amount of the difference. UCC § 9-615(d). Article 9 does not provide for the automatic issuance of a deficiency judgment; rather, the secured party must bring an action in the appropriate court to obtain the judgment.

If the secured party fails to abide by the requirements of Article 9 by properly taking possession of the collateral, by failing to give notice of its disposition or by not making a commercially reasonable disposition of the collateral, the secured party risks losing its right to a deficiency.

A. **Deficiencies in nonconsumer sales:** In the action for a deficiency, for business collateral, the secured party need not prove compliance with Article 9 unless the debtor raises it in a defense or counterclaim. If the debtor does raise it, the burden of proof is on the secured party to prove compliance.

   If the secured party fails to prove compliance as set out previously, the presumption arises that the debtor is damaged by the amount claimed in the action for deficiency. To recover a deficiency, the secured party must rebut the presumption by showing that the damages suffered by the debtor do not equal the amount of the deficiency.

   Before the recent revisions to Article 9, some courts held that the secured party forfeited its deficiency if the sale procedures were not in compliance with Article 9. Under the revised Article 9, courts can no longer follow this rule but must use the presumption set out previously, in nonconsumer sales.

   Example 7: David defaults on his obligation to Sally, which is secured by a security interest in his home entertainment system. Sally repossesses peacefully and sells the collateral to her brother Bob for $2,000 without giving notice to David. Since David owed her $3,000, there is a deficiency in the amount of $1,000. If Sally sues David, she will recover nothing because it is presumed that the amount of loss David suffered because she did not properly sell the collateral is equal to the amount of the deficiency. However, if Sally can show that the loss suffered by David is less than $1,000, she can recover $1,000 minus whatever the loss actually was.

   To review: In nonconsumer transactions, there is a presumption that the amount of damages suffered as a result of a noncommercially reasonable sale is equal to the amount of the deficiency. Thus, unless the secured party successfully rebuts the presumption, it receives no deficiency. UCC § 9-626(a).

B. **Deficiencies in consumer sales:** Article 9 applies the aforementioned rule only to nonconsumer transactions. The Code specifically states that it favors no particular rule in a consumer transaction. Before the revision of Article 9, most states applied the presumption rule to all transactions, but some took the position that a failure to follow the Article 9 rules on disposition resulted in the secured party forfeiting its rights to a deficiency. It is unlikely that those states that adopted the forfeiture rule, see *Emmons v. Burkett*, 353 S.E.2d 908 (Ga. 1987), will change it for consumer goods although they are mandated to do so for noncommercial transactions.

In other words, the Code is silent on the issue of whether a secured party can recover a deficiency if it holds a noncommercially reasonable sale in a consumer transaction.

VIII. CALCULATION AND EXPLANATION OF DEFICIENCY OR SURPLUS IN CONSUMER TRANSACTIONS

A. **Definition of deficiency or surplus:** If the sale does not bring the exact amount necessary to pay the costs and the amount owed to the secured party who sells after repossessing, there will be either a surplus that must be paid to someone or the secured party will be entitled to a deficiency judgment.

B. **Explanation of calculation:** Article 9 describes how the surplus or deficiency is to be calculated and requires that the secured party provide an explanation of the surplus or deficiency to the debtor in a consumer transaction. UCC § 9-616. This explanation is obligatory and must be given whether the debtor requests it or not. Article 9, unlike in many other situations in which a "record" suffices, requires that the explanation be in writing, but there is no requirement that it be signed. It must be given before or when the secured party makes any distribution of a surplus or demands that the debtor pay a deficiency.

The specific items that must be contained in this statement are highly technical. The explanation must contain the following information, in this order: (1) the aggregate amount of obligations secured by the security interest under which the disposition was made; (2) the amount of proceeds of the disposition; (3) the amount of the obligations after deducting the amount of proceeds; (4) the amount and types of expenses; (5) the amount of credits; and (6) the amount of the surplus or deficiency. UCC § 9-616(c). Substantial compliance with these requirements is acceptable. UCC § 9-616(d). In other words, the explanation need not be perfect.

The explanation must be given after the disposition and before or when the secured party makes any distribution of a surplus or makes a demand that the debtor pay a deficiency. Because the secured party may delay distribution or seek a deficiency, Article 9 allows the secured party to make a demand for one. The request must be an authenticated record and can be sent any time after the collateral is sold or otherwise disposed of. When requested, an explanation must be given by the secured party within 14 days after the request is received. UCC § 9-616(b)(2).

Example 8: Secured Party sells the collateral on May 1. Because the sale does not bring enough to cover both Secured Party's debt and the costs of sale, Debtor still owes a deficiency after the sale. Secured Party has until the statute of limitation runs to bring an action to collect the deficiency. By August 1, Secured Party has done nothing, and Debtor is concerned about whether there is a deficiency. Debtor can send a request for an explanation, which Secured Party must provide within 14 days.

When the debtor is liable for a deficiency, the secured party may, instead of sending an explanation after the debtor requests it, waive its rights to a deficiency in a record sent to the debtor. UCC § 9-616(b)(2).

If the secured party fails to fulfill its responsibility to either send an explanation or waive its right to a deficiency when one is due, the debtor is entitled to statutory damages in the amount of $500, in addition to any losses suffered by the debtor as a result of the secured party's inaction. UCC § 9-625(e)(5)(6).

IX. COLLECTION WHEN THE COLLATERAL IS ACCOUNTS, CHATTEL PAPER, OR GENERAL INTANGIBLES (INCLUDING PAYMENT INTANGIBLES) AND DEPOSIT ACCOUNTS

Recall the definitions of accounts, chattel paper, and general intangibles set out in Chapter 1. Although the paper evidence of these types of property can be possessed, the obligations themselves cannot. They are intangible! If they are in writing, the writing is only evidence of them—it is not the obligation.

Each of these types of property involves an "account debtor," someone who owes an obligation, usually money, *to the debtor*. It is important that the secured party be able to collect from the account debtors if there is a default. UCC § 9-102(a)(3).

The terminology here can become a little confusing, so we'll try to simplify it. Three parties are involved: the secured party, the debtor, and the account debtor. Refer to the following diagram.

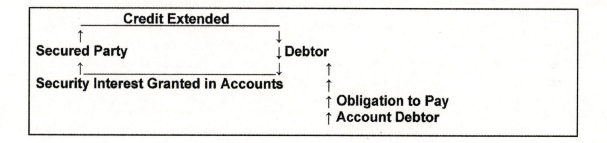

The account debtor owes something to the debtor. Perhaps he or she has purchased goods from the debtor and made a promise to pay in 60 days. As you know, that promise is an account, and in the diagram, the secured party has taken a security interest in the debtor's accounts. In most cases, the debtor will continue to collect from the account debtor and make payments separately to the secured party, but if the debtor defaults, the secured party wants to be able to collect directly from the account debtor.

Example 9: David owns and operates a retail appliance store. He sometimes sells on credit to contractors, taking back their promises to pay in 60 days. David gives a security interest in his accounts to Sabrina. If David defaults, Sabrina isn't really interested in getting possession of the invoices and sales slips that represent the contractors' debts to David. What she wants is to be able to get the money directly from these contractors, i.e., the account debtors.

Article 9 provides a method for the secured party to collect directly from the account debtors. The secured party after default can notify the account debtors that she has a security interest in the accounts and demand that they pay it. If they do not pay, the secured party can sue them directly. UCC § 9-607.

After notice, the account debtor may discharge its obligation only by paying the secured party. UCC § 9-406(a). The notice must: (1) reasonably identify the accounts, chattel paper, instruments, or payment intangibles in which the secured party has a security interest or which have been assigned to it; (2) require the account debtor to pay the secured party the entire obligation that it owes the debtor; and (3) be an authenticated record. UCC § 9-406.

The secured party must furnish the account debtor with reasonable proof of its right to payment. If it fails to do so, the account debtor may discharge its obligation by paying the debtor. UCC § 9-406(c).

If the account debtor refuses to the make payment and the secured party sues, the secured party will have whatever rights the debtor had against the account debtor: The secured party steps into the debtor's shoes.

For example, if the collateral is chattel paper, the account debtor will have given a security interest in some of its property, probably the property it purchased from the debtor that gave rise to its promise to pay, and the secured party may enforce that security interest just as the debtor could have done. UCC § 9-607(a)(3). And, in the lawsuit, the account debtor will have whatever defenses it had against the debtor.

Example 10: Donald gives a security interest in all of his accounts and chattel paper to Sabrina to secure a debt of $50,000. Pauline purchases a machine from Donald paying $5,000 down and promising to pay the remainder of the price, $20,000, in 90 days. Pauline gives Donald a security interest in the machine to secure her debt to him.

Donald defaults as to Sabrina. Sabrina has the right to inform Pauline that payment should be made to her rather than to Donald. If Pauline fails to pay, Sabrina may enforce the security interest that Pauline gave to Donald, and Sabrina may repossess the machine.

If the secured party has given notice to an account debtor, and the obligation of the debtor to the secured party is satisfied, e.g., if the debtor pays the obligation it owes to the secured party, then the secured party must notify the account debtor of that fact and also that the account debtor no longer should pay the secured party. UCC § 9-209. If the secured party fails to give this notice, the debtor can recover any actual loss that results plus an additional $500 as statutory damages. UCC § 9-625(e)(2).

A. **Remedies on outright sale of the accounts, chattel paper, or instruments compared to merely obtaining a security interest in these assets:** Remember that a person wanting to raise money using its accounts, chattel paper, or payment intangibles, can either give a creditor a security interest in them or sell them outright. Either approach gives rise to a secured transaction under Article 9. There is a difference in the remedy, however, when the debtor defaults.

  If the transaction is one in which the debtor gives a security interest in the accounts, chattel paper, or payment intangibles, the distribution of the proceeds that are collected from the account debtors is basically the same as when the collateral is goods. The secured party first pays expenses, then pays itself, then pays any subordinate secured parties who have given the required notice, and finally, gives anything left over to the debtor. UCC § 9-608(a).

  However, if the transaction is an outright sale of the accounts, chattel paper, promissory notes, or payment intangibles, the debtor is not entitled to any surplus, nor can the secured party recover any deficiency, unless the agreement provides for payment of a surplus or the obtaining of a deficiency judgment. UCC § 9-608(b). This makes sense given that the secured party, not the debtor, owns the assets.

B. **Secured party's contact with account debtors:** Article 9 allows the secured party to contact the account debtors only after default, but the secured party and debtor may agree, in the security agreement or otherwise, that the secured party can contact the account debtors directly, even before a default. If the debtor and the secured party agree to this, the secured party can inform the account debtors before default that the accounts, chattel paper, or general intangibles have been used as collateral or sold before default. UCC § 9-607(a). They can also agree that payment, even absent a default, should be made directly to the secured party.

  When the collateral is deposit accounts, e.g., savings or checking accounts in a bank, the secured party will perfect (a concept discussed in Chapter 6) by taking *control* of the account.

This is often done by making the bank account a joint account between the debtor and the secured party. In effect, this means that the debtor *and* the secured party will be able to make withdrawals from the account. On default, the secured party's remedy is simple: to withdraw the money in the deposit account and apply it to the debt.

X. RIGHTS OF A TRANSFEREE OF THE COLLATERAL TAKING FROM A REPOSSESSION SALE

A person who purchases or otherwise obtains the collateral at a foreclosure sale obtains all of the rights of the debtor in the collateral. Usually, the purchaser takes free of the security interest of the secured party conducting the sale and of all subordinate security interests and liens. The transferee, however, always takes subject to any security interests or liens that have priority over those of the foreclosing secured party. UCC § 9-617.

A. **Sales made to a purchaser in good faith:** If the transferee takes in good faith, it takes free of liens that others have on the collateral, even if the secured party does not conduct the sale in accordance with the requirements of Article 9, e.g., fails to give notice of the sale or holds a sale that is not commercially reasonable. UCC § 9-617(b).

B. **Sales without good faith:** If the transferee does *not* act in good faith, it takes subject to the rights of the debtor, the security interest of the person selling the collateral, and of all subordinate liens. UCC § 9-617(c). In other words, the purchaser who *is not* in good faith does not take free and clear of these liens.

C. **The implied warranty of good title:** When an Article 9 secured party sells collateral under the Code, it gives the purchaser an implied warranty of good title by law. Thus, the purchaser may have rights against the secured party if the property was encumbered or the debtor did not have title to it. UCC § 9-610(d). The warranty provides significant protection to one purchasing at a sale made by a junior secured party, who fails to disclose the existence of the superior security interest.

Note: The warranty can be disclaimed. Article 9 states that the following words are effective to disclaim the warranty: "There is no warranty relating to title, possession, quiet enjoyment or the like in this disposition." UCC § 9-610(e). These types of disclaimers are very common, and when the warranties are disclaimed, purchasers at Article 9 sales need to be very careful to look into the title issues themselves.

XI. ACCEPTANCE OF THE COLLATERAL IN SATISFACTION OF THE DEBT

A. **Introduction:** Another remedy the secured party may pursue when the debtor defaults is to accept the collateral in satisfaction of the debt. This is sometimes called *strict foreclosure*. Except where the goods are consumer goods, the acceptance of the collateral may be in full or partial satisfaction of the debt. UCC § 9-620(a). If the goods are consumer goods, the remedy of acceptance is only available if the secured party agrees to discharge the debtor from all of the obligations secured. UCC § 9-620(g). This remedy requires the consent of the debtor and of others interested in the collateral (e.g., people who have guaranteed the debt).

B. **Technical requirements for acceptance in satisfaction:** There are four requirements when the secured party wishes to accept the goods in satisfaction of the debts: (1) the debtor must consent, (2) there must be no objection by the debtor or another interested party, (3) the debtor cannot be in possession of the collateral if it is consumer goods, and finally, (4) the debtor must *not* have paid 60% or more of the debt if the collateral is consumer goods.

1. **The debtor must consent:** The debtor's consent is somewhat complicated.

    a. **Partial satisfaction:** When the proposal is that the debt will only satisfy part of the debt, the debtor must actually agree to the terms of the acceptance as proposed by the secured party. The consent must be in an authenticated record and must be after default. UCC § 9-620(c)(1).

    b. **Full satisfaction:** When the proposal is for full satisfaction of the debt, there are two ways in which the debtor consent can occur:

        i. the debtor may actually consent, UCC § 9-620(c)(1), or

        ii. the debtor will be deemed to have consented if the secured party sends a proposal to accept in full satisfaction and the debtor does not send an objection by an authenticated record so that the objection is received by the secured party within 20 days after the proposal is sent. For the consent to occur by the debtor's failure to object, the proposal must be unconditional. UCC § 9-620(c)(2).

    Like we said, complicated!

2. **There must be no objection to the proposal to accept:** The debtor can *object* to a proposal that the collateral be kept in satisfaction of the debt by avoiding consent. Also, other parties with an interest in the collateral have the right to prevent the acceptance in either partial or full satisfaction by objecting. No doubt, another interested person can object even if the debtor has consented, so this provision is not completely redundant of the last one.

    This means that the proposal must be sent not only to the debtor, but also to (1) any person notifying the secured party that it has an interest in the collateral, and (2) other secured parties or lienholders who had perfected by filing at least ten days before the debtor consented. When the proposal is for a partial acceptance, the proposal must also be sent to secondary obligors. Any of these parties can object and, if they do, the secured party must sell or otherwise dispose of the collateral. To be effective, the objection must be received by the secured party within 20 days after the proposal has been sent.

3. **Possession of consumer goods:** If the collateral is consumer goods, the debtor cannot be in possession of them at the time the debtor consents or is deemed to have consented.

4. **Mandatory disposal of consumer goods:** If the collateral is consumer goods and the debtor has paid 60 percent of the obligation, the secured party cannot accept the goods in satisfaction and must dispose of them in a commercially reasonable sale. UCC § 9-624(e). The disposal must be within 90 days of taking possession, but the debtor and secondary parties can agree, after default, to a longer period. UCC § 9-620(f).

C. **Effect of acceptance:** An acceptance in satisfaction transfers all of the debtor's right in the collateral to the secured party. The acceptance also terminates the security interest of the person accepting, as well as all subordinate security interests and liens. It does not terminate prior security interests, and to keep the collateral, the secured party will have to pay prior secured parties.

The acceptance in satisfaction terminates the debtor's obligations—all of them if it is a full satisfaction or that part of them specified in the proposal and consent if it is a partial satisfaction. Thus, if it is a full satisfaction, the secured party no longer has a right to a deficiency judgment, and the debtor has no right to any surplus if one would have resulted from a sale.

In effect, when there is a full satisfaction, the transaction is over and neither party has any further obligation to the other on the debt foreclosed. If the satisfaction is partial, the underlying debt is discharged to the extent of the agreement, but the debtor remains obligated to pay the portion that is not satisfied, and the secured party has a right to a judgment in the amount of the unsatisfied part of the debt.

For example, if the debtor owed $10,000 that was secured by a security interest and there was an agreement that the secured party would keep the collateral in satisfaction of $7,000 of the debt, the debtor would still owe $3,000 and the secured party could obtain a judgment for that amount.

XII. RIGHT TO REDEEM THE COLLATERAL

The debtor has the right to redeem the collateral until it is sold, accepted in full or partial satisfaction of the debt, or until the secured party has collected payment from the account debtors on accounts, chattel paper, general intangibles, or promissory notes. The right to redeem is also given to secondary obligors, other secured parties, and those who have involuntary liens on the property. UCC § 623(a).

To redeem, all the obligations the debtor owes to the secured party must be paid, including expenses the secured party incurred in retaking possession, preparing to dispose of the collateral, storing the collateral, processing the collateral, and, to the extent provided for in the agreement, attorneys' fees.

When the debt is to be paid in installments, once the debt has been *accelerated*, the debtor must pay all of it. Until that time, the debtor can redeem, or *cure*, by making past payments and any additional interest or late fees, and by reimbursing the secured party for any expenses incurred.

XIII. DEBTOR'S WAIVER OF RIGHTS

Many of the provisions regarding repossession and disposal of the collateral are for the benefit of the debtor. Generally, these rights cannot be waived either by a provision in the security agreement or otherwise, at least before default.

The rights of the debtor that cannot be waived prior to default include:
(1) the obligations of the secured party to care for collateral in its possession;
(2) the right of the debtor to an accounting of the collateral and the amount of the debt, and to an explanation of how a deficiency or surplus was calculated;
(3) the provisions dictating how the proceeds of a repossession sale shall be paid;
(4) the methods of collecting a debt from an account debtor;
(5) the duty to repossess by self-help only without breaching the peace;
(6) the provisions on the disposition of the collateral, including the requirement of giving notice; and
(7) the provisions regarding acceptance of the collateral in satisfaction of the debt.
UCC § 9-602.

Note: *After default*, the debtor may waive: (1) the right to notification of the disposal of the collateral, (2) the requirement of mandatory disposal when the goods are consumer goods, and (3) except as to consumer goods, the right to redeem. UCC § 9-624. The waiver must be made by an authenticated record.

XIV. DEBTOR'S REMEDIES FOR A SECURED PARTY'S FAILURE TO FULFILL ITS OBLIGATIONS ON A DEBTOR'S DEFAULT

A. **Court orders:** If the secured party is not proceeding in accordance with the provisions of Article 9 on foreclosure, a court may restrain a secured party's action or order the secured party to take action "on appropriate terms or conditions." UCC § 9-625(a).

Example 11: After repossessing the collateral, Secured Party sends notice that the collateral will be sold at auction three days after the notice is sent. The notice is almost certainly ineffective as it is sent too late. Debtor could obtain a court order restraining Secured Party from conducting the sale.

Example 12: After repossessing the collateral, six months have elapsed and Secured Party has done nothing to dispose of the collateral. Debtor could probably obtain an order from the court mandating that Secured Party arrange for a disposition of the collateral.

B. **Debtor's general right to recover damages:** We've already mentioned several situations in which the debtor is entitled to relief from the secured party, e.g., the possible loss of the secured party's right to a deficiency judgment and the right to sue in conversion for a wrongful repossession. Article 9 also has a general provision allowing damages for "any loss caused by the failure to comply with this article." Recoverable losses include those resulting from the debtor's inability to obtain credit or the increase in the cost of credit. UCC § 9-625(b).

Example 13: After repossessing the collateral, an automobile, Secured Party sends notice that the automobile will be sold at auction three days after the notice is sent. The notice is almost certainly ineffective as it is sent too late. As noted previously, Debtor could obtain a court order restraining Secured Party from conducting the sale. Assume, however, that Debtor does not seek this remedy.

The car is sold for $5,000 at the auction, which is the exact amount of the debt owed plus Secured Party's expenses in selling. It can be established that the market value of the car is $7,000, and that if it had sold for that amount, there would have been a surplus of $2,000 that would have gone to Debtor.

Debtor can recover $2,000, assuming Debtor can establish that the improper notice caused the loss.

XV. REAL ESTATE FORECLOSURES

When there is a default in an obligation secured by a mortgage on real property, the secured party has a right to foreclose. A mortgage foreclosure, however, is quite different from foreclosure (or sale) under Article 9.

To start with, the mortgagor is entitled to retain possession of the real property until it is actually sold, and, unlike the approach taken by Article 9, which provides the secured party wide latitude in determining the method of sale, statutes governing mortgages usually have detailed requirements that must be strictly followed. See *Edry v. Rhode Island Hospital Trust National Bank (In re Edry)*, 201 B.R. 604 (Bankr. D. Mass. 1996). Half of the states require a judicial sale of the property, and in others, a public sale is mandated. Frequently, even in the states allowing a public sale, a judicial sale is required unless the mortgage contains a "power of sale" provision allowing a private sale.

If the property is sold at a judicial sale, the time and method of sale will be set by the court when the petition for foreclosure is granted. When a judicial sale is not required, there are detailed rules governing the method of conducting the sale and giving notice. Judicial confirmation of the sale is frequently required.

In most states, the debtor can redeem the collateral after the sale, sometimes for as long as a year. Although in many states the time may be reduced by a provision in the mortgage, this extended redemption period often keeps the mortgage holder from getting a fair price for the property. Purchasers at real estate foreclosure sales are given little protection, other than to get back the money they paid in the event of an improper sale or redemption.

In some states, deficiency judgments on mortgage debts are prohibited when the land is farm or residential property. All in all, foreclosure of a mortgage is complicated, and the mortgagee has far less discretion and control than the holder of an Article 9 security interest. See *Farm Credit Bank v. Stedman*, 449 N.W.2d 562 (N.D. 1989).

In some states, a creditor may use a *deed of trust* to obtain a lien on the debtor's real property. In a deed of trust transaction the property is put into trust with a third person, with the instructions to transfer title to the debtor once the debt has been paid. If the debtor defaults, the trustee is instructed to deed the property to the creditor. Although this type of transaction was originally used to avoid the formalities of real estate foreclosure, today deed of trust transactions are also highly regulated and subject to many of the same rules as mortgage foreclosures.

XVI. BANKRUPTCY AND THE AUTOMATIC STAY

A description of Article 9 remedies would surely be incomplete (not to mention misleading) if it did not also describe the effects on the secured party of a debtor's bankruptcy. Everything we have just told you about secured party remedies under Article 9 is tempered by one reality: If a borrower goes into bankruptcy, all of a secured party's collection efforts must cease. The secured party must stop any act to repossess property, stop all collection letters and calls, and must stop selling any collateral it already has in its possession. This is mandated by the U.S. Bankruptcy Code, a federal statute that trumps Article 9. This is the most important thing that secured parties and their lawyers need to know about bankruptcy. A failure to halt collection efforts can result in actual and punitive damages in the borrower's bankruptcy.[1]

---

1. The approach to paying creditors also differs substantially in bankruptcy. The basic approach, subject to many exceptions, especially when one or more of the creditors is secured, is to divide up the debtor's property and distribute it to the creditors in proportion to their claims. Thus, if the debtor has $1,000 in assets and two creditors to whom he owes $500 and one to whom he owes $1,000, each would receive 50% of their claims. (The total available is $1,000, and the total debts are $2,000.) This example is, of course, far too simple, but it makes the point. As you have learned, or you will learn if you take a bankruptcy course, secured creditors are treated much better, as are certain preferred creditors.

Once a petition in bankruptcy is filed, all of the debtor's property flows automatically into a *bankruptcy estate*, which is under the supervision of the court and, in many bankruptcies, the trustee.

Quiz Yourself on REMEDIES: THE SECURED PARTY'S RIGHTS AGAINST THE DEBTOR

22. What are the primary differences in the remedies for secured and unsecured creditors? _____

23. What is the relevance of the concept of default in defining a secured party's remedies? _____

24. What is the most obvious default in any security agreement? _____

25. What is an insecurity clause and how are those interpreted? _____

26. What is an acceleration clause and why does a secured party need one? _____

27. When can a secured party engage in self-help repossession? _____

28. If violence is possible, how does the secured party get paid? _____

29. Once the secured party has obtained possession of its collateral, can it just keep the collateral in satisfaction of its debt? If no, why not? _____

30. Who gets paid from the proceeds of any secured party sale and in what order? _____

31. What is a deficiency claim? _____

32. Is the secured party always entitled to a deficiency claim? _____

33. What is a right of redemption and why does the Code provide for this right? _____

34. If a secured party has already repossessed collateral before hearing that the debtor has filed for bankruptcy, can the secured party proceed to sell the _____ collateral?

The following questions are true/false.

35. The following provision in a security agreement is enforceable unless the collateral is consumer goods:

    "Debtor agrees that if Secured Party elects to keep the collateral in satisfaction of the debt upon Debtor's default, no notice need be given to Debtor."

    True _____ False _____

To preserve this estate and provide control over it, the Bankruptcy Code (a federal statute applied to all bankruptcy cases) imposes a *stay* on all attempts by creditors to collect on their debts. They can do nothing to try to get money from the bankrupt debtor: no collection letters, no commencing or continuation of lawsuits, and, for our purposes here, no attempt to repossess or sell the debtor's property.

If the repo person is on the sidewalk ready to take the debtor's car, he or she must stop. If a secured party has repossessed and is in the middle of a sale, the sale must stop. In sum, *all* attempts to collect a debt or to obtain or perfect a security interest must stop on the filing of a bankruptcy.

There are ways in which a creditor can have the stay *lifted*, so that the collection activities can continue, but that is beyond the scope of this Outline. The point is, once a bankruptcy petition is filed, all of the actions discussed in this chapter must cease.

36. On January 15, *D* gave a security interest to S in all of his equipment. *D* never filed a financing statement. On March 1, *D* defaulted, and on March 15, *S* took possession of the equipment. *S* has sent a proposal to *D* proposing that *S* keep the equipment in satisfaction of the debt. Assuming *D* does not object, *S* can keep the equipment, but *S* will not be entitled to a deficiency judgment in the event that the value of the equipment is less than the amount of the debt, and will not have to account to *D* for any amount by which the value of the equipment exceeds the amount of the debt.

True _____ False _____

37. On January 15, *D* gave *S* a security interest in her equipment to secure a $50,000 loan from *S*. *S* filed a financing statement immediately in the proper office. On March 1, *D* borrowed $10,000 from *C*, giving *C* a security interest in the same collateral. *C* immediately filed. On August 1, *D* defaulted on her obligation to *C*. *C* has a right to repossess the equipment and sell it, and if she does, *S* has no right to the proceeds from the sale.

True _____ False _____

38. On January 15, *D* gave a security interest in its inventory to *S* to secure a loan made by *S* to *D* in the amount of $50,000. On March 1, *D* defaulted on the loan, and *S* repossessed the inventory on March 15. *D* gave notice to *S* of a public sale to be held on April 15. On April 1, *D* filed a petition in bankruptcy seeking relief under Chapter 7 of the Bankruptcy Code. If the inventory is worth less than $50,000, *S* may proceed with the sale without petitioning the Bankruptcy Court.

True _____ False _____

39. On January 15, *D* borrowed $10,000 from *S*. At *S*'s request, *X* promised in writing to repay in the event that *D* did not pay. *D* gave *S* a security interest in his computer, and *S* filed a financing statement with the Secretary of State. *D* defaulted and *S* repossessed the computer. If *S* plans to sell the computer at a public sale, *S* must give notice of the sale to both *D* and *X*.

True _____ False _____

40. On May 1, Denny borrowed $10,000 from Susy, giving to Susy a security agreement in equipment. The security agreement stated, among other things, that "a default shall occur whenever the Secured Party deems that payment of Debtor's obligation is insecure." Susy has never filed a financing statement. On June 1, Susy discovers that Denny has missed payments on several obligations including the mortgage he gave on his house. He has not missed any payments on the $10,000 loan that he received from Susy. Susy has a right to treat the obligation Denny owes her as being in default and to repossess the equipment unless Denny can prove that she is not acting in good faith.

True _____ False _____

41. On April 1, VX purchased a new automobile from Sylvia's Yugo dealership. He paid $5,000 down and agreed to pay the remainder of the price, $10,000, in 48 monthly installments on the first of each month. The security agreement provided that if a payment was missed, all future payments became due and payable immediately. VX made the May 1 payment but missed the June and July payments because he was laid off and had no income. On July 15, Sylvia repossessed the automobile. VX won $2,000 playing bingo on July 20. VX can require Sylvia to return the car to him if he tenders the payments he missed, the August 1 payment, and all of Sylvia's costs in repossessing the auto.

True _____ False _____

Answers

22. Secured parties can repossess their collateral and thus sidestep the painful process of getting a judgment and executing on it. The secured party can then sell the collateral and use of the proceeds to satisfy the debt. In some cases, the secured party can keep the collateral in satisfaction of the debt.

23. Default triggers the secured party's right to exercise its remedies, including its right to repossess.

24. The security agreement is the contract for a security interest. In all security agreements, a failure to make payments constitutes a default.

25. In most security agreements, there is an insecurity clause stating that if the lender feels insecure in the lending relationship (basically meaning that it believes that its collateral or its position in its collateral is at risk), this constitutes a default under the security agreement, allowing the secured party to exercise its remedies. Because of the possibility of abuse on the part of the lender flowing from these broad rights, insecurity clauses are interpreted to include an implied duty of good faith and fair dealing. Also, the insecure feeling must arise because of something that happens after the loan is made, not just from the lender's remorse.

26. It is a clause in a security agreement that states that if the debtor defaults, by missing a payment or some other way, the whole debt—not just the missed payment—becomes due. This is needed so the secured party does not need to sue separately for each payment as it comes due.

27. A secured party can use self-help repossession whenever this can be done without breaching the peace. The peace is breached whenever there is a possibility of violence at the repossession site.

28. If the secured party cannot repossess peacefully, then the secured party must proceed through judicial process, which involves bringing an action for repossession, and then using the resulting court order to obtain possession.

29. The secured party cannot just keep the collateral without selling it, at least not without proper notice. The secured party generally has an obligation to dispose of the collateral for a fair price.

30. First the secured party holding the sale gets its costs of sale. Next, that secured party has its claim paid from the collateral. Next, any junior secured parties or lienholders are paid. If there is anything left, it goes to the debtor. There are two interesting things about this. First, senior liens do not get paid from the proceeds but remain on the collateral. Second, unsecured claims get nothing from the sale.

31. A deficiency claim is the amount still owed on a secured party's debt after the collateral is sold by the secured party.

32. No, if the secured party does not hold a commercially reasonable sale or does not give the proper notice, its deficiency can be reduced by any harm caused by the improper sale. In nonconsumer cases, the loss to the debtor is presumed to be equal to the deficiency so that the secured party gets nothing.

33. The right of redemption is the debtor's right to get the collateral back at any time prior to the sale of the collateral, by paying the full amount due. Because the debtor must pay the whole debt, along with the secured party's attorneys' fees and costs, this right is seldom exercised.

34. After bankruptcy, all attempts to collect on a prebankruptcy debt must stop. This means the secured party cannot sell the collateral once the debtor's bankruptcy has been filed.

35. False. Section 9-602 prohibits the clause unless it is executed after default.

36. True. If the secured party keeps the inventory in satisfaction of the debt, there is no obligation to account to the debtor nor is there any right to a deficiency judgment. UCC § 9-620.

Note: Please do not forget that a failure to file a financing statement (to perfect a security interest) does not affect a secured party's rights against the debtor to pursue collateral, but only the creditor's priority vis-à-vis other creditors. This is something students often miss. Don't let that happen to you!

37. True. There is no restriction on the subordinate secured party's right to repossess, UCC § 9-609, or right to sell, UCC § 9-610. Nor does the Code provide that any of the proceeds must be given to the secured party with the prior security interest. See UCC § 9-608. The superior secured party is protected because the sale by the junior secured party is subject to the prior secured party's security interest, i.e., the purchaser at the repossession sale takes subject to the prior secured party's security interest.

Remember that the superior secured party has the right to repossess the collateral from the subordinate secured party—*S* could repossess it from *C* in this example—and then conduct the sale. If *S* does this, *C*'s security interest will be cut off, but *C* may be entitled to some of the surplus from *S*.

38. False. The bankruptcy stay prohibits a creditor from taking any action to collect a debt, including sale of property that has already been repossessed. 11 U.S.C. § 362. *S* must petition to have the stay lifted.

39. True. *X* is a secondary obligor and is thus entitled to notice.

40. True. This may be a judgment call and an inappropriate true/false question. However, we believe that it is clear that Susy has grounds for insecurity based on Denny's failure to make other payments. If she does, the clause allows her to accelerate the debt. The security agreement provides that the exercise of her right to accelerate constitutes a default. Of course, if she does not act in good faith, and Denny can carry his burden of proof on this issue, there is no default.

Again, the failure to file a financing statement is irrelevant here. By now, we bet that is starting to sink in.

41. False. VX must tender all of the unpaid balance in addition to the costs of repossession.

 Exam Tips on
REMEDIES: THE SECURED PARTY'S RIGHTS AGAINST THE DEBTOR

This was a long and detailed chapter with many potential testing areas. As a result, we have summarized the entire chapter here. We have also included a sample test question at the end.

☛ ***Collection rights of secured versus unsecured creditors:*** Some teachers ask students to compare the collection rights of secured versus unsecured creditors. To do this you will need to combine the knowledge you gained about the unsecured creditor remedies in Chapter 1 with the information in this chapter.

This is not too difficult but you should carefully describe the painstaking process of obtaining a judgment and collecting it, to which unsecured creditors are subjected. You'll compare this to the secured party's process of obtaining possession and selling the collateral, which is far easier.

☛ *Self-help repossession:* This has to be the most common testing area in the remedies section of the course. All the various fact patterns create a happy hunting ground for unusual test questions. Remember that whether there has been a breach of the peace depends on whether the creditor has created a potential for violence, not whether violence has actually occurred.

☞ Also remember that if the repossession is essentially completed before anyone comes out of the premises or approaches the secured party, the repossession was peaceful and did not breach the peace.

QUESTION

You represent Horrace Light, who just called about the following scenario. He bought a BIG MAN power tool kit for $5,000 from Sears to use in his construction business. According to the credit slip he signed at Sears, Sears retained a security interest in the power tool kit, but Sears never filed or otherwise perfected its security interest. When Horrace missed a few payments, Sears went to his house and saw the tool kit behind the fence. Horrace's guard dogs were asleep and Sears' representative was able to climb over the fence and lift the tool kit over the fence without harming the dogs or the fence. Horrace wants to know if this activity on the part of Sears gives him rights against Sears.

In analyzing this question and writing your answer, you should touch on the following points:

1. The fact that Sears did not perfect does not affect their rights against the debtor, Horrace;

2. The repossession has to be without a breach of the peace;

3. It is the likelihood or possibility of violence that is important, not whether it actually occurs;

4. The trespass to Horrace's property probably was not in itself a breach of the peace, because it was not an invasion of his house;

5. The presence of the dogs presents a situation that may result in violence. Even though they were asleep, it was likely that they would have awakened when the Sears person was climbing the fence, and they might have attacked him or they might have alerted Horrace who could have shot or injured someone coming on his property;

6. The fact that dogs were not harmed does not mean that there wasn't a breach of the peace.

This question and similar questions usually do not yield a nice, neat, definite answer. What is important is that you analyze the facts and state the law.

☛ *Default under the security agreement:* The security agreement can define a default in any way the parties choose and the definition is an enforceable contract provision. If the events of default are not defined in the security agreement, then a failure to make a payment is probably the only default.

☞ Testing in this area may require you to interpret contract language such as this example from the LoPucki and Warren textbook on secured transactions. See *Lynn M. LoPucki and Elizabeth*

Warren, SECURED CREDIT: A Systems Approach, p. 229, problem 13.2 (Aspen 2006). To answer the question, one would need to tell the teacher how long a payment can remain past due:

Payment default: Payment is due at the first of each month. A payment default occurs when the debtor has outstanding an amount exceeding one full payment that has remained unpaid for more than 10 days after the due date, at which time the creditor shall have all rights and remedies, including the right to accelerate.

Note in this example that there are no remedies for the creditor until at least the 11th of the month. Actually, because it says the amount outstanding must be at least 10 days late and also *exceed* one payment, not be equal to one, the default does not technically occur until one month and 11 days before a default occurs, assuming no late charges. Tricky!

☞ One common form of default clause is the *insecurity clause*. These are enforceable, despite their somewhat counterintuitive name, as long as the creditor believes in good faith that its prospect for payment has been impaired by some event in the debtor's business that occurred after the loan was given.

The secured party can waive a default under the security agreement by continually accepting late payments or otherwise ignoring default provisions in the agreement. Most well-drafted security agreements say that a failure to enforce a default does not waive the right to call future defaults but these clauses are not always enforced.

Example: John borrowed $10,000 from Bank, giving to Bank security interest in a car that he was purchasing. The loan was payable over 3 years. He made the first 3 payments on time, but the next 6 payments were sent from 10 to 15 days late. Although the security agreement provided for a late fee, Bank never charged him. Bank was sold to new owners, and when John sent his tenth payment 12 days late, Bank sent it back telling him that he was in default and that it would repossess the car unless he paid the entire amount still owed. In this case, not only would the prior defaults be waived, but Bank would be estopped from refusing to accept the tenth payment, even though it was late.

☛ *Acceleration:* If the debtor is to pay in installments, the secured creditor needs a provision in its security agreement providing that the secured party can accelerate the debt and thus make the whole amount due and payable upon the debtor's default. Practically speaking, this means the debtor cannot cure the default by just paying the past-due amounts.

☛ *Obtaining possession: Self-help repossession versus judicial action*

☞ The secured party can repossess or simply take back its collateral, as long as this can be done without breaching the peace. Again, whether there has been a breach of the peace depends on whether the creditor has created a potential for violence, not actually encountered violence.

☞ Judicial action (replevin) means getting a court order for possession. This is normally done only when the creditor is not able to get the collateral through self-help repossession.

Many state replevin statutes allow the secured party to get an order for possession or replevin without providing notice to the debtor. This may raise constitutional concerns and some of these state statutes have been struck down as a violation of the debtor's due process. Most recent cases uphold these statutes, however, at least as long as the debtor is entitled to a prompt hearing after the seizure.

☛ *Disposing of the collateral*

☞ **Public versus private sales:** The creditor can sell its collateral at either a public or a private sale. Either way, the sale must be commercially reasonable *in all aspects*, a test not defined in the Code.

☞ The *commercially reasonable sale* requirement is also a very common area for testing, as it is fact intensive.

☞ **Notice of the sale:** The creditor must give notice of the sale to the debtor and to any guarantors or third-party obligors. If the collateral is consumer goods, no other notice need be given, but if it is any other type of collateral, notice also must be given to other creditors who have filed a UCC financing statement on the collateral to be sold.

The notice must be sent within a reasonable time before the disposition. Notice sent at least ten days before the sale is timely in a nonconsumer transaction. For consumer transactions, it all depends what would be considered reasonable, but notice of less than ten days is most likely insufficient.

The purpose of the notice is to allow the debtor to redeem and to attend the sale and otherwise protect their interests at the sale.

☞ **Distribution of the proceeds:** Once the sale occurs, the proceeds go first to the costs of sale, next to pay the claim of the selling secured creditor, then to any junior lienholders (if they have demanded payment from the sale), and then to the debtor. Those with superior security interests or other liens get nothing.

Unsecured creditors have no interest in any particular property and get nothing out of the sale.

☞ **Caveat:** A very common thing to test on is the rights of a person with an unexecuted judgment. Please never forget that a judgment that has not been executed upon is nothing more than a piece of paper evidencing the unsecured debt. A person holding one of these would not recover anything from a secured creditor's sale.

☞ Also keep in mind that secured debts trump state law exemptions, so a secured party need not worry about a debtor's exemptions when holding an Article 9 sale.

☛ *A secured party's right to a deficiency judgment*

☞ If an Article 9 sale does not generate enough sales proceeds to pay the secured party's debt, the secured party can obtain an unsecured deficiency judgment and collect on it the same way as any other unsecured creditor.

☞ Before the most recent revision of Article 9, at least in some courts, a failure to comply with Article 9 would cause a secured party to forfeit its deficiency judgment.

☞ Under new Article 9 this is not the case for *nonconsumer transactions.* A failure to comply with Article 9 just creates a presumption that the sale would have covered the deficiency if it had been properly conducted. The secured party can defeat the presumption by proving that the defects in the sale did not affect the price.

☞ For consumer sales, most courts will probably follow the presumption rule applied in nonconsumer transactions, but some may hold that the secured party forfeits the deficiency after a nonconforming sale.

Example: ABC, Inc. borrowed $50,000 from Bank, giving Bank a security interest in three trucks that it used in its business. ABC defaulted on the loan, still owing Bank $40,000, and Bank repossessed the trucks. Without giving notice to ABC, Bank sold the trucks at an auction sale for $30,000. Bank has a right to a deficiency judgment in the amount of $10,000, but its failure to give notice of the sale gives ABC a right to any damages it suffered as a result of the failure to give notice, and the presumption is that ABC's damages are the amount of the deficiency, $10,000.

Unless Bank can rebut the presumption by showing that the failure to give notice did not cause ABC damages in that amount, Bank will get nothing in its deficiency suit.

☛ *Calculation of the deficiency or of a surplus:* The secured party must send the debtor an accounting of the sale if there is a surplus, or if it wishes to enforce its deficiency. If the secured party fails to send the notice, the debtor can demand it, in which case the notice must be sent to the debtor within 14 days of the request.

☛ *Collecting from accounts and other intangible collateral*

  ☞ If the collateral is accounts or other intangible collateral, the secured party obviously cannot repossess the collateral in the traditional sense. Instead, if the debtor defaults (and even before that if the security agreement so provides), the secured party can contact the account debtors (the people who owe the accounts to the debtor) and tell them to pay the creditor directly.

  ☞ The security agreement normally allows the secured party to contact the account debtors directly and collect from them, even before default.

  ☞ If the secured party has purchased the accounts outright from the debtor, the rights of the secured party are different when collecting accounts. While the purchase is generally treated as a secured transaction under Article 9, the remedies are different. After an outright sale to the secured party, there can be no deficiency or surplus.

☛ *Rights of the buyer of the debtor's property at the secured party's sale*

  ☞ Generally, a buyer in good faith steps into the debtor's shoes and acquires all the debtor's rights. The sale also wipes out the selling secured party's lien as well as all subordinate liens.

  ☞ A buyer who does not buy in good faith takes subject to the rights of all these creditors. In other words, the sale does not extinguish any of the claims or liens.

  ☞ The secured party warrants good title (that there are no senior liens on the property) to all buyers in an Article 9 sale, but this warranty can be disclaimed.

☛ *Acceptance of the collateral in satisfaction of the debt*

  ☞ Often called *strict foreclosure*, the secured party can accept the collateral in satisfaction of all or part of the debt in some cases. Strict foreclosure can be accomplished by obtaining the debtor's consent, as long as there is no objection to the proposed acceptance by others who have an interest in the collateral.

  ☞ If the goods are consumer goods, there are two additional rules. The debtor cannot be in possession of the collateral (the secured party must have repossessed it). And if the debtor has paid 60 percent or more of the loan which the property secures, the collateral must be sold. If the collateral is consumer goods, the secured party can only keep the collateral in full (not partial) satisfaction of the debt.

☛ ***Debtor's waiver of certain rights:*** The debtor can waive certain rights provided by the Code in the security agreement. The following rights, however, cannot be waived:

1. The right to have the secured party take care of the collateral while it is in its possession;

2. The right to an accounting after a sale, and to have the proceeds of the sale applied as stated above;

3. The rules regarding collecting accounts;

4. The rules regarding repossession without breach of the peace;

5. The rules regarding notice and disposition of collateral; and

6. The rules regarding strict foreclosure.

☞ Keep in mind that point 5, the rules regarding notice, may be waived after default but never in the security agreement.

☛ ***Debtor's right to redeem:*** A debtor can redeem property held by a secured party, by paying the full amount of the debt, plus costs and fees, at any time before the sale.

☛ ***Debtor's remedies on violation of Article 9:*** The debtor who is harmed by a violation of Article 9 can recover damages from the secured party. In some cases, the debtor also may be able to enjoin a creditor from taking certain action in violation of Article 9.

☛ ***The effect of bankruptcy on the secured party's remedies:*** A bankruptcy of any kind stays all collection activities of creditors. If a secured creditor is in the process of repossessing or selling collateral owned by a debtor who is now in bankruptcy, the creditor must stop the collection activity immediately.

☞ In some cases, the creditor can have the stay lifted and return to its prebankruptcy position.

Chapter 4

CREATION OF A SECURITY INTEREST

ChapterScope ━━━━━━━━━━━━━━━━━━━━━━━━━━━━━━━━━━━━

This chapter describes the process of obtaining a security interest, as well as the relevance of doing so. The key points in this chapter are as follows:

- **Creation versus perfection:** This chapter teaches you the difference between creation of a security interest, which involves an agreement between the debtor and creditor, versus perfection of a security interest, which involves filing notice of the security interest.

- **Scope:** Article 9 covers all transactions intended to create a security interest, even though some transactions are disguised with other names, such as conditional sales, sales of accounts, and consignments.

- **Default and enforcement:** A security interest allows a secured party to repossess and sell the collateral rather than obtaining a judgment.

- **Contract required:** A security interest is created by contract, usually (although not always) through a written contract called a security agreement.

- **Methods of creating a security interest:** A security interest can be created through a written security agreement, but also through possession of the collateral by the secured party or control of the collateral by the secured party.

- **Security agreement:** A security agreement must be a record, authenticated by the debtor, and must contain a description of the collateral.

- **Collateral description:** The description of the collateral is very important, perhaps *the* most important part of the security agreement, because it determines which assets are covered by the security interest.

- **Composite document rule:** A creditor without a description of its collateral in its written security agreement may save its security interest under the composite document rule, which will combine two or more documents to piece together a description of the collateral. In other words, the requirements of the security interest may be found in more than one document, e.g., the description may be found in one piece of paper and the language indicating an intent to grant a security interest in another.

- **Security agreement versus financing statement:** This chapter describes how the security agreement is different from another common Article 9 document, the financing statement.

- **After-acquired property:** A security agreement can extend to property that the debtor acquires after the security agreement is signed, but the loan agreement must specifically provide for this in most instances.

- **Proceeds:** Proceeds are whatever the debtor obtains if it sells or otherwise disposes of the collateral. A security agreement in particular property always extends to any identifiable proceeds of the collateral.

- **Future loans:** A security interest can secure future amounts lent by the creditor to the debtor and thus collateralize these later loans as well as the loan made at the time the security interest is given.

■ **Attachment:** In order for a security interest to attach (to be effective), the debtor must have rights in the collateral, the creditor must give value to the debtor (usually a loan or promise to loan), and the debtor must agree to give the creditor a security interest.

■ **Personal property lien versus real property mortgage:** This chapter explains that a security interest in personal property is far easier to create than a real property mortgage.

I. INTRODUCTION

A. **Creation versus perfection:** We think of creating and enforcing a security interest as a two-step process. First, we *create* a security interest or allow it to attach to specific property (the collateral). Second, we *perfect* the security interest, usually by filing in a public office, although there are other ways to "perfect."

   Step one (*attachment* or *creation*) often involves executing a written *security agreement* that describes the collateral and expresses the debtor's intent to create a security interest in favor of the creditor in that particular collateral. The security agreement is—pure and simple—the contract between the debtor and the creditor. This agreement describes when and how the creditor can exercise its right against the collateral. Step one is the subject of this chapter.

   However, we want you to know something about step two, perfection, right now. Perfection is often accomplished by filing a *financing statement,* but can be accomplished in other ways as well. In this chapter, we will help you learn the difference between a security agreement and a financing statement, which are the two most common documents in a secured transaction.

   Step two is *perfection* of a security agreement. Perfection can be accomplished through possession and in other ways, but as we just said, it is often accomplished by filing a *financing statement.* The financing statement is *not* the contract between the debtor and the creditor. In fact, it contains no contract terms—just the names and addresses of the parties and a description of the collateral. The financing statement is simply a brief notice document that a secured party files in a public place for the purpose of putting third parties on notice of the existence of the security interest.

   Step two is not necessary for the secured party to have a valid security interest in the collateral (to *create* a security interest), and for the creditor to have the right to repossess and sell the collateral. Step two *is* necessary, however, for the secured party to have the best possible rights in the collateral vis-á-vis the rights of other parties.

   Although step two is called "perfection," it does not create "perfect" rights, even by a long shot. It just helps assure that the secured party has the best possible rights under the circumstances, as you'll learn in more detail in Chapters 5 and 6.

   With that said, we are ready to move on to our discussion of step one, the creation of security interests.

B. **The elements or requirements for attachment:** This chapter is about "attachment" of the security interest. Putting it in a less technical way, it is about when a security interest is enforceable. For a security interest to attach, and thereby be enforceable, there are four requirements:

   1. The debtor must have intended to grant a security interest to the creditor-secured party;
   2. There must either be a writing evidencing this intent (a security agreement) or the secured party must be in possession of the collateral or in control of it;

3. The secured party must have given value to the debtor; and

4. The debtor must have rights in the collateral.

UCC § 9-203.

Note: Most law school texts and commercial outlines focus extensively on a formula of things needed to create an enforceable security interest. The formula is sometimes collapsed and shortened into the acronym VAR, which stands for value, agreement, rights. For a security interest to be enforceable, it must "attach," which is a technical status achieved once the creditor has given value, there is an agreement to grant a security interest, and the debtor has rights in the collateral.

In other words, for attachment to occur there must be:

VALUE	Meaning that the creditor must give value, often a loan, a promise to loan money, or a sale of goods on credit
AGREEMENT	Meaning that the debtor must agree to grant a security interest to the creditor, usually in writing but in some cases orally
RIGHTS	Meaning that the debtor must have rights in the collateral, usually but not always meaning that the debtor owns the collateral

We discuss the agreement part of this formula very early in this chapter as it is so integral to the creation of security interests. We save our discussion of the rest of this formula for the end of the chapter. We think the discussion of attachment makes a whole lot more sense once you have mastered the more conceptual (and intuitive) aspects of creating a security interest by use of a security agreement.

II. FUNCTION OF A SECURITY INTEREST

A. How does a security interest affect a creditor's rights? As the preceding chapters indicate, the purpose of a security interest is to secure a debt and make it easier to collect. Remember the legal rights of a creditor when there is no security interest?

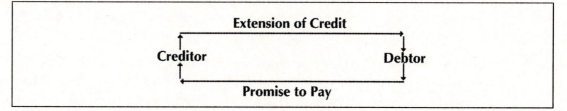

If the debtor doesn't pay, the creditor has *only* a cause of action against the debtor for breach of the lending contract, enforceable *only* by obtaining a judgment and then executing on that judgment.

What happens when the debt is secured? Refer to the following diagram:

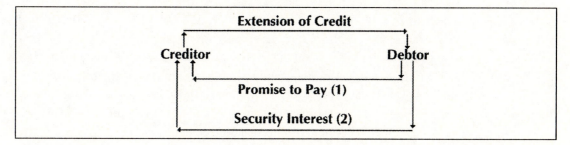

Now, in addition to the debtor making a promise to pay (1), the debtor has given the creditor a security interest in some of its property (2). That means the creditor becomes a secured party. One purpose of the security interest is to make it easier to collect the debt. The other is to make it more likely that the secured party will be the first (or one of the first) to get paid out of a sale of the collateral when there are many creditors, and the debtor has insufficient assets to pay them all.

This chapter describes how security interests are created, as well as when a security interest becomes enforceable.

B.   What is an Article 9 security interest? Remember that an Article 9 security interest is a "consensual" lien. The debtor must create it. To create a security interest, the debtor gives the creditor an interest in some or all of the debtor's property. The security interest, as a type of lien, gives the secured party (creditor) the right to possession of the collateral if the debtor fails to perform on its obligations (i.e., the debtor defaults). The underlying obligation can be of any kind, e.g., the security interest can secure an obligation arising out of tort, a divorce settlement, or a right arising out of property law, However in most cases, the obligation arises out of a contract, and the two most frequent types of transactions are loans and sales of property on credit.

A sale of property may be financed either by the seller or by some third person, such as a bank. In both cases it is likely that the resulting security interest will be a "purchase-money" security interest, which will be discussed later in this Outline. This phrase just means that the money borrowed was used to buy the property in which the security interest was given.

Credit may be advanced as a one-time event, such as when a debtor borrows $1,000 to be repaid in installments over a year. Or credit can be extended in installments over time, either fixed or in amounts and at times to be determined in the future. For example, the creditor may agree to provide a line of credit against which the creditor can draw part of the available funds whenever it needs money.

C.   Real property and personal property security interests

1. **Creation of personal property security interests versus real property:** Since the adoption of the UCC, there is only one type of personal property interest, which we call a *security interest.* Security interests are governed by Article 9 of the UCC. They are created when a debtor grants a security interest to the secured party in collateral in which the debtor has rights, and the secured party has given value in return.

2. **Different types of security interests in real property:** Several types of security interests can be created in real property. The most common is the *mortgage*, but in some states it is possible to create a security interest by what is called a *deed of trust.* Also, a few states permit the creation of a security interest by the use of a *real estate contract* or an *installment sales contract.* Each of these real property security interests is governed by state law outside of the UCC, and, although there are broad principles governing real property security interests, the details vary significantly from state to state and from one type of security interest to another.

3. **Formalism in real estate law:** Mortgages tend to be rather formal documents, and states have various requirements for their creation. The real property usually has to be defined in the mortgage document by its legal description to create a valid security interest in real estate. The description is very formulaic, and a simple reference to a street address may not suffice. In some states the document has to be notarized or witnessed, and in others it must be executed "under seal." These are ancient formalities, many of which survive today. Part of the reason for all the formal rules is that they demonstrate the seriousness of the transaction to the parties.

Under real property law, the amount of the debt being secured often must be included in the mortgage. Except in a very few instances, disputes involving mortgages are not governed by Article 9[1] and, although we occasionally refer to real property security interests, a detailed discussion of mortgage law is outside the scope of this Outline.

The point of all this talk about real estate mortgages is that they are much more formalistic than Article 9 security interests in personal property.

As discussed in Chapter 1, in the past there were several types of personal property security interests, but since the adoption of the UCC there is only one, which we simply call a *security interest.* Article 9 of the UCC governs these, and determines, among other things, how they are created.

III. METHODS OF CREATING A PERSONAL PROPERTY SECURITY INTEREST UNDER ARTICLE 9

A. Intent: To create a security interest, the debtor must have an intent to grant (or give) the creditor a security interest in some personal property. *Expeditors International v. Official Creditors Committee (In re CFLC, Inc.),* 166 F.3d 1012 (1999). The intent must be that the creditor will be entitled to sell the collateral in the event that the debtor defaults on its obligations.

The intent must be objectively manifested, but may be either explicit or implicit. In most cases, the intent is manifested in a *security agreement,* which contains what we often call "the granting language." Typically, the language is "I hereby grant a security interest to Max in my watch" or similar language. We'll talk about situations in which the security interest is valid without this language shortly, but it is common to have a written security agreement that contains this or similar language.

Example 1: Debtor signs an agreement that gives Creditor a security interest. The agreement states that "Debtor grants to Creditor a security interest in . . . ," or that "Debtor agrees that Creditor shall have a security interest in . . . ," or similar language. In each case the language expresses an intent to create a security interest.

A security interest is always in something in particular, never in the abstract. Moreover, the security interest will be only in the property in which the debtor intends to give the security interest. For example, if a retail establishment gives a security interest in its truck, the secured party will not have a security interest in the retailer's automobiles. A particular security interest, however, can be granted in a wide variety of property, including accounts, inventory, and even assets with which you may be completely unfamiliar. For example, a creditor might take a security interest in all of the debtor's "equipment, inventory, and accounts." In this case, the security interest extends to all of the debtor's property that falls within the categories of equipment, inventory, or accounts.

B. Disguised security interests: One situation in which the documents may grant a valid security interest without the granting language and thus without any express intent to grant a security interest is where the parties attempt to disguise a secured transaction as an outright sale. Mortgage law has long held that an absolute deed will be treated as a mortgage if that was the intent of the parties. Article 9 carries this over to personal property security interests. See Official Comment 3 to UCC § 9-203.

---

1. The notable exception is when a person with an Article 9 security interest has a security interest in fixtures and the dispute is between the Article 9 secured party and a mortgagee.

Example 2: Debtor borrows $1,000 from Creditor. The intent is that Creditor is to have the right to take possession of Debtor's ring in the event that the loan is not repaid. Debtor signs a document stating that it has "sold" the ring to Creditor. The transaction is a secured transaction governed by Article 9.

Language expressing the intent to grant a security interest may also be absent when the parties set up the transaction as a lease or consignment or when the transaction is structured as a conditional sales contract.

Example 3: Business leases copy machines from Supplier for 3 years. The agreement provides that Business will become owner of the machines at the end of the 3-year period by paying $1. If the machines were worth $1,000 at the end of the lease period, the transaction would be deemed a secured transaction (see Chapter 2, *supra*) even though there was no express or actual intent that a security interest be created. The supplier (lessor) would be deemed to have a security interest in the machines, and the lessee would have title.

Example 4: Retailer accepts diamonds "on consignment" from their owner. The agreement provides that the retailer will sell the diamonds for the owner and will pay the sales proceeds to the owner once the diamonds are sold. Still, even though there is no express or actual intent that the transaction creates a security interest, it is a secured transaction governed by Article 9, and the consignor is deemed to have a security interest in the goods.

Example 5: Store sells a piano to Buyer on credit. The document provides that "title shall remain in Store until all of the payments are made." This is a secured transaction: Title passes in spite of the language, and the seller is a secured party and the buyer is a debtor.

C. **Intent alone isn't enough—The requirement of possession, control, or a written security agreement:** In addition to requiring that the debtor intend to grant a security interest, Article 9 has another requirement for its creation. The secured party must have one of three things: (1) possession of the collateral, (2) control over the collateral or (3) a written security agreement executed by the debtor documenting the transaction.

Note: The security agreement is a big deal and will be one of the primary foci of your Secured Transactions class. Although a written security agreement is not always needed to create a valid security interest, it is necessary in most cases, as we'll soon explain in more detail.

1. **Creating a security interest through possession of the collateral:** If a creditor takes physical possession of the collateral with the debtor's understanding that the creditor is entitled to keep possession until the debt is repaid, and if the debt is not repaid, the creditor may dispose of the property and use the proceeds of the disposition to discharge the debt, a security interest is created.[2] UCC § 9-203(b)(3)(B). The most common example of the creation of a security interest by possession is the pawnbroker transaction. Sometimes, when a loan is made by a friend or relative, the lender will be given possession of the debtor's watch or other goods with the understanding that the goods will be returned when the debt is repaid. In these instances, a security interest has been created.

   Example 6: Juan asks Mary for a loan of $100 until his next payday. Mary agrees, but tells Juan that she wants to keep his watch as security for the loan. Juan gives Mary the watch. Mary has a security interest in the watch even though the transaction is oral.

_____

2. This is too simple, but sufficient for making the point that possession is a way of creating a security interest. As Chapter 3 discusses, the creditor's rights when the debtor defaults are far more complex than this statement might imply.

Example 7: Jenny asks Liz for a loan of $100, and Liz agrees and gives Jenny the $100. Liz then asks Jenny if she can borrow Jenny's sweater to wear while she walks home, and Jenny gives it to her. Liz does not have a security interest in the sweater because there was no intent that she keep it as security for Jenny's promise to repay the loan.

Another more complex form of "possession" recognized by the law is "field warehousing," a method of financing inventory by which the inventory is held in custody for the lender by an agent of the lender. In a field warehousing transaction, the lender will establish a place to store the collateral—either at the debtor's place of business or nearby. A person will be appointed as the agent of the lender and take control of the space. The collateral will be placed in the space and the debtor will be given possession of it only when the lender tells its agent to release it. Because the lender has possession of the goods through its agent, the lender has a security interest in it, even though there is no writing. However, once the collateral is released to the debtor, the security interest is lost unless there is a valid security agreement.

As the somewhat tortured concept of field warehousing demonstrates, it is often far easier to just execute a written security agreement.

When the lender has possession of the collateral there needn't be something in writing. But in actual practice, the agreement usually is written, except in the most casual transaction. Remember that if there is no writing, the creditor loses its security interest if it returns possession of the collateral to the debtor.

2. **Creating a security interest by exercising control over the collateral:** A security interest can also be created by "taking control" of the collateral if the collateral is one of the following types: (1) deposit accounts, (2) electronic chattel paper, (3) investment property, (4) letter-of-credit rights, or (5) electronic documents. UCC § 9-203(b)(3)(D). Basically, a secured party has "control" when it has the ability to engage in transactions regarding the collateral. How the secured party gains control differs depending upon the type of collateral. UCC §§ 9-104 (deposit accounts), 9-105 (electronic chattel paper), 9-106 (investment property), and 9-107 (letter-of-credit rights). You'll learn more about this later.

3. **A written security agreement:** If the secured party does not have possession of the collateral (or control when the collateral is deposit accounts, electronic chattel paper, investment property, letter-of-credit rights, or electronic documents) a security interest can be created only if there is a *security agreement*, a topic we'll pick up now.

IV. THE SECURITY AGREEMENT

A. The elements of a security agreement

1. **Intent to grant a security interest and other requirements:** The definition of a security agreement found in UCC § 9-102(a)(73) is not very helpful. The subsection says that a security agreement is "an agreement that creates a security interest." *Agreement* is further defined as "the bargain of the parties in fact as found in their language" and in the surrounding circumstances. UCC § 1-201(3) [UCC § 1-201(b)(3) of the revised version]. A *security interest* is "an interest in personal property or fixtures which secures payment or performance of an obligation." UCC § 1-201(37) [UCC § 1-102(b)(35) of the revised version]. The impact of these sections is that the document must evidence the debtor's intent to grant a security interest to the secured party. More concrete are the additional requirements set out in UCC § 9-203: the agreement must be (1) a record (2) authenticated by the debtor that (3) contains a description of the collateral.

2. Form over substance: As with all other areas of substantive law, the title or name given to a document does not determine whether it is a security agreement. Rather, the substance of the document controls. Although it is becoming less common, sometimes security agreements are titled "conditional sale contract," "chattel mortgage," or "trust receipt" using what is, in effect, pre-Code language. Today it is common to use the heading "retail installment sales agreement." Yet each of these documents will be a security agreement (regardless of its name), if it contains the necessary requirements.

To further confuse things, the substance of the agreement may use language that is taken from pre-Code forms and does not specifically say that a security agreement is intended. In short, any language showing that the intent of the debtor was to give the creditor a security interest is sufficient.

EXAMPLES OF THINGS THAT HAVE CONFUSING NAMES BUT ARE REALLY JUST SECURITY INTERESTS

In these three types of cases, a document that appears on its face to memorialize a transaction that is *not* a secured transaction operates to create a security interest:

(1) An installment sale of goods agreement states that a seller of goods retains title to the goods until the buyer pays all of the installments. This type of agreement has the effect of passing title to the buyer and all the seller retains is a security interest in the goods. UCC § 9-109(a)(1).
(2) Another type of agreement states that the owner of accounts sells its accounts to someone else.[3] This type of agreement operates as a secured transaction, and the buyer becomes the debtor and the seller the secured party. UCC § 9-109(a)(3).
(3) An agreement claims that the owner of goods is giving possession of the goods to another *on consignment.* This is a secured transaction. The owner becomes a secured party, and the buyer becomes a debtor under Article 9. UCC § 9-109(a)(4).

Note what is *not* required in a security agreement: (1) the security agreement need not be signed by the *secured party*, (2) no addresses need be included, (3) the document need not be witnessed or sealed, and (4) it need not contain any information about the terms of the loan. Also note that misspellings, even of the debtor's name, are not fatal. All in all, it is very easy to draft and authenticate a document that will have the effect of a security agreement.

Most security agreements contain many more provisions than are necessary to create a security interest. Typically, a security agreement will have (1) representations made by the debtor, such as the debtor's affirmation that there are no prior liens on the collateral; (2) obligations of the debtor, such as to keep the collateral insured; and (3) other details of the transaction. These provisions are not necessary to create a security interest. Their purpose is to specify the rights and obligations of the parties, the same as the provisions of any contract.

Look through the "typical" security agreement shown here as Figure 4-1. It will give you a more concrete idea of what a security agreement is like and make our discussion more meaningful.

---

3. Can't remember what *accounts* are? Go back and read the end of Chapter 2.

Figure 4-1
Security Agreement

Security Agreement
Last National Bank
23 Annette Drive NE
Albuquerque, NM 99999

_____(12) 20 _____(3)

Daniel Dilletant, Inc., *Debtor*, and Last National Bank, *Secured Party*, with addresses as they appear with their signatures below, agree as follows:

Debtor grants to Secured Party a security interest in the following equipment as *Collateral* and in any additions, accession, and substitutes and to the proceeds of it:

One 2005 Red Ford 21/2 Ton Truck VIN 98768734

The Security Interest granted by this agreement is to secure payment by Debtor to Secured Party of any and all Indebtedness and liabilities of any kind, direct or indirect, absolute or contingent, primary or secondary, joint and/or several, due or to become due, existing now or hereafter, whether evidenced by notes, drafts, open account or otherwise, and all renewals and extensions of any obligations.

DEBTOR EXPRESSLY WARRANTS AND COVENANTS:

1. [] If marked here Debtor is a duly organized and existing corporation under the laws of the State of New Mexico and is duly qualified and in good standing in every state in which it is doing business. Debtor's corporate registration number is 5151999777. The execution, delivery, and performance of this Security Agreement are within Debtor's corporate powers, have been duly authorized, are not in contravention of law or the terms of Debtor's articles of incorporation, by-laws, or other incorporation papers, or of any indenture, agreement, or undertaking to which Debtor is a party or by which Debtor is bound.

2. The Collateral will be kept at Debtor's address as stated below; otherwise the Collateral will be kept at the following address: 1505 Candelaria Avenue NW. Debtor will at all times advise Secured Party, in writing, of any change of address or location of Collateral.

3. Debtor is the owner of all Collateral, whether presently existing or hereinafter acquired, free of any adverse lien, security interest, or encumbrance other than this security interest granted to Secured Party hereby; and Debtor will defend the Collateral against all claims and demands of all persons who at any time claims the same or any Interest in it.

4. No financing statement covering the Collateral or any proceeds of it is on file in any public office.

5. Debtor will pay all taxes and assessments of every nature, which may be levied or assessed against the Collateral.

6. Debtor will not permit or allow any adverse lien, security interest, or encumbrance on the Collateral and will not permit the Collateral to be executed on, attached, or replevied.

7. Debtor will not sell, transfer, conceal, or dispose of the Collateral, nor take or attempt to remove the Collateral from the state where kept as above stated, without the prior written consent of the Secured Party.

8. The Collateral is in good condition and Debtor will, at Debtor's own expense, keep the same in good condition and from time to time, replace and repair all parts of the Collateral as may be broken, worn out, or damaged without allowing any lien to be created on the Collateral on account of any replacement or repairs, and the Secured Party may examine and inspect the Collateral at any time, wherever located.

9. At its option, Secured Party may discharge taxes, liens, or security interests or other encumbrances at any time levied or placed on the Collateral, and may pay for the repair of any damage or injury to the Collateral, and may pay for the maintenance and preservation of the Collateral. Debtor agrees to reimburse Secured Party on demand for any payment made or expense incurred by Secured Party pursuant to the foregoing authorization.

10. Debtor will, at Debtor's own expense, insure the Collateral with an insurance company approved by Secured Party against loss or damage by accident, fire, and theft for an amount equal to the value of the Collateral, and keep the same insured continuously until the full amount of the indebtedness secured by this security interest is paid, with loss payable to Secured Party as its interest may appear.

11. In the event that this Security Agreement is placed in the hands of an attorney for enforcement, Debtor will pay the reasonable attorneys' fees of Secured Party.

UNTIL DEFAULT Debtor may have possession of the Collateral and use it in any lawful manner not inconsistent with this agreement and not inconsistent with any policy of insurance, but upon default Secured Party shall have the immediate right to the possession of the Collateral.

DEBTOR SHALL BE IN DEFAULT under this agreement on the happening of any of the following events or conditions:

(a) default in the payment or performance of any obligation contained or referred to in this Security Agreement or in any note or other document evidencing any indebtedness to the Secured Party;

(b) if any warranty, representation, or statement made or furnished to Secured Party by or on behalf of Debtor proves to have been false in any material respect when made or furnished;

(c) failure to make any payment which results in the acceleration of the maturity of any indebtedness of Debtor to others under any indenture, agreement, or undertaking;

(d) loss, theft, concealment, damage, destruction, disposal, removal, sale or transfer, or encumbrance on any of the Collateral, or any levy, seizure, execution, or attachment of the Collateral;

(e) death, dissolution, termination of existence, merger, consolidation, reorganization, insolvency, business failure, suspension, or liquidation of the business, issuance of writ of garnishment or attachment or of notice of tax or other lien against the property of, appointment of a receiver of any part of the property of, assignment for the benefit of creditors by entry of judgment against or commencement of any proceeding under any bankruptcy or insolvency laws by or against Debtor or any guarantor or surety for Debtor,

(f) the good faith determination at any time by Secured Party that the prospect of its receiving payment of any obligation secured by this Security Agreement, the performance of any of the terms of this agreement or that the possibility of resorting to the Collateral for the purpose of satisfying any obligation, is impaired.

UPON DEFAULT and at any time thereafter, Secured Party may, without demand or notice, declare all obligations secured hereby immediately due and payable and shall have the remedies of a secured party under the Uniform Commercial Code as adopted in the State of New Mexico. Secured Party may require Debtor to assemble the Collateral and deliver or make it available to Secured Party at a place to be designated by Secured Party which is reasonably convenient to both parties.

No waiver by Secured Party of any right, remedy, or event of default with respect to any of Debtor's obligations shall operate as a waiver of any other right, remedy, or event of default on a future occasion.

This agreement shall be effective when signed by Debtor.

Daniel Dilletant, Inc.   **Last National Bank**

By _____ (14)   By _____ (14)
          DEBTOR   SECURED PARTY
          Address of Debtor: Address of Secured Party:
          1505 Candelaria Avenue NW   23 Annette Drive NE
          Albuquerque, NM 87934   Albuquerque, NM 99999

Note: The signature of the Secured Party (Last National Bank) is not required for the security agreement to be sufficient. However, the secured party usually signs it.

3. **The security agreement versus the financing statement:** As we told you in the beginning of this chapter, a *security agreement* is not the same as a *financing statement.* You'll need to know the difference between the security agreement, the contract granting the creditor a security interest, and the notice document known as a financing statement.

The financing statement is the document that a creditor files to give notice that the creditor has a security interest in some of the debtor's property. It is *not* the contract between the debtor and the creditor, but just a piece of paper that is filed on record to let third parties know about the security interest. You'll learn much more about financing statements in Chapter 5, reproduced over the following pages in Figure 4-2.

A financing statement has a different purpose and different requirements than a security agreement. It must contain (1) the names of both the debtor and secured party and (2) an indication of the collateral. UCC § 9-502. It need not be signed or otherwise authenticated. Also, the financing statement does not have any language indicating that the debtor's intent is to grant a security interest. Because a document that merely meets the requirements of a financing statement lacks those requirements of a security agreement, it will not, by itself, substitute for a security agreement. Thus, if a creditor does nothing more than file a financing statement, the creditor will not have a security interest in the property described in the financing statement.

In fact, a creditor is allowed to file its financing statement before it has made a loan or executed a security agreement. Thus, it is impossible to tell if the secured party actually has a security interest, based on the existence of a financing statement alone.

However, some courts have found the financing statement coupled with one or more other documents, read together, may contain all the requirements of a security agreement. Under the "composite document" rule, several documents may suffice as a security agreement. In some cases, there will be a reference on one of the documents to the others, but, lacking an express connection, the two or more documents can be shown to be linked by parol evidence.

Example 8: When a financing statement had been filed with a description of the collateral but with no clause stating that the debtor had given or granted a security interest to the creditor, and there was a signed promissory note stating that the note was secured, but which contained no description of the collateral, the court held that the financing statement supplied the description and the note supplied the granting language and the authentication. Thus, a security interest had been created, despite the lack of a formal security agreement. *In re Amex-Protein Development Corporation,* 504 F.2d 1056 (9th Cir. 1974).

Example 9: In another case, the court held that a sufficient security agreement existed when a note evidenced a debt, the financing statement described the collateral, and a resolution of the debtor corporation's board of directors authorized the granting of the security interest. The three documents representing the transaction, taken together, were a sufficient security agreement. *In re Bollinger Corp.,* 614 F.2d 924 (3d Cir. 1980).

B. **Requirement of a record:** Before the adoption of the current version of Article 9, a security agreement had to be in writing. To accommodate the possibility of security agreements being prepared and stored in electronic form, Article 9 now provides that the security agreement must merely be a "record." *A writing is always a record,* UCC § 9-102(a)(69), and almost all of

Figure 4-2
UCC Financing Statement

UCC FINANCING STATEMENT
FOLLOW INSTRUCTIONS (front and back) CAREFULLY

A. NAME & PHONE OF CONTACT AT FILER [optional]

B. SEND ACKNOWLEDGMENT TO: (Name and Address)

THE ABOVE SPACE IS FOR FILING OFFICE USE ONLY

1. DEBTOR'S EXACT FULL LEGAL NAME - insert only <u>one</u> debtor name (1a or 1b) - do not abbreviate or combine names

1a. ORGANIZATION'S NAME			
OR 1b. INDIVIDUAL'S LAST NAME	FIRST NAME	MIDDLE NAME	SUFFIX
1c. MAILING ADDRESS	CITY	STATE POSTAL CODE	COUNTRY

1d. TAX ID #: SSN OR EIN	ADD'L INFO RE ORGANIZATION DEBTOR	1e. TYPE OF ORGANIZATION	1f. JURISDICTION OF ORGANIZATION	1g. ORGANIZATIONAL ID #, if any	NONE

2. ADDITIONAL DEBTOR'S EXACT FULL LEGAL NAME - insert only <u>one</u> debtor name (2a or 2b) - do not abbreviate or combine names

2a. ORGANIZATION'S NAME			
OR 2b. INDIVIDUAL'S LAST NAME	FIRST NAME	MIDDLE NAME	SUFFIX
2c. MAILING ADDRESS	CITY	STATE POSTAL CODE	COUNTRY

2d. TAX ID #: SSN OR EIN	ADD'L INFO RE ORGANIZATION DEBTOR	2e. TYPE OF ORGANIZATION	2f. JURISDICTION OF ORGANIZATION	2g. ORGANIZATIONAL ID #, if any	NONE

3. SECURED PARTY'S NAME (or NAME of TOTAL ASSIGNEE of ASSIGNOR S/P) - insert only <u>one</u> secured party name (3a or 3b)

3a. ORGANIZATION'S NAME			
OR 3b. INDIVIDUAL'S LAST NAME	FIRST NAME	MIDDLE NAME	SUFFIX
3c. MAILING ADDRESS	CITY	STATE POSTAL CODE	COUNTRY

4. This FINANCING STATEMENT covers the following collateral:

5. ALTERNATIVE DESIGNATION [if applicable]:	LESSEE/LESSOR	CONSIGNEE/CONSIGNOR	BAILEE/BAILOR	SELLER/BUYER	AG. LIEN	NON-UCC FILING
6. This FINANCING STATEMENT is to be filed [for record] (or recorded) in the REAL ESTATE RECORDS. Attach Addendum [if applicable]		7. Check to REQUEST SEARCH REPORT(S) on Debtor(s) [ADDITIONAL FEE] [optional]		All Debtors	Debtor 1	Debtor 2

8. OPTIONAL FILER REFERENCE DATA

FILING OFFICE COPY — NATIONAL UCC FINANCING STATEMENT (FORM UCC1) (REV. 07/29/98)

Instructions for National UCC Financing Statement (Form UCC1)

Please type or laser-print this form. Be sure it is completely legible. Read all Instructions, especially Instruction 1; correct Debtor name is crucial. Follow Instructions completely.

Fill in form very carefully; mistakes may have important legal consequences. If you have questions, consult your attorney. Filing office cannot give legal advice.

Do not insert anything in the open space in the upper portion of this form; it is reserved for filing office use.

When properly completed, send Filing Office Copy, with required fee, to filing office. If you want an acknowledgment, complete item B and, if filing in a filing office that returns an acknowledgment copy furnished by filer, you may also send Acknowledgment Copy; otherwise detach. If you want to make a search request, complete item 7 (after reading Instruction 7 below) and send Search Report Copy, otherwise detach. Always detach Debtor and Secured Party Copies.

If you need to use attachments, use 8-1/2 X 11 inch sheets and put at the top of each sheet the name of the first Debtor, formatted exactly as it appears in item 1 of this form; you are encouraged to use Addendum (Form UCC1Ad).

A. To assist filing offices that might wish to communicate with filer, filer may provide information in item A. This item is optional.

B. Complete item B if you want an acknowledgment sent to you. If filing in a filing office that returns an acknowledgment copy furnished by filer, present simultaneously with this form a carbon or other copy of this form for use as an acknowledgment copy.

1. **Debtor name**: Enter only one Debtor name in item 1, an organization's name (1a) or an individual's name (1b). Enter Debtor's exact full legal name. Don't abbreviate.

1a. Organization Debtor. "Organization" means an entity having a legal identity separate from its owner. A partnership is an organization; a sole proprietorship is not an organization, even if it does business under a trade name. If Debtor is a partnership, enter exact full legal name of partnership; you need not enter names of partners as additional Debtors. If Debtor is a registered organization (e.g., corporation, limited partnership, limited liability company), it is advisable to examine Debtor's current filed charter documents to determine Debtor's correct name, organization type, and jurisdiction of organization.

1b. Individual Debtor. "Individual" means a natural person; this includes a sole proprietorship, whether or not operating under a trade name. Don't use prefixes (Mr., Mrs., Ms.). Use suffix box only for titles of lineage (Jr., Sr., III) and not for other suffixes or titles (e.g., M.D.). Use married woman's personal name (Mary Smith, not Mrs. John Smith). Enter individual Debtor's family name (surname) in Last Name box, first given name in First Name box, and all additional given names in Middle Name box.

For both organization and individual Debtors: Don't use Debtor's trade name, DBA, AKA, FKA, Division name, etc. in place of or combined with Debtor's legal name; you may add such other names as additional Debtors if you wish (but this is neither required nor recommended).

1c. An address is always required for the Debtor named in 1a or 1b.

1d. Debtor's taxpayer identification number (tax ID #) — social security number or employer identification number — may be required in some states.

1e,f,g. "Additional information re organization Debtor" is always required. Type of organization and jurisdiction of organization as well as Debtor's exact legal name can be determined from Debtor's current filed charter document. Organizational ID #, if any, is assigned by the agency where the charter document was filed; this is different from tax ID #; this should be entered preceded by the 2-character U.S. Postal identification of state of organization if one of the United States (e.g., CA12345, for a California corporation whose organizational ID # is 12345); if agency does not assign organizational ID #, check box in item 1g indicating "none."

Note: If Debtor is a trust or a trustee acting with respect to property held in trust, enter Debtor's name in item 1 and attach Addendum (Form UCC1Ad) and check appropriate box in item 17. If Debtor is a decedent's estate, enter name of deceased individual in item 1b and attach Addendum (Form UCC1Ad) and check appropriate box in item 17. If Debtor is a transmitting utility or this Financing Statement is filed in connection with a Manufactured-Home Transaction or a Public-Finance Transaction as defined in applicable Commercial Code, attach Addendum (Form UCC1Ad) and check appropriate box in item 18.

2. If an additional Debtor is included, complete item 2, determined and formatted per Instruction 1. To include further additional Debtors, or one or more additional Secured Parties, attach either Addendum (Form UCC1Ad) or other additional page(s), using correct name format. Follow Instruction 1 for determining and formatting additional names.

3. Enter information for Secured Party or Total Assignee, determined and formatted per Instruction 1. If there is more than one Secured Party, see Instruction 2. If there has been a total assignment of the Secured Party's interest prior to filing this form, you may either (1) enter Assignor S/P's name and address in item 3 and file an Amendment (Form UCC3) [see item 5 of that form]; or (2) enter Total Assignee's name and address in item 3 and, if you wish, also attaching Addendum (Form UCC1Ad) giving Assignor S/P's name and address in item 12.

4. Use item 4 to indicate the collateral covered by this Financing Statement. If space in item 4 is insufficient, put the entire collateral description or continuation of the collateral description on either Addendum (Form UCC1Ad) or other attached additional page(s).

5. If filer desires (at filer's option) to use titles of lessee and lessor, or consignee and consignor, or seller and buyer (in the case of accounts or chattel paper), or bailee and bailor instead of Debtor and Secured Party, check the appropriate box in item 5. If this is an agricultural lien (as defined in applicable Commercial Code) filing or is otherwise not a UCC security interest filing (e.g., a tax lien, judgment lien, etc.), check the appropriate box in item 5, complete items 1-7 as applicable and attach any other items required under other law.

6. If this Financing Statement is filed as a fixture filing or if the collateral consists of timber to be cut or as-extracted collateral, complete items 1-5, check the box in item 6, and complete the required information (items 13, 14 and/or 15) on Addendum (Form UCC1Ad).

7. This item is optional. Check appropriate box in item 7 to request Search Report(s) on all or some of the Debtors named in this Financing Statement. The Report will list all Financing Statements on file against the designated Debtor on the date of the Report, including this Financing Statement. There is an additional fee for each Report. If you have checked a box in item 7, file Search Report Copy together with Filing Officer Copy (and Acknowledgment Copy). Note: Not all states do searches and not all states will honor a search request made via this form; some states require a separate request form.

8. This item is optional and is for filer's use only. For filer's convenience of reference, filer may enter in item 8 any identifying information (e.g., Secured Party's loan number, law firm file number, Debtor's name or other identification, state in which form is being filed, etc.) that filer may find useful.

Instructions for National UCC Financing Statement Addendum (Form UCC1Ad)

9. Insert name of first Debtor shown on Financing Statement to which this Addendum is related, exactly as shown in item 1 of Financing Statement.

10. Miscellaneous: Under certain circumstances, additional information not provided on Financing Statement may be required. Also, some states have non-uniform requirements. Use this space to provide such additional information or to comply with such requirements; otherwise, leave blank.

11. If this Addendum adds an additional Debtor, complete item 11 in accordance with Instruction 1 on Financing Statement. To add more than one additional Debtor, either use an additional Addendum form for each additional Debtor or replicate for each additional Debtor the formatting of Financing Statement item 1 on an 8-1/2 X 11 inch sheet (showing at the top of the sheet the name of the first Debtor shown on the Financing Statement), and in either case give complete information for each additional Debtor in accordance with Instruction 1 on Financing Statement. All additional Debtor information, especially the name, must be presented in proper format exactly identical to the format of item 1 of Financing Statement.

12. If this Addendum adds an additional Secured Party, complete item 12 in accordance with Instruction 3 on Financing Statement. In the case of a total assignment of the Secured Party's interest before the filing of this Financing Statement, if filer has given the name and address of the Total Assignee in item 3 of the Financing Statement, filer may give the Assignor S/P's name and address in item 12.

13-15. If collateral is timber to be cut or as-extracted collateral, or if this Financing Statement is filed as a fixture filing, check appropriate box in item 13; provide description of real estate in item 14; and, if Debtor is not a record owner of the described real estate, also provide, in item 15, the name and address of a record owner. Also provide collateral description in item 4 of Financing Statement. Also check box 6 on Financing Statement. Description of real estate must be sufficient under the applicable law of the jurisdiction where the real estate is located.

16. Use this space to provide continued description of collateral, if you cannot complete description in item 4 of Financing Statement.

17. If Debtor is a trust or a trustee acting with respect to property held in trust or is a decedent's estate, check the appropriate box.

18. If Debtor is a transmitting utility or if the Financing Statement relates to a Manufactured-Home Transaction or a Public-Finance Transaction as defined in the applicable Commercial Code, check the appropriate box.

today's security agreements meet the record requirement by being in writing. But, if the information is stored on a tangible medium, for example in the hard drive of a computer or a computer storage device such as a disk, the requirement that the security agreement be a record is met.

The requirement that there be a record, along with the requirement of authentication discussed below, is basically a statute of frauds provision. The general law relating to the statute of frauds applicable in other transactions, such as the sale of real property, may provide persuasive authority by analogy. For example, if the record is destroyed, the record requirement should be held to have been met, and proof of its existence prior to its destruction should be allowed.

C. Authenticated by the debtor: Until the current version of Article 9 was adopted, the security agreement not only had to be in writing, but also had to be signed. The requirement that security agreements be authenticated broadens the signature requirement. Now, electronically prepared and stored security agreements can be authenticated by using an electronic symbol or encryption instead of a signature. Of course, you can use a signature, and this is still most common. UCC § 9-102(a)(7).

The important part of the requirement is that the symbol used, whether it is a signature or other mark on a written security agreement or an electronic name or symbol, be made with the present intention that it constitutes an authentication. Thus, an X on a document can authenticate the document if placed there with the intent to sign it.

Cases that discuss the question of a whether a writing is signed for the purposes of the Statute of Frauds are relevant to determine if a document was authenticated. It appears, for example, that the signature or other authentication need not be at the end of the document, but could be contained within it. For example, a document that said, "Dan Debtor hereby grants a security interest . . ." would be authenticated if Dan Debtor intended that the inclusion of his name operate as a signature, even through there was no signature at the end of the document.

Note that there is no requirement that the secured party sign or otherwise authenticate the security agreement. Only the debtor is required to authenticate it. This may seem odd considering that we view the security agreement to be the contract between the parties.

D. Description of the collateral

    1. General requirement that collateral be described: A security agreement must contain a description of the property in which the security interest is given (the collateral). UCC § 9-203(b)(3)(A). The basic test of whether words of description are sufficient to meet this requirement is whether the language "reasonably identifies" the property. UCC § 9-108(a). The flexibility of the requirement is emphasized by the approval of "any . . . method if the identity of the collateral is objectively determinable." UCC § 9-108(b)(6). Wide latitude is given to the drafter in meeting this test, but there are limits.

        When the security interest covers timber to be cut, the security agreement must also describe the land from which it is to be cut. UCC § 9-203(b)(3)(A). If there is no description of the real estate, then the security agreement is ineffective. *C & H Farm Serv. v. Farmer's Sav. Bank,* 449 N.W.2d 8676 (Iowa 1989). A description of the real estate will be sufficient if it "reasonably identifies" the realty, UCC § 9-108(a), and under the "composite document rule" the requirement that the land be identified will be met if it is not in the security agreement but is contained in the financing statement. *FDIC v. Cooners (In re Cooners),* 954 F.2d 596 (10th Cir. 1992).

    2. Methods of describing the collateral: The basic test of whether a description is sufficient is whether it "reasonably identifies what is described." The test takes a commonsense approach rather than a technical approach. Thus, if the court can determine the property in which the security interest has been given, the description should be held to be sufficient, even if it is in some ways inaccurate or sketchy.

Still, care must be taken in considering whether particular words constitute a sufficient description. Sloppiness and vagueness should obviously be avoided. If someone other than the drafter of the language cannot tell what the collateral is from the description, the security interest probably will be invalid, which would relegate the creditor to the status of an unsecured creditor.

The basic question is whether in reading the description it is possible to say whether the security interest was given in specific property. In other words, by reading the description, can you determine that the security interest attaches to this automobile? This inventory? These accounts?

The statute enumerates several ways in which collateral can be described: (a) by specific listing, (b) by category, (c) by type, with two exceptions, (d) by quantity, and (e) by the use of a computational or allocation formula. UCC § 9-108(b).

a. **By specific listing:** Clearly, the security agreement may contain a specific description of the property given as collateral. UCC § 9-108(b)(1). For example, the description may be "a 2010 Sony 27-inch television, serial number 1505268." If this description were in the security agreement, the security interest is only in that particular television. A couple of points:

   i. A mistake in the serial number usually will not invalidate the description unless it is misleading. Similarly, a mistake in other parts of the description is not necessarily fatal. For example, if the TV is 30 inches and it is described as "27 inches," the description will be sufficient if it is clear from other language that a particular television is described.

   ii. The description need not be as complete as the one given in the above example. Clearly, describing the television as "a 2010 27-inch Sony Television" would be sufficient, and it is likely that the description, "a 27-inch Sony Television" would pass muster. "Debtor's television set" would probably suffice if the debtor had only one television, but not if he or she had two or more. Clearly, the less information given about the collateral, the more likely that the description will be insufficient. For example, if the collateral were described simply as "a television," it probably would not be sufficient description.

   iii. The listing of the collateral may be on an attachment to the security agreement, and may contain an unlimited number of items. For example, if the debtor owned a number of trucks and other vehicles, the security agreement could refer to a separate piece of paper that listed each of them by make, model, VIN, etc. There are lots of cases in which security interests have been found invalid because the attorney forgot to attach the separate list, so be careful!

b. **By category:** It is unclear exactly what is meant by the word "categories." On an initial reading, it would seem to refer to the categories of collateral defined by Article 9 such as consumer goods, chattel paper, etc. However, describing the collateral in this manner appears to come under the provision allowing a description by "type." See UCC § 9-108(b)(3).

Probably, "categories" means that you can describe the collateral by such words as "all *goods* of the debtor," or "all *intangibles* owned by the debtor." It also appears to mean that you can describe it by the kind of property, e.g., "all automobiles owned by the debtor." In any event, the term "categories" clearly does not have any technical meaning but is designed simply to emphasize the generality of the ways in which the collateral can be described.

c. **By type:** A description by one or more of the types of collateral defined by Article 9 is sufficient. Thus, describing the collateral by using the words "inventory" or "chattel paper," for example, is permissible. UCC § 9-108(b)(3). However, using these words alone is not sufficient because it does not reasonably identify the collateral covered. There must be a reference to *what* inventory or chattel paper is covered. For example, the description would have to say something like "all of *debtor's* inventory," or the "inventory *located at 4520 Montoya Street.*"

Note: As discussed in Chapter 5, describing the type of collateral more generally is permitted in a financing statement.

Consumer goods cannot be described by type, nor can commercial tort claims, security entitlements, security accounts, or commodity accounts. UCC § 9-108(e). When the collateral is one of these types of collateral, the collateral must be defined specifically. For example, the description of a commercial tort would have to read something like "the right that the debtor has against X flowing from an action based on interference with debtor's contractual rights."

d. **By quantity or by use of a formula:** Section 9-108(b)(4)(5) speaks to describing the collateral by "quantity" or by "use" of a formula. Clearly, something more than a quantity term or a computation by a formula is needed. The description must also name a type or category of collateral or contain a specific listing. For example, simply saying "one half" would be insufficient. The description would have to say something like "one half of the grain stored in Silo #444."

Indeed, the quantity or formula of describing the collateral may be of very limited use anyway because a description reading "one half of debtor's inventory [or cattle or equipment]" might be insufficient because it does not identify which of the inventory [cattle or equipment] is covered.

e. **Supergeneric descriptions:** A description of the collateral as "all the debtor's personal property" or "all the debtor's assets" is not a sufficient description in a security agreement. UCC § 9-109(c). This does not mean that all of the debtor's assets cannot be given as collateral, but only that using that phrase, or a similar one, to describe the collateral in the security agreement is impermissible. A security agreement could, for example, provide that the collateral is "all of the debtor's inventory, accounts, general intangibles, equipment, . . ."[4]

f. **Extent to which description covers property:** The description contained in the security agreement will determine which collateral is covered by the security agreement. The question here is not whether the description is sufficient to meet the requirements of Article 9, but whether it includes or covers particular property.

---

4. As discussed in Chapter 5, a supergeneric description is permitted in financing statements.

Remember, a security interest is always in specific property, even when the description is broad. For example, if the collateral is described as "all accounts and inventory of the debtor" in the security agreement, no security interest will exist in the debtor's equipment even though "equipment" is included on the financing statement.

One of the dangers of listing the items of the collateral is that the listing may limit general language that is also placed in the description. For example, in one case, the security agreement specifically described items (including a truck) in a schedule attached to the security agreement. The security agreement also contained the following language:

> "in addition to all the above enumerated items, it is the intention that this mortgage shall cover all chattels, machinery, equipment, tables, chairs, work benches, factory chairs, stools, shelving, cabinets, power lines, switch boxes, control panels, machine parts, motors, pumps, electrical equipment, measuring and calibrating instruments, office supplies, sundries, office furniture, fixtures, and all other items of equipment and fixtures belonging to the mortgagor, whether herein enumerated or not, now at the plant of Laminated Veneers Co., Inc."

The court held that the description did not include two Oldsmobile automobiles owned by the debtor that were used as equipment because the description did not refer to automobiles or motor vehicles. The enumeration of property types was otherwise so inclusive or specific that the court thought that an omission showed an intent *not* to include those items. *In re Laminated Veneers*, 471 F.2d 1124 (2d Cir. 1973). Scary! Now the result may well have been different if the listing of specific items had been prefaced by a clause such as "including but not limited to."

In a similar case, *Citizens Bank and Trust v. Gibson Lumber*, 96 B.R. 751 (W.D. Kentucky, 1989), the court rejected *Laminated Veneers*, and held that parol evidence should be admitted to ascertain the intent of the debtor and creditor, requiring, however, clear and convincing evidence that the nonlisted items were intended to be included.

The composite document rule (that we briefly mentioned earlier) has not been held to extend the security interest to property that is not described in the security agreement, but that is named in the financing statement, *Allis Chalmers Corp. v. Straggs*, 453 N.E.2d 145 (Ill. 1983), or named in preloan documents, such as the application for the loan. *In Re Martin Grinding & Machine Works, Inc.,* 793 F.2d 592 (7th Cir. 1986). You need to describe your collateral accurately in the security agreement.

g. **Defective descriptions:** Although there are many ways in which to meet the requirement that the security agreement contain a description of the collateral, not all descriptions are sufficient. For example, when a security agreement described the collateral as all "merchandise" purchased by use of a charge card issued by an appliance retailer, the court held that the description did not sufficiently identify the collateral. *In re Shirel*, 252 B.R. 157 (Bankr. W.D. Okla. 2000). However, another court held that an almost identical description was sufficient—*In re Ziluck,* 139 B.R. 44 (S.D. Fla. 1992)—and another court held a similar description sufficient by using the composite document rule, given that it found a more complete description on the sales slip evidencing the sale of the goods. *In re Bradel*, 1990 Bankr. Lexis 1334 (Bankr. N.D. Ill. 1990).

h. **Parol evidence:** Article 9 does not have a parol evidence rule. Courts approach the issue of whether parol evidence is admissible by applying, or at least referring to, either the parol evidence rule for contracts in general or the parol evidence rule that applies to the sale of goods found in § 2-202.

As is generally true in cases applying the parol evidence rule, there is considerable inconsistency in the application of the rule to secured transactions. Some generally accepted principles can, however, be articulated.

Parol evidence is admissible when a word is ambiguous: When a description is ambiguous, parol evidence can be introduced to clarify that ambiguity. For example, when the collateral was described as "560-131 985894," parol evidence was admitted to show that the description referred to a typewriter. *In re A & T Kwik-N-Handi, Inc.,* 12 U.C.C. Rep. Serv. 765 (Bankr. M.D. Ga. 1973). Parol evidence is also admissible to determine whether a specific piece of property is being held by the debtor as equipment or as inventory.

However, parol evidence is not admissible to expand a clearly articulated description of collateral. For example, when the security agreement provided that the collateral was inventory at one address, parol evidence was inadmissible to show that the parties also intended to include inventory at a different address. *In re California Pump & Mfg. Co.,* 588 F.2d 717, 719 (9th Cir. 1978).

3. **After-acquired property:** Much to some students' surprise, a security interest can be taken in property to be acquired by the debtor in the future. UCC § 9-204(a). This is permitted in most but not all cases.

When the goods are consumer goods, a security interest can be taken *only* in the consumer goods that the debtor acquires within ten days after the secured party gives value. Additionally, after-acquired clauses are prohibited when the collateral is commercial torts. UCC § 9-204(b).

When the parties intend that the security interest exist as to after-acquired property, it is highly advisable to explicitly state that the security interest extends to the after-acquired collateral. However, if the collateral is accounts, some courts have held that the security interest extends to after-acquired accounts, even when the description is "all accounts" and there is no reference to "after-acquired" accounts. *Paulman v. Gateway Venture Partners III, L.P. (In re Filtercorp, Inc.),* 163 F.3d 570 (9th Cir. 1998). The theory is that accounts are so fluid that the parties must have intended to include the after-acquired accounts. The same theory has been applied to inventory. However, when the collateral is equipment or another type of collateral, the courts have consistently held that the security interest does not extend to after-acquired property, unless the agreement explicitly so states.

4. **Proceeds:** When the debtor sells or otherwise transfers the collateral, the secured party obtains a security interest in what the debtor got or received for the collateral. We call these things or amounts (whatever is received in exchange for the collateral) *proceeds*. The security interest in the proceeds arises automatically by virtue of law and need not be recited in the security agreement.[5] UCC § 9-315(a)(2).

5. **Accessions and products:** *Accessions* are goods that are united with other goods in such a way that the added goods do not lose their identity. UCC § 9-102(a)(1). For example, if a secured party has a security interest in a tractor and the owner-debtor has a new engine installed, the engine is an accession. Priority problems arise when one person has a security interest in the tractor and another in the engine. UCC § 9-335.

Products are not defined by Article 9, but are generally considered to be property produced by the collateral. The most common example of a product is the young of animals. If the

---

5. As Professor Martin is a belt-and-suspenders kind of gal, she still mentions the proceeds in her collateral descriptions, as you can see in the description above. Professor Hart, on the other hand, thinks this is both unnecessary and a waste of paper and ink.

security interest is in a cow and the cow gives birth to a calf, the calf is a product. Again, whether the calf becomes collateral under the security interest depends on the description. If the description is "all of debtor's presently owned and after-acquired cows and bulls," the calf would qualify as after-acquired property. If, however, the security agreement described the collateral as "one cow named Rose II of Abalone," the calf would not be covered by the security agreement unless some language such as "and all products" were included as part of the description.

Neither accessions nor products are proceeds because they do not result from the debtor *exchanging* the collateral.

6. **The debt secured:** The security agreement need not include a reference to the obligation (the amount initially owed or to be borrowed) secured by the security interest. In most cases, however, the security agreement includes a statement of what debt is secured by the collateral or a reference to some other document, such as a promissory note, that states the obligation.

A security agreement can secure any obligation, but usually it secures a promise to pay. It may secure one debt, such as the obligation to pay for an automobile that the debtor has purchased, or many obligations that the debtor owes to the secured party. It can secure present or past obligations and also obligations to be incurred in the future. An example would be "this collateral secures all debts of any kind and any nature, owed by the Debtor to the Creditor, whether now owed or owed at any time in the future." This language is known as a *dragnet clause.*

Traditionally, so-called *dragnet clauses* have been carefully scrutinized by the courts and limited where needed to promote justice. For example, a dragnet clause in *John Miller Supply Company, Inc. v. Western Bank*, 55 Wis.2d 385, 199 N.W.2d 161 (1972) read that the security interest secured "payment of [loans made at the time it was signed] and all other obligations" owed by the debtor. "Obligations" were then defined as "all Debtor's present and future debts, obligations and liability of whatsoever nature." The court held that the security interest secured neither warranty claims nor contract claims that the secured party had against the debtor.

The Official Comments to § 9-204 of the revised version of Article 9 reject the holding of *John Miller* and similar cases and state that whether a debt is covered by the security interest is to be determined by construing the agreement to determine the parties' intent. Assuming that courts give effect to the official comment, the *John Miller* case is probably no longer good law.

The inclusion in the security agreement of a provision that the security interest secures future advances is essential if it is anticipated that additional advances will be made. Without such a future advances clause, the later advances will not be secured.

SAMPLE DESCRIPTION OF COLLATERAL FOR A SECURITY AGREEMENT

The debtor hereby grants the secured party a security interest in all of the debtor's inventory, accounts, equipment, and general intangibles, whether now owned or hereafter acquired, as well as all proceeds, products, offspring, and profits of all of such collateral, and this collateral shall secure all obligations owed by the debtor to the secured party at any time, whether now owed or owed in the future.

V. ENFORCEABILITY OF A SECURITY INTEREST: ATTACHMENT

A. **Introduction to attachment:** In addition to the requirements that the debtor intend to create a security interest, and that the secured party have possession, control, or has an authenticated security agreement, there are two additional requirements in order for the security interest to be enforceable: (1) value must have been given, and (2) the debtor must have rights in the collateral or the power to transfer rights in the collateral to the secured party.

It is said that when all four requirements occur, the security interest *attaches* to the collateral. In many, if not most, transactions, value is given and the debtor has rights in the collateral when the security agreement is signed or around that time.

Many commercial textbooks summarize these requirements using the acronym VAR, meaning *v*alue, *a*greement, *r*ights. Again, these requirements are that the creditor must give value, usually in the form of a loan or a promise to make a loan, the debtor must agree to grant a security interest to the creditor, either in writing or in some cases orally, and the debtor must have rights in the collateral, usually but not always meaning that the debtor must own the collateral.

If you think about the reasons for these rules, it may help you to remember them. The creditor must give the debtor some value in order for the debtor to give the creditor a valid security interest. Why? Because secured creditors can always beat out unsecured creditors and usually a trustee in bankruptcy, a debtor could make him or herself judgment-proof just by granting security interests to friends and family members, even to those who never gave the debtor a loan or to whom the debtor never owed any money. If the law allowed these security interests to be valid, the property that was listed as collateral would not be available to legitimate creditors. The Code does not allow this and instead requires that for a security interest to be valid, the creditor must have given value.

What about agreement? Naturally, we only want to enforce a security interest that the debtor granted on purpose, voluntarily, thus the requirement of an agreement. We just finished a lengthy discussion of this requirement.

And rights? The debtor can only grant as collateral something that he or she has some interest in, right? In that light, this formula makes some sense. Here are a few examples of how these requirements play out.

Example 10: Debtor purchases a car from Secured Party, signing a security agreement that gives to Secured Party a security interest in the automobile to secure Debtor's promise to pay in installments. The Debtor will obtain rights in the collateral as a result of the sale, and Secured Party will give value by transferring title to the car. All three requirements of attachment occur simultaneously or almost simultaneously.

Example 11: Debtor borrows money from Secured Party, signing a security agreement that grants a security interest in her computer. The lending of the money is value, and because the debtor already owns the computer, he or she has rights in it. Again, the attachment occurs immediately.

In neither of these examples is there a problem with attachment. Problems can arise when either credit is extended at a later date or when the debtor does not have rights in the collateral at the time the transaction occurs.

Example 12: Debtor negotiates for a loan from Bank. Debtor signs a security agreement giving to Bank a security interest in its equipment, but at that time Bank does not make any commitment to make the loan. Debtor owns the equipment at the time. Bank agrees to make the contemplated loan a week later. No value is given and hence, there is no attachment, and the security interest is not enforceable until Bank agrees to make the loan.

Example 13: Debtor signs a security agreement giving Secured Party a security interest in all of its "present and after-acquired inventory" in return for a loan made on the day that the security agreement is signed. There is attachment as to the inventory that Debtor presently had on hand, but as to inventory purchased in the future, there is no attachment until Debtor has rights in it.

Attachment is important for three reasons: (1) until there is attachment, the secured party cannot enforce the security interest against either the debtor or a third party, and (2) there can be no perfection until there is attachment.[6] Chapters 5 and 6 will discuss the details of these rules, and (3) sometimes priority is determined by the time of attachment.

Because we already talked about the agreement in detail in the prior sections of the chapter, the remainder of our discussion focuses on the nuances of the creditor giving *value* and the debtor having *rights* in the collateral.

B. **Value:** There is no separate definition of *value* in Article 9. Thus, the Article 1 definition, UCC § 1-201 (44) [UCC § 1-204 of the revised version], applies to the determination of whether value has been given for the purpose of attachment. A secured party can give value:

1. in return for any consideration sufficient to support a simple contract;
2. as security for a preexisting claim;
3. in full or partial satisfaction of a preexisting claim; or
4. in return for a binding commitment to extend credit whether or not the credit has actually been given.

Probably because of this broad definition of value, there has been little litigation questioning whether a secured party has given value. Let's look at some examples of value.

Example 14: Debtor owes Creditor $1,000. The debt is unsecured. Creditor asks Debtor for a security interest to secure the debt, and Debtor gives one to Creditor in a home entertainment system. Value has been given even if the debt is not yet due because giving a security interest to secure a preexisting debt is value.

Example 15: Creditor agrees to loan money to Debtor on the condition that a review of Debtor's financial statement discloses that Debtor has the resources to repay the debt. Creditor has made a promise that would be good consideration under contract law, and if Debtor gives a security interest before the loan is actually made, the creditor-secured party has given value. The fact that the promise is conditional does not destroy its effectiveness as consideration or value.

Example 16: Debtor owes Creditor $1,000 based on a loan made on March 1, and $10,000 based on a loan made on April 1. Both loans are unsecured. Debtor gives Creditor a security interest to secure the $10,000 loan in return for a discharge of the $1,000 loan. Creditor has given value, both because the security interest secures a preexisting loan and because the security agreement was given in satisfaction of a debt.

C. **Debtor's rights in the collateral:** The requirement that the debtor have *rights* in the collateral is somewhat more complicated. In general, most issues arise when a security agreement covers collateral that the debtor does not presently own. This arises when the security agreement covers both present and after-acquired property.

---

6. The importance of perfection in determining priority problems is discussed in Chapter 6, *infra*.

Example 17: Debtor grants a security interest in "all of its present and after-acquired inventory and present and after-acquired equipment." As to the inventory and equipment presently owned by Debtor, the security interest attaches immediately. If Debtor acquires new inventory or a new truck sometime in the future, the security interest covers it, but there is no attachment until Debtor acquires an interest in the new inventory or the new truck.

Attachment can be delayed in other situations as well. Assume for example that Debtor intends to purchase a new automobile and obtains financing with a bank. At the time of the transaction, Debtor has not entered into a contract to purchase the automobile. If Debtor gives a security interest in the automobile that it intends to purchase, there is no attachment until Debtor actually obtains rights in a specific automobile.

The exact moment at which a debtor acquires *rights* in collateral that it is in the process of buying can be somewhat elusive. Assume that Secured Party takes a security interest in a specially equipped truck that Debtor plans to purchase from Retailer, and that Retailer has to order it from the manufacturer. Clearly, Debtor would have rights in the truck once it is manufactured, shipped to Retailer, and delivered to Debtor because title would pass from Retailer to Debtor at that time, absent a specific agreement as to when title would pass. See *Daniel v. Bank of Hayward*, 425 N.W.2d 416 (Wis. 1988).

However, the rule generally is that the Debtor obtains rights in the truck as soon as the particular truck is determined to be the one to be delivered under the contract between Retailer and Debtor. The reason is that under Article 2 of the UCC, a buyer of goods, the Debtor in our example, gets a special property interest in the truck upon *identification* of the goods to the contract. UCC § 2-501.

Example 18: Debtor contracts to purchase a computer that Seller is to assemble using parts obtained from various manufacturers. At the time of the contract, Debtor has no rights in the computer because it is not in existence. Seller completes the assembly and designates the computer as the one being sold to Debtor. At that time, Debtor obtains a property interest in the computer under Article 2 and has rights in the collateral under Article 9.

A debtor may have less than all of the rights in the collateral and still pledge it as collateral. For example, if a debtor owns a truck jointly with some other person, the debtor would have a sufficient interest in the truck to give a security interest in it and a sufficient interest to have the security interest attach to the truck. Of course, the secured party would have a security interest in only the debtor's interest in the truck.

Likewise, a lessee of goods under a long-term lease has a sufficient interest in the leased goods to give a security interest in the leased goods, and the security interest will attach to the goods. Again, the security interest would run only to the lessee's rights under the lease.

The collateral need not be owned by the debtor if the owner gives the debtor permission to grant a security interest in it. For example, if the owner of an automobile gives her brother permission to grant a security interest in the automobile, the brother has *the power to transfer rights* in the collateral and the requirement of attachment will be met.

Usually, the extension of credit goes to the person giving the security interest, but it need not. For example, the person owning the debt may give a security interest in collateral to secure a loan going to another person. In such a situation, Article 9 makes a distinction in the terminology used to describe the parties. The one giving the security interest is called the *debtor*, even if she is not obligated to repay the loan, UCC § 9-102(a)(28), and the person to whom the loan is made and who has the obligation to repay it is called the *obligor*. UCC § 9-102(a)(59).

The distinction between debtors and obligors is important only in a limited number of cases, e.g., in determining who is entitled to notice when goods are to be sold after repossession. In the vast majority of cases the distinction is unimportant because the obligor is also the debtor. For example, assume David borrows money from Sarah, giving to Sarah a security interest in his automobile. David is both a debtor and an obligor. In this case, it is convenient to call David simply a *debtor*. We use this vocabulary throughout this Outline.

Quiz Yourself on CREATION OF A SECURITY INTEREST

42. What does it mean for a secured party to create a security interest? What is the legal significance? _____

43. What are the technical requirements for attachment of a security interest? _____

44. How does a debtor show an intent to grant a security interest? _____

45. Can a security interest be granted in the abstract? _____

46. What are the technical requirements of a security agreement? _____

47. What makes a description of collateral sufficient? _____

48. Can the description of the collateral in the security agreement just read "all assets"? _____

49. Describe the composite document rule, its uses, and its limitations. _____

50. What are proceeds, product, and offspring of collateral? _____

51. If the secured party intends to obtain a security interest in proceeds, products, and offspring, does the security agreement need to specifically say this? _____

52. Can the security agreement grant a security interest not only in property the debtor owns now but also property the debtor will own in the future? If this is what the secured party wants, need this be mentioned in the security agreement? _____

53. Assume a debtor grants a security interest to Bank One and obtains a loan the same day. The security interest is "all now owned or after-acquired equipment." If the debtor obtains a new drill press one year after this, while the loan is still outstanding, when does Bank One's security interest in the drill press attach? _____

54. Does it matter when determining whether Bank One can enforce its security interest in the drill press if the drill press is worth $500,000 but the initial loan was only for $50,000? _____

55. At a typical loan closing table, when does attachment occur? _____

Answers

42. Creating a security interest means that the debtor has agreed to give the secured party a security interest in specific property and has fulfilled the legal requirements to do this. Without a properly created security interest, the creditor has no rights in any property. The creditor is then just a general unsecured creditor.

43. The technical requirements of attachment are: (1) an intention on the part of the debtor to grant a security interest; (2) a written security agreement in favor of the secured party, or the secured party has either possession or control of the collateral; (3) the secured party gave the debtor value; (4) and the debtor has rights in the collateral. Some teachers collapse the requirements into the easy-to-use acronym *VAR*, which stands for: (1) value, (2) agreement, and (3) rights.

44. Usually the intent to create a security interest is clearly set out in a written security agreement specifically stating that the debtor "grants" a security interest in particular property to the secured party. Because the secured party can also have possession of the collateral instead of a written security agreement, however, the intent to grant a security interest may not be so clearly articulated, such as in a case when a person borrows someone else's property but also loans them money.

45. No, a security interest can only be granted in specific property. This may be much or perhaps even everything the debtor owns but it is still in something specific, not in the abstract. A security agreement can give a security interest in "all of the debtor's inventory, present and to be later acquired."

46. A security agreement must be a record that is authenticated by the debtor and that contains a description of the collateral. A record is a written or electronic document, and authentication is a written signature or electronic authentication.

47. The description of the collateral must "reasonably identify" the collateral.

48. No, the description must be more specific than that. The collateral can of course be described very specifically, such as by serial number. It also can be described by category, such as "all equipment" or "all inventory." Remember that the test is whether the description reasonably identifies the collateral. Supergeneric collateral descriptions such as "all assets" are insufficient to describe the collateral in a security agreement, but are sufficient in financing statements. We will discuss financing statements further in Chapter 5.

49. Under the composite document rule, a party may be able to enforce its security interest even though its security agreement does not contain a description of its collateral. This is possible because some courts are willing to read the security agreement, along with another document (thus the name "composite"), to find the requirements of a valid security agreement. Courts will only engage in this inquiry if it appears clear that the debtor intended to grant the secured party a security interest.

50. Proceeds of collateral are money and other property generated when secured party sells or otherwise disposes of the collateral. Products are things that are created from the collateral, and offspring are calves from cows and so on.

51. Not as to the proceeds. The Code automatically grants the secured party a security interest in the proceeds of its collateral. Product and offspring, however, should be included in the secured party's collateral description in the security agreement.

52. This question refers to after-acquired property clauses. The Code grants the secured party an automatic security interest in the proceeds of its collateral, that is, things that are generated by the existing collateral. This question asks about something different. What if the debtor comes into new property that fits within a category of collateral in which the secured party claims an interest? The security agreement can extend the security interest to these new items as well, but the Code does not do this automatically. If the secured party wants a security interest in property acquired by the debtor after the initial security interest is granted, the secured party must include an after-acquired property clause in the security agreement. Typical language would be something like "all of debtor's inventory, present and to be acquired in the future."

53. When the last of these, value, agreement, rights, occurs. In this case, that would be when the debtor obtains rights in the drill press.

54. No . . . why would it? Remember, you can never be too rich or have too much collateral.

55. The agreement is usually signed before closing so it would be whenever the last of these two things occurs: (1) the bank promises to lend or hands over the check, or (2) the debtor acquires rights in the collateral.

Exam Tips on *CREATION OF A SECURITY INTEREST*

Although attachment doesn't cause too many problems in practice, it is a fertile ground for exam questions, and some professors (including us) seem almost obsessed with it.

☞ In approaching questions in an examination, don't forget to first determine whether the creditor has a valid security interest—in other words, whether it has a security interest that has attached to some of the debtor's personal property.

　☞ Check to see if *each* element of attachment exists: (1) did the debtor intend to grant a security interest; (2) did the secured party give value; (3) does the debtor have rights in whatever the security interest was given; and (4) is there a valid security agreement or does the secured party either have control of the collateral or possession of it?

☞ If there has to be a security agreement, check to see if *all* the elements exist: (1) is it a "record," which usually means is it in writing; (2) is it "authenticated," which usually means is it signed; (3) does the record contain language indicating that the debtor intends to grant a security interest; and (4) does it contain a proper description of the collateral?

　☞ Carefully consider whether the description is valid. Does it reasonably describe the collateral? Watch out for generic descriptions when the goods are consumer goods—they are invalid.

☛ What property of the debtor is covered by the description? Does it cover the property that is at issue in the question? If the security interest is only in accounts, the secured party will have no interest in the debtor's equipments or chattel paper!

    ☞ Does the security interest cover property that the debtor obtains after the security interest is given? Is there an after-property clause in the security agreement?

☛ What obligations of the debtor are covered? Does the security interest secure only a loan that was made contemporaneously with grant of the security interest or does it cover past and even future loans or other obligations?

☛ Has the secured party given value? Remember that value is a broadly defined term including preexisting debtors and promises to make a loan.

☛ Does the debtor have rights in the collateral? Usually the answer is yes, but the debtor doesn't own the collateral. Be careful to see whether the debt has some rights in it by virtue of a lease or under Article 2.

☛ Above all, pay attention to what your own teacher spends the most time on. For example, if he or she spends a lot of time talking about perfection in certain kinds of collateral, this will likely appear on his or her test.

CHAPTER 5

PERFECTION OF SECURITY INTERESTS

ChapterScope _____

This chapter covers the methods for perfecting a security interest, including possession, control, and the ever-important filing system used under Article 9. The most important concepts in this chapter are as follows:

■ **Notice:** Notice is the theme of Article 9. Article 9's primary goal is to provide a notice system through which people (usually lenders) can determine whether other people have already loaned to a debtor and taken back a security interest in certain of the debtor's assets, before making his or her own loan.

■ **Real property recording systems:** The real property system, through which people loan with real estate as the collateral, has its own recording or notice system, which varies from state to state. These systems involve the same concept as Article 9. They are designed to give people a place to look for prior liens before making another loan to the same debtor on the same assets. Because most people are familiar with mortgages on real estate, this chapter starts by looking at this analogous filing system.

■ **Why perfection matters:** Whether a security interest is perfected affects a secured creditor's rights in its collateral vis-à-vis other creditors, but not the debtor. Perfection establishes priorities among creditors, but even an unperfected secured creditor can repossess and exercise its other rights against the debtor.

■ **The basics of perfection—Methods of giving notice:** There are four basic ways to perfect a security interest—by filing, by possession, by control, and automatically.

  ■ *Perfection by filing:* To perfect by a public filing, one must file a financing statement, a copy of which is contained in this chapter. This document is short and contains only the most basic information. This is because it is a notice-only system. If a future lender wants more information about a prior loan, the new creditor must ask for more information from the debtor or the current lender.

    ■ *Where does one file a financing statement?* First, one must determine which state to file in, which is based on the state in which the debtor is located. If the debtor is a corporation, this is its state of incorporation. If the debtor is an unregistered organization such as a partnership, one files where the debtor does business or has its executive offices. If the debtor is an individual, one files where the debtor's principal residence is. Once the state is determined, one must then determine whether to file in the state Secretary of State's office, the real estate office, or some other office.

    ■ *The requirements of a financing statement:* A financing statement contains just very basic information, such as the name of the debtor, the name of the secured party, the address of both the debtor and the secured party, and a description of the collateral, and if the debtor is an organization, a statement to that effect along with its organizational number.

    ■ *The description of the collateral:* The description of collateral can be broader in the financing statement than the one required in the security agreement.

■ *The effects of mistakes or omissions in the financing statement:* Mistakes that are seriously misleading will invalidate the financing statement.

■ *The steps to take when the collateral changes its form, or the debtor moves, and as a result, the financing statement is no longer accurate:* Some changes in the debtor's name, the debtor's location, or the collateral require the debtor to refile the financing statement to correct what has changed and some do not.

■ *How long does a financing statement last?* Five years. After that the financing statement lapses. One needs to continue the financing statement if the loan is to remain outstanding after 5 years or the creditor may lose priority.

■ *Perfection by possession:* Many assets can be perfected by the secured party taking possession of the collateral, including goods, instruments, tangible negotiable documents of title, money, tangible chattel paper, and certificated securities.

■ *Automatic perfection:* Perfection can occur automatically in certain limited situations. The most common situation in which this occurs is when a secured party has a PMSI in consumer goods. The other instances in which perfection occurs automatically are when the security interest is in promissory notes, and sometimes when the security interest is in accounts created by an assignment. In most transactions of consequence, i.e., those involving a lot of money, automatic perfection does not apply so don't overemphasize the importance of automatic perfection.

■ *Perfection by control:* This is a relatively new way to perfect, created by recent changes to Article 9. A secured party can perfect by control when the collateral is investment property, deposit accounts, letter of credit rights, electronic chattel paper, and electronic documents.

■ **Continuous perfection:** A secured party can change its method of perfection, but to retain its priority, its perfection must be continuous. This means there can be no gaps in perfection.

■ **Perfection of security interests in proceeds:** Sometimes the secured party needs to amend its financing statement if its collateral changes its form. Although the secured party's security interest clearly continues in its proceeds, to stay perfected an amendment may be required.

I. INTRODUCTION

In this chapter, you will learn what many consider to be the backbone of Article 9, the filing system. So important is this filing system that some lawyers even call the little piece of paper that one files to "perfect" a security interest in personal property a "UCC-1."[1] Actually, the little piece of paper is called a *financing statement*, and filing it "perfects" a security interest that a debtor grants in the collateral.

But what is perfection? Perfection is the general process of providing notice to the world of one's security interest in collateral. Perfection by filing is constructive notice because the notice is given by sending notices to a particular place so that people who are interested can come and find them. Notice is sometimes also given by having the creditor retain possession of the collateral.

---

1. As you know, UCC is short for the Uniform Commercial Code, or the entire series of uniform statutes governing not just all Article 9 secured transactions, but also the sale of goods, leases, negotiable instruments, bank deposits and collections, letters of credit, documents of title, and investment securities.

The theory behind this kind of notice is that creditors who wish to take collateral for an obligation can and should ask the debtor to see the collateral. If the debtor cannot produce it, the assumption should be that another person, for example a creditor, has rights in it.

While perfection of a security interest is important, students and lawyers alike tend to overstate the importance of perfection. Perfection is very important, but it does not control the rights of the creditor vis-à-vis the debtor. A creditor with a security interest that has attached (the subject of Chapter 4) can repossess its collateral even if the security interest is not perfected. Give this some thought before moving on.

Perfection does not control whether a creditor can exercise its rights against the debtor—rather, it affects only the relative rights between creditors. Thus, it only matters where there is more than one creditor claiming an interest in the same collateral. This is still very important of course, because a creditor must always assume there will be other creditors, but a failure of a secured party to perfect does not protect a debtor from repossession or the other Article 9 remedies.

Another instance in which perfection is important is when the debtor sells the collateral to a third party. Frequently, if the secured party has perfected, it has the same rights against the purchaser as it had against the debtor.

As we mentioned, Article 9 provides four ways in which a security interest can be perfected: (1) by filing, (2) by the secured party taking possession of the collateral, (3) by the secured party taking control of the collateral, and (4) automatically (the security interest is perfected even though the secured party does nothing to perfect it). In some cases, the secured party has a choice of how to perfect. For example, if the collateral is equipment, the secured party may perfect either by filing or by taking possession. However, sometimes only one method of perfection is available, for example, if the collateral is accounts, the only way to perfect is by filing. And, even when the secured party has a choice of how to perfect, one method of perfection may provide protection against more parties than another.

This chapter is about perfection, which can occur by filing as well as by other means. The three primary ways to perfect a security interest are by filing, by possession, and by control. The most effective way to perfect, between these three ways, will vary depending on the type of collateral involved.

We said previously that the primary purpose of perfection is to give notice to the world of the existence of a security interest. The notice essentially tells later creditors, "stay away if you do not want to have a lower priority than this other secured party." Thus, it provides invaluable information to future lenders and purchasers from the debtor about the value the collateral will have to them if they take an interest in it.

We start our discussion below by talking about the most common method of perfection, filing a UCC-1 Financing Statement. But before we even do that, we tell you a little about the real estate filing system. Because many of you probably are familiar with the notion of filing a real estate mortgage, this will help put the rest of our discussion into context.

A. **Real property recording systems:** If the owner of a home sells the house, the transaction will be enforceable as between the two parties as long as certain formalities are met. For example, a contract for a sale of real property must be in writing, and a deed is required to pass title. The transaction is between the two of them, and most other people could care less that the home has been sold. However, for certain third parties, the fact that the sale has been made will be important. The real property system is particularly important to buyers because it allows them to determine the condition of the title, including whether there are prior liens on the property.

   Assume for a moment that you are about to purchase a farm from Velma who has occupied it for many years. You probably presume that Velma owns the farm because she has lived there, but before you buy you want to be certain. Perhaps she has already sold it to someone else who is letting her live there. Perhaps she is only a tenant. Perhaps she has only a life estate in the farm. You, your lawyer, or a title company will do a title search to make certain that she has title and that there are no liens on the farm.

Because the farm is real property, the title search process is pretty straightforward. There will be a file containing the documents (deed, mortgage, etc.) that represent every transaction involving that particular piece of property: sales, mortgages, the granting of easements, etc. The file is located in a state office, frequently the office of the clerk of the county in which the property is located, and the search may be by the legal description of the property. If the last deed on record is one to Velma, she probably is the owner.

What if Velma had in fact deeded the property to Patrick a few months before, but the sale does not turn up in the search? Well, until Patrick records his deed, the transfer to him is ineffective as to subsequent purchasers without notice of the sale. Hence, if you buy the farm, you will get good title even as to Patrick, provided you file your deed before he does. Although as between Velma and Patrick the transfer is immediately effective, and Patrick can enforce it and is the owner of the farm as between them, the law does not recognize the effectiveness of the transfer as to third parties unless and until the deed is filed.

The process of selling property or encumbering it with a mortgage is initially a secret one because only the parties to the transaction know about it. The essence of a recording system is that it provides a method of discovering interests in property that would otherwise be unknown to third parties. It protects parties who purchase the property or loan money against the property from interests that would otherwise be unknown and undiscoverable.

Because there is no uniform act covering real property transfers or mortgages that has gained acceptance by the states, one must consult the law of the state in which the land is located to determine how to file notice of a mortgage and the exact consequences of a failure to record a deed or mortgage. In general, however, unless a deed or mortgage is recorded, the deed or mortgage is ineffective as against others who subsequently deal with the property without knowledge, e.g., subsequent purchasers and subsequent mortgagees.

Although there are exceptions, the filing system determines priorities based on who files the operative document first. Here are some examples.

Example 1: Victor, the owner of Blackacre, sells it to Andy for $100,000 and gives Andy a deed. The next day, Victor sells Blackacre to Brigid for $75,000 and gives her a deed. Assuming Brigid does not know of the sale to Andy, if she files her deed before Andy files his, Brigid has title to the property, even as against Andy. Priority is based on who files his or her deed first.

Example 2: Victor, the owner of Blackacre, sells it to Andy for $100,000 and gives Andy a deed. Before Andy files his deed, Victor borrows $50,000 from Bank and gives Bank a mortgage on Blackacre. Bank files its mortgage before Andy files his deed. The mortgage is valid, and if Victor defaults, Bank can foreclose on Blackacre even though Andy is the owner of the property. As the example shows, priority among deeds and mortgages is also determined based on who files first.

Example 3: Victor, the owner of Blackacre, borrowed $75,000 from Bank, giving Bank a mortgage on Blackacre. If Bank does not file the mortgage, a subsequent purchaser of Blackacre without notice takes the property free of the mortgage, and if Victor gives another mortgage to Creditor, Creditor's mortgage has priority over Bank's if Creditor did not know of Bank's mortgage when it made the loan and Creditor filed its mortgage first. This example shows that filing provides notice of the mortgage and thus "perfects" the mortgage on real estate. Before this perfection has occurred, the mortgage is valid against the debtor but is not valid against subsequent purchasers without knowledge of the existence of the mortgage. Again, the first-in-time rule prevails.

B. Perfection under Article 9: As is true with real property, there can be secret ownership interests in personal property, but unlike the real property recording system, there is no comprehensive system of recording sales or ownership rights in personal property.[2] Thus, if I purchase a television from an appliance store or I sell a refrigerator to my neighbor, the transaction is not recorded and the only way in which third parties would discover the sale is if they were told about it. Similarly, if I take my watch to a jeweler to have it repaired, there is nothing on file to show that the jeweler is only a bailee of the watch or that I am its owner. With some significant but limited exceptions, we assume that the person in possession of personal property is its owner.

When we are talking about security interests rather than an ownership interest, it is a different story. A security interest is effective as to third parties only if it is "perfected." Thus, if a secured party has a security interest in a debtor's property, the security interest is valid as between the parties so long as it is properly created. See Chapter 4, *supra*. However, unless it is perfected, it is most likely not valid as to those who deal with the collateral, i.e., purchasers from the debtor, other creditors who take a security interest in the same collateral, and those who have judicial or statutory liens on the collateral. UCC §§ 9-317 et seq. We will discuss this in greater detail in Chapter 6, which deals with priorities among creditors.

The rationale of perfection of an Article 9 security interest is the same as that of recording real property transactions. Perfection is merely a method of giving third parties notice that property is encumbered by a security interest. The details of the process, however, are quite different.

The differences in the details result from various things. To start with, personal property is moveable, whereas real property is not. A refrigerator may go from one town to another, from one county to another, from one state to another. Secondly, as you have seen, personal property falls into various types of categories, some tangible and some intangible. Finally, Article 9 governs a number of different types of transactions running the gamut from a security interest in a television that a consumer purchases to a complicated transaction in which a business borrows money and gives a security interest in its inventory, accounts, equipment, etc. Collateral also can change forms or turn into something else, which creates other perfection issues.

The result is that perfection of a security interest under Article 9 is complicated, with many rules to be learned.

II. METHODS OF PERFECTION UNDER ARTICLE 9

A security interest cannot be perfected until it has attached (UCC § 9-308(a)), and, in most cases, something more than attachment must occur. Filing is the most common method of perfection under Article 9, but the Article provides four methods of perfection:

1. Filing,
2. Possession of the collateral by the secured party,

---

2. The exception is when the property involves motor vehicles, airplanes, and sometimes other types of goods such as boats. "Certificate of title" statutes that require registration of these types of property will be discussed later.

3. Perfection that occurs automatically upon attachment without any action required by the secured party, and
4. Perfection by taking control of the collateral.

Frequently, the secured party has a choice of how it will perfect. For example, when the collateral is goods, perfection by either filing or taking possession is effective. In other cases, only one method is permitted. For example, perfection of a security interest in accounts can only be accomplished by filing. As will be discussed in this chapter, as well as in Chapter 6, when the secured party has a choice, one method of perfection may provide protection against more parties than another.

To determine the proper method of perfection, correctly categorizing the collateral is critical. In some cases, the nature of the transaction, e.g., whether the security interest is a purchase-money security interest (PMSI), is also important.

III. PERFECTION BY FILING

A. **Introduction:** Filing is certainly what most of us think of when we think about perfecting a security interest in personal property. This is because most security interests can be perfected by filing and because filing is a lot more convenient than the other most common method, possession.

The only exceptions to the rule that perfection can be accomplished through filing are deposit accounts, letter-of-credit rights, or money. UCC § 9-312(a).[3] One cannot file for these things.

Moreover, in some cases, the secured party may obtain better rights, and thus be better protected against third parties, by perfecting in some way other than by filing. For example, when the collateral is a negotiable instrument the secured party can perfect by filing, but the security interest will not be valid against a person who subsequently takes the instrument as a holder in due course.[4] If, however, the secured party perfects by taking possession of the instrument, there can be no holder in due course, and the secured party is better protected.

Unlike the real estate recording system in which the actual contract between the parties (the deed or mortgage) is filed, Article 9 adopts what is commonly called a "notice" filing system. The document filed, called a "financing statement," provides little information and is designed to simply put third parties on notice that the debtor may have given a security interest in the described property.

Throughout the filing system, the drafters of Article 9 tried their best to balance the needs of filers and searchers. At times, the system allows the filer to leave a financing statement in place that is no longer accurate, rather than making the filer update the financing statement. At other times, the drafters required the filer to fix the financing statement once it becomes inaccurate. Obviously, a financing statement that is still considered effective but is no longer accurate is a big problem for searchers. On the other hand, having to change the financing statement a great number of times is inconvenient for the filer. Throughout the system, you can see the Code reflecting a balance between the needs of searchers and filers.

---

3. Deposit accounts and letter-of-credit rights can be perfected only by the secured party taking control of them, and a security interest in money can be perfected only by the secured party taking possession.

4. Basically a holder in due course is a person who purchases a negotiable instrument in good faith. There are, however, technical requirements. To be a holder in due course a person must be a holder who has given value and who takes without notice of defenses to the instrument or that others claim an interest in it. The person must also take without notice that the instrument is overdue, that it has been dishonored, or that there are unauthorized signatures on it. UCC § 3-302. If the secured party takes possession of it, no other person can be a holder; hence, no one else can be a holder in due course.

The determination of whether a security interest is perfected involves a two-step process:

1. Where must the filing be made, and
2. What must be filed?

B. Where to file a financing statement

1. **Introduction:** In determining where to file a financing statement, two inquiries must be made: (1) In which jurisdiction or state must the filing be made, and (2) in which office should it be filed within that jurisdiction? The question of which state or jurisdiction is the proper one is the more complicated question.

2. **The proper state in which to file**

   a. **Baseline rule—Location of debtor:** In most cases the rule is simple: filing must be in the state where the debtor is located. UCC § 9-301(1). Article 9 provides where a debtor is located in UCC § 9-307.

      i. **Registered organizations:** If an organization is registered in a state, the organization is located in that state for legal purposes and that state is the proper place to file. Corporations, limited partnerships, and limited liability companies come within this rule. UCC § 9-307(e). This rule is convenient because, as you'll see, when debtors move it causes problems, but registered organizations cannot move.

   Example 4: ABC Inc. does business only in Washington and Oregon, but was created as a Delaware corporation. Delaware is the proper state in which to file.

      ii. **Individuals:** Filing as to individuals must be done in the state of the individual's principal residence. UCC § 9-307(b)(1). The term "principal residence" is not defined by the Code, and its location may present problems in some cases. Clearly, if an individual has a home in Nebraska in which he or she lives most of the year, Nebraska is the proper state in which to file, even though the person has a winter home in Florida where he or she lives for the months of December, January, and February. If an individual has homes in Colorado, Illinois, and Hawaii, and he or she spends approximately four months per year in each home, the principal residence would be determined by where he or she pays taxes, registers to vote, etc.

      iii. **Sole proprietorships:** Because sole proprietorships have no legal existence, filing must be done where the owner has his or her principal residence.

   Example 5: Dave Debtor is the sole owner of an appliance business in Kansas City, Missouri that he operates under the name "A-1 Appliances." If Dave lives across the river in Kansas City, Kansas, the proper place to file is Kansas.

      iv. **Organizations that are not registered:** Some organizations are generally considered to be entities, although not necessarily legal entities, even though they are not registered with a state. These include partnerships, unincorporated associations, business trusts, governments, and governmental subdivisions. See UCC § 1-201(b)(25) [2001 version]. The proper state to file for these types of organizations is as follows:

   - If the organization has only one place where it conducts its affairs, in that state. UCC § 9-307(b)(2).

- If the organization conducts its affairs in more than one state, in the state where it has its executive offices. UCC § 9-307(3).

Example 6: Margaret and Andrew decide to purchase rental property as an investment. Each contributes half of the necessary capital with the agreement that they will share in the profits. Although there is no formal partnership agreement, the law will treat them as a partnership.

- If they purchase property only in Texas, then a financing statement must be filed in Texas to perfect an Article 9 security interest because they are conducting their business only in that state.
- If they purchase property in both Texas and Oklahoma, then filing must be in the state where they have their "executive office." This is not necessarily where they own the most land, it is where they pay the partnership bills, have their business bank account, where the partnership pays taxes, etc.

Example 7: Ajax Partnership, a retailer of shoes, has its principal store in New Jersey, but also has stores in Pennsylvania and Connecticut. It has its executive office in New York City. The proper place to file is New York.

b. Exceptions to baseline rule

  i. Goods covered by a certificate of title: When goods are governed by a certificate of title—motor vehicles in all states and boats in some states—the location of the debtor does not determine the proper state in which to file. Rather, it is the state that issued the certificate of title. UCC § 9-303.

Example 8: Debtor is a trucking company that has its chief executive office in Iowa but does business in several states. If it registers its trucks in a number of different states, perfection as to any security interests in the trucks would have to be in the state that issued the certificate of title on that particular truck.

  ii. Fixture filings; timber to be cut and as-extracted collateral: To obtain maximum protection for a security interest in fixtures, the secured party must file a "fixture filing." Fixture filings are discussed in more detail below, but for now, just know that a fixture filing must be filed in the state where the real property to which the goods are affixed is located. UCC § 9-301(3)(A). When the collateral is timber to be cut or as-extracted minerals, the law where the timber to be cut or minerals are located controls. UCC § 9-301(3)(B), (4).

  iii. Agricultural liens: Agricultural liens must be filed under Article 9. The proper state in which to file is the state in which the real property is located. UCC § 9-302.

3. The proper office in which to file

  a. Statewide office for most transactions: For the vast majority of transactions, the office in which to file is a statewide office established for that purpose. UCC § 9-501(a)(2). In most states, one files financing statements in the Secretary of State's office.

  b. Exceptions

  i. Goods for which a certificate of title has been issued: When a certificate of title has been issued for a registered vehicle, a motor vehicle for example, the certificate of title law of the state will apply. UCC § 9-303. In almost all states, the filing office will be different from the one used for other secured transactions filing. Usually, it will be called the "Department" or "Registry" of Motor Vehicles or by some similar name. The security interest will be noted on the certificate of title itself when it is filed, and anyone dealing with the certificate will be able to see that the vehicle is encumbered. The only way to perfect a security interest in goods covered by a certificate of title statute is to comply with the statute.

If a motor vehicle is held as inventory by a seller, the certificate of title statute will not apply as it is not registered for use on the roads and the filing will be in the Secretary of State's office treating the vehicle as inventory. For example, if Good Buy Autos Inc. has new and used automobiles for sale, these vehicles are not registered while they are held for sale, and a security interest in them will be filed the same as for other inventory in the Secretary of State's office.

ii. **Property subject to federal perfection rules:** Federal statutes regulate how perfection is to occur as to some property such as airplanes and copyrights. In such cases, the only way in which to perfect is by following the federal law. *National Peregrine, Inc. v. Capitol Federal Savings and Loan Association of Denver (In re Peregrine Entertainment, Ltd.),* 116 B.R. 194 (C.D. Cal. 1990). A federal statute that provides for perfection may not, however, have any priority rules. If it does not, the Article 9 priority rules will be applied. *Aircraft Trading and Services, Inc. v. Braniff, Inc.,* 819 F.2d 1227 (2d Cir. 1987).

iii. **Fixture filings:** When the collateral is fixtures, a fixture filing must be filed in the office that is designated by state law for the filing of real property mortgages. UCC § 9-501(a)(1)(B). In most states, this is the Office of the County Clerk in the county where the real property to which the fixture is affixed is located.

iv. **Timber to be cut and as-extracted minerals:** Like fixture filings, security interests in as-extracted minerals and timber to be cut are filed in the office where real property mortgages are filed. UCC § 9-501(a)(1)(A).

v. **Transmitting utilities:** Most states have established a separate office for the filing of security interests in collateral, including fixtures, of transmitting utilities. See UCC § 9-501(b).

C. What must be filed

1. **Introduction:** Unlike real property recording systems that require filing of the actual document, e.g., the deed or mortgage, Article 9 requires only that a "financing statement" be filed. There is a form of financing statement in Article 9 at § 9-521. We have reproduced a sample here as Figure 5-1, as well as in Chapter 4. Again, the financing statement is also sometimes called a UCC-1, after the form that is used to do an initial filing. There are also Financing Statement Amendments, which are used for other purposes and are discussed below.

Figure 5-1
UCC Financing Statement

UCC FINANCING STATEMENT
FOLLOW INSTRUCTIONS (front and back) CAREFULLY

A. NAME & PHONE OF CONTACT AT FILER [optional]

B. SEND ACKNOWLEDGMENT TO: (Name and Address)

THE ABOVE SPACE IS FOR FILING OFFICE USE ONLY

1. DEBTOR'S EXACT FULL LEGAL NAME - insert only <u>one</u> debtor name (1a or 1b) - do not abbreviate or combine names

1a. ORGANIZATION'S NAME			
OR 1b. INDIVIDUAL'S LAST NAME	FIRST NAME	MIDDLE NAME	SUFFIX

1c. MAILING ADDRESS	CITY	STATE	POSTAL CODE	COUNTRY

1d. TAX ID #: SSN OR EIN	ADD'L INFO RE ORGANIZATION DEBTOR	1e. TYPE OF ORGANIZATION	1f. JURISDICTION OF ORGANIZATION	1g. ORGANIZATIONAL ID #, if any ☐NONE

2. ADDITIONAL DEBTOR'S EXACT FULL LEGAL NAME - insert only <u>one</u> debtor name (2a or 2b) - do not abbreviate or combine names

2a. ORGANIZATION'S NAME			
OR 2b. INDIVIDUAL'S LAST NAME	FIRST NAME	MIDDLE NAME	SUFFIX

2c. MAILING ADDRESS	CITY	STATE	POSTAL CODE	COUNTRY

2d. TAX ID #: SSN OR EIN	ADD'L INFO RE ORGANIZATION DEBTOR	2e. TYPE OF ORGANIZATION	2f. JURISDICTION OF ORGANIZATION	2g. ORGANIZATIONAL ID #, if any ☐NONE

3. SECURED PARTY'S NAME (or NAME of TOTAL ASSIGNEE of ASSIGNOR S/P) - insert only <u>one</u> secured party name (3a or 3b)

3a. ORGANIZATION'S NAME			
OR 3b. INDIVIDUAL'S LAST NAME	FIRST NAME	MIDDLE NAME	SUFFIX

3c. MAILING ADDRESS	CITY	STATE	POSTAL CODE	COUNTRY

4. This FINANCING STATEMENT covers the following collateral:

5. ALTERNATIVE DESIGNATION [if applicable]:	LESSEE/LESSOR	CONSIGNEE/CONSIGNOR	BAILEE/BAILOR	SELLER/BUYER	AG. LIEN	NON-UCC FILING

6. ☐ This FINANCING STATEMENT is to be filed [for record] (or recorded) in the REAL ESTATE RECORDS. Attach Addendum [if applicable]	7. Check to REQUEST SEARCH REPORT(S) on Debtor(s) [ADDITIONAL FEE] [optional]	All Debtors	Debtor 1	Debtor 2

8. OPTIONAL FILER REFERENCE DATA

FILING OFFICE COPY — NATIONAL UCC FINANCING STATEMENT (FORM UCC1) (REV. 07/29/98)

Instructions for National UCC Financing Statement (Form UCC1)

Please type or laser-print this form. Be sure it is completely legible. Read all Instructions, especially Instruction 1; correct Debtor name is crucial. Follow Instructions completely.

Fill in form very carefully; mistakes may have important legal consequences. If you have questions, consult your attorney. Filing office cannot give legal advice.

Do not insert anything in the open space in the upper portion of this form; it is reserved for filing office use.

When properly completed, send Filing Office Copy, with required fee, to filing office. If you want an acknowledgment, complete item B and, if filing in a filing office that returns an acknowledgment copy furnished by filer, you may also send Acknowledgment Copy; otherwise detach. If you want to make a search request, complete item 7 (after reading Instruction 7 below) and send Search Report Copy, otherwise detach. Always detach Debtor and Secured Party Copies.

If you need to use attachments, use 8-1/2 X 11 inch sheets and put at the top of each sheet the name of the first Debtor, formatted exactly as it appears in item 1 of this form; you are encouraged to use Addendum (Form UCC1Ad).

A. To assist filing offices that might wish to communicate with filer, filer may provide information in item A. This item is optional.

B. Complete item B if you want an acknowledgment sent to you. If filing in a filing office that returns an acknowledgment copy furnished by filer, present simultaneously with this form a carbon or other copy of this form for use as an acknowledgment copy.

1. **Debtor name**: Enter only one Debtor name in item 1, an organization's name (1a) or an individual's name (1b). Enter Debtor's exact full legal name. Don't abbreviate.

1a. Organization Debtor. "Organization" means an entity having a legal identity separate from its owner. A partnership is an organization; a sole proprietorship is not an organization, even if it does business under a trade name. If Debtor is a partnership, enter exact full legal name of partnership; you need not enter names of partners as additional Debtors. If Debtor is a registered organization (e.g., corporation, limited partnership, limited liability company), it is advisable to examine Debtor's current filed charter documents to determine Debtor's correct name, organization type, and jurisdiction of organization.

1b. Individual Debtor. "Individual" means a natural person; this includes a sole proprietorship, whether or not operating under a trade name. Don't use prefixes (Mr., Mrs., Ms.). Use suffix box only for titles of lineage (Jr., Sr., III) and not for other suffixes or titles (e.g., M.D.). Use married woman's personal name (Mary Smith, not Mrs. John Smith). Enter individual Debtor's family name (surname) in Last Name box, first given name in First Name box, and all additional given names in Middle Name box.

For both organization and individual Debtors: Don't use Debtor's trade name, DBA, AKA, FKA, Division name, etc. in place of or combined with Debtor's legal name; you may add such other names as additional Debtors if you wish (but this is neither required nor recommended).

1c. An address is always required for the Debtor named in 1a or 1b.

1d. Debtor's taxpayer identification number (tax ID #) — social security number or employer identification number — may be required in some states.

1e,f,g. "Additional information re organization Debtor" is always required. Type of organization and jurisdiction of organization as well as Debtor's exact legal name can be determined from Debtor's current filed charter document. Organizational ID #, if any, is assigned by the agency where the charter document was filed; this is different from tax ID #; this should be entered preceded by the 2-character U.S. Postal identification of state of organization if one of the United States (e.g., CA12345, for a California corporation whose organizational ID # is 12345); if agency does not assign organizational ID #, check box in item 1g indicating "none."

Note: If Debtor is a trust or a trustee acting with respect to property held in trust, enter Debtor's name in item 1 and attach Addendum (Form UCC1Ad) and check appropriate box in item 17. If Debtor is a decedent's estate, enter name of deceased individual in item 1b and attach Addendum (Form UCC1Ad) and check appropriate box in item 17. If Debtor is a transmitting utility or this Financing Statement is filed in connection with a Manufactured-Home Transaction or a Public-Finance Transaction as defined in applicable Commercial Code, attach Addendum (Form UCC1Ad) and check appropriate box in item 18.

2. If an additional Debtor is included, complete item 2, determined and formatted per Instruction 1. To include further additional Debtors, or one or more additional Secured Parties, attach either Addendum (Form UCC1Ad) or other additional page(s), using correct name format. Follow Instruction 1 for determining and formatting additional names.

3. Enter information for Secured Party or Total Assignee, determined and formatted per Instruction 1. If there is more than one Secured Party, see Instruction 2. If there has been a total assignment of the Secured Party's interest prior to filing this form, you may either (1) enter Assignor S/P's name and address in item 3 and file an Amendment (Form UCC3) [see item 5 of that form]; or (2) enter Total Assignee's name and address in item 3 and, if you wish, also attaching Addendum (Form UCC1Ad) giving Assignor S/P's name and address in item 12.

4. Use item 4 to indicate the collateral covered by this Financing Statement. If space in item 4 is insufficient, put the entire collateral description or continuation of the collateral description on either Addendum (Form UCC1Ad) or other attached additional page(s).

5. If filer desires (at filer's option) to use titles of lessee and lessor, or consignee and consignor, or seller and buyer (in the case of accounts or chattel paper), or bailee and bailor instead of Debtor and Secured Party, check the appropriate box in item 5. If this is an agricultural lien (as defined in applicable Commercial Code) filing or is otherwise not a UCC security interest filing (e.g., a tax lien, judgment lien, etc.), check the appropriate box in item 5, complete items 1-7 as applicable and attach any other items required under other law.

6. If this Financing Statement is filed as a fixture filing or if the collateral consists of timber to be cut or as-extracted collateral, complete items 1-5, check the box in item 6, and complete the required information (items 13, 14 and/or 15) on Addendum (Form UCC1Ad).

7. This item is optional. Check appropriate box in item 7 to request Search Report(s) on all or some of the Debtors named in this Financing Statement. The Report will list all Financing Statements on file against the designated Debtor on the date of the Report, including this Financing Statement. There is an additional fee for each Report. If you have checked a box in item 7, file Search Report Copy together with Filing Officer Copy (and Acknowledgment Copy). Note: Not all states do searches and not all states will honor a search request made via this form; some states require a separate request form.

8. This item is optional and is for filer's use only. For filer's convenience of reference, filer may enter in item 8 any identifying information (e.g., Secured Party's loan number, law firm file number, Debtor's name or other identification, state in which form is being filed, etc.) that filer may find useful.

Instructions for National UCC Financing Statement Addendum (Form UCC1Ad)

9.   Insert name of first Debtor shown on Financing Statement to which this Addendum is related, exactly as shown in item 1 of Financing Statement.

10.   Miscellaneous: Under certain circumstances, additional information not provided on Financing Statement may be required. Also, some states have non-uniform requirements. Use this space to provide such additional information or to comply with such requirements; otherwise, leave blank.

11.   If this Addendum adds an additional Debtor, complete item 11 in accordance with Instruction 1 on Financing Statement. To add more than one additional Debtor, either use an additional Addendum form for each additional Debtor or replicate for each additional Debtor the formatting of Financing Statement item 1 on an 8-1/2 X 11 inch sheet (showing at the top of the sheet the name of the first Debtor shown on the Financing Statement), and in either case give complete information for each additional Debtor in accordance with Instruction 1 on Financing Statement. All additional Debtor information, especially the name, must be presented in proper format exactly identical to the format of item 1 of Financing Statement.

12.   If this Addendum adds an additional Secured Party, complete item 12 in accordance with Instruction 3 on Financing Statement. In the case of a total assignment of the Secured Party's interest before the filing of this Financing Statement, if filer has given the name and address of the Total Assignee in item 3 of the Financing Statement, filer may give the Assignor S/P's name and address in item 12.

13-15. If collateral is timber to be cut or as-extracted collateral, or if this Financing Statement is filed as a fixture filing, check appropriate box in item 13; provide description of real estate in item 14; and, if Debtor is not a record owner of the described real estate, also provide, in item 15, the name and address of a record owner. Also provide collateral description in item 4 of Financing Statement. Also check box 6 on Financing Statement. Description of real estate must be sufficient under the applicable law of the jurisdiction where the real estate is located.

16.   Use this space to provide continued description of collateral, if you cannot complete description in item 4 of Financing Statement.

17.   If Debtor is a trust or a trustee acting with respect to property held in trust or is a decedent's estate, check the appropriate box.

18.   If Debtor is a transmitting utility or if the Financing Statement relates to a Manufactured-Home Transaction or a Public-Finance Transaction as defined in the applicable Commercial Code, check the appropriate box.

As you can see, the financing statement contains only enough information to alert one searching the files that a debtor has, or at least may have, given a security interest in the described property. UCC § 9-502. To be *sufficient*, a financing statement must:

1. Provide the debtor's name,
2. Provide the name of the secured party or the name of a representative of the secured party, and
3. Indicate the collateral covered by the financing statement.

In addition, if the financing statement covers as-extracted collateral, timber to be cut, or is a fixture filing, it must:

1. Indicate that the collateral is of the type, i.e., must state the collateral is "timber to be cut,"
2. Indicate that it is to be filed in the real estate record,
3. Provide a description of the real property to which the collateral is related, and
4. If the debtor is not the owner of the real property and does not have an interest in it, the name of the record owner.

UCC § 9-502(b).

These minimal requirements for the *sufficiency* of a financing statement do not tell the whole story. Section 9-520, which provides grounds for a filing officer's refusal to file a financing statement, includes several provisions that go to the contents of the financing statement. A filing officer is authorized to, and indeed is required to, refuse to accept a financing statement if it does not contain the following: (1) the address of the secured party, (2) a mailing address for the debtor, (3) an indication of whether the debtor is an individual or an organization, and (4) the organizational number if there is one. UCC § 9-520.

The requirements for determining whether a financing statement should be *filed* by the filing officer do not go to the *sufficiency* of the financing statement. If the financing statement is not sufficient, i.e., lacks debtor's name, the secured party's name, or an indication of the collateral, it cannot result in an effective filing even if filing officer in fact does file it. However, if the financing statement lacks only one of the other *additional* bits of information, such as the organization's organizational number, it is effective if the filing officer files it.

Example 9: Secured Party prepares a financing statement that does not contain the name of the secured party. The filing officer should reject the financing statement, and if he/she does, there is no filing. If the filing officer instead accepts the financing statement and adds it to the files, the filing still is not effective because it lacks one of the requirements of sufficiency.

Example 10: Secured Party prepares a financing statement that does not contain the address of the secured party. The filing officer should reject it, and if he/she does, there is no filing and the security interest is unperfected. If, however, the filing officer files the financing statement without the secured party's address, the filing is effective and the security interest is perfected.

Example 11: Secured Party prepares a financing statement that contains all of the information required and tenders the filing fee. At that point, the financing statement is filed even though the filing officer refuses for some unauthorized reason to accept it or the filing officer loses the financing statement before it is entered into the filing system.

2. **Name of the debtor:** It is critical that the name of the debtor be correctly stated on the financing statement because the statement will be filed under the debtor's name and those searching will search by the debtor's name. Any mistake in naming the debtor is almost certain to render the filing ineffective. The only exception is if a search of the records under the incorrect name used on the financing statement would in fact disclose the financing statement. UCC § 9-506(c).

Section 9-503 has directions on how a name must be stated:

a. **Individuals:** As you would expect, you state the name of the individual in the appropriate boxes.

b. **Sole proprietorships:** The name of the owner of the business must be listed. If the person uses a trade name it may be listed, but this is not required. The listing of only the trade name is insufficient.

Example 12: Mary Smith owns and operates a grocery store as a sole proprietorship. She uses the trade name "Mary's Grub." The name on the financing statement must be "Mary Smith." The trade name "Mary's Grub" can be added but is not needed, and if the financing statement uses only the name "Mary's Grub" without naming Mary Smith, the filing is ineffective.

c. **Registered organizations:** If the debtor is a corporation, limited partnership, or limited liability company, the name must be the official registered name of the organization. Again, if the organization uses a trade name, it may be included but need not be. Using only the trade name makes the financing statement insufficient.

d. **Other organizations:** When the debtor is an unregistered organization or partnership, the name of the organization or partnership must be used in the financing statement. If the organization or partnership does not have a name, the name of the members of the organization or the names of the partners must be used. As you can imagine, this vague rule causes plenty of confusion.

Example 13: *A* and *B* have a partnership that owns rental property. The property is in the name of *A* and *B* and they do not use any partnership name. The names of *A* and *B* must be used in the financing statement as the debtors.

Example 14: *A* and *B* operate a retail shoe store under the name "Tired Feet" and use that name in all of their partnership transactions. For example, they have letterhead with that name, a checking account in that name, and they enter into contracts using that name. The name to be used on the financing statement is "Tired Feet."

Example 15: A group of people form a neighborhood association. If they give it a name and use that name, the association's name must be in the financing statement. If they do not operate under a name, all of the members of the association must be listed as the debtor.

3. **Indication of the collateral:** The requirement that the collateral be "indicated" in the financing statement is similar to the requirement that a security agreement contain a "description" of the collateral, but be careful. There are some differences between the collateral descriptions required in security agreements and those used in financing statements.

Any description of collateral that is sufficient for a security agreement can be used as the indication of the collateral for the financing statement as well. UCC § 9-504(1). Thus, the collateral may be described by specific listing, category, type, quantity, formula, or by any other method if the identity of the collateral is objectively determinable. See Chapter 2, *supra.*

However, because the financing statement need merely "indicate" the collateral whereas the security agreement must "describe" it, the test of what is sufficient for a financing statement is more liberal. *Grabowski v. Deer & Company (In re Grabowski)* 277 B.R. 388 (Bankr. S.D. Ill. 2002). For example, a description in the security agreement that simply said "inventory" might be insufficient because it doesn't state whether all inventory is covered or only some, and if only some, which parts of the inventory. However, use of the word "inventory," even without more, would be sufficient in a financing statement.

The financing statement must indicate all of the collateral in which a security interest is given. For example, if the security agreement gives a security interest in inventory and equipment, but the financing statement lists only inventory, the security interest in the debtor's equipment is not perfected.

When the security agreement grants a security interest in after-acquired property, the financing statement need not contain any reference to after-acquired property to perfect the security interest in after-acquired property. Official Comment 7 to UCC § 9-204. Thus, if the security agreement grants a security interest in "all of debtor's presently owned and after-acquired inventory," and the financing statement lists the collateral only as "all of the debtor's inventory," the secured party has a perfected security interest in any after-acquired inventory. Likewise, there is no need to include "proceeds" in the financing statement description because a security interest in proceeds is created automatically under Article 9.

Although a generic description of the collateral such as "all of the debtor's assets," or "all of the debtor's personal property" is insufficient in a security agreement, it is permitted in a financing statement. UCC § 9-504(2). In fact, many financing statements in very large loans simply describe the collateral as "all assets." As long as this is in fact the collateral for the loan, this description works fine in the financing statement although it would be too broad for the security agreement.

D. Effect of mistakes or omissions

1. **Introduction:** Since Article 9 has adopted a "notice" theory of filing, some errors in a financing statement will not invalidate a filing. A financing statement may be effective even though it contains minor errors or omissions, as long as

   a. it substantially satisfies the requirement of Article 9, and
   b. the error or omission does not make it seriously misleading.

   The basic test is whether the filing actually puts someone who searches the database on notice that a particular person, the debtor, gave or might have given a security interest in particular property. Another way of putting this is to ask whether a reasonably diligent searcher, using the existing filing system, could find this financing statement.

2. **Debtor's name:** As previously noted, an error of any kind in the debtor's name is fatal unless a search under the improperly stated name would disclose the financing statement. Searches for financing statements are now done by computer, and whether a search will disclose a financing statement when there is an error in the debtor's name depends on the

search engine used by the applicable state. In most cases, the computer is unforgiving, and this exception will rarely validate a financing statement when there is a mistake in the debtor's name.

Example 16: Debtor's name is Brigid Darwin, but Secured Party lists her name as Brigitte Darwin. A search under Brigid Darwin, her real name, will not turn up the financing statement in most states. The filing is ineffective.

Example 17: Debtor's name is Carl Contractor Construction Company. The financing statement has the name Carl Contractor. Only if a search under the name "Carl Contractor" will disclose the financing statement is it effective. In most states, it will not, and the filing is ineffective.

3. **Indication of the collateral:** A small error in the description of the collateral will not invalidate the filing. For example, a mistake in a product's serial number or a simple misspelling is not fatal so long as it would not seriously mislead someone reading the financing statement. Thus, spelling "accounts" with only one "c" would not destroy the effectiveness of the filing, nor would spelling "refrigerator" without the second "r."

4. **Name of the secured party and addresses:** Mistakes in the name of the secured party are less critical, and, unless they make the filing seriously misleading (meaning that a reasonably diligent searcher could not find it), they will not render the filing ineffective. The same is true of the addresses of the debtor and secured party. A financing statement has been held to be effective when the individual's business address was listed rather than the home address. *Grabowski v. Deere & Company (In re Grabowski)*, 277 B.R. 388 (Bankr. S.D. Ill. 2002).

E. **Subsequent changes:** A number of events may occur after the filing that will affect the likelihood that one searching the filings will discover the financing statement. Although there are some exceptions, the starting point is that changes will not invalidate the filing. UCC § 9-507(b).

  We just described the basic rules for getting an effective financing statement on record in the first place. This will create the highest possible priority under the circumstances. Moreover, this priority can be enjoyed indefinitely assuming certain facts, namely that the financing statement is renewed if the loan could remain outstanding for more than five years, that the debtor's name and location do not change, and that the collateral never transforms itself into a different kind of property. Truthfully, that is a lot to assume, and you'll need to know what to do *if* these changes occur.

  As we've discussed before in this Outline, the filing system tries its best to balance the needs of filers and searchers. We could have adopted a set of rules that proclaimed that as long as a filer got it right initially, meaning that he or she filed it in the correct place, under a debtor's name that is not seriously misleading, and correctly described its collateral at least as of the time the initial financing statement was filed, then the filing remains effective forever, regardless of what happens after that. As you might have guessed, however, such a system would cause a great inconvenience to searchers because a good percentage of the time, searchers would not be able to locate the information needed to see if a prior security interest existed on the collateral.

  To balance the needs of both searchers and filers, the Code compromises by allowing some changes to occur without requiring a corrected filing, while requiring a corrected filing in other situations. Moreover, the Code gives filers extended grace periods to discover that a change has occurred and thus to do a new amended filing where it is necessary.

1. **Change in the location of the debtor:** If a debtor changes its location within the state in which the financing statement is filed, the financing statement will become inaccurate because it no longer contains the correct address of the debtor. However, the financing statement does not become ineffective, and there is no need to file a new financing statement. UCC § 9-507(b). This is true even though the financing statement may be considered to have become seriously misleading.

    If the debtor moves to a different jurisdiction, the rule is different. In that case, the secured party will need to file a new financing statement subsequent to the debtor's move in the new state. However, filing in the old state remains effective for four months after the move. It then becomes ineffective and the security interest becomes unperfected, unless the secured party files in the new state. UCC § 9-316(a).

    If there is no perfection in the new state, the security interest is deemed never to have been perfected as to purchasers of the collateral for value. It is important to note that the word "purchasers" includes secured parties, so the filing is as though it never happened not only as to buyers of the collateral but also as to other secured parties.

    Example 18: Claudette operates a bakery in Fargo, North Dakota as a sole proprietorship. She borrows $10,000 from Fargo Bank to purchase a new oven, giving the bank a security interest in the oven. At the time, Claudette lives in Fargo and when Fargo files with the Secretary of State in North Dakota it correctly states her address on the financing statement.

    - Claudette moves to Bismarck, North Dakota, taking the oven and the rest of the equipment to that city, where she sets up a new bakery. The perfection of Fargo Bank's security interest remains effective.
    - Claudette moves her residence to Moorhead, Minnesota, across the river from Fargo. Whether she moves the business or not, the bank's perfection will cease within four months if it does not file in Minnesota. As to purchasers for value, it will be as though Fargo Bank never perfected.
    - If Claudette had incorporated her business under Delaware law and the bank had filed in Delaware, neither the change in her residence nor in the place where the business is operated will invalidate the filing because the place to file for a corporation is not dependent on her residence or place of business.

2. **Change in the name of the debtor:** As you saw earlier, because searches are done by the debtor's name, the name is a critical part (perhaps *the* critical part) of the financing statement. You can imagine, therefore, that if the debtor's name changes, this can really frustrate the searcher. The drafters dealt with this problem by requiring a secured party to amend its financing statement after a name change if the name change makes the financing statement seriously misleading. Practically speaking, the secured party has four months from the time the name changes to file its new financing statement to remain continuously perfected in all of its collateral, but this is a bit of an oversimplification.

    Note: Whatever one is doing to change the original filing, the amendment has to reference the original filing.

    If the name of the debtor changes and, as a result, the financing statement becomes seriously misleading, the filing remains effective but only as to collateral that was obtained before the change in name or within the four months following the change in name, unless an amendment to the financing statement is filed to show the name change. UCC § 9-507(c).

Because the filing remains effective as to all collateral acquired by the debtor before the name change, the danger of losing perfection because of a change in name only applies when there is an after-acquired property clause and where the security interest is secured by collateral obtained by the debtor more than four months after the change in name.

Example 19: Mike and Andy operate a retail shoe store as a general partnership under the name "Mike and Andy Partnership." As this is an organization that has a name, Secured Party I and Secured Party II file under that name. Mike and Andy decide to change the name of the partnership to "Quality Shoes Partnership," a change that makes the name under which Secured Party I and Secured Party II filed seriously misleading.

- If Secured Party I has a security interest only in the equipment that existed at the time of the filing, Secured Party I need not file an amendment.
- If Secured Party II has a security interest in "present and after-acquired inventory," and Secured Party II does not file an amendment showing the name change, the filing will be ineffective as to any inventory obtained by the partnership four months after the name change.

What if the secured party files an amendment *after* the four months subsequent to the name change? In this case, as explained above, the filing is effective as to collateral acquired before the name change and for four months thereafter. It is also effective as to any collateral that the debtor acquires after the late filing, but it is ineffective as to collateral obtained after the four-month period and before the new filing of the amendment.

Example 20: Secured Party I files a financing statement on all of Debtor's present and after-acquired inventory on February 1. Debtor changes its name in a way that is seriously misleading on June 1. Secured Party I does not file an amendment until November 1.

- Secured Party II filed a financing statement on all of Debtor's present and after-acquired inventory on July 1 using Debtor's new name. As to any collateral in existence on June 1 and any that is acquired during the following four months (until October 1), and as to all collateral obtained after November 1, Secured Party I's filing is effective and Secured Party I will have priority. As to the collateral that was obtained during October, the filing is ineffective and Secured Party II will have priority.
- Secured Party II filed a financing statement under Debtor's new name on November 15. Secured Party I's security interest is effective as to all inventory of Debtor. Even though there was a gap, the gap does not help Secured Party II because it filed after Secured Party I filed the amendment.

Again, the rules are a compromise between causing inconvenience to searchers and to filers. The rules make the searchers suffer for four months, during which time there may be no way to know that a debtor's assets are encumbered by prior security interests. This will come as a great inconvenience and can even cost the creditor money if it has not been able, even through diligent searching, to find the existing security interests.

After the four months, it is the original filer who suffers. How, you might wonder, is a creditor supposed to find out about a name change? One way is by asking the debtor to tell the secured party when it has changed its name. The skeptics among you should wonder how well this works, and we think the answer is not very well. Other things can be done to discover this type of change. The secured party can keep an eye on the debtor's business and see if the signs have changed, can look over the addresses on checks, letterhead, and so on. It pays to ask the debtor to disclose future changes in name in the terms of the security agreement, but to stay alert as well.

If the debtor is an individual, then it will be harder to detect a name change—for example, one that might result from a marriage. Again, the secured party should watch the names on checks and stationery.

You should now be concluding that all these changes create a dicey situation, from which the secured party can only do its best to protect itself. There is no foolproof way to ensure that the debtor will not change his or her name to the detriment of both searchers and filers.

How A Secured Party Can Best Protect Itself Against Losses Resulting from Name Changes

For searchers: Inquire to the extent possible (based on the size of the loan) into the names the debtor has used during the past four months, or perhaps to be safe, the past six months. Search under those names as well.

For filers: Require notification of changes and stay alert to changes through the debtor's documents, and for big loans, a periodic (at least every four months) search of public documents.

---

3. **Changes affecting the description of collateral—When bad things happen to good collateral:** Lots of things can happen while a loan is outstanding to make the collateral description in the financing statement less than accurate. Sometimes, a debtor grants a security interest in certain collateral and then changes the way it uses the collateral. In other cases, the debtor trades or barters pieces of collateral for other kinds of assets, or simply sells collateral and buys something else with the money.

In all of these situations, the new assets acquired, or the old asset being used differently, are proceeds of the secured party's collateral and thus remain part of the collateral. The question is whether the security interest in these new or transformed items remains *perfected*.

Adding to the confusion, as you may recall, the same item of collateral may be characterized differently at different times. For example, a television will be inventory when it is in the hands of an appliance store. When it is sold, it becomes consumer goods or equipment in the hands of the buyer. Assuming the security interest was properly perfected by filing, the filing remains effective after the sale. Whether the security interest continues in the collateral after the sale is a separate question that depends on whether the purchaser takes free of the security interest. This is a priority problem covered in priority rules. See Chapter 6, *infra*.

a. **Changes in use:** In some cases the person who gave the security interest in the collateral will keep it but use it in a way that changes its characterization. For example, a business selling copiers may take one of the copiers out of its inventory and use it in its business, thereby changing it from inventory to equipment. If the financing statement describes the collateral as "all of debtor's inventory," the financing statement is now misleading, probably seriously so, as to the copier that has become equipment. However, the secured party's filing remains effective. UCC § 9-507(b).

b. **Changes in collateral through barter, sale, or proceeds:** Sometimes collateral changes from one form to another, say from inventory to equipment, because the debtor trades inventory for a piece of equipment. These kinds of transactions are called *barters* and do not involve any cash changing hands, just a trade. In these situations, the secured party obtains a security interest in the property received by the debtor as a result of the trade under the proceeds provisions of Article 9. UCC § 9-315. We discussed this topic in Chapter 2, *supra*. Whether the security interest in this property is perfected is a separate question. Although we will consider the perfection of security interests in proceeds in more detail later in this chapter, we can tell you now that the security interest in the received property—the proceeds—is perfected if the secured party perfected by filing as to the original collateral. UCC § 9-315(d).

Example 21: A secured party has a security interest in inventory and has filed a financing statement for inventory. The debtor, a hardware store for the rich and famous, trades a gold hammer (inventory) for a forklift, which is equipment. Must the secured party file a new financing statement to reflect this change? No. There is nothing to do just by virtue of a change of use. This will confuse a searcher but still the filing is all set. Yes, this is misleading too! UCC § 9-315.

c. **Changes in the collateral description resulting from cash sales or involving proceeds of proceeds:** Let's say that the debtor sells the hammer and uses the resulting cash to buy equipment. When cash proceeds are involved, the rule changes. Now the secured party must file an amended financing statement to reflect the transformation of inventory to equipment, even though it's all proceeds, unless the financing filed as to the inventory also included equipment as collateral. This is about perfection, not creation of a security interest. UCC § 9-315(d). The new filing must take place within 20 days of the debtor obtaining the new collateral, purchased with the cash proceeds.

Also, a secured party remains continuously perfected in cash proceeds no matter what. UCC § 9-315(d)(2).

d. **Changes in the filing office:** Finally, any time collateral changes its form from something that is filed in one office to something that is perfected by filing in another office, an amended financing statement must be filed. One example is where a piece of inventory transforms itself into a fixture. One perfects in the inventory by filing in the Secretary of State's office, but the fixture filing should be filed in the real estate office to protect the secured party from those who claim an interest in the real property. UCC §§ 9-315(d)(2), 9-507(b).

These rules are technical, but they do make sense for the most part. The most common situation is one in which a secured party has a perfected security interest in inventory. This inventory is likely in many businesses to transform itself into accounts when the inventory is sold by the debtor on credit.

Even if the secured party does not have a security interest in accounts, the accounts are proceeds of the inventory so the security interest remains in the accounts. But is the security interest perfected? The answer is yes.

The financing statement for accounts would be filed in the same office as for inventory so there is no need to file an amendment based on a different filing location. Moreover, there has been no cash changing hands here, no proceeds of proceeds. The inventory just turned into accounts through normal business operations.

Although the financing statement does not mention accounts and could be seen by some as misleading, sophisticated lenders know that inventory becomes accounts and would thus know that the accounts are part of the inventory lender's collateral. Lenders would also know, probably just intuitively, that perfection continues in the accounts. Tricky, but sensible in the world of commercial lending.

4. **Change in form of business:** A person operating a business as a sole proprietor may incorporate or form a limited liability company or partnership. When this occurs, the filing may be in the "wrong place." For example, if the sole proprietor is located in Illinois and incorporates in Delaware, filing of financing statements after the incorporation would be in Delaware rather than Illinois.

If the person has granted security interests before the incorporation, the financing statements will be filed in Illinois; after the incorporation, the correct state is Delaware. In effect, the debtor has "moved" from Illinois to Delaware. Any financing statements filed in Illinois are effective for only four months after the move. UCC § 9-316(a). Unless a new financing statement is filed in Delaware, perfection will not only cease but it will be as though there never was a filing in Illinois as to purchasers for value (which includes secured parties). UCC § 9-316(b). If a new financing statement is filed in Delaware during the four-month period, perfection will be continuous. UCC § 9-316(b).

If a sole proprietorship becomes a corporation under the law of the state in which the original filing occurred, then it has not moved across state lines and the filing is still in the same state. No new filing is necessary unless the name is changed in a seriously misleading way.

5. **The so-called "new debtor" problem:** When there is a change in the form of a business, frequently there is a transfer of the assets to the new business form and the new form assumes the debts of the original entity. For example, if a sole proprietorship or general partnership incorporates, the assets of the business will be transferred to the new corporation that will also assume all of the debts of the prior business. The security interest in goods existing at the time of incorporation will not be cut off as a result of the transfer of the assets, UCC § 9-315. A problem arises, however, if the security interest is in after-acquired property.

Example 22: Sandy, while operating her business as a sole proprietorship, gives Bank a security interest in all of her present and after-acquired inventory. She then incorporates transferring all of the business assets to the corporation, and the corporation assumes all the debts incurred while she was doing business as a sole proprietorship. The corporation then purchases new inventory.

Does Bank have a security interest in the inventory acquired after the transfer by the corporation, and, if it does, is the security interest perfected? The answer to both questions is "yes."

By assuming the debts of the sole proprietorship, the corporation becomes a "new debtor." UCC § 9-102(a)(56). Although it has never signed a security agreement giving Bank a security interest in the inventory it acquires, it is bound by the security agreement that Sandy signed, and the filing as to that security agreement is effective as to the inventory it purchases. UCC §§ 9-203(d), 9-508(a). Of course, if the name of the business is changed in a way that makes the financing statement ineffective, the rules on change of name discussed previously apply. UCC § 9-508(b).

F. **When to file:** A security interest cannot be perfected until it has attached, UCC § 9-308(a), i.e., until there is an agreement that it attach, value has been given by the secured party, and the debtor has rights in the collateral. See Chapter 4, *supra*. It would seem, logically, that the filing must come after attachment, but this is not the case. UCC § 9-502(d).

As will be discussed in Chapter 6, *infra*, it is important for the secured party to file as soon as possible because priority often depends on the time of filing. Thus, prefiling one's financing statement, meaning filing it before a loan is even made, is always the safest thing to do. Think of this as saving your place in line.

Early filing is important in determining whether other parties have taken a security interest in the collateral. In fact, the only way for a secured party to actually know in advance of lending what its position in the collateral will be is to first obtain the debtor's authority to file a financing statement, then to file the financing statement, and then, after several days have passed, search for all filings under the debtor's name. If the search shows this secured party's filing and no prior filings made earlier in time, then it is safe to extend credit to the debtor.

Example 23: David is in the process of negotiating a loan from Bank. They reach an agreement, and David is to give Bank a security interest in his equipment. The prudent procedure for the bank to follow is:

1. Obtain a security agreement from David;
2. File a financing statement;
3. Wait for a few days to let the filing office record Bank's financing statement;
4. Order a search under David's name; and
5. Extend the credit if the search shows the Bank's financing statement and none earlier in time (or none on the same collateral, anyway).

Although there will be no *perfection* until Bank extends the credit, the date of filing will be earlier in time and may well be important to give Bank priority over other persons. You will learn much more about this in Chapter 6.

Timely filing is also important if the debtor subsequently files a petition in bankruptcy. If the filing is made significantly after the credit is extended, the security interest may be avoidable by the trustee in bankruptcy as a preferential transfer. 11 U.S.C. § 547. The possibility of a preferential transfer stems from two rules: (1) under the Bankruptcy Code the granting of a security interest is a transfer, and (2) the transfer does not occur until the security interest is perfected. 11 U.S.C. § 347(e)(1).

If the filing of the financing statement is delayed, the "transfer" will be to secure an antecedent debt because of the gap between the date the credit that was secured was given and the time of the transfer, i.e., when the security interest was perfected by the filing. If this occurs within 90 days of the filing of the bankruptcy petition, it is almost certain to be avoidable by the trustee as a preference.

Example 24: On May 1, Sally lends David $10,000 and takes a security interest in all of David's equipment. Sally does not file a financing statement until August 1. David files a petition in Bankruptcy on October 1. The trustee can avoid Sally's security interest as a preferential transfer. The debt was incurred on May 1, the transfer of the security interest did not occur until August 1, therefore it was a transfer for an antecedent debt, and August 1 is within 90 days of David's filing of his petition in bankruptcy. In order to be a preferential transfer, David must have been insolvent at the time of the transfer, August 1, but there is a presumption that debtors are insolvent during the 90 days preceding the filing of the petition. 11 U.S.C. § 547.

G. **Authority to file:** The former version of Article 9 required that the debtor sign the financing statement, but this requirement has been eliminated by the present version of Article 9. Instead, the person filing, usually the secured party, must have authority to file given by the debtor. UCC §§ 9-509, 9-510(a). If the debtor signs a security agreement, its signature constitutes authority to file a financing statement, but only as to the collateral that is described in the security agreement. UCC § 9-509(b). Thus, if the security agreement only creates a security interest in inventory, the secured party has no authority to file as to equipment.

If the debtor has not signed a security agreement, authority to file a financing statement must be given by the debtor in an authenticated record. For example, if a lender and borrower are negotiating a loan, they may be close to closing the transaction but the terms of the security agreement may not be final. To speed things up, the lender may wish to file a financing statement so that it can begin the process of determining whether its financing statement will be the first one filed. In this case, the lender would have to obtain authority from the debtor to file an authenticated record.

If a secured party files a financing statement without the authority to do so, it is liable for any loss resulting, including the debtor's inability to obtain other financing or to obtain other financing only at an increased cost. In addition, the secured party is liable for statutory damages in the amount of $500. UCC § 9-625(e).

H. **Duration of filing, continuation statements, and termination statements**

1. **Lapse after five years:** Financing statements do not last forever. They must be refiled or extended every five years, assuming the loan in question is still outstanding. A financing statement that has not been refiled or extended will lapse five years after it is filed. UCC § 9-515(a). The financing statement that one files to extend the security interest is called a "continuation statement." UCC § 9-515(d). Somewhat oddly, a continuation statement is effective only if it is filed within the 6-month period prior to the lapse. This means the continuation statement (which must refer to the prior financing statement in order to be effective) must be filed between 4 1/2 and 5 years after the filing of the original financing statement. It understandably cannot be filed after this time, but somewhat inexplicably also cannot be filed before this time. See UCC § 9-515(d).

   A note about satisfaction: If the loan is satisfied before five years runs, the secured party is required to file a termination of the financing statement. This terminates the financing statement and makes it ineffective. See below.

   Both continuation and termination are accomplished by filing a UCC-2 Financing Statement (as opposed to a UCC-1, which is an initial filing). Section 9-521 contains the uniform UCC-2 form, which is also reproduced below.

   Thus, a financing statement remains of record and effective for five years[5] after it is filed unless it is extended by a continuation statement or earlier terminated by a termination

---

5. A financing statement is effective for 30 years if the collateral is a manufactured home or is filed in connection with a public-finance transaction. UCC § 9-515(b).

statement. UCC § 9-515(a). As to most other parties, e.g., other secured parties, lienholders, the trustee in bankruptcy, the security interest is treated as being perfected during the five-year period, but not thereafter unless a continuation statement is filed. However, if a continuation statement is not filed, as to purchasers for value of the collateral, it is deemed never to have been perfected. UCC § 9-515(c).

Example 25: Susan takes a security interest in machinery that Daniel uses in his factory, and files a financing statement on June 1, 2001. She does not properly file a continuation statement, and the filing becomes ineffective (through lapse) on June 1, 2006. The filing is ineffective as to Sally who took a security interest in the equipment on March 1, 2006, and also as to Paul, who purchased the machinery on May 1, 2006. They both take free of the security interest.

The five-year period runs from the date of filing, not the date of attachment. Hence, if a filing statement is filed on February 1, but the loan is not finalized until March 1, the filing would terminate five years after February 1.

2. **More on continuation statements:** As briefly stated previously, the life of a financing statement may be extended beyond the five-year period by the filing of a continuation statement, but there is a short window of time during which a continuation statement can be filed. UCC § 9-515. The statement must be filed no earlier than six months before the expiration date and no later than the expiration date of the original financing statement. UCC § 9-515(d). Only during that six-month period is extension possible: A continuation statement filed either before the period begins to run or after the original financing statement has expired is of no effect. UCC § 9-510(c). Once a security interest has lapsed, the only action the secured party can take is to file a new financing statement, and the new financing statement will have the date of *its* filing, not a date reverting back to the original filing that has lapsed.

3. **More on termination statements:** As discussed briefly above, once a debtor has paid off an obligation secured by the security interest, the security interest terminates and the debtor is entitled to have this termination reflected in the filing system. The document that is filed is called a termination statement. UCC § 9-513. If the collateral is consumer goods, the secured party has an obligation to file the termination statement without any demand by the debtor. UCC § 9-513(a). The termination statement must be filed within 30 days of the time that the obligation is extinguished, but the time is shortened to 20 days from the time of demand if the consumer debtor demands that it be filed.

Example 26: Bank takes a security interest in Debtor's home entertainment system. The obligation is paid on March 1. The Bank has until March 31 to file a termination statement but if Debtor makes a demand on March 2 that a termination statement be filed, the Bank must file it by March 23.

If the collateral is something other than consumer goods, the debtor must make a demand for a termination statement by an authenticated record. Otherwise, no termination statement will be filed. The secured party must supply the statement within 20 days of the demand. It is up to the debtor to file it.

The debtor is not entitled to a termination statement if the secured party has a continuing obligation to make future advances to the debtor, even if there is no present debt due. Thus, if the security agreement contains a future advances clause, the secured party is entitled to the debtor's agreement that the future advances clause is no longer binding before supplying a termination statement.

The rights of a debtor to obtain a termination statement apply even though the security interest is perfected by filing under a certificate of title statute, unless the certificate of title statute provides an alternate method of terminating the filing. Official Comment 1 to UCC § 9-513.

If the secured party fails to file the satisfaction despite being requested by the debtor to do so, and the debtor is injured by the failure to satisfy, the debtor can recover actual damages as well as a civil penalty of $500. See UCC § 9-625(b), (e)(4).

Terminating, continuing, or amending a financing statement is accomplished by filing a UCC Financing Statement Amendment, which is reproduced on the next page as Figure 5-2.

IV. PERFECTION BY SECURED PARTY TAKING POSSESSION OF THE COLLATERAL

A. **Introduction:** Before the development of filing systems that operate to give constructive notice of security interests, the only way in which a secured party could obtain rights against third parties, i.e., other secured parties, purchasers of the collateral from the debtor, and lien creditors, was to take possession of the collateral. Called a "pledge," this method of "perfection" greatly limited the availability of secured credit because frequently the purpose of a secured transaction was to allow the debtor to retain possession of assets it needed to run its business. For example, if the debtor is financing its equipment, it needs the equipment to run its business and to make money to repay the loan.

The rationale for allowing the debtor to perfect by taking possession of the collateral is that one thinking of lending to a debtor should be able to view its collateral before lending. Moreover, such a lender should be suspicious if the person with whom he or she is dealing does not have possession.

As we will see, sometimes when the secured party has the choice of perfecting by filing or by taking possession, perfection by taking possession provides better protection. In other cases, it is more convenient and is the normal method of doing business, such as when someone borrows money from a pawnbroker.

Perfection by possession also has the advantage of allowing the secured party to protect the collateral—to ensure that it will not be damaged by the debtor—and it also may make enforcement of the security interest easier because the secured party has possession and does not have to repossess the collateral if the debtor defaults. Finally, when the collateral is cash, possession is the only method of perfecting.

B. **Types of collateral subject to perfection by possession:** Although filing is the most common method of perfection under Article 9, the Article allows perfection by possession for many types of collateral. Under UCC § 9-313, perfection by possession is allowed when the collateral is any of the following:

1. goods;
2. instruments;
3. tangible negotiable documents of title;
4. money;
5. tangible chattel paper; or
6. certificated securities.

Figure 5-2
UCC Financing Statement Amendment

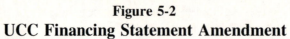

UCC FINANCING STATEMENT AMENDMENT
FOLLOW INSTRUCTIONS (front and back) CAREFULLY

A. NAME & PHONE OF CONTACT AT FILER [optional]

B. SEND ACKNOWLEDGMENT TO: (Name and Address)

⌐   ¬

∟   ⌟

THE ABOVE SPACE IS FOR FILING OFFICE USE ONLY

1a. INITIAL FINANCING STATEMENT FILE #	1b. ☐ This FINANCING STATEMENT AMENDMENT is to be filed [for record] (or recorded) in the REAL ESTATE RECORDS.

2. ☐ **TERMINATION:** Effectiveness of the Financing Statement identified above is terminated with respect to security interest(s) of the Secured Party authorizing this Termination Statement.

3. ☐ **CONTINUATION:** Effectiveness of the Financing Statement identified above with respect to security interest(s) of the Secured Party authorizing this Continuation Statement is continued for the additional period provided by applicable law.

4. ☐ **ASSIGNMENT** (full or partial): Give name of assignee in item 7a or 7b and address of assignee in item 7c; and also give name of assignor in item 9.

5. **AMENDMENT (PARTY INFORMATION):** This Amendment affects ☐ Debtor or ☐ Secured Party of record. Check only one of these two boxes.

Also check one of the following three boxes and provide appropriate information in items 6 and/or 7.

☐ CHANGE name and/or address: Give current record name in item 6a or 6b; also give new name (if name change) in item 7a or 7b and/or new address (if address change) in item 7c.   ☐ DELETE name: Give record name to be deleted in item 6a or 6b.   ☐ ADD name: Complete item 7a or 7b, and also item 7c; also complete items 7d-7g (if applicable).

6. CURRENT RECORD INFORMATION:

6a. ORGANIZATION'S NAME			
OR 6b. INDIVIDUAL'S LAST NAME	FIRST NAME	MIDDLE NAME	SUFFIX

7. CHANGED (NEW) OR ADDED INFORMATION:

7a. ORGANIZATION'S NAME			
OR 7b. INDIVIDUAL'S LAST NAME	FIRST NAME	MIDDLE NAME	SUFFIX
7c. MAILING ADDRESS	CITY	STATE POSTAL CODE	COUNTRY

7d. TAX ID #: SSN OR EIN	ADD'L INFO RE ORGANIZATION DEBTOR	7e. TYPE OF ORGANIZATION	7f. JURISDICTION OF ORGANIZATION	7g. ORGANIZATIONAL ID #, if any ☐ NONE

8. **AMENDMENT (COLLATERAL CHANGE):** check only one box.

Describe collateral ☐ deleted or ☐ added, or give entire ☐ restated collateral description, or describe collateral ☐ assigned.

9. NAME OF **SECURED PARTY** OF RECORD AUTHORIZING THIS AMENDMENT (name of assignor, if this is an Assignment). If this is an Amendment authorized by a Debtor which adds collateral or adds the authorizing Debtor, or if this is a Termination authorized by a Debtor, check here ☐ and enter name of DEBTOR authorizing this Amendment.

9a. ORGANIZATION'S NAME			
OR 9b. INDIVIDUAL'S LAST NAME	FIRST NAME	MIDDLE NAME	SUFFIX

10. OPTIONAL FILER REFERENCE DATA

FILING OFFICE COPY — NATIONAL UCC FINANCING STATEMENT AMENDMENT (FORM UCC3) (REV. 07/29/98)

Instructions for National UCC Financing Statement AMENDMENT (Form UCC3)

Please type or laser-print this form. Be sure it is completely legible. Read all Instructions, especially Instruction 1a; correct file number of initial financing statement is crucial. Follow Instructions completely.

Fill in form very carefully; mistakes may have important legal consequences. If you have questions, consult your attorney. Filing office cannot give legal advice.

Do not insert anything in the open space in the upper portion of this form; it is reserved for filing office use.

An Amendment may relate to only one financing statement. Do not enter more than one file number in item 1a.

When properly completed, send Filing Office Copy, with required fee, to filing office. If you want an acknowledgment, complete item B and, if filing in a filing office that returns an acknowledgment copy furnished by filer, you may also send Acknowledgment Copy, otherwise detach. Always detach Debtor and Secured Party Copies.

If you need to use attachments, use 8-1/2 X 11 inch sheets and put at the top of each sheet: "AMENDMENT" and the file number of the initial financing statement to which this Amendment relates; you are encouraged to use Amendment Addendum (Form UCC3Ad).

Always complete items 1a and 9.

A. To assist filing offices that might wish to communicate with filer, filer may provide information in item A. This item is optional.

B. Complete item B if you want an acknowledgment sent to you. If filing in a filing office that returns an acknowledgment copy furnished by filer, present simultaneously with this form a carbon or other copy of this form for use as an acknowledgment copy.

1a. **File number:** Enter file number of initial financing statement to which this Amendment relates. Enter only one file number. In some states, the file number is not unique; in those states, also enter in item 1a, after the file number, the date that the initial financing statement was filed.

1b. Only if this Amendment is to be filed or recorded in the real estate records, check box 1b and also, in item 13 of Amendment Addendum, enter Debtor's name, in proper format exactly identical to the format of item 1 of financing statement, and name of record owner if Debtor does not have a record interest.

Note: Show purpose of this Amendment by checking box 2, 3, 4, 5 (in item 5 you must check two boxes) or 8; also complete items 6, 7 and/or 8 as appropriate. Filer may use this Amendment form to simultaneously accomplish both data changes (items 4, 5, and/or 8) and a Continuation (item 3), although in some states filer may have to pay a separate fee for each purpose.

2. To terminate the effectiveness of the identified financing statement with respect to security interest(s) of authorizing Secured Party, check box 2. See Instruction 9 below.

3. To continue the effectiveness of the identified financing statement with respect to security interest(s) of authorizing Secured Party, check box 3. See Instruction 9 below.

4. To assign (i) all of assignor's interest under the identified financing statement, or (ii) a partial interest in the security interest covered by the identified financing statement, or (iii) assignor's full interest in some (but not all) of the collateral covered by the identified financing statement: Check box in item 4 and enter name of assignee in item 7a if assignee is an organization, or in item 7b, formatted as indicated, if assignee is an individual. Complete 7a or 7b, but not both. Also enter assignee's address in item 7c. Also enter name of assignor in item 9. If partial Assignment affects only some (but not all) of the collateral covered by the identified financing statement, filer may check appropriate box in item 8 and indicate affected collateral in item 8.

5,6,7. To change the name and/or address of a party: Check box in item 5 to indicate whether this Amendment amends information relating to a Debtor or a Secured Party; also check box in item 5 to indicate that this is a name and/or address change; also enter name of affected party (current record name, in case of name change) in items 6a or 6b as appropriate; and also give new name (7a or 7b) and/or new address (7c) in item 7.

5,6. To delete a party: Check box in item 5 to indicate whether deleting a Debtor or a Secured Party; also check box in item 5 to indicate that this is a deletion of a party; and also enter name (6a or 6b) of deleted party in item 6.

5,7. To add a party: Check box in item 5 to indicate whether adding a Debtor or Secured Party; also check box in item 5 to indicate that this is an addition of a party; also enter all required information in item 7: name (7a or 7b) and address (7c); also, if adding a Debtor, tax ID # (7d) in those states where required, and additional organization Debtor information (7e-g) if added Debtor is an organization. Note: The preferred method for filing against a new Debtor (an individual or organization not previously of record as a Debtor under this file number) is to file a new Financing Statement (UCC1) and not an Amendment (UCC3).

8. Collateral change. To change the collateral covered by the identified financing statement, describe the change in item 8. This may be accomplished either by describing the collateral to be added or deleted, or by setting forth in full the collateral description as it is to be effective after the filing of this Amendment, indicating clearly the method chosen (check the appropriate box). If the space in item 8 is insufficient, use item 13 of Amendment Addendum (Form UCC3Ad). A partial release of collateral is a deletion. If, due to a full release of all collateral, filer no longer claims a security interest under the identified financing statement, check box 2 (Termination) and not box 8 (Collateral Change). If a partial assignment consists of the assignment of some (but not all) of the collateral covered by the identified financing statement, filer may indicate the assigned collateral in item 8, check the appropriate box in item 8, and also comply with instruction 4 above.

9. Always enter name of party of record authorizing this Amendment; in most cases, this will be a Secured Party of record. If more than one authorizing Secured Party, give additional name(s), properly formatted, in item 13 of Amendment Addendum (Form UCC3Ad). If the indicated financing statement refers to the parties as lessee and lessor, or consignee and consignor, or seller and buyer, instead of Debtor and Secured Party, references in this Amendment shall be deemed likewise so to refer to the parties. If this is an assignment, enter assignor's name. If this is an Amendment authorized by a Debtor that adds collateral or adds a Debtor, or if this is a Termination authorized by a Debtor, check the box in item 9 and enter the name, properly formatted, of the Debtor authorizing this Amendment, and, if this Amendment or Termination is to be filed or recorded in the real estate records, also enter, in item 13 of Amendment Addendum, name of Secured Party of record.

10. This item is optional and is for filer's use only. For filer's convenience of reference, filer may enter in item 10 any identifying information (e.g., Secured Party's loan number, law firm file number, Debtor's name or other identification, state in which form is being filed, etc.) that filer may find useful.

Instructions for National UCC Financing Statement AMENDMENT Addendum (Form UCC3Ad)

11.   Enter information exactly as given in item 1a on Amendment form.

12.   Enter information exactly as given in item 9 on Amendment form.

13.   If space on Amendment form is insufficient or you must provide additional information, enter additional information in item 13.

As to other types of collateral, there is nothing to possess that would give the "possessor" dominion over the collateral. Consider accounts. Although accounts usually will be represented by a writing that can be possessed, possession of the writing does not constitute legal right to the account; it is possession only of evidence of the account. Thus, generally, a security interest in intangibles cannot be perfected by possession.

Some intangibles, however, are so integrated into a writing that possession of the writing is tantamount to possession of the intangible. Consider negotiable notes, which are governed primarily by Article 3 of the UCC, but which are defined as instruments under Article 9. Security interests in them can be perfected by filing (UCC § 9-310), but they can also be perfected by possession. UCC § 9-313. Indeed, perfection by possession provides better protection to the secured party with instruments.

Under Article 9, a note can be enforced only by the "holder"[6] of the note; to be a holder, one must be in possession of the note. Thus, if the secured party has possession of the note, no one else can enforce it and possession of it constitutes perfection. See *Coral Petroleum, Inc. v. Banque Paribus (In re Coral Petroleum, Inc.)*, 50 B.R. 830 (S.D. Tex. 1985). Thus, perfection by possession of an instrument, and of chattel paper as well, provides better protection.

Example 27: Andy's appliance store sells mainly to contractors, usually on credit. Andy takes back a security interest in the goods sold along with a negotiable note in the amount that Buyer owes for the goods. Andy then borrows money from Bank I and gives Bank I a security interest in the obligations of Buyer to Andy's. This is, of course, chattel paper.

Bank I can perfect its security interest in the chattel paper by filing or by taking possession of it. If Bank I perfects by filing and allows Andy to keep possession of the chattel paper, Andy can sell it to Bank II or to someone else. If Andy sells the chattel paper to Bank II, and if Bank II gives new value, takes possession of the paper, in good faith and in the ordinary course of business and without knowledge of Bank I's security interest, Bank II takes free of Bank I's security interest. See UCC §§ 9-330(b), 9-331.

If, however Bank I perfects by taking possession of the chattel paper, no one else can have possession of it and no one else can take over Bank I.

The same is true of tangible (paper) negotiable documents of title. If the owner of goods stores the goods with a warehouse, the warehouse will issue a "warehouse receipt." If the owner of goods ships the goods by a common carrier, the carrier will issue a "bill of lading." Both are documents of title under Article 9. UCC § 1-201(b)(16) [2001 version].

Warehouse receipts and bills of lading can be either negotiable or nonnegotiable. UCC § 7-104. Warehouse receipts and bills of lading contain the contract between the owner and the warehouse or carrier, and they are also representative of the goods. If they are negotiable, they are, in a sense, more representative because the warehouse or carrier will require that the piece of paper, the warehouse receipt or bill of lading, be surrendered before the warehouse or carrier will give the goods to whomever claims them. Thus, transfer of the piece of paper is tantamount to transfer of the goods themselves; possession of the piece of paper gives the possessor dominion over the goods, and perfection can be obtained by taking possession of the bill of lading or warehouse receipt. Again, although the secured party has a choice of perfection by filing as to the goods, or filing as to the documents of

---

6. There are very narrow exceptions to this proposition. For example, if the note is destroyed it can be enforced by one who is the owner of the right.

title, the best way to perfect for these assets is to take possession of the negotiable ware-house receipt (a document of title).

Nonnegotiable documents of title, however, cannot be perfected by possession as the piece of paper is nothing more than evidence of the owner's rights. The document need not be surrendered when possession of the goods is demanded. In effect, the piece of paper isn't very important. Under UCC § 9-312(d), a security interest in the goods bailed to the carrier or warehouse under a nonnegotiable document can be perfected only by the following:

1. Filing as to the goods;
2. Having the bailee issue a new document of title in the name of the secured party; or
3. Receipt of notice by the bailee of the secured party's security interest.

Although motor vehicle and other certificates of title are the best *evidence* of title, and possession of them is generally important in the transfer of title, neither possession of the vehicle nor possession of the certificate of title constitutes perfection of a security interest in the vehicle unless the applicable certificate of title law permits it. Usually, the only way to perfect a security interest in a vehicle is to have the department or registry of motor vehicles note or list the security interest on the certificate of title. For the most part, title loans are not perfected and, thus, any security interests created in favor of title lenders by people who file for bankruptcy can be avoided in bankruptcy.

C. **What constitutes possession:** The UCC does not define what is meant by possession; rather it is left to non-Code law. (Your first-year course in property will be of use here!) In most cases in which perfection occurs by possession, of course, the secured party has physical possession, has exclusive dominion and control over the property, and can exclude others from using the property. For example, when a watch is pawned, the pawnbroker will put it in a safe, and when a certificated security is given to a bank, the bank will put it in a vault.

Possession by an agent of the secured party is sufficient so long as the agent is holding the collateral solely as agent of the secured party. Official Comment 3 to UCC § 9-313. In one case, a court held that the debtor's lawyer was the secured party's agent because of a specific agreement by the attorney to answer to the secured party. *In re Rolain*, 823 F.2d 198 (8th Cir. 1987). However, if the goods are given to an escrow agent with instructions to return them to either the secured party or the debtor, depending on the happening of some event, the secured party would not have possession because the escrow agent has obligations running to both the debtor and the secured party. Official Comment 3 to UCC § 9-313.

"Field warehousing" is a method of collateralizing loans secured by inventory. Used primarily to obtain better control over the collateral, the secured party sets up a "warehouse" near the debtor, perhaps on the same premises where the debtor operates its business, and the inventory is kept in that warehouse. Sometimes the so-called warehouse is just an area of the debtor's premises that is cordoned off in some way from the rest of the premises. As long as the secured party has control over when the inventory is released to the debtor, the secured party has possession of it. This also may be accomplished by having an employee or agent of the secured party operate the warehouse. Of course, the cautious secured party will also perfect by filing, because you can imagine that this "warehousing" could have its limitations in real life.

D. **Possession as substitute for security agreement—Necessity of attachment:** Remember from Chapter 3 that no *written* security agreement is necessary when the secured party takes possession of the collateral. Hence, possession has a twofold use: (1) it substitutes for the writing usually required to create a security interest, and (2) it may operate to perfect the security interest.

Keep in mind, however, that *attachment* occurs only when the debtor has rights in the collateral, has granted a security interest in the collateral, and the secured party has given value.

And, as you might recall, attachment is necessary for perfection. Thus, even though a creditor has possession of the goods belonging to its debtor, the secured party may not have a perfected security interest in the property.

Example 28: David owes Susan $1,000. While they are having dinner together at the restaurant, David asks Susan to take his diamond cuff links and put them in a safe located in her house. Susan takes possession of the cuff links. Even though Susan is owed money by David, she does not have a security interest in the cuff links because David never granted her one, either orally or in writing. Because she does not have a security interest, there can be no perfection.

Example 29: Building on the same facts, assume that a few days later, Susan asks David to pay her the $1,000 he owes her and he does not have the money. She says that he can have an extra week, but only if he gives her a security interest in the cuff links. If he agrees, even orally, she has a security interest in them even though there is no writing, and the security interest is perfected.

V. AUTOMATIC PERFECTION

Article 9 provides that perfection occurs automatically as soon as the security interest attaches in a few very narrow situations. UCC § 9-309. In other words, the secured party need do nothing to perfect its security interest; it need not file nor take possession of the collateral.

The most important situation in which perfection is automatic is when the collateral is consumer goods and the security interest is a PMSI. UCC § 9-309(1).

The purpose is to avoid cluttering the filing records with numerous filings and to make the sale of consumer goods less complicated. The rule applies most often to sales by a retailer to a consumer when the seller takes back a security interest to secure payments in installments on the purchased goods. One example is where a department store or appliance store sells a refrigerator on time and takes back a security interest in the refrigerator to secure payment.

Consumer goods can, however, be quite valuable. For example, a boat worth over $30,000 has been held to be consumer goods, giving rise to automatic perfection when the secured party held a PMSI in it. *Gallatin National Bank v. Lockovich (In re Lockovich)*, 124 B.R. 660 (W.D. Pa. 1991).

Note: It is important to remember that both of these requirements must be present. For example, a PMSI in equipment is not automatically perfected, and a non-PMSI in consumer goods is not automatically perfected. The provision does not apply when the security interest is in a motor vehicle or other property covered by a certificate of title statute.

Even though a PMSI in consumer goods is automatically perfected, the secured party can file. By filing, the secured party obtains greater perfection. As will be discussed in Chapter 6, if the secured party relies on its automatic perfection and does not file, a casual buyer takes free of the security interest. UCC § 9-320(b). However, if the secured party *does* file, a casual buyer takes subject to the security interest, so defeating the casual buyer is the main reason to do a filing. It probably makes sense to do one only if the collateral is very valuable, like the boat referred to earlier.

Sales of promissory notes, a subclass of instruments, are secured transactions. They are perfected automatically, UCC § 9-309(4), but again, buyers of a promissory note in the ordinary course take free of the security interest. By also perfecting by taking possession, the secured party can protect itself from holders in due course because, as noted previously, no one will be able to become a holder in due course if the secured party is in possession of the collateral.

Security interests in an account created by an assignment of the account are automatically perfected, if the assignment "does not by itself or in conjunction with other assignments to the same assignee, transfer a significant part of the assignor's account." UCC § 9-309(2).

A Final Note of Caution: Students notoriously believe that automatic perfection is common when in fact it is rare indeed, especially in large transactions.

VI. PERFECTION BY TAKING CONTROL

The word "control" is often used in the context of describing whether someone has possession of property. Generally, possession requires that the person have dominion and control over the property. Control, as used in Article 9 as a means of perfection, is a technical term and means something completely different. Under UCC § 9-314, perfection by control is possible only when the collateral is any of the following:

1. investment property;
2. deposit accounts;
3. letter-of-credit rights;
4. electronic chattel paper; or
5. electronic documents.

As to deposit accounts and letter-of-credit rights, control is the *only* way in which perfection can be accomplished.

How a secured party obtains control depends on the type of collateral. UCC §§ 9-104, 9-105, 9-106, 9-107. The secured party need not necessarily have exclusive control. For example, if the collateral is a deposit account, an agreement with the bank giving both the secured party and the debtor access to the account constitutes sufficient control. UCC § 9-104.

VII. CONTINUOUS PERFECTION

If a financing statement is filed after the security interest has attached, perfection remains continuous from the time of filing, which is the moment when the financing statement is given to the clerk, until the filing terminates either by the passage of time (five years if no continuation statement is filed), or by the filing of a termination statement.

When perfection is by possession, questions may arise regarding whether the perfection is continuous from the time that the secured party obtains possession. If the secured party returns the property to the debtor, perfection will cease, and, if the secured party subsequently gives possession back to the secured party, the date of perfection becomes the time that the property was returned.

When there is a change in the method of perfection, e.g., the secured party takes possession and some time later files a financing statement, the perfection is continuous so long as there is no time during which there was no perfection by one or the other method. UCC § 9-308(c).

Example 30: Susan has possession of David's watch, in which she has a security interest. On Saturday, she returns the watch to David because he has to time a cross-country race. On Monday, he returns the watch to her. Her perfection relates back only to Monday.

Example 31: Sally has possession of David's diamond ring, in which she has a security interest. On Monday she files a financing statement, and on Tuesday she gives possession of the ring to David. Her perfection is continuous and it dates back to the time that she originally took possession of the ring.

Example 32: Sally has possession of David's diamond ring, in which she has a security interest. On Monday, she gives possession of the ring to David. On Wednesday she files a financing statement. Her perfection dates back only to Wednesday, and her security interest will be subordinate to (lower than) one that arose on Tuesday.

VIII. PERFECTION OF SECURITY INTERESTS IN PROCEEDS

As discussed in Chapter 4, a secured party automatically obtains a security interest in identifiable proceeds. UCC § 9-315(a)(2). The security interest in the proceeds is perfected automatically for 20 days. UCC § 9-315(c) and (d). If the proceeds are cash proceeds, the perfection continues automatically after the 20 days. UCC § 9-315(d)(2). Perfection in the security interest in proceeds also continues if the secured party perfects the security interest in the proceeds by taking possession or by filing within the 20-day period. UCC § 9-315(d)(3).

Perfection in proceeds is discussed in a slightly different context in Section III.E of this chapter. We repeat part of that conversation here. There is a third way in which the perfection is continued beyond the 20 days. This method is called the "same office rule." If (1) the security interest on the original collateral was perfected by filing, (2) the collateral that constitutes the proceeds could also be perfected by filing in the same office, and (3) the proceeds were not acquired with cash proceeds, then the perfection continues. UCC § 9-315(d)(1).

The third condition requires some explanation. It refers to a case involving "proceeds of proceeds." For example, assume that the secured party has a security interest in inventory, that some of the inventory is sold for cash, and that the debtor then takes the cash and buys a computer that it will use as equipment. The computer is proceeds and the secured party has a security interest in it. It is "proceeds acquired with cash proceeds" and subsection (3) of § 9-315 applies. The same office rule does not give the secured party perfection. As a result, the secured party would have to file as to the new collateral, the computer.

However, if the financing statement happened to include "equipment" as well as "accounts" in the description, the security interest in the computer would be perfected, not under the same office rule, but because the description already includes equipment.

Example 33: Bank has a security interest in all of Debtor's inventory, and the description in the financing statement is "inventory." Debtor sells inventory with the buyer obligated to pay for it in 60 days. The sale gives rise to an account which is proceeds. If Bank filed as to the original collateral, the inventory, Bank's security interest in the accounts remains perfected automatically and Bank need take no steps to continue the perfection in the accounts.

Example 34: Bank has a security interest in all of Debtor's inventory. Debtor sells inventory for cash. The cash is proceeds and the secured party has a perfected security interest in it so long as it is identifiable. If Debtor then uses the cash to purchase a machine (which would be equipment under Article 9), Bank has a security interest in the machine as proceeds of the cash proceeds, but in order to perfect it, Bank must file a financing statement describing the collateral as equipment, describing the machine specifically, or must take possession of it.

Example 35: Bank has a security interest in Debtor's copier, which Debtor is using as equipment. The financing statement describes the collateral as "One QuickPic copier Serial Number 132457." Debtor sells the copier for cash and uses the cash to purchase a "Truepic" copier. Bank has a security interest in the Truepic as proceeds of proceeds, but it is not perfected. The same office rule does not apply, and the description in the financing statement covers only the specific copier described.

Example 36: Bank has a security interest in all of Debtor's inventory, perfected by filing on January 15. On March 10, Debtor sells some of the inventory and the buyer promises to pay for it in 60 days. Bank's security interest in the resulting account is perfected under the same office rule and the date of filing of the security interest in the account dates back to January 15.

If the security interest in the proceeds continues under any of these rules, the date of filing is the date of filing as to the original collateral.

IX. PERFECTION OF SECURITY INTERESTS IN FIXTURES

Chapter 2, *supra*, defines fixtures. Briefly, fixtures are goods that are so affixed to realty that they have characteristics of both personal and real property. UCC § 9-102(a)(41). Chapter 6, *infra*, discusses the priority rules that govern disputes when the collateral is fixtures. Although there can be disputes between two secured parties over who has the better rights in a fixture, as well as disputes between a secured party and a lien creditor or a trustee in bankruptcy, the more common disputes are between a secured party under Article 9 and someone who has an interest in the real property, such as a purchaser or a mortgagee.

A security interest can be perfected in fixtures by filing a regular UCC financing statement, as with other goods, but the perfection obtained by simply filing in the central office does not provide much protection. It is totally ineffective as to purchasers of the real property and mortgagees. To obtain protection against those who have an interest in the real property, the secured party must file a "fixture filing." Both the contents of the fixture filing and the location in which it is filed are different than filings as to other collateral.

Example 37: Secured Party I takes a security interest in an air conditioning unit that is to be installed in a house and will then become a fixture. Secured Party I files only an ordinary financing statement with the Secretary of State, and does not file otherwise. If Secured Party II subsequently takes a security interest in the same air conditioner, Secured Party I has priority even though Secured Party II files both an ordinary financing statement and a fixture filing. Secured Party I, however, has no rights as against a purchaser or mortgagee of the real property to which the air conditioner is affixed.

A "fixture filing" is a financing statement that contains additional information. In addition to the requirements of an ordinary financing statement, according to UCC § 9-502(b), a fixture filing statement must:

1. state that the goods are fixtures;
2. state that the financing statement is to be filed in the real property recording system;

3. contain a description of the real property to which the fixture is or will be affixed; and
4. include the name of the record owner of the real property if the debtor does not have an interest in the real property.

The description of the real property is sufficient if it complies with the requirements of the real property filing rules of the jurisdiction. Official Comment 5 to UCC § 9-502.

A fixture filing must comply with the real property recording rules of the jurisdiction. In most states, this means filing with the County Clerk or some other office in the county where the real property is located. The filing is done in the same place where one would record a mortgage or a deed, making it convenient for searchers interested in information about that piece of property. The priority rules between parties who have filed a fixture filing and persons with interest in the real property are covered in Chapter 6, *infra*.

Note: Students sometimes confuse proceeds with "after-acquired property." Remember that *proceeds* are property that the debtor obtains from selling the collateral in which the secured party has a security interest. *After-acquired property* is *new property* of the same type as the original collateral that is purchased subsequent to the time that the security interest is given. Remember that the rules for the perfection of each are quite different.

X. PERFECTION OF AGRICULTURAL LIENS

Agricultural liens can be perfected only by filing. UCC § 9-308(b). The perfection becomes effective when the financing statement has been filed and the lien has become attached under the state law creating it.

XI. ASSIGNMENT OF SECURITY INTERESTS

If a perfected security interest is assigned by the secured party, no new filing is required to continue the perfection. UCC § 9-310(c).

Quiz Yourself on *PERFECTION OF SECURITY INTERESTS*

56. The four methods of perfecting a security interest are

a. _____

b. _____

c. _____

d. _____

57. You cannot perfect by filing if the collateral is (1) _____, (2) _____, or (3) _____.

58. To determine the correct office in which to perfect a security interest you must first _____, and then you must _____.

59. When the debtor is a corporation, limited liability company, or limited partnership, the proper state in which to file is _____.

60. When a security interest is taken in property used by the ABC Company, which is a sole proprietorship doing business in Fargo, ND, in what state should the financing statement be filed if the owner of the business lives in Moorhead, MN? _____

61. ABC Corporation is registered in Delaware, but operates its only store in Philadelphia. If it owns a truck that is registered in Pennsylvania, a security interest in the truck must be perfected in _____.

62. XYZ Corporation is registered in Iowa. It gives a security interest in a furnace located in its Nebraska factory. If the furnace is a fixture, a security interest in the furnace must be filed in _____.

63. If a creditor takes a security interest in a debtor's crops, the financing statement should be filed in _____.

64. To be *sufficient*, a financing statement must contain the following information: (1) _____, (2) _____, and (3) _____.

65. If the collateral is timber to be cut, as-extracted minerals, or is a fixture filing, the financing statement must also contain the following information: (1) _____, (2) _____, (3) _____, and (4) _____.

66. Even if a financing statement is sufficient, a filing officer can, and is supposed to, refuse to accept it for filing if it lacks any of the following information: (1) _____, (2) _____, (3) _____, or (4) _____.

67. If a financing clerk accepts for filing a financing statement that is sufficient but does not have the secured party's address, the security interest is perfected.
True _____ False _____

68. If a financing statement that contains all of the information is given to a filing officer with the required fee, and the filing officer refuses to file it, or files it and loses it before entering it into the records, the filing is effective. True _____ False _____

69. John Black operates "John's Shoe Store" as a sole proprietorship. The correct name to be placed on a financing statement representing a security interest in the store's inventory is _____.

70. A financing statement that describes the collateral as "all of the debtor's assets" contains an adequate description. True _____ False _____

71. A security agreement states that the security interest is in all of "debtor's presently owned and hereinafter acquired equipment." If the financing statement describes the collateral as "all of debtor's inventory," the filing is good as to both presently owned inventory and that which is after-acquired. True _____ False _____

72. The debtor's name is John Gallegos. A financing statement filed under the name "John Guyagos" is sufficient. True _____ False _____

73. Creditor takes a security interest in Debtor's red Honda Accord automobile with the following vehicle identification number (VIN): 1A2B3C4D5E. Creditor files a financing statement with the Secretary of State with the description "One red Honda Accord automobile, VIN 1B2A3C4D5E." Creditor's security interest is perfected. True _____ False _____

74. If a security interest is perfected by filing and the debtor's location changes to a different state, to continue perfection the secured party must _____.

75. If a debtor changes its name, the secured party should _____

76. Danny operates a retail shoe store in Minnesota under the name "Danny's Happy Feet." He gives a security interest in all of his present and hereinafter inventory to Susan, who perfects by filing. On May 1, Danny incorporates in Minnesota under the name "Danny's Happy Feet, Inc." If Susan does nothing, she has a perfected security interest in inventory purchased by Danny before _____ and during the _____ months after May 1.

77. Bank has a perfected security interest in all of the inventory of Dick's retail television store. Dick takes one of the TVs he has for sale and puts it in his waiting room for the entertainment of his customers. To continue perfection of the security interest in that TV, Bank must _____.

78. On October 1, 2000, Bank filed a financing statement on all of Dave's inventory. On February 1, 2006, Bank filed a continuation statement because it was still lending Dave money. Bank's security interest will be perfected in the collateral until _____.

79. Bank takes a security interest in a promissory note payable to Dan. To perfect its security interest, Bank should _____.

80. Sally's Appliance store sells a TV to Dilbert on time. Sally takes back a security interest in the TV to secure payment. To perfect her security interest, Sally must _____.

81. On September 1, Sarah loans Dilbert $1,000 and takes a security interest in his diamond ring and takes possession of it. On October 1, she gives the ring back to Dilbert as he is going to his class reunion and wants to show it to his friends. On October 5, Sarah files a financing statement in the proper office, and on October 10, Dilbert gives the ring back to her. Sarah's perfection dates from _____.

82. Bank has a security interest in Dave's entire inventory of appliances. It filed a financing statement on July 1. On September 1, Dave sold ten refrigerators to Contractor on credit, taking back a security interest in the refrigerators. Bank has a perfected security interest in the obligation of Contractor to pay and in the security interest that Contractor gave Dave, and Bank's security interest is perfected as of _____.

83. Bank has a security interest in Dan's egg washing machine, which is perfected by filing. The financing statement describes the collateral as "one egg washing machine Serial number 56678." Dan sells the machine for cash and purchases a new egg washer with the proceeds of the sale. Bank has a security interest in the new egg washer, which is perfected.
True _____ False _____

84. Heating and Air Conditioning Company sells a furnace to Dick. The furnace is installed in a house in such a manner that it becomes a fixture. To perfect its security interest, Heating and Air Conditioning must _____.

Answers

56. a. Filing, b. possession, c. control, and d. automatic.

57. (1) Money, (2) deposit accounts, and (3) letter-of-credit rights.

58. Determine the correct state, and then you must determine the correct office within that state.

59. The state in which the organization is chartered.

60. The state of the owner's residence—Minnesota.

61. Pennsylvania. Security interests in motor vehicles must be perfected in the state in which the vehicle is registered.

62. Because the collateral is a fixture, the correct office is the office that has the filing records for the real property to which the fixture is attached, probably the Office of the County Clerk where the real property is located.

63. The office for central filing, usually the Secretary of State's office.

64. (1) Name of debtor, (2) name of secured party, and (3) indication of the collateral.

65. (1) Indication that the collateral is timber to be cut or as-extracted minerals, (2) indication that it is to be filed in the real estate records, (3) a description of the real property, and (4) the name of the owner of the real estate if the debtor does not have an interest in it.

66. (1) Address of secured party, (2) mailing address of the debtor, (3) an indication of whether the debtor is an individual or an organization, and (4) the organization's registration number if it has one, e.g., the registration number of a corporation.

67. True. Even though the filing officer was supposed to refuse to accept it, if the financing statement is accepted, the filing is valid.

68. True. Also, if the financing statement contains all of the information and the filing officer wrongfully refuses to file it, the attempted filing becomes valid as a filing.

69. John Black, because John's Shoe Store is not a corporation or other legally recognized entity.

70. True. Remember, that would not be sufficient in the security agreement but it is OK in the financing statement.

71. True. The financing statement need not refer to after-acquired property.

72. False. Almost any defect in the name of the debtor will invalidate the filing.

73. True. The filing would not be "seriously misleading" and would be valid.

74. File in the new state within four months. If the secured party files in the new state within the four-month period, the perfection dates back to the original filing in the old state. If it does not file within four months, it is as though there never was perfection as to purchasers of the collateral for value, which includes other buyers and other secured parties.

75. File an amendment to the financing statement stating the new name if the secured party has a security interest in hereinafter-acquired collateral. Note that the perfection remains valid as to any collateral that was obtained by the debtor before or within four months of the name change. It is only as to after-acquired collateral obtained after the four-month period that the amendment must be filed. The amendment must refer to the original financing statement.

76. May 1 and during the four months.

77. Do nothing. Although the collateral has changed from inventory to equipment, no new filing is required.

78. September 30, 2006. Because the continuing statement was filed more than six months prior to the expiration of the financing statement, it is ineffective, and the filing ends five years after the original filing.

79. Take possession of the note. There is automatic perfection as to the note, but the perfection does not protect the secured party as to holders in due course of the note. Therefore, the bank should take possession of the note to prevent anyone from becoming a holder in due course of it.

80. Do nothing to gain perfection because it is automatic. However, she should file if she wants protection against casual buyers because they take free of all unfilled secured interest. This will be revisited in Chapter 6, *infra*.

81. October 5. Because there was a gap in perfection—she gave back the ring before she filed—the perfection does not relate back to the time that she originally took possession.

82. July 1. The obligation to pay coupled with the security interest that Contractor gave Dave is chattel paper. It is proceeds of the original collateral, the inventory, and is perfected under the same office rule. The date of perfection reverts to the time of the filing as to the inventory.

83. False, unless it files as to the new egg washer. In this case, the original proceeds were cash. The cash was then converted into the new egg washer. Because the financing statement described only the old egg washer, there must be a new filing. Note that if the financing statement described the collateral as "equipment," the filing would be good as to the new egg washer, not under the same office rule, but because the new egg washer was equipment.

84. Heating and Air Conditioning Company should file a fixture filing to protect itself against subsequent purchasers of the real property and subsequent mortgagees. The fixture filing would have to include additional information and would have to be filed with the real estate record. Heating and Air Conditioning can file with the Secretary of State, and the filing would perfect its security interest, but the perfection would not be good as against those who have an interest in the real property.

Exam Tips on
PERFECTION OF SECURITY INTERESTS

☞ *The notice theme:* Remember that the theme of perfection is providing notice to subsequent third parties, namely searchers and lenders. The *filing system* and *possession* provide this notice constructively, because they do not actually give notice to anyone in particular. Instead they set up systems where people who understand the system know where to look for filings, or know enough to find out whether the collateral is in the debtor's possession before lending on it.

☞ *Automatic possession* and *possession by control* give constructive notice in an even more tangential way. If you know the rules, you know that consumer goods could have automatically perfected security interests on them and that bank accounts are subject to security interests by the depositary bank as well as others. To many people, these perfection methods do not fit well within the notice theme of Article 9.

☞ *The categories of perfection:* The first task in tackling perfection is to know the four basic ways to perfect: (1) filing, (2) possession, (3) control, and (4) automatically.

    ☞ *The best way to perfect for each asset:* Next you need to study your chart of the various ways to perfect each different type of Article 9 collateral, and learn which methods of perfection beat out other methods for the different types of collateral.

    ☞ *Perfection by possession:* Don't forget that possession can serve two purposes: perfection as well as a substitute for a written security agreement. Sometimes an exam question will involve a situation where a creditor clearly has possession of an asset, but there is no agreement (oral or written) to grant a security interest. In such a case, there can be no perfection because perfection requires attachment and without an oral agreement to grant a security interest, possession cannot substitute for a written security agreement.

☞ *Intangible assets:* Don't forget that you cannot perfect by possession of intangible assets. The biggie in this category is accounts, which can be perfected only by filing. Other assets for which one cannot perfect by possession include general intangibles, contract rights, and so on. Think of it this way: If you can't hold it or there is no piece of paper locking up the rights embodied in the assets, you cannot perfect the asset by possession. Understanding this may require a review of the different types of collateral to make sure you actually know what each one is. To do this, go back to Chapter 2.

☞ *The filing system*

    ☞ At times, approximately 40 percent of our exams test on the filing system. The rules are complex and there are many nuances on which to test.

    ☞ Remember that one cannot file for deposit accounts, letter-of-credit rights, or money, but one can file for everything else. This does not mean that filing is always the best way to perfect. One can file for negotiable promissory notes but it is better, for priority purposes, to possess negotiable promissory notes.

☛ **Where to file**

☞ One must first decide *in which office to file*. There are at least three places within each jurisdiction in which one could file: the Secretary of State's office, the Department of Motor Vehicles (or some other filing office for road-going collateral), and the real estate office, often called the County Recorder of Deeds. There is also federal filing for airplanes and copyrights.

☞ Remember that *motor vehicles* and *fixtures* get filed in offices other than the Secretary of State's office.

☞ Once one determines in which office to file, one must determine the *state or jurisdiction in which to file;* the proper state depends upon the debtor's location.

☞ If the debtor is an individual or a sole proprietorship, one must file where the debtor (or the owner) has his or her *principal residence*. Exam questions often have the debtor living in more than one place throughout the year, in which case the principal residence depends on where the debtor votes and pays taxes, etc.

☞ If the debtor is a *registered organization*, such as a corporation, a limited partnership, or a limited liability company, one must file in the state of *incorporation or registration.*

☞ The trickiest location situations involve *organizations that are not registered*, such as partnerships, unincorporated associations, business trusts, and governments and governmental subdivisions. For unincorporated or unregistered organizations, one must file where the company *does business* if it does business in only one jurisdiction or state. If it has more than one place of business, one must file where it has its *executive office.* Where an executive office is located depends upon where the major decisions are made. Oftentimes on exams, one needs to watch where the chief executive officer lives and/or conducts business. Sometimes, this person moves in the middle of an exam question. Just look for the place from which the organization pays its bills, has its bank accounts, and makes important decisions.

☛ **What information goes into a financing statement**

☞ Financing statements must contain the debtor's name, the name of the secured party, and an indication of the collateral. If a financing statement does not contain at least these three pieces of information, it is ineffective even if the filing office accepts it. It is as if it were never filed at all. It need not be signed by either the debtor or the secured party, but the secured party must have authority to sign it.

☞ The filing office can (and is supposed to) refuse to accept a financing statement that fails to include the following information as well: the secured party's address, the debtor's address, whether the debtor is an organization or an individual, and the organizational number for the debtor if it has one. If the officer takes the financing statement without these things, it is effective even though he or she was supposed to refuse it.

☛ **The debtor's name**

☞ Searches are done by the debtor's name, so it is important to get this right. If the debtor is an individual or sole proprietorship, one must file under the individual owner's exact correct legal name, not the name of the business. A secured party should ask for a birth certificate or other proof of the correct name.

☞ Registered organizations should be filed under the exact legal name of the organization. Unregistered organizations, including general partnerships, should be filed under the name of the business, or if there is none, the names of all of the members or partners.

☞ ***Indications of the collateral:*** The financing statement must indicate the collateral for the loan. One can use general categories of assets, describe the collateral specifically, or even say, if this is the case, ***all assets.*** This broad description would not suffice for a security agreement but works for a financing statement, which is filed only to give notice.

☞ *The effect of mistakes*

☞ Whether a financing statement is ***seriously misleading*** depends on ***whether the searcher can still find the financing statement*** and whether it is sufficient once found to put the searcher on notice of the prior loan.

☞ A financing statement is effective unless an error or omission in it makes the financing statement ***seriously misleading.*** Even ***small mistakes in the debtor's name*** will most likely invalidate the financing statement because they will make it difficult if not impossible for a searcher to find the financing statement.

☞ If there is a small mistake in the indication of the collateral, such as a mistake in a serial number, this usually will not invalidate the filing. Nor will mistakes in the address of the secured party or the debtor invalidate the filing in most cases.

☞ *Subsequent changes*

☞ Sometimes the ***debtor's name changes*** and, if so, the secured party must find out about the change and file a corrected financing statement within ***four months*** of the change to maintain its priority in collateral obtained by an after-acquired property clause subsequent to the four-month period.

☞ If the ***debtor's location changes***, the secured party need do nothing if the governing law does not change, e.g., an individual debtor moves from one city to another in the same state. However, if the governing law changes, e.g., an individual debtor moves to a city in another state or a sole proprietorship incorporates in a different state, the secured party must file within four months as to after-acquired property the debtor obtains after the four-month period.

☞ Sometimes the ***collateral*** itself is ***transformed*** into some category of collateral that the secured party has not listed on its financing statement. If this happens as a result of a mere change of use of the collateral, the secured party need not file a new financing statement unless the new one would be filed in a different office, e.g., as a fixture filing in the county recorder of deeds.

☞ If the debtor trades the collateral for collateral of a different category, again the secured party need not file a new financing statement unless the new asset, the proceeds, would be filed in a different office.

☞ If, however, the debtor sells collateral and receives cash proceeds and then uses the cash to buy a different category of collateral, then the secured party must file a new financing statement to reflect the change within 20 days of the change.

☞ *When to file a financing statement*

☞ Don't forget that a secured party can file its financing statement before lending any money. In fact, it must do so if it wants to make sure there are no prior security interests in the collateral.

☞ A financing statement lasts for five years, after which the financing statement must be continued if the loan is still outstanding and the secured party wants to continue being perfected. The secured party has only the six months before the time the security interest expires in which to file a continuation statement.

☛ *Perfection by control:* A secured party can perfect in some assets by control, namely deposit accounts, investment property, letters-of-credit rights, electronic chattel paper, and electronic documents. The only area likely to be tested on here is deposit accounts, which have become an important form of collateral.

☛ *Automatic perfection:* Perfection is automatic for ***PMSIs in consumer goods.*** Students forget that this is a narrow rule. The loan has to ***be a PMSI and also be in consumer goods***. Teachers often test on this by describing a loan that is a PMSI in equipment. Remember that one does not get automatic perfection for this loan, because collateral cannot be both equipment (a business asset) and consumer goods.

☛ *Continuous perfection:* If a party changes its mode of perfection, it must make sure that perfection is continuous. There can be no gap in perfection, or the secured party loses its place in the line. This is also a common testing area. Sometimes a secured party has possession and gives the collateral back to the debtor, later filing a financing statement.

☛ *Perfection in proceeds:* A security interest in properly perfected collateral, that becomes cash, remains perfected in the cash proceeds indefinitely. However, if those cash proceeds are used to buy something not described in the financing statement, then the secured party must refile in the new category or item within 20 days to remain perfected.

☛ *Amended financing statements:* All amendments, which include continuation statements and termination statements, and statements used to correct a previously filed financing statement, must reference the original financing statement in order to protect the secured party's position in the line.

CHAPTER 6

PRIORITIES

ChapterScope ━━━

This chapter examines problems when two or more parties, one of whom is a secured party, claims an interest in the same property—the collateral in which the secured party claims a security interest. The focus is on the types of priorities problems that may arise and on a systematic method for solving them. The key points in this chapter are as follows:

■ **The three most common types of priorities problems:** Article 9 governs three common priorities competitions, as well as a series of less common competitions. The three most common competitions are those between two or more secured parties, competitions between a secured party and a lien creditor, and competitions between a secured party and buyers or transferees from the debtor. The rules are different for each of these different types of competitions.

■ **Asking the four questions—Methodology for answering priorities problems:** It will help you immensely if you use a systematic method for tackling priorities problems. The one we have devised asks you to pose and answer four questions each time you see a priorities problem:

    1. Is the claimed security interest valid?
    2. What is the type of collateral?
    3. Is the security interest a purchase-money security interest (PMSI)?
    4. Is the security interest perfected, and, if so, when and how was it perfected?

Once you have gone through this analysis, you will be ready to apply the priorities rules of Article 9.

■ **Secured party versus secured party:** Priority goes to the first to file or perfect. A secured party can save the secured party's space by filing its financing statement before funding its loan, thus before attachment.

  ■ **PMSI:** If one party has a PMSI, then the PMSI usually beats a regular secured party regardless of the first to file or perfect rule. This is often an issue when the debtor has granted a security interest to a secured party in both present and after-acquired property and the debtor buys new inventory giving the seller a PMSI in the purchased collateral. Although the first creditor filed first, the PMSI still wins in the new property, as long as the requirements of timely filing and notice are met.

    There are more rules regarding inventory versus equipment loans, PMSIs in livestock, and conflicting security interests in proceeds.

  ■ **Perfected interests:** Perfected security interests beat unperfected security interests.

  ■ **Unperfected interests:** Between two unperfected security interests, the first to attach has priority.

■ **Secured party versus transferee:** Three types of buyers or transferees get special treatment in the Code, and thus can beat out a secured party's security interest in purchased goods.

  ■ **Purchasers for value without knowledge:** A buyer without actual knowledge of an existing security interest who gives value and takes delivery buys free of the security interest.

■ **Casual buyers:** A person who buys consumer goods from someone else who also held the goods as consumer goods takes security interests that are perfected automatically. They are not perfected by filing.

■ **Buyer in the ordinary course (BIOC) of business:** A buyer who buys goods in good faith, without knowledge that the sale violates the rights of a third party, and who buys from someone who is in the business of selling goods of that kind, takes free of all security interests created by the seller.

■ **Secured party versus lien creditor:** The general rule, although it has exceptions when the security interest is a PMSI, is that priority goes to the first to file or to become a lien creditor.

■ **Future advances and priorities:** The priorities rules change when it comes to future advances made by the lender after the original loan, lent either pursuant to a binding legal commitment to lend, or otherwise lent voluntarily.

■ **Secured party versus secured party:** The usual rule is still first to file or perfect, at least between secured parties. A secured party with a financing statement can continue to lend and beat out someone who made a later loan and filed a later financing statement.

■ **Secured party versus buyer or transferee:** A secured party can continue to lend without regard to whether the collateral has been sold to a third party for 45 days. In other words, during this period, the buyer takes the property subject to the prior security interest that covers the old advances as well as the future advances. After the 45 days, the buyer is not subject to the security interest for future advances.

■ **Secured party versus lien creditor:** If the secured party has no knowledge of the lien or has made its future advance pursuant to a commitment to lend, it can continue to lend to its heart's content and still retain its first position. On the other hand, if it has knowledge that a lien has been filed *and* is lending voluntarily and not pursuant to a prior obligation, the lienholder will jump the line as to the future advances, made 45 days after the lien becomes a lien (attaches).

■ **Priorities and fixtures:** The most common dispute regarding fixtures is between the secured party and the owner of the real estate to which the fixtures are now attached. The rule is that the first to file or record has priority.

I. AN INTRODUCTION TO PRIORITIES PROBLEMS

A. **What is a "priorities problem"?** Priorities problems under Article 9 involve situations in which a security interest has been created in certain personal property, the collateral, and someone other than the secured party also claims an interest in this property. The debtor may have sold the collateral to a third party. In that case, the question is whether the secured party can enforce its security interest against the third party by taking possession of the collateral on the debtor's default. Alternatively, the debtor may have given a second security interest to a third party, and the question might be who, as between the secured parties, will be satisfied first when the collateral is sold. Another possibility is that a third party may claim a lien on the collateral arising from execution on a judgment against the debtor or arising from a statute or the common law.

In all of these cases, the task is to determine who as between the parties has priority in the collateral. Solving these problems involves determining the status of the secured party, the status of the other claimant, and then applying the priorities rules found in Article 9.

The perfection of agricultural liens and the resulting priorities problems are also covered by Article 9. The rules for the perfection of agricultural liens and security interests are identical (see Chapter 4, *supra*), and except in a few instances, creditors holding agricultural liens are treated the same as persons holding Article 9 security interests for the purpose of determining priorities. When agricultural liens are treated differently from secured parties, the differences will be discussed in the text. Otherwise, when the term "secured party" is used, the rule also applies to agricultural liens.

B. The three types of priorities problems: Article 9 governs three basic types of priorities problems:

1. Disputes between the secured party or holders and persons to whom the collateral has been sold by the debtor;
2. Disputes arising when the debtor has given a security interest in the same collateral to two or more persons; and
3. Disputes in which a secured party and a creditor with a judicial, statutory, or common law lien (other than an agricultural lien) are contesting who has better rights in the collateral.

To help you keep this all straight, we'll treat each of these types of disputes separately. Try to learn one set of rules well before moving on.

In addition, special priorities rules apply to certain types of collateral. We'll discuss these rules after the discussion of the general priorities rules.

C. An approach to priorities problems: In analyzing priorities problems, the first step is to determine the status of the parties. At least one of the parties will be claiming a security interest under Article 9. The other party may also be a secured party, or might instead be a transferee of the collateral from the debtor, or a lien creditor.

Analyzing Priorities Problems

A. Each time you analyze a priorities problem, we suggest you answer four questions about the secured party, before applying the priorities rules.

1. Is the claimed security interest valid?
2. What is the type of collateral?
3. Is the security interest a purchase-money security interest (PMSI)?
4. Is the security interest perfected, and, if so, when and how was it perfected?

B. After asking these four questions, then apply the priorities rules.

---

1. **Validity of the security interest:** Chapter 4, *supra*, discusses in detail how to create a security interest. As you may recall, there are four requirements for creation of a security interest: (1) there must be an intent by the debtor that the creditor is to have a security

interest; (2) unless the secured party has possession, the agreement must be a record that is authenticated by the debtor; (3) the agreement must contain a description of the collateral; and (4) the agreement must contain language indicating that the purpose of the transaction is to create a security interest.

2. **Type of collateral:** In Chapter 2 we discussed the various types of collateral in detail. A significant distinction is made between tangible personal property (goods) and intangible personal property.

     a. **Tangible personal property:** Goods are subdivided into consumer goods, equipment, inventory, and farm products (including livestock and crops). Also to be considered separately in the context of priorities are a few tangible categories of collateral that are special kinds of goods, namely fixtures, accessions, and commingled goods.

     b. **Intangible personal property:** Intangible collateral includes accounts, chattel paper, commercial tort claims, deposit accounts, electronic chattel paper, general intangibles, health-care insurance receivables, instruments, letter-of-credit rights, payment intangibles, software, and tangible chattel paper. Although this is a formidable list, some of these types of collateral are relatively esoteric, and for the purpose of applying the priorities rules, many of the classes can be treated together.

3. **Purchase-money security interests (PMSIs):** A PMSI is one in which the credit was extended to allow the debtor to obtain the collateral. When the debtor is buying goods and is to pay for them in the future, perhaps in installments, and gives back to the seller a security interest in the goods, the seller-secured party has a PMSI. Also, if a third party extends credit to allow the debtor to obtain the goods in which a security interest is granted to the creditor, the creditor has a PMSI.

4. **Perfection:** Chapter 5 covers the perfection of a security interest. Perfection usually occurs as a result of filing a financing statement, but may be accomplished by the creditor taking possession of the collateral, if the collateral is of a certain type. Also, in a few cases, perfection occurs automatically. In still other types of cases, perfection occurs by the creditor taking "control" of the collateral.

     a. **Time of perfection:** The time that perfection occurs is often critical in determining priorities problems. However, as will be seen by subsequent discussions, a secured party often gets the earlier date of filing or perfection when perfection occurs at a time different from the time of filing. This can happen, for example, when a financing statement is filed covering after-acquired inventory. In that case, there can be no perfection until the debtor gets rights in the after-acquired inventory, but the secured party gets the advantage of an earlier filing date. Also, a secured party can file its financing statement before making a loan. Because perfection cannot occur before attachment, which usually requires a loan, such a party would be filing before perfection.

     b. **Importance of steps in perfection:** Why is it important to go through these steps in setting up the status of the secured party? Well, what if the security interest was never properly created? Then the "secured party" is not a secured party, but rather, a general creditor. The type of collateral is important because (1) the method of perfection may depend on the type of collateral, and (2) the priorities rules are different in competitions among security interests in different types of collateral. Whether the security interest is a PMSI is important because the priorities rules sometimes give preferential treatment to PMSIs. Finally, perfection is important because priority usually depends on the time of perfection or filing.

The analysis seems complicated, but it builds on prior chapters of this material and an understanding of those chapters is necessary to the solving of priorities problems.

Completion of the analysis of the secured party's status will yield a conclusion similar to this: "*S* has a perfected non-PMSI in equipment that was perfected by filing on January 15." That sentence is succinct, but understanding it requires detailed knowledge of the law. Here is where your prior knowledge, built through reading the past chapters of this Outline, will come together.

5. **Apply the priorities rules:** The final step is to apply the priorities rules. Article 9 contains a significant number of rules governing priority, and they cannot be condensed into a "general rule" that applies to all transactions. A starting point, but only a starting point, is the rule "first in time–first in right," which means that the first person to acquire a right will have priority over parties whose rights arise later. Thus, priorities problems involve a sequence of events that determine which of the competing secured parties has priority. The sequence can be illustrated by a time line specifying each event that occurs, indicating those that establish the critical date for each of the parties. Illustration of time lines will accompany several of the examples that follow. If you find it helpful, you should develop a time line for the other examples as you analyze them.

6. **Agricultural lien:** Analysis of the status of one holding an agricultural lien is somewhat simpler. Whether it exists (has been created) will depend on state law outside the Uniform Commercial Code (UCC). Whether the collateral falls within the scope of agricultural lien and how it should be characterized and described also will depend on the non-Code statute. No distinctions are made in the priorities rules based on the type of property subject to the lien. Whether it is perfected, however, depends on Article 9, and in all cases requires filing with the same office in which security interests are filed. Article 9 does not provide any special preferences for "purchase-money" agricultural liens, so that part of the analysis is unnecessary.

After the analysis of the secured party's status, it is necessary to analyze the status of the other parties to the priority dispute. If a second party is also claiming a security interest in the collateral, the analysis of that party's status is the same as that of the first secured party. If the other party is a transferee of the collateral from the debtor, the type of transferee must be determined, and if the other party claims a lien on the collateral, the type of lien and the time that it arose must be determined. Priorities problems will be discussed in the context of the types of the other parties to the dispute: other secured parties, transferees, and lienholders.

II. PRIORITIES INVOLVING PARTIES EACH CLAIMING A SECURITY INTEREST IN THE COLLATERAL: SECURED PARTY VERSUS SECURED PARTY

A. **Introduction:** A debtor may give a security interest to more than one creditor resulting in a question of which of the two or more secured parties has priority, i.e., which of the secured parties would be paid first if the collateral was sold and the sale did not bring enough money to pay all secured parties. Two security interests in the same collateral may also arise because one party has a security interest in property that is proceeds of the collateral in which it took the original security interest, and another party has taken a security interest directly in that collateral.

The time that a secured party perfects or files is the most important event in determining priority between two secured parties. However, PMSIs are given preferential treatment in some instances.

B.   When none of the secured parties has a PMSI: If the debtor has given a security interest to two or more parties, and none of the secured parties has a PMSI, three rules determine priority.

1.   Perfected versus unperfected: If only one of the secured parties has perfected its security interest, the perfected security interest has priority over the other unperfected security interests.

Example 1: If *D* gives security interests to *S1*, *S2*, and *S3*, and *S3* is the only party to perfect, *S3* prevails over *S1* and *S2*. UCC § 9-322(a)(2). Wow! A simple, straightforward rule!

2.   Unperfected versus unperfected: When none of the parties has perfected, the first security interest to attach prevails. UCC § 9-322(a)(3). Attachment requires (1) that there be an agreement that the security interest attach (the security agreement), (2) that the secured party has given value, and (3) that the debtor has rights in the collateral. See Chapter 3, *supra.*

Example 2: If *S1*, *S2*, and *S3* all have unperfected security interests (and agreement and rights have already been taken care of in each loan), and *S1* gave value on February 1, *S2* on January 1, and *S3* on March 1, *S2* would prevail, *S1* would be second in line, and *S3* would be last.

3.   Perfected versus perfected: When all of the security interests are perfected, the first to either perfect or file has priority if neither party has a PMSI. UCC § 9-322(a)(1). It is important to note that the rule is *not* that the first to **perfect** prevails, but that the first to **either file or perfect** prevails. Another way of saying this is that a secured party gets the benefit of the earlier of either the time of perfection or the time of filing. Thus, if *S* files a financing statement on June 1, but does not give value until August 1 (and hence does not have a perfected security interest until August 1 because perfection requires that the security interest attach), *S* will prevail over a secured party who perfected by giving value and filing on July 1.

For these examples, assume that none of the parties has a PMSI.

Example 3: On January 1, Debtor gave *S1* a security interest in existing inventory to secure a loan made on that date. *S1* perfected by filing on April 1.

On February 1, Debtor gave *S2* a second security interest in the same collateral and *S2* filed on that day, but did not give value until March 15.

On March 1, Debtor gave a third security interest in the same collateral to *S3* and *S3* gave value and filed on that day.

S1 has a valid non-PMSI in the inventory that was perfected and filed on April 1. The critical date for *S1* is April 1, the date of filing and perfection.

S2 has a non-PMSI in the same inventory that was filed on February 1. Although *S2*'s security interest was not perfected until *S2* gave value on March 15, the critical date for *S2* is February 1, the date of filing.

S3 has a valid non-PMSI filed in the same inventory that was filed and perfected on March 1. *S3*'s critical date is March 1.

In determining priority, because *S1*'s critical date is April 1, *S2*'s critical date is February 1, and *S3*'s critical date is March 1, the priorities are *S2*, *S3*, and then *S1*. When the collateral is sold, *S2* will be paid first. If there is anything left, *S3* will be paid next, and *S1* will get anything remaining after both *S1* and *S2* have been paid.

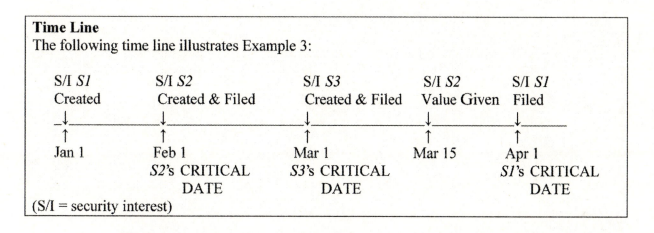

Time Line
The following time line illustrates Example 3:

S/I *S1*	S/I *S2*	S/I *S3*	S/I *S2*	S/I *S1*
Created	Created & Filed	Created & Filed	Value Given	Filed
Jan 1	Feb 1	Mar 1	Mar 15	Apr 1
	S2's CRITICAL DATE	*S3*'s CRITICAL DATE		*S1*'s CRITICAL DATE

(S/I = security interest)

Example 4: On August 1, *S1* took a security interest in all of Debtor's present and after-acquired inventory. *S1* filed a financing statement on the same day. On September 1, Debtor gave a second security interest in its present and after-acquired inventory to *S2*, who filed immediately. Debtor purchased new inventory that is delivered on October 1.

As to that new inventory, *S1* prevails over *S2*. Even though the security interest of *S1* and *S2* are perfected on the same date, October 1, *S1* gets the earlier date of filing because that is the date on which the Debtor acquires an interest (rights) in the collateral.

Time Line
The following time line illustrates Example 4:

S/I *S1*	S/I *S2*	New Inventory
Created & Filed	Created & Filed	Acquired
Aug 1	Sept 1	Oct 1
S1's CRITICAL DATE	*S2*'s CRITICAL DATE	

(S/I = security interest)

Example 5: Debtor gave *S1* an interest in a guitar on March 1. *S1* took possession of the guitar on that date. Debtor gave *S2* a security interest in the same guitar on April 1, and *S2* filed a financing statement for the guitar on that date. *S1* filed on May 1 and returned the guitar to Debtor on May 2.

As between *S1* and *S2*, *S1* has priority because it perfected by taking possession on March 1, and there was never a gap in the perfection.

Note: If *S1* had returned the guitar (gave up perfection by possession) after April 1 and before filing its financing statement to continue its perfection, *S2* would have jumped the priority line because of the gap in perfection.

Time Line
The following time line illustrates Example 5:

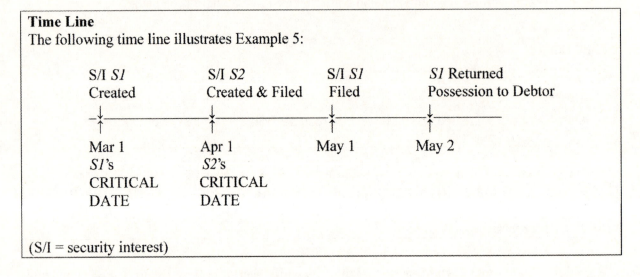

(S/I = security interest)

C. When one of the secured parties has a PMSI

1. **Introduction:** Only when the collateral is goods (other than crops) or software can there be a PMSI. Article 9 gives special priority treatment to PMSIs under several different rules. Distinctions among the various types of goods are important in the consideration of these rules. The rules for software and livestock are also distinct.

2. **PMSIs in goods other than inventory and livestock:** A PMSI in goods *other than* inventory or livestock has priority over all other security interests in the same collateral if it is perfected within 20 days of the date on which the debtor obtains possession of the goods. This is a straightforward rule and is easy to remember as long as you can remember what a PMSI is. UCC § 9-324(a).

Note: The 20 days starts to run when the debtor obtains possession, not when the security interest is created.

Example 6: On February 1, *S1* took a security interest in all of Debtor's equipment, including after-acquired equipment and perfected by filing on that day. On March 1, Debtor purchased a new computer for use in its business, giving to the seller, *V*, a security interest to secure payment of the price in installments over the next year. The computer was delivered to Debtor on March 15, and *V* perfected by filing on April 1.

S1 has a valid non-PMSI in the computer (as equipment) perfected by filing on February 1.

V has a PMSI in the same computer (as equipment) perfected by filing on April 1, within 20 days of Debtor obtaining possession.

As between *S1* and *V*, *V* has priority because it has a PMSI that was perfected within 20 days of the time Debtor obtained possession of the computer.

Time Line

The following time line illustrates Example 6:

S/I *SI*		New Computer	Computer	*V* Files
Created in		Purchased	Delivered	
Equipment (After-Acquired Included)		*V*'s S/I Created		

↓   ↓   ↓   ↓

↑   ↑   ↑   ↑

Feb 1   Mar 1   Mar 15   Apr 1

SI's CRITICAL   *V*'s CRITICAL

DATE   DATE[*]

(S/I = security interest)

[*] But *V* still wins because it had a PMSI.

Example 7: On July 1, Debtor purchased a computer and gave the seller, *V*, a security interest in it to secure the purchase price, which was to be paid in installments. *V* never filed a financing statement.

Debtor used the computer to play computer games, balance a checkbook, etc.

On August 1, Debtor borrowed $100 from *Happy Finance* and gave *Happy* a security interest in the same computer. *Happy* perfected by filing on the same day.

As between *V* and *Happy*, *V* has priority. Here, *V*'s security interest is automatically perfected because it is a PMSI in consumer goods.

One explanation for this seemingly curious result is that *V* perfected first and prevails under UCC § 9-322(a). Another, and better, approach is that *V* prevails because *V* has a PMSI that was perfected within 20 days of Debtor obtaining possession. The fact that possession occurred automatically is irrelevant. The second rationale is more technically correct because UCC § 9-322(a) (which contains the rule about being first) applies only when there is no other priority rule covering the problem.

Time Line

The following time line illustrates Example 7:

PMSI *V*	S/I *HF*
Created in	Created & Filed
Consumer Goods	

↓   ↓

↑   ↑

July 1   Aug 1

V's CRITICAL   *HF*'s CRITICAL

DATE   DATE

(S/I = security interest)

3. PMSIs in inventory: When the collateral is inventory, the preferred treatment given to a PMSI is narrower. A PMSI in inventory prevails over another security interest in the same collateral only if

    1. The security interest is perfected *before* the debtor obtains possession of it; and
    2. Notice is given to the conflicting secured party.

UCC § 9-324(b).

The notice must be given to all conflicting secured parties who have perfected by filing before the date that the purchase-money secured party files, or, if the goods are held by a bailee, during the 20 days of automatic perfection granted under UCC § 9-312(f). The notice must identify the inventory and inform the conflicting secured party that the new PMSI secured party has or expects to take a security interest in the inventory. The notice must be received by the conflicting secured party within the five year period before the debtor receives possession of the inventory.

Example 8: On May 1, *S* loaned money to Debtor and took a security interest in all of Debtor's inventory, present and after-acquired. *S* perfected by filing on the same day. On June 1, Debtor purchased new inventory from *V*, giving *V* a security interest in the newly purchased inventory to secure the purchase price that is to be paid in 60 days. *V* perfected by filing on June 5, and delivered the collateral to Debtor on June 15.

If *V* gave notice to *S* that it intended to take a security interest in the inventory, and the notice was received by *S* within five years before June 15, *V*'s security interest has priority over *S*. If proper notice was not given, *V* does not get the benefit of special priority, and thus *S*'s security interest has priority.

Time Line
The following time line illustrates Example 8:

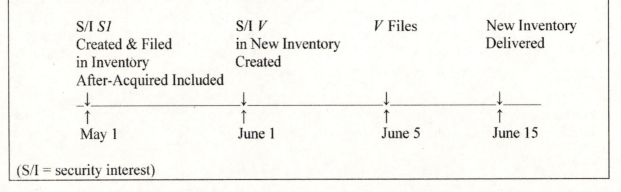

(S/I = security interest)

Example 9: On July 1, *S* loaned money to Debtor and took a security interest in all of Debtor's inventory, present and after-acquired. On August 1, *S* purchased new inventory from *V*, giving *V* a security interest in the newly purchased inventory to secure the purchase price that was to be paid in 60 days. The new inventory was delivered to Debtor on August 5, and *V* perfected by filing on August 10. Even if *V* gave the proper notice to *S*, *S*'s security interest has priority over *V*'s security interest because *V* did not file before August 5, the date on which Debtor obtained possession. Thus, *S* continues to have priority.

Time Line

Create your own time line for Example 9 here:

_____

---

4. **Consignments:** With only very limited exceptions, a consignment (an agreement that a seller will provide a debtor with goods to sell for the seller and the seller will retain ownership of the goods) is a secured transaction (see UCC §§ 9-102(a)(20), 9-109(a)(4)). A consignor's security interest in the goods consigned is a PMSI, (UCC § 9-103(d)). Because the goods are held by the consignee for the purpose of sale, the collateral is inventory and the PMSI rules for inventory apply. Official Comment 7 to UCC § 9-324.

Example 10: On May 1, S took a security interest in all of Debtor's inventory, present and after-acquired. S filed on the same day. On June 1, C agreed to consign goods to Debtor, and filed a financing statement on that day. C delivered the consigned goods on June 5. If C gave the required notice to S before the goods were delivered, C's security interest has priority over S.

Time Line

Create your own time line for Example 10 here:

_____

---

5. **PMSIs in livestock:** A PMSI in livestock, a subcategory of farm products, is treated similarly to a PMSI in inventory. You can probably imagine why. Livestock is the inventory of a farm, at least part of it anyway. It is sold and replaced with new stock. To gain priority, the purchase-money secured party must perfect before the debtor obtains possession of the livestock. Also, the purchase-money secured party must give notice, this time within the six years preceding the time that the debtor received possession of the livestock in which the purchase-money secured party claims a security interest. The notice must state that the purchase-money secured party has or intends to take a security interest in the livestock and must describe the livestock.

D. **Conflicting security interests in proceeds**

1. **Introduction:** The Code provides that a secured party obtains a security interest not only in the collateral described in its security agreement but also in any proceeds. UCC § 9-315(a)(2). See Chapter 4, *supra*. A security interest in proceeds is perfected automatically for 20 days and remains perfected if (1) the proceeds are identifiable cash, (2) there is a new

filing as to the proceeds, or (3) the proceeds are of a type that can be perfected by filing in the same manner as the original collateral, as long as there was a filing as to the original collateral. UCC § 9-315(d) and Chapter 5, *supra*.

Thus, if a creditor takes a security interest in all of the debtor's inventory and properly files a financing statement, the creditor has a perfected security interest in everything that the debtor receives when it sells the inventory, e.g., accounts, cash, chattel paper, trade-ins, etc. Also, if a debtor purchases a computer and gives a security interest in it, for example to the seller or a financial institution, and the debtor trades it for a different computer, the secured party has a security interest in the computer obtained by the debtor in the trade.

Conflicts may arise between the secured party who has a security interest in the collateral as proceeds and a secured party who specifically took a security interest in the collateral that constitutes the proceeds. Perhaps the most common conflicts arise when the debtor has given a security interest in inventory to one person and a security interest in accounts to a second person. When inventory is sold and generates accounts, both secured parties will have a security interest in the accounts, and the question may arise as to who has priority. If neither has a PMSI, priority goes to the first to file or perfect.

2. **Priorities in proceeds when there is no PMSI:** If neither the secured party with the security interest in the collateral as proceeds nor the secured party who took a security interest in the collateral as original collateral has a PMSI, the first in time–first in right rule is applied to conflicts between security interests in the same collateral. UCC § 9-322(a). This rule applies even though one of the parties took a security interest in the collateral as original collateral and the other obtained its security interest as proceeds.

Thus, if both security interests are perfected, the secured party who is first to file or perfect prevails. In making the determination as to which secured party has filed or perfected first, the secured party who has the security interest in the property as proceeds of the original collateral gets the date when it perfected or filed as to the original collateral. UCC § 9-322(b)(1).

Example 11: On September 1, *S1* loaned money to Debtor and took a security interest in all of Debtor's existing inventory to secure Debtor's promise to repay. *S1* filed a financing statement perfecting its security interest on the same day. On October 1, *S2* took a security interest in all of Debtor's present and after-acquired accounts, and perfected by filing on the same day.

On November 1, Debtor sold inventory to *P* and took back *P*'s promise to pay in 60 days. Now both *S1* and *S2* have a security interest in *P*'s promise to pay. As between *S1* and *S2*, *S1*'s security interest has priority in the account because *S1* filed as to the original collateral, the inventory, before *S2* filed as to the accounts. The perfection of the inventory permanently perfects the security interest in the accounts because financing statements as to accounts and inventory are filed in the same office, and the date for perfection as to the proceeds is the date of filing as to the original collateral.

Time Line
Create your own time line for Example 11 here:

Example 12: On February 1, *S1* loaned money to Debtor and took a security interest in all of Debtor's existing inventory. On March 2, *S2* took a security interest in all of Debtor's accounts. *S2* filed on the same day. On April 1, Debtor sold part of the inventory to *P*, and *P* promised to pay for the goods sold in 60 days. On April 5, *S1* perfected its security interest by filing. As between *S1* and *S2*, *S2* has priority in the account that arose when *P* promised to pay because *S2* filed first.

Time Line
Create your own time line for Example 12 here:

_____

---

3. **Priorities in proceeds when the security interest in the original collateral is a PMSI:** A PMSI in the original collateral retains its preferred status as a PMSI in all proceeds if the original collateral is anything other than inventory. UCC § 9-324(a). Thus, as to the proceeds, a secured party who has perfected its security interest in the original collateral within 20 days of the delivery of the original collateral prevails over all other secured parties who have a security interest in the proceeds of the original collateral.

When the original collateral is inventory, the PMSI preference given to proceeds is much narrower. Although in some cases the preference extends to instruments and chattel paper, it basically extends only to cash proceeds that are received by the debtor on or before the date that the inventory is delivered to the debtor. UCC § 9-324(b). Thus, in most cases, the first-in-time rule applies to priority disputes in the proceeds of inventory.

Example 13: On March 1, *S1* sold an Orange computer to Debtor for Debtor's own personal use. *S1* took a security interest in the computer but never filed a financing statement.

On April 1, Debtor traded the computer to *P* and obtained a more powerful Plum computer. On May 1, *P* borrowed $1,000 from *S2*, giving *S2* a security interest in the Plum computer. As between *S1* and *S2*, *S2* has priority.

Although *S1*'s security interest was perfected automatically, *S1*'s security interest in the proceeds was perfected only for 20 days because the requirements that would make perfection permanent were not met, e.g., the same-office rule. UCC § 9-315(d) and Chapter 5, *supra*.

Thus, *S2* prevails because it has a perfected security interest in the Plum computer and *S1* has an unperfected security interest in it. If *S1* had filed, as it could have, its security interest in the Plum computer, as proceeds of the Orange computer, would have been perfected beyond the 20-day period, and *S1* would have prevailed. This is true because *S1* had a PMSI in the original collateral and the preference given to PMSIs would carry over to the Plum computer.

Time Line
Create your own time line for Example 13 here:

_____

Example 14: On August 1, *S1* took a security interest in all of Debtor's present and after-acquired equipment, which it perfected on the same day by filing.

On September 1, *S2* sold a new X2 machine to Debtor taking back a security interest in the machine to secure Debtor's promise to pay in 90 days. *S2* immediately filed a financing statement in the X2.

On October 1, Debtor traded the X2 machine to *P* in return for a smaller X1 machine. In addition to giving the X1 machine to Debtor, *P* agreed to pay Debtor $1,000 on December 1.

As between *S1* and *S2*, *S2* has superior rights to both the X1 machine and the $1,000 account. Both *S1* and *S2* have security interests in the X1 machine and in the account because they are proceeds of collateral in which each creditor has a security interest. *S2* has priority because it had a perfected PMSI in the X2 machine that it filed within 20 days of the debtor gaining possession of the X2, which carried over to all proceeds and thus to the X1 machine and the account.

Time Line
Create your own time line for Example 14 here:

_____

III. PRIORITIES BETWEEN A SECURED PARTY AND A TRANSFEREE (OR BUYER) FROM THE DEBTOR

A. Introduction: After a debtor has granted a security interest to a secured party, the debtor may transfer the collateral to a third person. Also, a debtor whose property is subject to an agricultural lien may transfer it. The transfer raises the question of whether the secured party's security interest or the agricultural lienholder's lien continues in the collateral after the transfer, or whether it is cut off as a result of the transfer. Some texts refer to these transferees as buyers or purchasers, but we'll generally use the more inclusive word, transferee.

While not all teachers consider competitions between buyers and secured creditors priorities problems, your authors do. When this is considered to be a priorities problem, the question is: Who has priority, the secured party or the transferee? The same question arises when a party has an agricultural lien on the debtor's property and the debtor sells the property. The starting point is that a security interest or agricultural lien continues in the collateral and the secured party or lienholder can repossess the collateral from the transferee *unless* there is a provision in Article 9 giving the transferee better rights. UCC § 9-315(a)(1). The resolution of a dispute requires an inspection of situations in which Article 9 protects the transferee by providing that the security interest *does not* continue in the collateral.

In solving these disputes, it is necessary first to examine the status of the secured party using the same approach described in the last section: (1) Is the security interest properly created? (2) What kind of property is the collateral? (3) Is the security interest a PMSI? (4) Is the security interest perfected, and, if so, when and how?

The next step is to classify the status of the transferee. Is the transferee a purchaser for value who has taken delivery without knowledge of the security interest or agricultural lien? UCC § 9-317(b). Or is the transferee a buyer in ordinary course (BIOC) of business? UCC §§ 1-201(9), 9-320(a). Or is the transferee a casual buyer? UCC § 9-320(b). Once the status of the secured party and the transferee are established, the applicable priorities rules determine who has priority.

B. Transferees who are donees or who take with knowledge of the security interest: The easiest dispute to resolve is one between a secured party and a transferee who does not give value to the debtor-transferor. Because there is no provision in Article 9 protecting donees, the secured party prevails and its security interest can be asserted against the donee. Indeed, the secured party wins even though the secured party has failed to perfect its security interest.

With one exception that will be discussed later in connection with BIOCs, the same is true of transferees who take with knowledge of the security interest. Security interests, even though unperfected, beat out transferees who had knowledge of the existence of the security interest at the time they purchased the collateral.

C. Transferees who give value without knowledge of the security interest and receive delivery of the collateral

1. **When the security interest is not a PMSI:** One type of transferee protected under Article 9 is a purchaser who gives value and takes delivery, without knowledge of an existing security interest. Yes, it's awkward, but we call this person a "P/V w/o K." The priority rule applied is first in time–first in right. The critical times are the time that the buyer meets all of the requirements of a P/V w/o K (value and delivery without knowledge of an existing security interest) and the time that the secured party perfected. UCC § 9-317(b). To put it another way, a buyer without knowledge of the security interest who gives value and takes delivery takes free of unperfected security interests. Note that the buyer must take delivery of the goods, and that the critical time for the secured party is the time of perfection, which is not necessarily the time of filing. Perfection could occur (first) in another way.

   Knowledge is actual knowledge, not simply notice. *Value* is broadly defined to include any consideration, including a preexisting debt. See UCC § 1-202 [2001 version].

   Example 15: *S* took a security interest in a truck that Debtor was using as equipment on June 1. On July 1, Debtor sells and delivers the truck to *B* in payment of a debt that Debtor owed *B*. On August 1, *S* perfected by filing.

   If *B* did not have actual knowledge of *S*'s security interest, *B* takes free of it and *S* has no right to repossess the truck from *B* if Debtor defaults.

Time Line

Create your own time line for Example 15 here:

_____

Example 16: *S* takes a security interest in Debtor's computer on August 1. Debtor sells the computer to *B* for $5,000 on September 1. *S* perfects by filing on September 5. Debtor delivers the computer to *B* on September 10. *S*'s security interest survives the sale to *B* because *B* did not meet all the requirements of being a P/V w/o K until *B* took delivery, at which point *S* had filed a financing statement.

Time Line

Create your own time line for Example 16 here:

_____

2. **When the security interest is a PMSI:** If the security interest is a PMSI, and the secured party files within 20 days of the time that the buyer met all of the requirements of being a P/V w/o K, the secured party prevails over the buyer who purchased during the 20-day period. See UCC § 9-317(e). Thus, purchase-money secured parties have 20 days in which to file, and the 20 days start when the buyer does what is necessary to become a P/V w/o K.

Example 17: On February 1, *S* advances credit to Debtor to allow Debtor to purchase a computer for use as equipment and takes a security interest in the computer. On March 1, Debtor sells the computer to *B* who takes without notice of *S*'s security interest and gives value. Debtor delivers the computer to *B* on March 15, and *S* perfects by filing on April 1.

S's security interest continues in the computer and *S* may repossess it from *B* if Debtor defaults because it perfected within 20 days of the time *B* met the requirements to become a P/V w/o K. This is true even though nothing had been filed by *S* as of the time that *B* bought the computer.

Time Line

Create your own time line for Example 17 here:

_____

D. Casual buyers: Casual buyers, sometimes called "consumer buyers" or "garage-sale buyers," are buyers who (1) buy the goods for their own personal, family, or household use; and (2) purchase the goods from a seller who is holding the goods as consumer goods. UCC § 9-320(b). The transaction is relatively rare, or casual, usually involving one person buying from a neighbor or at a garage sale. One who buys goods from someone engaged in selling goods, a retailer, is not a casual buyer and not protected under this provision of Article 9, although the buyer probably enjoys different protection as a BIOC. See discussion below.

Casual buyers take free of all security interests that are not perfected by filing, but take subject to security interests that are perfected by filing. The protection for casual buyers applies most frequently when the secured party had a PMSI that was perfected automatically because the debtor purchased the goods as consumer goods, and the debtor then sells the goods to someone who also intends to use the goods as consumer goods.

Note: For some reason, the rules were drafted so that casual buyers do not take free of security interests perfected by filing, even though it is pretty clear that casual buyers don't typically check the filing system before buying used goods.

A secured party who has perfected by possession and is still in possession of the collateral also can enforce its security interest against a casual buyer even if there is no filing. See UCC § 9-320(e). Presumably, not many people buy used goods without first asking the seller to see the goods and then taking immediate possession of the goods, so this scenario should be rather rare.

Example 18: On March 1, *S* sold Debtor a computer, taking back a security interest in it to secure the purchase price, which was to be paid over the next year. *S* did not file. Debtor purchased it for use in his home, e.g., to download from iTunes, keep track of his photos and music, and to balance his personal checkbook. On April 1, Debtor sold the computer to *B*, who used it to blog about celebrities at home.

S's security interest in the computer was perfected automatically, UCC § 9-309(1), because it had a PMSI in consumer goods. However, if *S* did not file its security interest in the computer, *S*'s security interest would not be enforceable against *B*. On the other hand, if *S* did file, as it had a right to do despite automatic perfection, *S*'s security interest would continue in the collateral after the sale, and *S* could repossess it if Debtor defaulted.

Time Line
Create your own time line for Example 18 here:

_____

This protection against casual buyers might explain why some creditors with security interests in high-end consumer goods perfect by filing even though they are already automatically perfected.

Example 19: On August 1, Debtor purchased an expensive television from *S* and gave *S* a security interest in it to secure the price, which was to be paid over the next year. *S* did not file a financing statement. Debtor purchased it for use in his home. On September 1, Debtor sold the television to *P*, a store that bought and sold used TVs. *P* put it in its inventory. On October 1, *B* purchased the television from *P*.

S's security interest was perfected automatically, and it continued in the TV after the sale to *B*. *B* was not a casual buyer because the person from whom *B* purchased, *P*, was not holding the goods as consumer goods.

Time Line
Create your own time line for Example 19 here:

_____

E. Buyers in ordinary course (BIOCs)

1. **Who is a BIOC?** BIOCs are sometimes said to be the most favored transferee under Article 9. Although this is an accurate general statement, BIOCs do not always take free of a security interest on the goods purchased.

   The definition of a BIOC is critical to an analysis of priorities problems. UCC § 9-201(a)(9). A BIOC is a person:

   1. who buys goods,
   2. in good faith,
   3. without knowledge that the sale violates the rights of another person,
   4. in the ordinary course of business,
   5. from someone selling goods of the kind purchased,
   6. who takes possession, or who has the right to possession from the seller.

   The requirement that a person be a "buyer" excludes donees. Also, the definition excludes persons who acquire the goods as security for, or in total or partial satisfaction of, a debt. Good faith requires acting honestly and observing reasonable commercial standards of fair dealing.

   The definition does not prevent one from knowing of the existence of a security interest; rather, it requires no knowledge that the sale is in violation of another's rights. Thus, a buyer may know that the seller who has given a security interest can still be a BIOC, but if the buyer knows that the security agreement or some other agreement prohibits the sale of the goods without the secured party's permission, the buyer is not a BIOC unless permission is given.

   The sale must be in the ordinary course of business. The test is whether the sale comports with usual or customary practices. In most cases, a BIOC purchases from a retailer, but a sale from a wholesaler or manufacturer to a retailer can be in the ordinary course. Purchasers at sales where the price is reduced can be BIOCs, as can be purchasers who buy on credit.

   Connected with the requirement that the sale be in the ordinary course is the requirement that the seller be in the business of selling goods of that kind. Manufacturers, wholesalers, and retailers clearly meet this test as to goods that they normally sell. However, a retailing clothing store would not be a seller of goods of the kind if it sold its computer. A sale by a pawnbroker is excluded from this exception, so a buyer who purchases from a pawnbroker cannot be a BIOC.

The buyer must either take possession of the goods or have a right to possession as against the seller. A buyer who has paid for the goods has a right to possession of them under Article 2, and a sale to a buyer who directs that the goods be delivered to someone else as a gift also meets the possession test.

2. **Rights of a BIOC:** A BIOC takes free of all security interests *created by its seller,* even if the security interest is perfected. Thus, if a retail appliance store has given a security interest in all of its inventory, a purchaser of goods from the inventory takes free of the security interest and the secured party may not repossess the goods from the purchaser. However, the security interest of a secured party in possession of the goods is not cut off by a sale to a BIOC, and the security interest can be enforced against the buyer.

A buyer of farm products does not enjoy the protections given by Article 9 to BIOCs, but may be protected under the Federal Farm Security Act. See Chapter 2, *infra.*

Example 20: On September 1, *S* takes a security interest in all of the inventory of ABC Appliance Store and files a financing statement on the same day. On October 1, ABC has a sale discounting all appliances, and *P* purchases a refrigerator during the sale.

Even though *P* may know that ABC has given a security interest in the refrigerator, *P* takes free of *S*'s security interest, and *S* cannot repossess it even though ABC defaults.

Time Line
Create your own time line for Example 20 here:

_____

Example 21: On March 1, *S* takes a security interest in all of the inventory of RST Appliance Store and perfects by filing on the same day. RST decides to stop selling microwave ovens and sells all of its stock to XYZ Appliance Store. *P*, who meets all the requirements of a BIOC, purchases a microwave from XYZ. *P* does not take free of *S*'s security interest because it was not created by XYZ.

Time Line
Create your own time line for Example 21 here:

_____

Tricky, tricky, tricky. Watch out for exam questions involving security interests created by someone other than a BIOC's seller. This is a common testing area.

F.   Transferee's derivative rights: A transferee of goods gets all of the title and rights of its transferor, and if the transferor took free of an existing security interest, so does the transferee. This is true even though the transferee is a donee or took with knowledge of the security interest.

Example 22: On May 1, Debtor gave a security interest to *S* in all of its equipment. On June 1, Debtor sold a piece of the equipment to *P*, a purchaser for value without knowledge, who took delivery on that date. On July 1, *S* perfected by filing. On August 1, *B* purchased the piece of equipment from *P*.

B takes free of *S*'s security interest. Although *B* took after *S* filed, and hence is not protected in its own right, *B* took all of the rights of *P* and *P* took free of *S*'s security interest.

Time Line
Create your own time line for Example 22 here:

_____

IV. PRIORITIES BETWEEN A SECURED PARTY AND A LIEN CREDITOR

A.   Introduction: A security interest itself is a type of lien, called a *consensual lien* because it arises by agreement of the debtor. In the terminology of Article 9, however, it is not referred to as a lien but rather as a *security interest*. Article 9 reserves the term "lien" for judicial liens which arise by virtue of the collection process and for the liens obtained by trustees in bankruptcy, assignees for the benefit of creditors, and receivers. UCC § 9-102(a)(52). When Article 9 uses the term "lien" by itself, the reference is only to these types of liens.

Judicial liens usually arise as a result of a creditor obtaining a judgment and then executing on the debtor's property. States vary as to when such a lien arises: some states take the position that the lien does not arise until the sheriff actually takes possession of (or exerts dominion and control over) the property under the writ; other states hold that the lien arises as soon as the writ of execution is delivered to the sheriff. See Chapter 1, *supra*.

Liens also may arise as a result of statutes or even by the common law (through cases). For example, a landlord usually has a lien on all of the tenant's property that is on the leased premises. Article 9 calls these "possessory liens" and treats them separately from judicial liens. UCC § 9-333.

Agricultural liens are another separate type of lien defined under Article 9. UCC § 9-102(a)(5). For most purposes, agricultural liens are treated the same as security interests, and the priorities rules for them are generally the same as for security interests.

B. Priorities between security interests and judicial liens: The basic rule determining priority between a security interest or an agricultural lien and a judicial lien is first in time–first in right. The critical time for the lienholder is the time that the lien arose or attached to the property. The critical time for the secured party is a little more complicated. In most cases, it is the time of perfection. However, if the secured party has filed earlier, and there is a security agreement granting the secured party a security interest in the property, the secured party is given the benefit of the earlier filing. UCC § 9-317(a).

Example 23: On April 1, Debtor purchases equipment from *S* and gives *S* a security interest in it to secure Debtor's promise to pay in 60 days. The goods are delivered on April 5. On May 1, *L* obtains a judgment against Debtor and obtains a lien by execution on the next day. As between *S* and *L*, *S* will prevail if *S* filed a financing statement and thus perfected its security interest before May 1. Otherwise, *L*'s lien will have priority.

Time Line
Create your own time line for Example 23 here:

_____

Note: *S*'s security interest here was not automatically perfected because, although it was a PMSI, it was not in consumer goods. Remember that the most important PMSIs, those involved in the largest commercial loans, are not in consumer goods. Thus, automatic perfection is of limited use in a commercial lending practice.

While automatic perfection is a common testing area, it is far less common in practice than many students think.

A secured party with a PMSI has 20 days in which to perfect to retain its preferred PMSI status. If the purchase-money secured party files during that period, the secured party has priority over intervening lien creditors, meaning those who obtain their liens during the 20-day period. UCC § 9-317(e).

As you can see, this makes the PMSI a secret lien during the 20 days. As we really dislike secret liens in this notice filing system, this gives you an idea how badly the drafters wanted to protect the PMSI lender. The PMSI lender is seen as a white knight of sorts, adding to the debtor's assets and thus improving the debtor's overall financial situation.

Keep in mind that while a secured party can prefile a financing statement, the security interest is not perfected until the requirements of attachment have been met. Also recall that while the date of relevance in competitions between two secured parties is the first to file or perfect, as between a lien creditor and a secured party, the only relevant date for the secured party in this competition is when the secured party perfected, not when it filed. Again, this is tricky!

Example 24: On April 1, Debtor signed a security agreement giving *S* a security interest in all of its existing inventory. *S* filed on the same day. *L* obtained a lien by execution on the inventory on May 1. *S* gave value to Debtor on June 1.

Because *S* did not perfect until June 1, value was not given until that day, and its security interest did not attach. Therefore, *L* prevails.

Time Line

Create your own time line for Example 24 here:

_____

V. FUTURE ADVANCES AND PRIORITIES

A. **Introduction:** In addition to securing obligations owing to the secured party at the time the security interest is given, a security interest may also secure advances made in the future. UCC § 9-204(c). See Chapter 4, *supra.* A lender may be required to make future advances of money to the debtor in its loan agreement, or it may have no obligation to do so. The loan agreement also may be silent as to future advances.

Note: The provisions on future advances only apply when the security agreement states that the security interest secures obligations made in the future.

If the security agreement only secures a debt made at the time it was given, or only secures past obligations, it does not secure loans made by the secured party to the debtor in the future. However, if the debtor signs a new security agreement when the new loan is given, the secured party gets the benefit of the date of filing as to the first loan, because the filing applies to all security agreements given by the debtor. Remember, you can file early, and that rule applies here. If the debtor does not give a new security interest when there is no future advance clause, the new loan is unsecured and the secured party is a general (unsecured) creditor as to the new loan.

If the secured party is required to extend credit in the future, these promises to lend are made, in the words of Article 9, "pursuant to commitment." UCC § 9-102(a)(68). This is important because, as you'll see below, a secured party who makes a future advance pursuant to commitment may have better rights than one who makes an advance without any obligation to do so.

In almost all cases, the secured party who makes future advances gets the earlier of the time of either perfection or filing in determining priority. A limited exception applies when the collateral is certificated securities, negotiable documents, or instruments, and perfection is only temporary. In these cases, an earlier date of filing does not help the secured party and the perfection does not occur until the future advance is made. UCC § 9-323. See also Official Comment 3 to UCC § 9-323(c). The exception for those types of collateral does not apply to buyers of accounts, chattel paper, payment intangibles, or promissory notes; or to a consignor. Hence, buyers of these types of collateral, who are secured parties under Article 9, always get the benefit of an early filing.

The extent to which the secured party obtains priority as to the future advance is complicated and is discussed below in detail.

B. **Future advances in competitions between two or more secured parties:** When the debtor has given a security interest to two parties and one of them is claiming that its security interest secures a future advance, the first-in-time rule applies in most cases. In effect, the time that the advance is made is immaterial. See Official Comment 3 to UCC § 9-323. Whether the future advance is made "pursuant to commitment" is immaterial in determining the priority between two or more voluntary secured parties with interests in the same collateral.

Example 25: On June 1, Debtor gives a security interest in all of its inventory to *S1* to secure a loan of $10,000 made on that date. The security agreement contains a future advance clause. *S1* files immediately. On July 1, *S2* takes a security interest in the same inventory to secure a loan of $5,000. *S2* files on the same day. On August 1, *S1* makes another advance of $20,000 to Debtor secured by the same security interest that it took on June 1.

S1's security interest has priority over *S2*'s to the extent of $30,000, the sum of both advances, even if *S1* did not have any obligation to make the August 1 advance. The same result would occur if on August 1, Debtor signed a new security agreement. The June 1 date of filing would apply to the new security interest as well. See Example 1 in Official Comment 3 to UCC § 9-323.

Time Line

Create your own time line for Example 25 here:

C. **When the competing party is a transferee (buyer) or lessee of the collateral from the debtor:** When the competing parties are a secured party and a transferee or buyer, however, the rules start to get tricky. Assume that after a debtor has given a security interest in collateral, the debtor sells or leases the collateral and that the transfer does not cut off the security interest. Clearly, the secured party may repossess the collateral and take from the sale enough money to satisfy the debt incurred before the sale. However, if the secured party makes an advance to the debtor subsequent to the sale, the question arises as to whether the amount of that advance also has priority as to the buyer or lessee. In other words, when the collateral is repossessed, and sold by the secured party, can the secured party take enough money out of the proceeds of the sale to satisfy both the debt incurred before the sale and also the debt incurred by the advance made after the sale? UCC § 9-323(d), (f).

If the future advance is not made "pursuant to commitment," Article 9 provides that the priority of the secured party extends to future advances made less than 45 days after the purchase, or the lease, becomes enforceable if they are made by the secured party without knowledge of the security interest. UCC § 9-323(c), (g). Thus, the secured party will lose its priority over the transferee as to any future advance that is made after 45 days from the time of the transfer *or* after having knowledge of the transfer.

Example 26: On June 1, Debtor gives a security interest in a machine to *S* to secure a loan made on that day in the amount of $10,000. The security agreement provides that the security interest secures all present and future obligations that Debtor owes to *S*, but *S* does not agree to make any future loans. *S* perfects by filing on the same day. On July 1, Debtor sells the machine to *P*. On August 1, *S* agrees to loan Debtor an additional $10,000, to be secured by the same machine. At the time, *S* does not know that the machine has been sold to *P*.

If Debtor defaults and the machine is sold for $20,000, *S* can keep the entire $20,000 because the future advance was made within 45 days of the sale and without *S*'s knowledge that the sale had been made.

Time Line
Create your own time line for Example 26 here:

_____

Example 27: On September 1, Debtor gives a security interest in a machine to *S* to secure a loan made on that day in the amount of $10,000. The security agreement does not contain a future advances clause. The security agreement provides that the security interest secures only the obligation of Debtor to repay the $10,000 and *S* does not agree to make any future loans. *S* perfects by filing on the same day. On October 1, Debtor sells the machine to *P*. On November 1, *S*, without knowledge of the sale to *P*, loans Debtor an additional $10,000, taking back a new security interest in the same machine to secure the debt.

If Debtor defaults and *S* sells the machine in a repossession sale for $20,000, *S* may retain only $10,000. The rules on future advances do not apply, because the original security agreement did not contain a future advances clause. When Debtor gave a new security agreement to secure the new loan, it was perfected because the original financing statement would cover it. However, the perfection did not occur until November 1 because there was no attachment until then. Assuming that *P* was a purchaser for value without notice who took delivery on October 1, *P* takes free of a security interest that was not then perfected.

Time Line
Create your own time line for Example 27 here:

_____

Example 28: On March 1, Debtor gives a security interest in a machine, to secure a loan made on that day in the amount of $10,000. The security agreement provides that the security interest secures all present and future obligations that Debtor owes to *S*, but *S* does not agree to make any future loans. *S* perfects by filing on the same day. On April 1, Debtor sells the machine to *P*. On June 1, *S* loans Debtor an additional $10,000, secured by the same machine. At the time, *S* does not know that the machine has been sold to *P*.

If Debtor defaults and the machine is sold for $20,000, *S* has priority only as to the $10,000, because the future advance was made more than 45 days after the sale.

Time Line
Create your own time line for Example 28 here:

_____

If the future advance was made "pursuant to commitment," the rule is a bit different. The secured party has priority over a buyer so long as the ***commitment*** was made before the sale or within 45 days thereafter without knowledge of the sale. UCC § 9-323(e).

Example 29: On June 1, Debtor gives a security interest in a machine to *S*, to secure a loan made on that day in the amount of $10,000. The security agreement provides that the security interest secures all present and future obligations that Debtor owes to *S*, and that *S* agrees to advance an additional $10,000 on September 1. *S* perfects by filing on the same day. On July 1, Debtor sells the machine to *P*. On September 1, *S* advanced the additional $10,000 to Debtor although *S* knows of the sale.

If Debtor defaults and the machine is sold for $20,000, *S* can keep the entire $20,000 because the future advance was pursuant to a commitment and that commitment was made within 45 days of the sale. Indeed, it was made before the sale.

Time Line
Create your own time line for Example 29 here:

_____

D. When the competing party has a lien: When the competition is between a secured party and a lienholder, the rules regarding future advances are downright complicated. The priority rule between a secured party making an advance and a lienholder uses a 45-day period, but in a very different way than the time period used in relation to buyers. The rule is much more favorable to the secured party. During the 45 days after the transfer, an advance by the secured party has priority even if the secured party knows that a lien creditor now has a lien. After the 45 days has run, the secured party still has priority if it made the advance either (1) without knowledge of the lien, *or* (2) in fulfillment of a commitment. UCC § 9-323(b).

Lien Creditors and Future Advances

As long as the secured party has no knowledge of the lien or has made its future advance pursuant to a commitment to lend, it can continue to lend to its heart's content and still retain its first position. On the other hand, if it has knowledge that a lien has been filed *and* is lending voluntarily and not pursuant to a prior obligation, the lienholder will jump the line as to the future advances, 45 days after the lien becomes a lien.

Example 30: On June 1, Debtor gives a security interest in a machine to *S*, to secure a loan made on that day in the amount of $10,000. The security agreement provides that the security interest secures all present and future obligations that Debtor owes to *S*, but *S* does not agree to make future advances. *S* perfects by filing on the same day. On July 1, *L* obtains a lien by executing on the machine. On August 1, *S* makes a future advance of $10,000.

S's security interest has priority as to the total of the two advances, $20,000, because the future advance was made during the 45-day period even if *S* had knowledge of *L*'s lien.

Time Line
Create your own time line for Example 30 here:

_____

Note: The previous example describes a future advance made without a future commitment to lend, with knowledge of a lien, and inside the 45-day period.

Example 31: On June 1, Debtor gives a security interest in a machine to *S*, to secure a loan made on that day in the amount of $10,000. The security agreement provides that the security interest secures all present and future obligations that Debtor owes to *S*, and *S* agrees to advance an additional $10,000 on October 1. *S* perfects by filing on the same day. On August 1, *L* obtains a lien on the machine by execution. *S* learned of the lien on August 15, but nevertheless advanced $10,000 on October 1.

S's security interest has priority as to $20,000 because it made the advance pursuant to a commitment that was made before the time *L* obtained its lien.

Time Line

Create your own time line for Example 31 here:

_____

Note: The previous example describes a future advance made pursuant to a commitment, with knowledge of a lien, but outside the 45 days.

Example 32: On June 1, Debtor gives a security interest in a machine to *S*, to secure a loan made on that day in the amount of $10,000. The security agreement provides that the security interest secures all present and future obligations that Debtor owes to *S*, but *S* does not agree to make any future advances. *S* perfects by filing on the same day. On August 1, *L* obtains a lien on the machine by execution. Without knowledge of *L*'s lien, *S* makes an advance of $10,000 on October 1.

   S's security interest has priority as to $20,000 because it made the advance without knowledge of *L*'s lien.

Time Line

Create your own time line for Example 32 here:

_____

Note: That was an example of a future advance made without a future commitment to lend, without knowledge of an existing lien, but outside the 45 days.

VI. FIXTURES

A. **Introduction to fixtures:** Fixtures exist in the never-never land somewhere between real property and personal property. They are goods that have been attached to real property in a way that gives them some of the characteristics of realty in a way that causes an interest in them to arise under real property law. UCC § 9-102(a)(41). See Chapter 2. Still, they retain sufficient aspects of personal property to allow a creditor to take an Article 9 security interest in them. UCC § 9-334(a). However, an Article 9 security interest cannot be created in ordinary building materials that become a part of the structure.

   If the goods that are fixtures were not attached to the realty, they would be classified under Article 9 as either equipment or consumer goods. Thus, if a heating unit is attached to an office building and becomes a fixture, it would also be equipment; if attached to a home, it would be consumer goods.

And, so long as no person claiming an interest in a fixture has an interest in the real property to which it is attached, the normal rules of perfection and priority apply. Perfection is by filing a financing statement with the Secretary of State, and the rules discussed previously also apply.

For example, if two parties have Article 9 security interests in a fixture and both have filed a financing statement, the first to file or perfect will prevail if neither has a PMSI.

If one of the parties has an interest in the fixture because it has an interest in the real property to which the fixture is affixed, different rules on both perfection and priority apply. UCC § 9-334. These rules apply when the dispute:

1. is between a creditor with a security interest in the fixture and a purchaser of the building in which the fixture is installed; or
2. is between a secured party and someone claiming a consensual lien on the building, for example a mortgagee, or between a secured party and a person claiming a judicial lien on the real property.

Perfection of the security interest is different if the secured party is to have any rights against people with interests in the real estate to which the fixtures are affixed. This is discussed in more detail in Chapter 5. The secured party must file a "fixture filing," and the filing must be with the real property records.

To reiterate, for the secured party to have rights against an owner of the real property, or a person holding a consensual lien on the realty (e.g., a mortgagee), the secured party must have filed a "fixture filing." Otherwise, the secured party will have no rights against the person claiming an interest in the realty.

B. **Priority when a security interest in fixtures is not a PMSI:** As between a non-PMSI secured party and the person having an interest in the real property, the first to file or record rule applies. In most cases, for the secured party to prevail, (1) it must have filed a fixture filing before a recording of the real property interest, i.e., the mortgage or deed, and (2) the debtor must have been in possession of the real property or have an interest in it when the security interest was given. UCC § 9-334(e)(1). The debtor will have an interest in the property as long as it is the owner or has a lease that is recorded. A secured party also must have priority over the predecessor in title to the one claiming a real property interest. *Id.*

Example 33: On June 1, *S* obtains a security interest in an air conditioning unit that is attached to real property owned by the debtor in such a way as to make it a fixture. *S* files a fixture filing on the same day. On July 1, the owner grants a mortgage on the real property to *M* in return for a loan. *M* records the mortgage on the same day.

S has priority over *M* as to the air conditioning unit because it filed a fixture filing before the time that *M* recorded.

Time Line

Create your own time line for Example 33 here:

_____

Example 34: On October 1, *O*, the owner of a building grants a mortgage to *M1* in return for a loan. *M1* records the mortgage on the same day. On November 1, *S* takes a security interest in an air conditioning unit presently in the building, and files a fixture filing on that day. On December 1, *O* grants a second mortgage to *M2*, and *M2* records on the same day.

M1 has priority over *S*, but *S* has priority over *M2*.

Time Line

Create your own time line for Example 34 here:

Example 35: On May 1, *O*, the owner of Blackacre grants a mortgage to *M* in return for a loan. *M* records on the same day. On June 1, *S* obtains a security interest in an air conditioning unit that is attached to real property owned by the debtor in such a way as to make it a fixture. *S* files a fixture filing on the same day.

M has priority over *S* because it recorded before *S* filed. If *M* assigns its mortgage to *A* on August 1, and *A* records the assignment on the same day, *A* has priority over *S* because *A*'s predecessor in title, *M*, had priority.

Time Line

Create your own time line for Example 35 here:

In three classes of cases, the secured party need not file a fixture filing, and thus a regular financing statement will suffice: (1) when a financing statement is filed before the goods become fixtures and the fixture is factory or office machinery, equipment which is not used in the operation of the realty, and when the goods are replacements of appliances that are consumer goods, UCC § 9-334(e)(2); (2) when the contest is between a secured party and one having a lien on the realty that was obtained through the judicial process, UCC § 9-334(e)(3); and (3) when the security interest is on a manufactured home and the security interest is recorded under a certificate of title statute. See UCC § 9-334(e)(4).

C. **Priority when a security interest in fixtures is a PMSI:** A PMSI in fixtures takes priority over a conflicting interest of a mortgagee or owner of the property if:

1. the interest of the mortgagor or owner arose before the goods became fixtures, and
2. the secured party filed a fixture filing within 20 days of the time the goods became fixtures.

UCC § 9-334(d).

Example 36: On March 1, *O*, who owns real property, gave a mortgage on the property to *M*, which *M* recorded on the same day. On April 1, *O* purchased a heater for the property, which was installed and became a fixture on April 15. *O* gave a security interest in the heater to the seller, *S*, to secure the purchase price. *S* filed a fixture filing on May 1.

As between *S* and *M*, *S* has priority.

Time Line

Create your own time line for Example 36 here:

_____

VII. CROPS

Crops, a subtype of farm products (see UCC § 9-102(a)(34)(A)), are not fixtures but bear a similarity to them in that crops are a part of the real property, and a person having an interest in the realty has an interest in the crops. Crops, however, can be collateral for an Article 9 security interest.

As is true with fixtures, when the dispute is between a security interest in crops and a second security interest in the same crops, or a creditor with a lien on the crops, the default priority provisions apply. The same applies when there is a dispute between a secured party and one having an agricultural lien because agricultural liens are treated as security interests. As between a secured party and one having a judicial lien, the rule is that the lien creditor prevails if the lien attached before the time that the secured party perfected.

Article 9 does not give the usual protection given to BIOCs if the collateral is crops. UCC § 9-320(a). Thus, a buyer of crops prevails only over unperfected security interests. UCC § 9-317(b). However, BIOCs of crops will take free of security interests under the Federal Farm Security Act unless there is compliance with the notice or filing requirements of that Act.

Note: The special preferences given to purchase-money secured parties do not apply, but can you guess why?

Because it is impossible to have a PMSI in crops, the drafters of the 1999 version of Article 9 offered suggestions for providing a preference to security interests that secured debts incurred to allow a farmer to produce crops. The sections, termed "model provisions," were not made a part of the Official Version, but suggested new §§ 9-103A and 9-324A that provide for "production-money security interests." In states adopting these provisions, money provided for the production of crops is given a preference similar to the preference given to PMSIs.

As between a security interest in crops and those having an interest in the real property, the security interest has priority so long as the security interest is perfected and the debtor has possession of the land or has a recorded interest in it. The time of perfection is immaterial.

Example 37: On January 1, *O*, the owner of a farm, gave a mortgage in the land to *M*, which *M* immediately recorded. On June 1, *O* gave a security interest in all of its crops to *S*.

As between *S*'s security interest and *M*'s mortgage, *S*'s security interest has priority.

Time Line
Create your own time line for Example 37 here:

_____

VIII. ACCESSIONS AND COMMINGLED GOODS

A. **Accessions:** An *accession* is a good that is physically united with another good without losing its identity. UCC § 9-102(a)(1). For example, if an engine is installed in an automobile, the engine is an accession. A security interest may be created in an accession and will continue in the accession after it becomes part of the other goods. Perfection of the accession also continues after it is united with the other goods.

The regular priorities rules apply to any conflict between the person having a security interest in the accession and the person who has a security interest in the goods of which the accession becomes a part. Thus, if the party having the security interest in the accession has filed before the person who has the security interest in the goods of which the accession becomes a part, the accession-secured party has priority. A secured party in accessions also gains the preference given to PMSIs.

Example 38: On February 1, *S1* takes a security interest in a cotton gin owned by Debtor to secure a loan to Debtor. *S1* perfects on the same day. On March 1, *S2* takes a security interest in an extra motor that Debtor had, and files a financing statement on that day. On June 1, the original motor in the cotton gin fails, and Debtor installs the motor in which *S2* has a security interest.

As between *S1* and *S2*, *S1* has priority as to the motor.

Time Line
Create your own time line for Example 38 here:

_____

Example 39: On February 1, Debtor gives a security interest in its tractor to *S1* to secure a loan. *S1* perfects immediately. On March 1, Debtor purchases a new motor for the tractor from *S2* and gives *S2* a security interest in the new motor. Debtor installs the new motor in the tractor.

As between *S1* and *S2*, *S2* has priority because it has a PMSI.

Time Line

Create your own time line for Example 39 here:

_____

B. **Commingled goods:** *Commingled goods* are goods that are united with other goods in a way that causes them to lose their identity. UCC § 9-336(a). For example, if a farmer stores grain in a commercial silo with the grain of other farmers, the grain loses its identity. Article 9 provides that there can be no security interest in goods that are commingled with other goods, UCC § 9-336(b), but that a security interest in the goods before they are commingled becomes a security interest in the whole of goods. UCC § 9-336(c). Thus, if *S* has a security interest in a farmer's grain, and the grain is commingled with other grain, *S* loses its security interest in the farmer's grain but gets a security interest in all of the grain.

    If the secured party has perfected its security interest in the goods before they are commingled, its security interest in the whole is also perfected. If more than one secured party has a security interest in the whole, perfected security interests have priority over unperfected security interests. If more than one security interest is perfected, the security interests rank in proportion to the value of the collateral at the time it was commingled. UCC § 9-336(f).

    Example 40: *S1* has a perfected security interest in grain owned by Farmer A worth $10,000. *S2* has a perfected security interest in grain owned by Farmer B worth $20,000. Farmers A and B each store their grain in a silo owned by *X*.

    As to the whole of the grain stored by Farmers A and B, *S1* has priority as to one-third of it, and *S2* has priority as to two-thirds of it.

Time Line

Create your own time line for Example 40 here:

_____

IX. MISCELLANEOUS PRIORITIES RULES

A. **Licensee of general intangibles:** A person who obtains a licensee of general intangibles in good faith, without knowledge that the license violates the rights of another and in the ordinary course of business, is called a "licensee in the ordinary course of business." A licensee in the ordinary course of a nonexclusive license takes free of all security interests created by the licensor even if they are perfected and the lessee knows of their existence. UCC § 9-321(a).

For example, *O*, who owns the trademark "Good and Best Widgets," grants a security interest in the trademark to Bank. *O* then grants *L* a license to use the trademark. *L* takes free of the security interest of Bank.

B. Lessee in ordinary course of business: A lessee in the ordinary course of business of goods takes free of all security interests created by the lessor even if they are perfected and the lessee knows of their existence. UCC § 9-321(b).

For example, Goodcopy grants a security interest in all of the copiers it holds as inventory to Bank. Goodcopy leases a copier to *L*, who takes in the ordinary course of business. *L* takes free of the security interest of Bank. The rule, as you will observe, is similar to the rule protecting BIOCs.

C. Priority of security interests in deposit accounts: A security interest in deposit accounts (which are bank accounts, and should not be confused with Article 9 "accounts," which are accounts receivable), can be perfected only by the secured party taking control of the deposit account. UCC § 9-312(b)(1). See Chapter 5, *supra*. When the secured party has taken control of the deposit account, and thus perfected its security interest, the security interest takes priority over all unperfected security interests and security interests that were perfected later. UCC § 9-327.

Transferees of money from a deposit account take free of any security interests in the account, even if perfected, unless the transferee acts in collusion with the debtor in violating the rights of the secured party. UCC § 9-332.

D. Purchasers of chattel paper

    1. When the secured party claims an interest in the chattel paper as proceeds: A purchaser of chattel paper (as opposed to a person who takes a security interest in chattel paper to secure a loan) has priority over a security interest in chattel paper if the security interest arises solely because it is proceeds of collateral in which the secured party has a security interest when the purchaser (1) is in good faith, (2) buys in the ordinary course of the purchaser's business, (3) gives new value, (4) and either takes possession of the chattel paper or obtains control of it, provided that the chattel paper does not contain a legend on it that indicates that the chattel paper has been assigned to someone other than the purchaser. UCC § 9-330(a). New value is defined as "(i) money; (ii) money's worth in property, services, or new credit; or (iii) release by a transferee of any interest in property previously transferred to the transferee." UCC § 9-103(a)(57). New value does not include an obligation substituted for another obligation. *Id.* When the secured party's security interest in the chattel paper exists because the chattel paper is proceeds, a purchaser who meets these requirements takes free of the security interest even if the purchaser knows that the sale violates the rights of the secured party.

    Example 41: *S* takes a security interest in all of Debtor's inventory. Debtor sells a piece of the inventory to Buyer, who gives *S* a promise to pay for the goods in 30 days and a security interest in the goods purchased (chattel paper). Debtor then sells the chattel paper to Purchaser. If Purchaser takes in good faith, in the ordinary course of Purchaser's business, takes possession or control of the chattel paper, and gives new value, Purchaser takes free of *S*'s security interest so long as the paper does not contain a legend on it stating that it had been assigned to *S* or to someone else.

Time Line
Create your own time line for Example 41 here:

_____

---

2. **When the security interest in chattel paper does not arise as proceeds:** A secured party may take a security interest directly in chattel paper as the collateral securing a loan. In these cases, a purchaser takes free of the security interest only if it meets the requirement noted previously—the purchaser (1) takes for new value, (2) takes possession or control of the chattel paper, (3) takes in the ordinary course of the purchaser's business, (4) takes in good faith, and also takes without knowledge that the sale violates the rights of the secured party. UCC § 9-330(b)). "Knowledge" is actual knowledge, and there is no obligation on the purchaser to check the filing records or otherwise attempt to obtain knowledge that the sale violates the secured party's rights. Even if the purchaser knows that a security interest has been given in the chattel paper, this does not mean that it knows (has actual knowledge) that the sale violates the rights of the secured party.

    Again, this is similar to the rule protecting BIOCs.

    Example 42: *S* takes a security interest in all of Debtor's chattel paper. Subsequently, Debtor sells some of the chattel paper to Purchaser, who takes in good faith and in its ordinary course of business, gives new value, and takes possession of the chattel paper. Purchaser knows that a financing statement has been filed by *S* listing the chattel paper as the collateral for its security interest, but has no other information about the transaction between *S* and Debtor.

    Purchaser takes free of *S*'s security interest.

E. **Purchasers protected under other Articles of the Code:** Certain bona fide purchasers are protected under other Articles of the Code. In Article 3, a "holder in due course" is given significant rights against ownership claims to a negotiable instrument by another person. Similarly, under Article 7, persons who take a negotiable document of title by "due negotiation," and "protected persons" under Article 8, generally take free of adverse claims.

    Because negotiable instruments, documents of title, and investment securities can be collateral under Article 9, the person protected in Articles 3, 7, and 8 are given the same protection against secured parties. UCC § 9-302. In other words, a holder in due course's rights are not impaired by any priority rule in Article 9, and a holder in due course takes free of all security interests in the transferred instrument. UCC § 9-302.

Quiz Yourself on
PRIORITIES

85. Priorities rules govern disputes between:

_____ and _____,

_____ and _____, and between

_____ and _____.

86. The following steps are important in deciding priorities problems:

a. the validity of the _____.

b. the type of _____.

c. whether the security interest is a _____.

d. whether and how the security interest is _____.

e. when a financing statement was _____.

87. When the collateral is fixtures, the most likely dispute will be between the secured party and _____.

88. As between two secured parties, neither of whom has perfected, the first security interest to _____ prevails.

89. In determining priority between two secured parties, each secured party gets the earlier date of _____ or _____.

90. A PMSI in equipment has priority over all other security interests in the same collateral if the holder of the PMSI _____.

91. The holder of a PMSI in inventory has priority over all other security interests in the same collateral and is the holder of the PMSI _____ and _____.

92. One who purchases goods without notice of *S*'s security interest, for value and who takes delivery, takes the goods free of *S*'s security interest even if perfected provided that _____.

93. If *S* has a PMSI in consumer goods that is perfected automatically, *S*'s security interest will not be enforceable against a casual buyer if _____.

94. A BIOC takes free of all security interest created by _____.

95. When the secured party has a non-PMSI, the secured party will prevail over judicial lien creditors if _____.

96. When the secured party has a PMSI, the secured party will prevail over judicial lien creditors provided the secured party has _____.

97. When the security agreement has a future advances clause, the secured party will prevail over other secured parties as a future advance provided that the _____.

98. When the security agreement contains a future advance clause, a secured party who has perfected by filing will prevail over judicial lien creditors as to an advance made with knowledge of the judicial lien provided the advance is made _____ or _____.

99. When the security agreement contains a future advance clause, a secured party will prevail over a buyer who takes delivery for value in good faith and without knowledge of the transfer _____.

100. When goods in which a party has a security interest become accessions, the security interest of the party _____.

101. If the goods are fixtures, to have rights against mortgagees of the real property to which the goods are affixed the secured party must _____.

102. If the secured party has properly filed, it will prevail over prior mortgagees if _____.

Answers

85. Secured parties and other secured parties; secured parties and transferees from the debtor; secured parties and lien creditors

86. a. Security interest

 b. Collateral

 c. PMSI

 d. Perfected

 e. Filed

87. someone who has an interest in the real property, e.g., a mortgagee or a purchaser from the debtor

88. attach

89. perfection or filing

90. perfects within 20 days of the debtor obtaining possession of the collateral

91. perfects before the debtor obtains possession of the collateral and gives notice to secured parties who have filed a financing statement

92. the perfection was after the purchaser met all of these requirements

93. it is unfilled

94. the person selling the goods to the BIOC

95. it has perfected before the lien arose

96. perfected within 20 days of time from when the debtor obtained possession of the collateral

97. secured party has perfected first

98. within 45 days of the time the lien arose even if the secured party knows of the lien or even after the 45 days if the secured party did not know of the lien

99. if the advance is made within 45 days of the transfer without knowledge of the sale or if there was a commitment to make the transfer within that 45-day period and the secured party did not know of the transfer

100. continues in the accession, and, as to a person with a security interest in goods to which the goods are added, has the same priority as it has as to other secured parties

101. file a fixture filing

102. the secured party has a PMSI

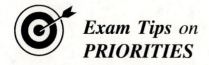

Exam Tips on PRIORITIES

Except for the material in Chapter 4, everything you have learned up to now was leading up to this chapter on priorities problems. Priorities problems are the most common type of question on most tests. These questions look difficult, and they are, but if you take a systematic approach to them, you can answer them. Because it is like a puzzle, solving these problems can actually be fun!

☞ *A system for solving them:* Remember the system that we have suggested in this chapter. Use it. What you do is:

1. Set up the status of the secured party.

   a. Is there a valid security interest?

   b. What is the collateral?

   c. Is it a PMSI?

   d. Is it Perfected? How? When?

2. Set up the status of the other parties. The other party must be one or more of the following:

   a. Another secured party

   b. A transferee of the collateral from the debtor

   c. A person with a judicial or possessory lien

3. Apply the correct priority rule.

☞ *Using the system:* Each of the steps is independent of the others. You need not go through all of them in writing your answer in some questions, but *think* about them while you are planning your answer. For example, if the question tells you that *D* gave a security interest to *S*, you need not question whether the security interest exists and is valid.

☛ *Step 1: Status of the secured party*

☞ *1. Is the security interest valid?* Remember what you learned in Chapter 4. The debtor must intend to create a security interest, and *either* there must be a security agreement *or* the debtor must have possession. If there is a question on this issue, it will usually give you facts about the security agreement and raise a problem with it: Is it an authenticated record? Does it have a description of the collateral? If there are facts given about the description, especially if the description is in quotes, consider whether the description in the agreement is sufficient: Does it describe the goods? Remember, an overbroad description, e.g., "All of debtor's property" is *not* sufficient" for use in a security agreement.

☞ *2. What is the collateral?* Go back to Chapter 2. Memorize the definition of the types of collateral, especially consumer goods, equipment, inventory, accounts, and chattel paper. These are the assets that most often come up in questions. Again, if your professor has covered other types of collateral, make sure you know the definition of those types as well.

☞ *3. Is the security interest a PMSI?* It is if the credit was extended to allow the debtor to obtain the collateral.

☞ *4. Is it perfected?* There must be attachment for perfection and then there must be a filing *or* the debtor must have possession *or*, as for deposit accounts, the debtor must have control. Remember, you cannot perfect by taking possession if the collateral is accounts. If there is a filing, carefully note the time of the filing, because often, but not always, the secured party gets the benefit of earlier of the date of perfection or the date of filing. For example, if the secured party files before it gives value, there will be no perfection until the value is given, but in many cases the critical date for the secured party will be the earlier date when it was filed. This analysis leads you to be able to say something like, "the secured party has a PMSI that was perfected by filing on May 1." There's a lot of analysis in that little sentence. Even if you only get to this point in your answer, if your analysis is accurate, you will get points.

☛ *Step 2: Status of other parties:* Other parties will be (1) other secured parties, (2) transferees, or (3) lien creditors or a combination of these types.

☞ *1. Other secured parties:* If there is a second (or third) secured party in the question, analyze those secured parties in the same way as suggested previously.

☞ *2. Transferees:* Transferees will be either

☞ *(a) Ordinary purchasers for value without knowledge who have taken delivery (P/V w/o K):* Remember the requirement of physical delivery. Remember also, that it is "knowledge" not "notice" that prevents one from attaining this status.

☞ *(b) Buyers in the ordinary course of business (BIOCs):* Persons who buy from a retailer, or retailers who buy from a wholesaler, are BIOCs. Remember that one can be a BIOC even though they know of a security interest, but they cannot be a BIOC if they know that the sale to them is in violation of the secured party's rights, e.g., they know that the security agreement has a provision forbidding the sale unless the debtor obtains possession from the secured party. Again, remember that to be a BIOC, the transferee must take possession of the goods.

☞ *(c) Casual buyers: A very limited group:* You have to buy **for** your own personal, family, or household purposes and you have to buy **from** someone who is holding the goods as consumer goods. A consumer who buys a refrigerator from a department store is ***not*** a casual buyer. Some teachers and writers call casual buyers "consumer buyers" or "garage-sale purchasers."

If a transferee does not fall into one of these categories, the transferee will lose to a secured party. For example, a donee loses.

☛ *Lien creditors*

☞ **First point:** General creditors, those without a lien, will always lose to a secured party.

☞ The most important type of lien creditor is the ***judicial lien creditor,*** one who gets a lien by virtue of the legal process. The most common judicial lien creditor is a creditor who gets a judgment and who then executes on the property. Depending on the jurisdiction, the lien can arise at the time the writ of execution is delivered to the sheriff or when the sheriff takes possession of (or get control over) the property—levies on it. Remember that a trustee in bankruptcy is a lien creditor as of the time that the petition in bankruptcy is filed.

☞ What Article 9 calls "***possessory liens***" are those that arise because of a statute and depend on the creditor having possession of the property. Frequently, they are called "statutory lien creditors." Liens given to mechanics and repairers of jewelry are frequent, but you have to look outside the Code to find who has a possessory lien.

☞ Another type of lien is the ***agriculture lien***. These are also created by statutes outside the Code, and usually give liens to those who supply credit to farmers. For the most part, Article 9 treats agricultural liens the same as security interests and the priorities rules applying to secured interests also apply to them.

☞ *When a question involves a lien creditor, it is important when the lien arose for the purposes of priorities.*

☛ *Step 3: Apply the correct priority rule:* An initial look at the priorities rules can lead to confusion. There are a lot of them, and they are so detailed. If you divide them into three types, they become more manageable. There are priorities rules that determine who wins as between: (1) two secured parties; (2) a secured party and a transferee, and (3) a secured party and a lien creditor.

☞ *1. Secured party versus secured party*

☞ *When neither has a PMSI* the rule is straightforward: first in time–first in right. **REMEMBER:** In applying this rule, the secured party gets the earlier of the date of perfection or of filing. Thus, if the security interest is first perfected by possession and then by filing, the secured party gets the advantage of the date it took possession *so long as there is no gap in the perfection.* Also, if there is a filing before perfection because there was no attachment at the time of filing, the date of filing is the critical time.

☞ *When one of the secured parties has a PMSI IN ANYTHING OTHER THAN INVENTORY:* A really simple rule: The secured party with the PMSI wins if it has perfected within 20 days of the debtor getting possession.

Note: The 20 days start at the time the debtor gets possession, not at the time the security interest was given or when value was given.

Also remember that a secured party with a PMSI in consumer goods gets automatic perfection—no need to file. The automatic perfection is just as good (at least in this competition) as perfection by filing or possession. The critical time is the time that the security interest has attached. This means that the secured party with a PMSI in consumer goods is going to win.

☞ ***When one of the secured parties has a PMSI in inventory:*** Here the rule is a little more complicated: the secured party with the PMSI wins if (1) it has perfected before the debtor obtains possession and (2) it has given notice that it is taking its security interest to other secured parties who have filed.

These are the two major rules that you must know when the dispute is between two secured parties. Unless your professor has emphasized some of the other, more detailed rules, you are probably better off not spending too much time studying them.

☞ ***2. Secured party versus transferees:*** Here it is necessary to consider carefully the status of the transferee. Is the transferee a BIOC? A causal buyer? A purchaser for value without notice?

   ☞ ***When the transferee is a BIOC:*** If the transferee is a BIOC, it takes free of all security interest *created by its seller.* A pretty simply rule, but watch out for the last four words, "created by its seller."

   A popular question involves a situation in which the security interest was created by someone else. For example, *D* gives a security interest to Bank. *D* then sells the property to Retailer, who deals in used goods of that kind. *T* then buys from Retailer. Even if *T* is a BIOC, which *T* might well be, *T* does NOT take free of Bank's security interest because it was not created by its seller, Retailer.

   ☞ ***When the transferee is a casual buyer:*** Again the rule is simple: a casual buyer takes free of all ***unfiled*** security interests. **REMEMBER:** Casual buyers must buy for their own personal, family, or household purposes ***and*** they must buy from someone who is holding the goods for their own personal, family, or household purposes. This limits casual buyers pretty much to those who buy from a neighbor, perhaps at a garage sale. **REMEMBER ALSO:** A secured party with a PMSI in consumer goods gets automatic perfection, ***but the secured party can file if it wants to*** and if it does file, it will prevail over casual buyers.

   ☞ ***When the transferee is a purchaser for value without knowledge (P/V w/o K):*** Here the basic rule is also simple: first in time–first in right. The critical time for the secured party is the time of ***perfection.*** If a filing occurs before perfection, the secured party does not get the benefit of the earlier filing date. The critical time for the transferee is the time that it meets ***all of the requirements*** of that status. Be careful, for example, of situations in which the transferee makes a contract for the sale of the collateral but does not take delivery until after the secured party has perfected.

   With P/V w/o K, the rule changes when the secured party has a ***PMSI***. In that case, the secured party always wins if it has perfected within 20 days of the time the debtor receives possession.

☞ ***3. Secured parties versus lien creditors:*** As to ***judicial lien creditors,*** the rule is the same as it is with regard to P/V w/o K. The first-in-time rule applies: time of perfection versus time that the lien arises in the collateral. Also, a secured party with a ***PMSI*** has 20 days in which to file.

   As to ***possessory liens,*** the holder of the lien wins over all secured parties unless the statute establishing the lien provides otherwise.

These are the primary and most tested priorities rules. If your professor has spent time on some of the other rules discussed in this chapter, go back to the text of the chapter and study them some more.

☛ ***Using time lines:*** As you go through the process of determining the status of the secured party or parties, and of third parties, we strongly suggest that you develop a time line such as we have done in the first few examples of this chapter. It's a great way to visually represent what has happened in the question and it makes it much easier to figure out the priorities among the parties. If you have constructed time lines as you worked though this chapter, they will become second nature.

CHAPTER 7

SOME BASIC BANKRUPTCY CONCEPTS

ChapterScope _____

This chapter exposes you to a few bankruptcy concepts, particularly those most important to a secured lender. The concepts discussed in this chapter are as follows:

- **The different kinds of bankruptcy:** This chapter describes the basic principles governing bankruptcy cases filed under Chapter 7, Chapter 13, Chapter 12, and Chapter 11 of the Bankruptcy Code.

- **The automatic stay:** The automatic stay is an injunction against all collection activities on the part of creditors. This section tells the secured party's attorney what to watch out for once a borrower files for bankruptcy.

- **Relief from the automatic stay:** This chapter also describes how a secured party goes about having the automatic stay removed or lifted.

- **Treatment of secured creditors in bankruptcy:** This chapter outlines how secured creditors are treated in bankruptcy, by describing the different treatment for oversecured and undersecured creditors, by walking through the calculations for bifurcated claims, and by describing the secured creditor's likely treatment in a Chapter 11 plan.

- **The avoidance powers:** This chapter also describes a few of the bankruptcy avoidance powers, particularly preferential transfers and the trustee's strong-arm powers, which allow a bankruptcy trustee to avoid unperfected security interests.

I. INTRODUCTION

Bankruptcy and secured transactions are intricately woven together. It would be hard to learn one of these topics without at least knowing something about the other. For that reason, we have included some basic bankruptcy concepts in this last chapter.

Most textbooks we have reviewed address the topic of bankruptcy at the end of the course, just as this Outline will do. Bankruptcy topics can be interspersed throughout a course, but for a more cohesive approach, we choose to address them at the end of the text here. Some Secured Transactions courses follow this approach as well; however, we suspect that most barely touch on the information we have included in this chapter. We therefore assume that you'll learn most of this in another law school course, and discuss only the basic types of bankruptcy here: the automatic stay, the treatment of secured claims in bankruptcy, and certain of the bankruptcy avoidance powers. We will also tell you here if the bankruptcy topic discussed below is substantively connected in some way to something we covered already in another chapter of this Outline.

II. THE DIFFERENT TYPES OF BANKRUPTCY

Federal bankruptcy law is a uniquely American phenomenon. It is an intricate system designed, in part, to fuel and support capitalism. The system has in the past been quite lenient on debtors in many ways, and has allowed people to get out from under their debts with few societal repercussions.

Just as we saw under state law, secured creditors have superior rights in bankruptcy when compared to creditors that do not have any collateral. In the United States, all the different kinds of bankruptcy are designed to balance two things: the rights of debtors to a fresh start or a second chance, and the rights of creditors to be paid. This tension is present in all aspects of the system.

Bankruptcy cases in the United States fall into two models or categories. They are either (1) "sellout" or liquidation-style cases, (also sometimes called straight bankruptcy cases), in which the assets available for creditors are sold and distributed to creditors, quickly ending the case, *or* (2) "payout" cases in which the debtor promises in a plan of repayment to pay some or all creditors from future income over time. Both the phrases "sellout" and "payout" can be misnomers, but they are quick generalizations that should help you learn the basics.

A. **Chapter 7:** In the past, approximately 70 percent of all personal bankruptcy cases filed in the United States have been Chapter 7 cases. These are called "liquidation" or "sellout" cases, and are quickly resolved. In each Chapter 7 case, a trustee is appointed to gather all assets available to pay creditors and to sell them and distribute the proceeds, according to a structured priority scheme. The trustee is a fiduciary for all creditors and is charged with maximizing value for estate creditors, usually by rooting around for nonexempt assets to be used to pay creditors' claims.

Some property is exempt in a bankruptcy, just as it is under state law. As a result, in 96 percent of Chapter 7 liquidation cases, none of the debtor's property is liquidated. The debtor therefore loses no property. Instead, in exchange for a complete and full disclosure of all financial information, the debtor receives a discharge of most of his or her debts within 90 days of filing the Chapter 7 case. Secured debts are not discharged, nor are certain other debts, such as student loans, most taxes, alimony and support, and others.

Most Chapter 7 cases are simple and uneventful. What issues might come up in an individual's Chapter 7 case? First, if the debtor's disclosures are not complete or are false, the case could be a total disaster, and the debtor could even end up in jail.

What else? The trustee could disagree with the debtor about which property is exempt and may challenge the values of the debtor's property as too low, thus arguing that there would be assets available to creditors if the property (or some part of it) were sold. The trustee or an individual creditor might object to the debtor's discharge due to wrongdoing on the part of the debtor right before or during the bankruptcy case (if, for example, the debtor hid assets). It is possible that a creditor will object to the dischargeability of its particular debt, or perhaps the United States Trustee's office (an arm of the Justice Department) or the court might object to the case because the debtor has income over and above his expenses and thus could afford a Chapter 13 plan.

In most cases, though, the case will be administered by the Chapter 7 trustee within 90 days of the filing; there are no court hearings, and after these 90 days are over, the debtor will obtain a discharge of most of his or her debts.

If a Chapter 7 case is for a business, there are no exemptions and whatever funds are generated from the sale of the business's property are distributed to creditors under a priority scheme. If a secured party has a business borrower who files for Chapter 7, the lender can frequently get their collateral back. This is explained in more detail below.

B. **Chapter 13:** Chapter 13 cases, as compared to Chapter 7 cases, are payout rather than sellout cases. As a general matter, the debtor does not sell its nonexempt assets and instead is allowed to keep all the assets as long as the debtor is paying at least the value of these nonexempt assets to creditors under the plan.

The idea is that the debtor will propose a repayment plan for paying creditors and will make the proposed payments for three to five years. During that time, the debtor will pay all secured claims in full (this is not necessarily the whole debt), all priority claims in full, and will pay a distribution to unsecured creditors as well, assuming the debtor has sufficient disposable income to do so.

The case is administered by a Chapter 13 trustee, who, like the Chapter 7 trustee, is a fiduciary for creditors and is charged with creating the best possible recoveries for the debtor's creditors. The trustee may do this by trying to get the debtor to contribute more of his income to the plan, by objecting to the debtor's expenses as profligate, or by encouraging the debtor to sell some property if this is the only way the plan will work.

Common issues in cases arising in a Chapter 13 case include: (1) the value of the underlying collateral, and thus the value of the allowed secured claims, (because in some cases the debtor can just pay the value of the collateral, rather than the whole loan); (2) the priority treatment of certain claims; (3) whether the debtor has contributed all of his disposable income to the plan, which is required under Chapter 13; and (4) the value of the debtor's exempt property, as that bears on the minimum distributions the debtor must pay under the plan.

The Chapter 13 trustee plays a very large role in the success of Chapter 13 cases and is often the one to object to the plan and otherwise ensure that it complies with the Bankruptcy Code. Chapter 13 is used most often for the purpose of curing past due amounts on secured debts.

C. Chapter 12: Chapter 12 is a bankruptcy scheme for family farmers and fishermen. A family farmer or fisherman is a person who receives more than 80 percent of his or her gross income from farming or fishing and who (with his or her family) owns a large part of the business that generates that income.

Chapter 12 is very similar to Chapter 13 but has slightly easier repayment rules and higher debt limits. The debt limit for a family farmer is $3,792,650, and for a family fisherman, $1,757,475. That means a person can file a Chapter 12 bankruptcy if his or her debts are at this level or lower. These numbers change periodically so make sure you look them up before using them.

Family farmers and fishermen are allowed to pay less on their secured debts, so this type of bankruptcy can be very beneficial for some debtors but not so beneficial for secured creditors.

D. Chapter 11: Chapter 11 is a payout-style case, available to individuals but almost always used by business entities like corporations. You can read about big Chapter 11 cases that are currently pending simply by reading the front page of the *Wall Street Journal*. Recent cases include Chrysler, GM, Kmart, Enron, WorldCom, and even the Texas Rangers!

Most individuals only file a Chapter 11 case if they are over the Chapter 13 debt limits, which, as of 2010, are $360,475 in unsecured debts and $1,081,400 in secured debts. These eligibility numbers increase on April 1 every year. The reason individuals prefer Chapter 13 to restructure their debts, even if they are business debts, is that Chapter 13 is far less complex and far cheaper than Chapter 11.

Chapter 11 cases involve restructuring the debts and other obligations of companies that need help. The general idea, as with Chapter 13, is that the debtor will repay a portion of its debts over time, from its future operations. Its plan will need to pay its allowed secured claims in full (up to the value of the collateral), its priority claims in full, and will usually pay a distribution to its unsecured creditors as well.

The plan approval process will be different, however. The debtor solicits votes from classes of creditors, on what it hopes will turn out to be a consensual Chapter 11 payout plan. If all classes of creditors vote to go along with the plan, then generally the court usually approves the plan. If there are holdouts ("no" votes), the court can sometimes force the creditors to accept the plan, assuming various tests are met by the plan and the debtor.

There is one huge difference between a case under Chapter 13 and a case under Chapter 11. Although both are payout-style cases, in a Chapter 11 case, the company in bankruptcy is run by the same people who were in management before the filing, or by some newly appointed management, but in any event, by management!

Some might say that the fox is in the henhouse, because in most Chapter 11 cases, there is *no* trustee. The debtor continues to run the company, although it does get a different name. The debtor is now called the "debtor in possession," or DIP. The DIP has, under the Bankruptcy Code, all of the duties and powers of a trustee. The DIP is a fiduciary and is charged with creating the best possible distributions for creditors.

III. THE AUTOMATIC STAY

As you know, outside bankruptcy, creditors can sue the debtor and then ***execute,*** or try to seize, the debtor's nonexempt assets. A bankruptcy petition acts as an immediate injunction order, directing creditors to cease all collection activity of any kind. This is accomplished through the ***automatic stay,*** which is the equivalent of a temporary restraining order that makes the creditor leave the debtor alone. As soon as the debtor files his bankruptcy petition, all creditors must stop any and all collection efforts against the debtor or the debtor's property, regardless of where that property is located.

The automatic stay stops all kinds of creditor collection activities, including the following:

■ *any* attempt to collect on a debt including phone calls and letters

■ *any* continuing lawsuit to collect a debt

■ *any* repossession of a debtor's assets

■ *any* attempt to exercise control over property of the debtor's estate

■ *any* attempt to perfect a security interest

■ pretty much *anything else* you can think of that would allow a creditor to improve its own position against the debtor compared to other creditors

The automatic stay continues in place until the bankruptcy case is over, or until a creditor gets the stay lifted or removed to pursue its own particular debt.

Secured creditors should be careful not to try to repossess or foreclose on property once a debtor has filed for bankruptcy. Secured creditors also are forbidden from perfecting a security interest after a bankruptcy, at least in most cases. Finally, a secured creditor cannot sell property in its possession that it has repossessed but not sold as of the filing of the debtor's bankruptcy petition. This is because the debtor still has an interest in the property.

Example 1: First Bank is suing Danny Debtor for a deficiency judgment resulting from a car loan gone bad. First Bank has already repossessed and sold the car, but its unpaid debt is still $4,000. First Bank has just received a piece of paper in the mail indicating that Danny has filed a Chapter 13 bankruptcy case. The state court hearing on the deficiency judgment case is tomorrow. First Bank should not appear at the hearing but, instead, should notify the court that the case has been stayed. In addition, it is unlikely that First Bank will receive much for the unpaid debt, but more on this later.

Example 2: Danny Debtor is way behind on his car payments to First Bank. First Bank was just about to send out the repo man to pick up the car when it received a notice in the mail that Danny Debtor had filed for Chapter 7 bankruptcy. First Bank should not repossess the car now that Danny has filed for bankruptcy. First Bank may be able to get the stay lifted in Danny's case, as we'll discuss later, but cannot proceed with the repossession until the stay is lifted.

Example 3: Danny Debtor is way behind on his car payments to First Bank. First Bank repossessed the car and is getting ready to sell it. While the car is in First Bank's possession, but before it is sold, First Bank receives a notice in the mail that Danny Debtor has filed for Chapter 11 bankruptcy. First Bank should not sell the car now that Danny has filed for bankruptcy. First Bank may be able to get the stay lifted to sell the car, as we'll discuss later, but cannot proceed with the sale now. Even though it was repossessed pre-bankruptcy, First Bank is forbidden from selling an asset of Danny's estate after the bankruptcy notice.

Note that the type of bankruptcy case filed is irrelevant. Also, if a creditor continues to try to collect from a debtor after a bankruptcy filing, the creditor can be held liable for actual and pecuniary damages, so be careful!

IV. RELIEF FROM THE AUTOMATIC STAY FOR SECURED CREDITORS

Even where the stay does go into effect, it can be removed by certain secured creditors, putting the debtor and the creditor back at square one, as if there had been no bankruptcy. In other words, sometimes secured creditors are able to have the automatic stay removed or lifted so that they can continue trying to collect the debt, just as if there was no bankruptcy.

In a Chapter 7 bankruptcy, the most common situation in which the stay will be lifted is when a secured creditor is *undersecured* or *upside-down*. This means the debt is larger than the value of the collateral.

Example 4: A debtor gets a loan from a dealership to buy a car. As part of the standard contract, the dealership gets a security interest in the car to secure payment on the loan. Everything goes fine for a year and then hard times hit. The debtor can't make the payments and the dealership, as a secured creditor, is threatening to repossess the car. Hoping to get some relief, the debtor files a Chapter 7 bankruptcy.

If the secured creditor, in our example the car dealership, is owed $10,000 and the automobile that is the collateral for the loan is worth only $8,000, the bankruptcy court will usually lift the stay. In practical terms this means the dealership, which couldn't even phone the debtor two paragraphs ago when he filed bankruptcy, can now repossess the auto and sell it to satisfy at least part of its debt.

Why should this be allowed when the debtor went through the trouble to declare bankruptcy? The rationale is that realistically, there is no value in the car for the debtor or the estate, meaning the debtor's other creditors. In fact, the debtor has no equity in the auto. A Chapter 7 debtor who is behind on his obligations to secured creditors will find very little relief under a Chapter 7 case. The creditor should be able to get the car back and sell it, although it may have trouble collecting its deficiency judgment.

The debtor would have no auto exemption to claim in such a case because he has no equity in the auto. In any case, a secured creditor's rights in collateral come ahead of a debtor's exemptions, even though the exemptions come ahead of the claims of unsecured creditors. This is true both inside and outside bankruptcy.

Getting back to the automatic stay, technically, there are two common ways for a secured creditor to get the stay lifted in order to pursue its rights under state law.[1] These standards for relief from the automatic stay are contained in Bankruptcy Code § 362(d)(1) and (2). Under § 362(d)(1), the stay shall be lifted if the court finds that there is "cause, including a lack of adequate protection of an interest in property of the moving party." This test requires that the creditor's interest in its collateral be safe and steady.

The creditor is not adequately protected if its position might be worsened through the debtor's use of the collateral. In practical terms, this often means that the debtor has no significant equity cushion in the property, that the property also is depreciating, and that as a result of this combined condition, the creditor is not protected against loss resulting from the debtor's continuing possession and use of the collateral.

Naturally, if the creditor is already undersecured, there is a good chance that there is a lack of adequate protection, but this also may be true if there is a small equity cushion (i.e., some value over and above the loan) but not one large enough to cover any diminution in the value of the collateral resulting from the debtor's use. Sometimes even an undersecured creditor (i.e., one in which the loan is larger than the value of the collateral) may not actually be entitled to relief from the stay in the rare case in which the debtor's use is not further diminishing the value of the collateral, but instead the value of the collateral will simply remain constant in the case. Most of the time, however, an undersecured creditor will not be adequately protected and thus the only requirement of Bankruptcy Code § 362(d)(1) will be met. As you can see by reading the section, Section 362(d)(1) is a one-part test.

Under the second way to obtain relief from the automatic stay, the creditor must prove two things, first that the debtor has no equity in the property (meaning the collateral), and second, that the property is not necessary to an effective reorganization of the debtor. While § 362(d)(1) often deals with equity in the sense that it identifies the size of the equity cushion, the section further involves looking only at the position of the moving party and whether there is equity in the property over and above *that* secured party's claim.

The equity described in Bankruptcy Code § 362(d)(2) refers to total equity in the property, which requires that one add up all the secured claims against the property (not just the moving party's claim) and determine if the debtor has any equity over and above all of those secured claims. In other words, for § 362(d)(2), we look at the total of all secured claims, not just the amount of the moving party's claim. This distinction makes a big difference.

For the second prong of § 362(d)(2), whether the property is necessary for an effective reorganization, the court must first determine if it is the kind of property that the debtor needs for its reorganization and then determine whether an effective reorganization is likely. This second part of the test is easiest for the creditor to prove that several months have passed without progress in the case.

After a certain amount of time has passed, the court may grant relief from the stay when there is no equity, because even if this property *would* be necessary in an effective reorganization of this debtor, an effective reorganization looks unlikely given all the time that has passed without progress.[2] Note that § 362(d)(2) requires the creditor to prove two things and thus tends to be harder to prove than § 362(d)(1), depending on the facts, of course. In a sense, § 362(d)(2) gives the debtor at least a few

---

1. To pursue rights under state law just means to pursue whatever rights the creditor had before the debtor invoked the federal Bankruptcy Code and interfered with its foreclosure, collection, repossession, etc. The phrase refers to a return to the status quo.

2. Extremely large cases are an exception to the rule that the debtor has just several months before relief from the stay is usually granted. In large cases debtors are often permitted to remain in operation, despite a lack of equity in a secured party's collateral, for years rather than months. This is true because very large reorganizations are highly complex and often take several years to complete.

months to reorganize, even if the debtor has no equity in the secured party's collateral. On the other hand, § 362(d)(1) requires that the court grant relief from the stay if it finds that the secured party lacks adequate protection, unless the debtor has another way of providing adequate protection.

Let's look at a situation in which the collateral is a $20,000 certificate of deposit (CD), and the secured creditor's claim against the collateral is $22,000 in a business bankruptcy case. This CD is not the type of collateral that the debtor needs to run its business. Not at all, in fact. The debtor can run its business quite aptly without this asset, and moreover the debtor has no equity in the collateral. Thus, one of the two tests for granting relief from the stay is met, even though it is the very beginning of the case. This is quite rare because most assets would be needed to run the business. This asset, however, is not. Thus, the creditor could get the stay lifted under § 362(d)(2). In a sense this test is consistent with common sense. If the debtor does not need the collateral for its operations (unlike equipment or inventory, for example) and if the debtor has no interest in the collateral anyway, why would we let the debtor keep it? It would make much more sense to just give it back to the creditor and let the creditor do whatever it wants to do with it, consistent with its state law rights. There are no overriding reorganization goals that would justify keeping the collateral from the creditor under these facts.

On the other hand, in the example in which the same debtor financed its operations through a $10 million line of credit secured by all of its inventory, its accounts, and its equipment, with a total value of about $9 million and a loan amount of about $9 million as well, the equities and circumstances are different. The creditor may or may not be adequately protected depending on whether the collateral is depreciating. If the creditor is not adequately protected, the court will need to grant relief from the stay or look for other adequate protection. If the collateral is not declining in value, then the creditor will need to rely on § 362(d)(2) and prove a lack of equity and that the property is not necessary to an effective reorganization. Because the creditor is required to prove both of these elements and because the collateral is clearly critical to the debtor's reorganization efforts, reorganization policy—as well as § 362(d)(2)—mandates that the debtor be given some chance to reorganize its affairs before the creditor is permitted to shut it all down.

V. THE TREATMENT OF SECURED CLAIMS IN BANKRUPTCY

As you know by now, when an Article 9 secured creditor's borrower is not in default and not in bankruptcy, the borrower pays the loan as promised and eventually the creditor releases it security interest on the collateral and the debtor owns the property "free and clear" of the security interest.

If the borrower does not pay the loan on time, and the loan instead goes into default, then the secured creditor has the right to repossess its collateral, sell the collateral to pay down the loan, and then pursue the debtor for a ***deficiency judgment***, the part of the loan that was not paid off from the sale of the collateral.

The creditor is, of course, an unsecured creditor for this deficiency judgment because the collateral is already gone, right? There is no longer any collateral to cover the part of the loan that is still unpaid. If the creditor wants to get a judgment for this remaining debt, it will need to execute on other property of the debtor to be paid, just as any unsecured creditor would.

This state law theme of being paid on default up to the value of the collateral, but not in excess of the value of the collateral, continues into the bankruptcy process. In a Chapter 7 case, if the debtor is a business and the business is now out of business, then the secured party can get the automatic stay lifted to gain the right to repossess and sell its collateral, just as it would outside bankruptcy.

If the debtor is an individual Chapter 7 debtor, then a number of things could happen. First, the debtor may just keep paying the loan and the creditor will not be affected by the bankruptcy. The debtor could also reaffirm the debt or redeem the collateral, something you'll learn more about in your bankruptcy class.

Alternatively, if the debtor is in default (i.e., behind on the payments), the secured creditor may get the stay lifted and again gain the right to repossess and sell the collateral. If this happens, then the creditor is limited in its recovery to the value of its collateral. Once it has sold it, the deficiency claim becomes an unsecured claim in the bankruptcy, and in most Chapter 7 cases, it is simply discharged.[3]

A. **Undersecured and oversecured creditors:** The creditor whose claim is bigger than the value of its collateral is called an ***undersecured creditor***. Conversely, a creditor whose collateral value more than covers the amount due on their loan to the debtor is an ***oversecured creditor***. The two are treated quite differently in bankruptcy.

The oversecured creditor gets extra benefits not available to either unsecured or undersecured creditors, including interest that continues to accrue after the bankruptcy case has been filed, at the contract rate,[4] as well as allowed fees for the creditor if the creditor must go to bankruptcy court or another court to enforce its right to be paid. Essentially, the oversecured creditor's claim can grow during the case, just as it would if there was no bankruptcy (through the continuing accrual of interest and fees), whereas the unsecured claim and the undersecured claim do not increase during the case, they stay the same.

The way that secured claims are calculated is covered in § 506 of the Bankruptcy Code. The special rights granted to creditors that are oversecured are spelled out in § 506(b).

Another thing about secured claims is that if they are undersecured, the claim ends up being split, for bankruptcy treatment purposes, into two parts. The part that is covered by the collateral is treated as secured, and the part that is not covered is treated as unsecured. We call this *bifurcation of the claim* because it is split into two parts.

The practical result is that the secured claim is really only as large as the value of the collateral. This concept is explained in § 506(a). The secured creditor's claim is allowed in the amount of the value of the collateral for the purposes of payment in bankruptcy. Whatever is left over of the claim is an unsecured claim.

Example 5: Brazen Bank holds a perfected security interest in all of Dominique's Boutiques's inventory. The current inventory in stock is worth approximately $45,000. Brazen's loan balance is now $60,000 with interest still accruing according to the terms of the loan documents. Because Brazen is owed $60,000 but has collateral worth just $45,000, Brazen is underwater, or undersecured.

Question: Can you calculate the size of Brazen's secured and unsecured claims? That would be $45,000 for the secured portion, and $15,000 for the unsecured portion, right?

B. **Practicing the calculations:** As you will soon see, it is always good from the creditor's perspective to have more collateral than one needs. Sometimes cases can drag on for some time. This is particularly true in a Chapter 11 case. We noted previously that the secured creditor's claim continues to accrue interest and attorneys' fees at the contract rate, if it is

---

3. This assumes there are no assets to distribute to creditors, which is often, although not always, the case.

4. The debtor and the secured creditor are usually parties to a written loan contract that provides that interest will accrue at a certain interest rate and also that attorneys' fees will be charged to the debtor if the loan goes into default and the creditor has to hire an attorney to help collect the loan.

oversecured. Section 506(b) makes it clear, however, that such postpetition interest and fees can accrue only for as long as there is still value left in the collateral over and above the secured party's claim.[5]

In other words, once the claim equals the value of the collateral (remember that the claim continues to increase during the case for the oversecured creditor), all the fees and interest cease to accrue. They do not become part of the unsecured claim either. Due to the timing issues, this can make for some tricky calculations.

Here we will borrow a question or two from the *Glannon Guide to Bankruptcy, Second Edition* (Nathalie Martin, Aspen Publishers, 2006). These are multiple-choice questions. See if you can answer them before reading the answers.

Example 6: John Carl Enterprises ("JCE") owes First State Bank $450,000 at the time it files its Chapter 11 case. JCE has pledged an office building worth $500,000 as collateral for the loan. The loan agreement provides that interest will accrue on the loan at the rate of 12% per annum or 1% per month. Assuming that there are no attorneys' fees to add to this claim, and that the building neither appreciates nor depreciates in value, how long can this case go on (assuming no payments of any kind to First State Bank during the case) before this loan stops earning interest?

a. 5 months
b. 9 months
c. 11 months
d. 18 months

Answer: The answer is **C**, 11 months. How did we calculate this? We divided the equity in the building by the interest expenses each month. The loan is currently at $450,000, and the collateral is worth $500,000. This leaves $50,000 in equity that can be used to pay future interest. But interest is accruing at the rate of 1% per month or $4,500 per month. After 11 months, this interest will equal $49,500. Yipes! If the case goes on for one year, not all that long in reality, then the loan will stop accruing interest after 11 months and a few days. This is an unrealistic problem because the creditor did not charge the debtor attorneys' fees. Thus, realistically, interest will actually be allowed in the claim for less than 11 months. This will be cured in the next problem.

Example 7: Use the same facts as in the previous example, but also assume that First State Bank's attorneys have been spending approximately $2,500 per month on attorneys' fees in JCE's Chapter 11 case. Now how many months can pass before First State Bank's loan will stop accruing interest, and until it also will need to begin paying its own attorneys' fees?

a. 6 months
b. 8 months
c. 7 months
d. 11 months

Answer: Instead of dividing the remaining equity in the building—$50,000—by $4,500 a month for just the interest, you now add to those payments $2,500 a month for attorneys' fees, for a total cost of $6,000 a month for both the interest and the fees. When this is done, it turns out that the equity is eaten up after just over 7 months. So the answer is **C**.

---

5. Any value in the collateral over and above the secured creditors' claim is called *equity*.

C. Secured creditor treatment under a Chapter 11 plan: As you will very shortly see, a Chapter 11 debtor can also drastically reduce the amount that the debtor pays on some secured loans, namely those in which the collateral for the loans is worth less than the debt. As you just learned, these are situations in which the secured party is undersecured. For these undersecured loans, the debtor can pay just the value of the secured property, along with interest, over the life of the plan.

1. **Bifurcation and "stripdown":** Because many personal property items depreciate rapidly after they are purchased, they are often worth far less than the amount still owed on them. Because the debtor can reduce the debt to the amount of the value of the collateral, this makes Chapter 13 very beneficial. The authority for this is Bankruptcy Code § 506(a), which defines a secured debt as secured "to the extent of the value of such creditor's interest . . . in such property." The process of reducing the loan to the value of the collateral is called, in bankruptcy parlance, the "stripdown" or "cramdown."

   One of the biggest benefits of both Chapter 13 and Chapter 11 is the ability to strip down the secured debt to just the value of the collateral. In its 2005 amendments to the Bankruptcy Code, Congress limited stripdown in Chapter 13 cases. Now one can no longer strip down a personal property purchase-money security interest (PMSI) loan secured by a car, if the car loan was taken out during the 2 1/2 years before the Chapter 13 case. One also cannot strip down a PMSI secured by household goods, if the loan was taken out within the one-year period before the Chapter 13 case. All other loans, including real estate loans, secured loans that are not PMSIs, and PMSIs outside these time frames, can still be stripped down.

2. **Valuation:** Stripdown requires that one determine the value of the collateral. Valuation is often accomplished in large business cases, as well as in some consumer cases, through an appraisal of the property in question. Appraisals may vary greatly depending on the purpose of the valuation, as well as the assumptions made by the appraiser. Judges often pick the most credible appraiser when asked to value a property. If both parties' appraisers are equally credible then the court will often just split the values down the middle. Normally only business assets and real estate are appraised. Smaller items of personal property are rarely appraised due to the cost of an appraisal. When it comes to vehicles and mobile homes, most parties use the Kelley Blue Book, an N.A.D.A. appraisal guide, or another similar resource.

   In *Associates Commercial Corp. v. Rash*, 520 U.S. 953 (1997), the U.S. Supreme Court decided whether the proper measure of value for stripdown purposes is the *wholesale* or the *retail* value, as both are offered by these Blue Book resources. After a long-standing split among the federal circuit courts about which of these two rules was preferable,[6] the U.S. Supreme Court declined to follow either approach, instead choosing the *replacement value*, a number somewhere in between wholesale and retail. The Supreme Court indicated in *Rash* that the proper value of a debtor's used personal property, for stripdown purposes, is the price at which the debtor could purchase a comparable used item.

   Regardless of how value is determined, it is the single most important determination with respect to whether a debtor will be able to afford to pay the crammed down value of a big-ticket item under his or her plan.

3. **The present value interest rate:** The other variable in determining the cost of paying off property that has been stripped down is the *present value* rate that the debtor will be required to pay. Section 1129 of the Bankruptcy Code requires that to strip down a secured creditor

---

6. Because the valuation sets the amount that the debtor must repay the secured party, the wholesale value tended to be lower and thus favored the debtor, while the retail value tended to be higher and thus favored the secured party.

class, the treatment the secured party receives must be "fair and equitable." Courts have determined that what is *fair and equitable* is to pay the secured party the *present value of its claim over the life of the collateral, and also to allow the secured party to retain its liens during the payment period.* This has been interpreted to mean that the creditor is entitled to the value of that claim as if it were being paid all at once on confirmation. Because the Code allows the payment over time, the debtor must compensate the creditor for the time value of money. A dollar paid a year from now is worth less than a dollar paid today. Thus, the debtor must pay the creditor for what the creditor loses in interest or other income by not receiving all of its money up front.

Practically speaking, we provide the secured party with the present value of its claim, and compensate it by assigning an interest rate to the debt. We somewhat cavalierly refer to this as the "present value interest rate" or simply the interest rate, but it is important to understand that it is not really interest. Rather, it is a payment to the secured party to provide it with the present value of its allowed secured claim.

VI. THE AVOIDING POWERS

Trustees and DIPs have the power to bring certain property that has been transferred away before a debtor's bankruptcy back into the debtor's estate. These powers are called the *avoiding powers.* There are many avoiding powers, and here we'll focus on just the main ones. Avoiding powers play an important role in most Chapter 11 cases and in some Chapter 7 and Chapter 13 cases.

The three most commonly avoided types of transfers are preferential transfers, fraudulent transfers, and invalidation of security interests that were never perfected in the first place. We will touch briefly only on those avoiding powers that most affect a secured party and the way these avoidance powers come up in a secured loan.

When a debtor makes a transfer of either money or a security interest, within the particular time set by the Code, the trustee or the DIP can avoid or undo the transfer, and thus bring the property (or a security interest) or its value back into the debtor's estate for the benefit of all creditors.

The policy behind reversing these transfers of property is equality of treatment between creditors. Avoidance of such transfers softens the transition period between the pre-petition period, during which some creditors may have improved their position using the state court collection processes, and the post-bankruptcy period, which is marked by equality of treatment rather than a race to the courthouse.

In some cases, a judgment creditor may have executed on property right before the bankruptcy. In other cases, the debtor may simply have transferred property or payments to another entity, either to keep them from taking action, or just because the debtor wants to pay one creditor over another. At other times a debtor may simply give a secured creditor a security interest, which is a transfer, for an old debt, right before a bankruptcy. Remember that the debtor can transfer money or other tangible property outright, or can transfer a *security interest* in something. All are transfers and are subject to potential avoidance.

A. **Preferential transfers:** Assume that the debtor pays its security company's bills for the past four months all at once and, a few weeks later, files for bankruptcy. This is a transfer of money or property (this one is money) on account of a past due or antecedent debt, within 90 days of the bankruptcy petition. If the debtor was insolvent at the time of the transfer, then this transfer would be avoidable by the trustee or the debtor-in-possession under § 547(b).

Section 547(b) contains the elements of an avoidable preferential transfer, and requires:

a. a transfer of property,
b. for or on account of an antecedent debt,
c. made within 90 days before the filing (one year for transfers to insiders such as family members),
d. while the debtor was insolvent,
e. that allowed the creditor to receive more than it would have received in a Chapter 7 case.

Why is insolvency required for a transfer to be a preference? Perhaps it is because at the time of insolvency, even if that precedes the bankruptcy filing, the policy of equality of treatment among creditors kicks in. More importantly, if the debtor is not insolvent at the time of a purportedly preferential transfer, there is no harm to other creditors because the remaining property should be sufficient to cover all creditors' claims.

The policy reasons behind preference avoidance should now be clear, and these policy reasons should help you remember the rule. Bring back the transferred property and allow it to be distributed among creditors equally, or at least according to the priority scheme.

1. **When the transfer is a security interest:** When the property transferred is a security interest, collateralizing an old or antecedent debt rather than a new one, avoiding the transfer can change the entire course of the case.

    Example 8: Assume Don's Auto is way behind on its payments to Karl's Parts, who has recently insisted that Don's come current on its account, or it will obtain a judgment and execute. Don's can't come current, so instead grants a security interest in all of its parts to Karl's to secure the past due amounts. Two months later, under the crush of other debt problems, Don's files a Chapter 11 petition, and moves to avoid the security interest. The transfer of this security interest to Karl's is an avoidable preferential transfer as long as the debtor was insolvent at the time the transfer of the security interest was made, or as long as no one proved otherwise.

    If the transfer of a security interest is made in connection with a new loan (not to secure an old debt), this transfer of a security interest is *not* a preference. The reason for this is that the security interest is not transferred "for or on account of an antecedent debt." Thus one element is not met. The security interest is given for a new debt, not an old or antecedent one.

    Caution: A secured party must make sure it files its financing statement as soon as it completes a loan, if not beforehand. If a creditor waits too long after the loan is made, the old loan might indeed be considered an antecedent debt.

2. **When the transfers are payments made to secured creditors during the preference period:** Note that the elements of a preference require that the transfer allow the creditor to get more than the creditor would receive in a Chapter 7 bankruptcy. By now, you probably know that in a Chapter 7 bankruptcy, fully secured creditors get their debts paid in full. This means that all payments made to fully secured creditors during the preference period are not preferences. The fully secured creditor does not meet the last element needed in order to get the transfer back from the creditor. More specifically, the secured creditor will not receive more than the creditor would get in a Chapter 7. In either case, the secured creditor would be paid in full. If the creditor receiving the payments is not fully secured, but rather is only partially secured, some of the payments may indeed be preferential transfers.

B. Avoidance of unperfected security interests under the trustee's strong-arm powers contained in § 544(a): Unperfected security interests can be avoided in bankruptcy. When this happens, the previously secured creditor is turned into a general unsecured creditor. The security interest is, in essence, returned to the estate, and the property is now unencumbered and its value can be distributed to unsecured creditors.

You'll recall from Chapter 6 that when determining the priority of claims between two secured creditors, the one that has perfected its security interest has priority over one who has not perfected. Moreover, the judgment lien creditor also has priority over the unperfected voluntary security interest, which is why perfection is important to maintaining one's position.

Outside bankruptcy, however, the fact that a secured party has failed to perfect does not wipe out the security interest completely. Rather, the secured party still has the rights of a secured party as against the debtor, and can repossess its collateral and sell it to realize on its claim.[7]

The priority themes contained in Article 9 (dealing with secured transactions) are continued in the Bankruptcy Code, although the avoidance powers go a step farther and allow the trustee to wipe out the unperfected security interest entirely rather than letting it linger around in its low priority state. The reason? Because we hate secret liens and fear that they could mislead creditors into thinking the debtor has more unencumbered assets from which to pay creditors than the debtor actually has.

The policies here are obvious, but the Code reaches this result in a way that is probably more complex than it needs to be. Following the theme of Article 9, the Code gives the trustee the rights of a hypothetical judgment lien creditor. Since lien creditors beat out unperfected security interests under Article 9, this means that the trustee can beat out an unperfected security interest. We call these avoidance powers the trustee's *strong-arm powers,* although we are not sure why.

Example 9: Bank One gets a security interest in accounts worth $100,000 on March 1 to secure a prior debt (as well as future debts) under a line of credit. Bank One never perfected this security interest. On August 1, the debtor who gave it to the Bank files for Chapter 11 bankruptcy. Bank One's security interest in the accounts can be avoided, thus relegating Bank One to the status of an unsecured creditor, because the security interest was never perfected.

The strong-arm powers are but one example of the bankruptcy trustee's avoiding powers, but are clearly one of the most important powers from the perspective of the secured creditor. For more avoiding powers, see 11 U.S.C. §§ 547, 548, and 550.

Quiz Yourself on BANKRUPTCY CONCEPTS

103. Briefly describe the differences between Chapter 7, 13, 12, and 11. _____

104. Which types of bankruptcy cases are available to individual debtors? _____

105. What is the purpose of the automatic stay? _____

---

7. This is true, assuming no senior lienholder's rights are impaired.

106. Can a creditor who has already repossessed a car but has not sold it go ahead and sell it after a bankruptcy has occurred? _____

107. What are the two primary grounds for lifting the automatic stay? _____

108. Define oversecured and undersecured. _____

109. Assume a creditor has security worth $50,000 and its loan is for $40,000. Its borrower has just filed for bankruptcy. What type of treatment can it expect in a Chapter 11 case? _____

110. Now assume those two numbers are reversed. The collateral is worth $40,000 and the loan is for $50,000. Now what can the creditor expect to receive in a Chapter 11 case? _____

111. Describe stripdown and its uses and limitations. In which bankruptcy chapters can it be used and for what? _____

112. The elements of a preference are _____, _____, _____, _____, and _____.

113. Why must a secured party make sure to file its financing statement very soon after it makes its loan? _____

114. Describe the strong-arm powers and their purposes. _____

Answers

103. Chapter 7 is a sellout- or liquidation-style bankruptcy. It can be used by individuals or business entities. The other bankruptcy chapters are all payout-style cases. They involve payment plans over time, usually from future income. Chapter 13 is used by individuals whose debts are below a certain amount. The payment plan for creditors is paid over three to five years. It is common to use a Chapter 13 to cure past due secured debts like home mortgages and car loans, because Chapter 7 does little to help a debtor save these items pledged as collateral for secured loans.

   Chapter 12 is similar to a Chapter 13 but is for family farmers and fishermen. Chapter 12 has higher debt limits than Chapter 13. Chapter 11 is a payment plan case used primarily by business debtors. The Chapter 11 debtor is managed by its current managers, not a trustee.

104. Chapters 7 and 13 can be used by individuals or natural persons. Chapter 12 also can be used by an individual if he or she is a farmer or fisherman.

105. The purpose of the stay is to stop all collection activity so the debtor can either use his or her assets to pay creditors in an organized way, or pay the debts over time.

106. No, not without getting the stay lifted.

107. The two most common grounds to have the stay lifted are: (1) for cause, including a lack of adequate protection of the secured party's position, or (2) the debtor has no equity in the collateral and the collateral is not necessary to an effective reorganization. The first test has one element and the second one has two.

108. Oversecured creditors have collateral worth more than the amount of their loans. Undersecured creditors have collateral worth less than the amount of their loans.

109. This creditor is oversecured, so it will likely be paid in full on its whole claim in the debtor's Chapter 11 case, with present value interest over the life of the plan. It can also receive attorneys' fees and interest on its claim post-petition (assuming the loan documents provide for this), while waiting for the debtor's Chapter 11 plan to be confirmed.

110. Now the secured party has an undersecured claim, so its claim will be bifurcated into two parts—the secured part worth $40,000 and the unsecured part worth $10,000. The secured party will get paid the full amount of the $40,000 secured claim under the plan, with present value interest, and will get an unsecured creditor distribution on the $10,000 unsecured part of the claim. This creditor will not earn post-petition interest or get attorneys' fees while waiting for a plan to be confirmed, regardless of what the loan documents say.

111. In a Chapter 11 case, all secured loans can be stripped down to the value of the collateral (except home loans for individual debtors). In a Chapter 13 case, all secured loans can be stripped down to the value of the collateral, except home loans, PMSI loans on cars taken out within 2 1/2 years before the filing of the Chapter 13 case, and PMSIs in household goods taken out within a year of the filing of the case.

112. a. a transfer of property

b. for or on account of an antecedent debt

c. made within 90 days before the filing (one year for transfers to insiders such as family members)

d. while the debtor was insolvent

e. that allowed the creditor to receive more than it would have received in a Chapter 7 case.

113. Waiting too long to file a financing statement after the loan is made can make the security interest a transfer on account of an antecedent or old debt. If it is filed on time, the transfer of the security interest is not a preference, but if it is filed late it could be avoidable.

114. The strong-arm powers allow a bankruptcy trustee to avoid a security interest that is not perfected and thus relegate the secured party to the status of an unsecured creditor. The purpose of the strong-arm powers are to invalidate security interest in which there has been no notice of the security interest, and thus to invalidate secret liens.

 Exam Tips on
BANKRUPTCY CONCEPTS

☞ To answer any exam question pertaining to bankruptcy, you will need to know at least the basic concepts behind the different *types of bankruptcy,* such as *Chapter 7, Chapter 13, Chapter 12, and Chapter 11.*

☞ Some secured transactions exams test on the ***automatic stay.*** To prepare for this, you should read § 362 of the Bankruptcy Code and also remember that these things are ***forbidden*** once a borrower has filed any form of bankruptcy: ***filing or continuing lawsuits to collect debts, repossessing collateral, selling collateral already repossessed, or doing anything else at all to collect on a debt.***

☞ Exams that test on bankruptcy concepts frequently ask students to determine whether the ***stay should be lifted.*** This requires a student to determine if there is ***equity in the collateral,*** whether the ***collateral is necessary to an effective reorganization,*** and also whether the secured party's ***interest*** in the collateral is ***adequately protected.***

☞ Many exams require students to determine whether a claim is ***oversecured*** or ***undersecured***; whether the secured party is entitled to ***interest, costs, and fees*** on its claim; and also whether these amounts can continue to accrue on the claim indefinitely. The exam also may ask you to determine how the secured party is entitled to be ***treated in a Chapter 11 plan.***

☞ Some exams test on the bankruptcy trustee's avoiding powers. The ones that most affect secured creditors are ***preferential transfers*** and the ***trustee's strong-arm powers,*** which allow a bankruptcy trustee to avoid unperfected security interests.

PRACTICE EXAMS

PRACTICE EXAMS

Three different forms of exams are provided here, all of which are popular with different teachers around the country. The exams are as follows: a traditional essay exam (one and a half hours), a true/false exam (two hours), and a short-answer exam (two and a half hours). Before each practice exam, instructions are given that tell you how best to approach each type of exam. Good luck, and we hope this practice helps you.

PRACTICE ESSAY QUESTION: (One and a half hours)

TIPS ON ANSWERING THE PRACTICE ESSAY QUESTION:

1. The first and most important tip is to avoid getting frustrated. DON'T PANIC. This is a complicated, difficult question that may, on first reading, appear impossible. You may not know where to start.
2. Read the question several times. Reading the question and the preparation that you do for your answer are just as important as actually writing the answer.
3. Think about the different types of collateral that appear in the question and determine who has a security interest in each type. Some of the creditors do not have any security interest in some of the collateral; if a creditor does not have a security interest in a particular item of the property, that party need not be considered in determining priority as to that property.
4. Consider what happens to each piece of the original collateral. Does it result in proceeds?
5. Analyze the status of each of the parties. As to a particular creditor, does the party have a valid security interest? If so, in what type of collateral? Is it a purchase-money security interest (PMSI)? Was it perfected? How? When? As to transferees of the collateral, is the transferee a casual buyer, a buyer in ordinary course (BIOC), a purchaser for value without knowledge? If there are creditors who do not have a security interest, are they lien creditors? If you know the materials in this course, this should be relatively easy, and should get you started. This step is essential to a determination of who has priority.
6. As you read the question, take notes and prepare one or more diagrams. Your diagram will probably get quite complicated, but don't worry about that. Its purpose is to help you understand the questions. Do not hesitate to change the diagram as you better understand the question. As you are preparing the diagram, include the status of the parties.
7. Try a time line (i.e., what happened when).
8. All of this is in preparation for writing your answer. As you work with the facts in this way, you will better understand the question, and it will be much easier to answer it. It is important to understand who is who and what is what before you start writing.
9. Remember, this is a practice question. It is probably more complicated than those on the typical law school Secured Transactions examination, and it is designed to show you how to approach these types of questions. After you have written an answer and studied the analysis, go back to your answer. You almost certainly will have left something out, and perhaps have made some mistakes. Ask yourself why you omitted some of the discussion and why you wrote something that is incorrect. This should help you determine what parts of this Outline you should read again.

THE QUESTION: Andy, a master carpenter, decided to become a contractor. After obtaining his license, he went to the First Bank to borrow some money. On January 5, First Bank agreed to give him a line of credit of up to $25,000. Andy gave the bank a security interest in "all my inventory and equipment." At the time he owned a truck, but no inventory. First Bank filed a financing statement on January 6 with the Secretary of State describing the collateral as "all inventory, equipment, and accounts."

Andy's first job as a contractor was to build an addition for Brigid. The contract with Brigid was signed on January 7. The work was to be finished on February 1, and she was to pay him $125,000 as soon as the addition was completed. In preparation for the work, Andy purchased $50,000 worth of lumber from Lumber, Inc. on January 8. He gave Lumber, Inc. $10,000 down using some of the money First Bank had lent him, and agreed to pay the rest of the price in 30 days. The lumber was delivered to the job site on January 9. Lumber, Inc. took a security interest in the lumber, and filed a financing statement in the proper office on January 10.

On January 12, Andy bought a selection of tools from Queen Hardware. The price was $2,000, which he paid with a check drawn on his bank line of credit. This exhausted the money in the line of credit, as he had used $13,000 of it to pay past bills that he had accumulated while he was studying for the contractor examination, advertising, rent on the premises he was using, etc.

On January 15th, Andy went to Second Bank and asked for a loan of $10,000. Based on the contract Andy had with Brigid, Second Bank loaned him the $10,000, which he put into a checking account that he opened at Second Bank. Second Bank, which did not know of First Bank's loan to Andy, took a security interest in "all of his equipment and accounts, presently owned and hereinafter to be acquired." A financing statement was properly filed on the same day.

On January 20, Andy purchased a new truck from Chris Sales. He received a credit of $5,000 for his old truck, which he traded in, and he agreed to pay the balance of the purchase price, $15,000, on a monthly basis over the next two years. He gave Chris a note for $15,000 and a security interest in the truck. Chris filed a financing statement in the office of the Secretary of State on January 25. On January 26, Chris sold the note and security interest to Third Bank for $13,500. Third Bank has not filed any documents with regard to the transaction.

Andy used approximately 75 percent of the lumber on the Brigid job, completing it on February 1. When he asked Brigid for payment, she said that she was sorry, but she could not pay him the full amount immediately. She gave him a check drawn on an account with Fourth Bank for $50,000 and signed a note for the remaining $75,000, payable in 90 days. She also gave him a security interest in "all of my jewelry." Andy has not filed a financing statement regarding this transaction. Andy has the right to file a mechanic's lien on Brigid's property under state law. The lien would give him the right to sell her house for the purpose of satisfying his claim against her. He has not filed, however, and presently has no mechanic's lien. When Andy deposited Brigid's check, it was returned marked "Insufficient funds."

On February 7, being short of money, Andy sold the remaining lumber he had to Mike, his neighbor, for $3,000. Mike intended to use it in the construction of a garage at his home. On the same day, he also took the tools he purchased from Queen Hardware (which now have a market value of $1,000) to Patrick, a pawn-broker, and pawned them. Patrick lent him $500 on the tools and took possession of them. Patrick gave Andy a claim check that makes no mention of anything like a security interest.

You are a young lawyer working for the First Bank. The General Counsel has given you these facts and has asked you to tell him the rights of all the parties as to the property now existing.

Please do so.

ANALYSIS OF PRACTICE ESSAY QUESTION:

> [*We have added comments at various places to help you understand better our analysis and to indicate why we have included or omitted some discussions. Our comments appear in italics between brackets.*]

In this answer we will treat the priority problems as to each item of property separately.

> [*When there are two or more items of collateral in the question, it is probably best to treat each one separately as we have done.*]

I. LUMBER:

a. The lumber used in the building is no longer personal property and cannot be the subject of a security interest. It would be too integrated into the structure to be a fixture, so it became part of the real estate.

b. Twenty-five percent of the lumber is in Mike's hands, assuming he has not yet used it. There is a priority problem with respect to this lumber involving First Bank, Lumber, Inc., and Mike.

Second Bank did not have a security interest in the lumber because its security interest is only in "equipment and accounts" and the lumber is inventory.

Mike is a transferee. He is not a casual (consumer) buyer because Andy was not holding the lumber as consumer goods. He is not a BIOC because Andy was not in the business of selling lumber. As a purchaser for value without knowledge, he takes subject to perfected security interests, and because First Bank and Lumber, Inc. have perfected, the lumber can be repossessed from him.

> [*When there is a transferee and more than one secured party vying for priority, we find it easier to determine the rights of the transferee first.*]

First Bank has a PMSI in "all inventory and equipment." There is no reference in the security agreement to after-acquired inventory, and whether later-purchased inventory is covered is a question of the intent of the parties to the security agreement. Because Andy did not have any inventory at the time that the security agreement was signed, it would appear that their intent was to cover after-acquired inventory. The failure to mention after-acquired property in the financing statement generally does not affect perfection of later acquired collateral. Here, however, it might be taken as evidence of an intent not to include it. Assuming that a court will hold that the intent of the parties was to include after-acquired inventory, First Bank has a security interest in the lumber that was perfected by filing. It is a PMSI to the extent that money advanced by First Bank was used to purchase it. Here, Andy used $10,000 of that money as a down payment and First has a PMSI to that extent.

> *[We have raised the issue of whether the First Bank has a security interest
> in after-acquired property and come to a conclusion. The conclusion is
> less important than the fact that issue has been raised.]*

Lumber, Inc. clearly has a PMSI in the lumber as inventory that was perfected by filing on January 10, within 20 days of the time that the lumber was delivered.

> *[Note that this short sentence contains all of your analysis of the status of
> Lumber, Inc. Its security interest is valid, the collateral is equipment, it is a
> PMSI, and it was perfected in a certain way and on a certain date. You
> have told the examiner that you know a lot about the course just by writing
> this sentence. There is no need to include a more extensive discussion
> because there would not be an issue raised as to any of these points.]*

Although Lumber, Inc. perfected later than First Bank, the special preference given to PMSIs must be considered. A PMSI in inventory prevails over all other security interests if it is perfected before the debtor obtains possession and the PMSI secured party has given notice to all other secured parties of record that it is taking a security interest in their collateral. Here, Lumber, Inc. failed to perfect on time and failed to give notice. Thus, it is not entitled to the preference and its security interest is treated as a non-PMSI.

Because Lumber, Inc. does not have the preference, First Bank can repossess the lumber in Mike's hands, sell it, and apply the money obtained for the sale to Andy's debt.

Note that if both First Bank and Lumber, Inc. had PMSIs, as between them, Lumber, Inc. would have priority because it was a seller of the lumber.

> *[Technically, there is no need for this last sentence, but it tells the examiner
> that you know that rule and it would probably earn you some points.]*

II. THE $3,000 THAT ANDY HAS FROM THE SALE OF THE LUMBER TO MIKE: The $3,000 represents proceeds of the collateral (the lumber) in which First Bank and Lumber, Inc. each has a security interest. Assuming that the money is identifiable, they will have a security interest in the money. The lowest intermediate balance test can be used to trace the $3,000 if it has been commingled by Andy with other funds. Both have perfected security interests in the $3,000 because there is automatic perfection as to the proceeds when the proceeds are cash.

> *[The facts are unclear as to whether the $3,000 is still identifiable. Hence,
> you state the tracing rule.]*

As between First Bank and Lumber, Inc., the first to file or perfect has priority. Because First Bank filed first, it is entitled to the $3,000.

III. THE $50,000 CHECK GIVEN BY BRIGID TO ANDY: Although this check was dishonored, a cause of action exists on the check, and whoever is entitled to the check is entitled to enforce that cause of action against Brigid.

The check is an instrument. It is also proceeds of the account that arose from Brigid's promise to pay for the extension. Thus, to have a security interest in it, a party must have either a security interest in instruments or in the accounts. First Bank, Second Bank, and Lumber, Inc. lack a security interest in instruments, and only Second Bank has a security interest in accounts. Although First Bank claimed a security interest in accounts in its financing statement, the financing statement cannot enlarge the scope of the security agreement, and accounts are not listed as collateral in that agreement. Hence, Second Bank will have a right to obtain possession of the check and the rights that flow from it.

Although it might be argued that the account (Brigid's promise to pay for the addition) is proceeds of the lumber and that the check is proceeds of that promise, it does not appear that lumber was "exchanged" for the promise to pay in the sense required for the account to become proceeds. The check was given for the addition, not the lumber, and once the lumber was integrated into the building, it was no longer personal property.

> [*This paragraph tells the examiner that you recognized that there could be an argument that the account is not proceeds, and it gives the reasons for concluding that it not. Again, the important thing is that the answer recognizes this as a possible issue.*]

Thus, Second Bank is entitled to the check.

IV. NOTE AND SECURITY INTEREST GIVEN BY BRIGID: The note and security interest given to Andy by Brigid is chattel paper, and is proceeds of the obligation that Brigid owed Andy for his completion of the building. Thus, only those parties who either took a security interest in chattel paper or who had a security interest in Andy's accounts have a security interest in this chattel paper.

None of the parties took a security interest in chattel paper, and only Second Bank took a security interest in Andy's accounts. Therefore, Second Bank has a right to the note and security interest given by Brigid.

Second Bank can enforce the note given by Brigid and, if she defaults, the bank can repossess the jewelry.

V. THE TOOLS: The tools would be equipment. Because only First Bank took a security interest in equipment, it would have the only security interest in them. The priority contest would be between the bank and Patrick, the pawnbroker. Patrick is neither a casual buyer nor a BIOC, and has rights only as a purchaser for value without knowledge. As such, he takes subject to previously perfected security interests, and hence First Bank can repossess the tools from Patrick.

VI. THE $500 ANDY GOT FROM PATRICK: The $500 is proceeds of the tools. Because only First Bank had a security interest in the tools, only that bank will have a security interest in the $500. If it is still identifiable, the bank has a right to it.

VII. THE OLD TRUCK THAT WAS TRADED IN: The old truck was equipment in which First Bank had a security interest. First Bank's security interest was not perfected, however, because it did not file in accord with the certificate of title statute. Chris, as a purchaser for value without knowledge, takes free of all unperfected security interests. Thus, First Bank cannot repossess the old truck from Chris.

VIII. THE NEW TRUCK: The contest here is between First Bank, which has an unperfected security interest in the truck as equipment, and Third Bank, which took an assignment of Chris's rights. Because Chris also filed in the wrong place, its security interest is unperfected. Third Bank would have only Chris's rights as a result of the assignment. There is no requirement that notice of the assignment be filed. As between two unperfected security interests, the first to attach has priority. Here, however, they both attached at the same time: when Andy obtained rights in the collateral. There is no Article 9 rule for determining priority in this situation.

Perhaps a court would look to the rule to be applied when two parties, one a seller of the goods and the other a lender, both have PMSIs. In that case, the seller has priority. Although the rule does not apply here, a court may find that the PMSI rule expresses an intent to favor sellers.

TRUE/FALSE EXAM: (Two hours)

A NOTE ABOUT TRUE/FALSE AND SHORT-ANSWER EXAMS:

> Many commercial law professors, including the two authors, prefer not to use essay exams on technical subjects like secured transactions. It is difficult to test on the smaller details in a big essay question. Additionally, teachers using true/false or short-answer exams can write a very inclusive exam. That means a teacher can literally test on every topic covered in the class, even if just a bit.
>
> True/false questions tend to be extremely literal and very tricky. For this type of test, please make sure you read each question and every word within each question *very* carefully. Take most of the time allotted and you should do well. Rush and you'll probably be unpleasantly surprised.
>
> We allow students taking our true-false exams to explain their answers if they wish. That way, if they get the answer wrong, they can still receive some points for a sound explanation.

THE TEST:

1. Debtor is a manufacturer of cotton shirts. If Secured Party takes a security interest in all of debtor's cotton cloth and thread, Secured Party has a security interest in equipment because equipment is the catchall category for goods that do not fit into any of the other subclasses of goods.

   TRUE   FALSE

2. A security agreement must always be an authenticated record to create a valid security interest.

TRUE   FALSE

3. A security agreement is not valid unless it contains all of the following elements: (1) a clause indicating that a security interest is being created, (2) a description of the collateral, and (3) authentications of the debtor and the secured party.

TRUE   FALSE

4. The following provision in a security agreement is enforceable unless the collateral is consumer goods:

"Debtor agrees that if Secured Party elects to keep the collateral in satisfaction of the debt upon Debtor's default, no notice need be given to Debtor."

TRUE   FALSE

5. Dave purchased a stereo from Sally for $1,000. He paid $200 down and agreed to pay the remainder in installments of $100 on the first of each of the next eight months. Dave gave Sally a security interest in the stereo to secure his promise to pay. Dave made three payments, but did not make the fourth payment. Sally repossessed the stereo. Before Sally had disposed of the stereo, Dave tendered Sally $200, $100 in payment of the missed installment and the other $100 as payment of the next installment, which was not due for another two weeks. Assuming that the security agreement has an acceleration clause, Dave has properly exercised his right to redeem the stereo and Sally must return the stereo to him.

TRUE   FALSE

Questions 6 through 8 are based on the following facts.

On May 1, Dave purchased a truck from Sally for use in his business for $15,000. He paid $5,000 down and promised to the pay the remainder in six months. Dave gave Sally a security interest in the truck. Sally filed a financing statement with the Secretary of State on May 2. On June 1, Dave borrowed $1,000 from Happy Finance, giving Happy a security interest in the same truck. Dave agreed to repay Happy on July 1. Happy did not perfect its security interest. When Dave failed to pay Happy on July 1, Happy repossessed the truck and sold it in a commercially reasonable sale to Patricia for $12,000. Happy did not know of Sally's security interest. Happy took $1,000 and gave the other $11,000 to Dave.

6. Happy had an obligation to give Sally notice of the sale.

TRUE   FALSE

7. Patricia took the truck subject to Sally's security interest.

TRUE   FALSE

8. If Sally, before Happy had distributed the $11,000 to Dave, had made a demand on Happy Finance that it pay her any money realized at the sale in excess of what was necessary to satisfy Happy's debt, Happy should have paid her the $11,000 rather than give it to Dave.

TRUE   FALSE

9. On February 1, Sally lent Dave $20,000 and took a security interest in all of his present and after-acquired inventory. On February 1, Dave's bank account had $5,000 in it. On February 5, Dave deposited $3,000, which he had received as rent on a building that he owns. On February 10, Dave deposited $10,000, which he obtained from the sale of the inventory in which Sally had a security interest. On February 15, Dave withdrew $15,000 from the account and used the money to pay rent and to meet his payroll. As of February 16, Sally had a security interest in the $3,000 remaining in the bank account.

TRUE   FALSE

10. Dave's Ranch, Inc., a Delaware corporation engaged in the ranching business with its principal place of business in Lubbock, Texas, borrowed $100,000 from Big Bank in Denver, Colorado. Dave's Ranch gave a security interest in cattle that are located near Clovis, New Mexico. The proper place for Big Bank to file a financing statement is with the Delaware Secretary of State.

TRUE   FALSE

Questions 11 through 15 are based on the following facts:

On February 1, Dave purchased a Peach computer from Sally for his own non-business use. He paid $500 down and promised to the pay the remainder of the purchase price, $2,000, on August 1. To secure the debt, Dave gave Sally a security interest in the computer. Sally has never filed a financing statement. On March 1, Dave traded the Peach computer to Rosy's Computer Store for an Orange computer. Rosy's is a retail computer store that sells both used and new computers. The Orange computer cost $3,000, and Rosy allowed Dave $2,500 for the Peach computer. David paid the difference in cash. On April 1, Rosy's sold the Peach computer to Peter for $2,700 cash. Peter took in good faith and without notice of Sally's security interest. Peter purchased the computer for his home, and has not used it in his business. Dave failed to pay Sally the $2,000 he owed her on August 1, and Sally has just discovered the above facts.

11. Sally has a perfected security interest in the Peach computer.

TRUE   FALSE

12. Sally cannot repossess the Peach computer from Peter because Peter is a buyer in the ordinary course of business.

TRUE   FALSE

13. Sally cannot repossess the Peach computer from Peter because he is a casual (or consumer) buyer under § 9-320.

TRUE   FALSE

14. Sally cannot repossess the computer from Peter because he is a Purchaser for Value Without Knowledge under § 9-317.

TRUE   FALSE

15. Sally has a security interest in the Orange computer, but it is unperfected.

TRUE   FALSE

16. On June 1, Dave purchased a new machine from Sally, giving her a security interest in it to secure his promise to pay the purchase price on July 1. The machine was delivered to Dave on June 4. On June 8, Dave borrowed $50,000 from Big Bank giving to the bank a security interest in all of his present and

after-acquired equipment. Big Bank filed on the same day. On June 12, Sally filed a financing statement with the Secretary of State. Sally has priority over Big Bank as to the machine that she sold Dave.

TRUE   FALSE

17. On April 1, Big Bank loaned Dave $10,000 and took a security interest in all of Dave's inventory. The bank filed a financing with the Secretary of State on the same day. On May 1, Sally loaned Dave $5,000 and took a security interest in all of Dave's accounts. Sally filed a financing statement in the proper office on the same day. By July 1, Dave had sold all of the inventory and had defaulted on both loans. He has accounts worth $3,000 resulting from sales of the inventory in which Big Bank took a security interest. As between Big Bank and Sally, Big Bank has priority as to all of these accounts.

TRUE   FALSE

Questions 18 through 20 are based on the following facts:

On July 1, Dave purchased a new stereo for his home from Sally for $1,200. He gave her a security interest to secure the purchase price, which he agreed to pay at the rate of $100 a month over the next year. On August 1, Dave borrowed $500 from Happy Finance, giving Happy a security interest in the stereo he had purchased from Sally to secure his promise to repay the loan on September 1. Happy filed a financing statement in the proper office on August 1. On August 15, Dave sold the stereo to his neighbor, Peter, for $1,000 cash. Peter bought the stereo for use in his home, and took in good faith and without knowledge of either of existing security interests. Dave has defaulted on his obligations to both Sally and Happy.

18. As between Sally and Happy, Sally has priority.

TRUE   FALSE

19. Peter took subject to the security interest of Happy.

TRUE   FALSE

20. Peter took free of the security interest of Sally.

TRUE   FALSE

21. Big Bank has a security interest in "all of Dan Debtor's accounts." Dan sells a refrigerator to Paula on credit and takes back from Paula her promise to pay and a security interest in the refrigerator to secure her promise. Big Bank has a security interest in the debt owed Dan by Paula.

TRUE   FALSE

22. On October 1, Dave borrowed $1,000 from Sally, giving her a security interest in his equipment to secure his promise to repay the money on December 1. Sally has never filed a financing statement. Dave failed to repay the loan and on December 15 filed a Chapter 7 petition in bankruptcy. The trustee in bankruptcy may avoid Sally's security interest under § 544(a) of the Bankruptcy Code.

TRUE   FALSE

23. On May 1, Dave borrowed $50,000 from Sally, giving her a security interest in his inventory to secure repayment of the loan. On June 1, Dave borrowed $20,000 from Carla. Before she lent him the money, she checked the UCC filings to make sure that no one had filed a financing statement on any of Dave's property. On October 1, Dave was in default on the loan made to him by Carla. She obtained a judgment on October 5. On October 6, having heard of Carla's judgment, Sally perfected her security interest by

filing in the proper office. Carla obtained a writ of execution on October 10. As between Carla and Sally, Sally has priority as to Dave's inventory.

TRUE   FALSE

24. On January 15, *D* gave *S* a security interest in its "present and after-acquired inventory." *S* filed a financing statement in the Secretary of State's office on February 1. On February 15, *D* acquired new equipment from *W*. *S*'s security interest in the new equipment was perfected on February 1.

TRUE   FALSE

25. *D*, a retailer of men's clothing, gave a security interest in all of her present and after-acquired inventory to *S* on January 15. On February 1, *D* sold six shirts to *B* and *B* paid by giving *D* a check in the amount of $120. The check is cash proceeds of the inventory.

TRUE   FALSE

26. *D* gave *S* a security interest in all of its inventory of commercial washing machines on January 15 to secure a loan of $10,000. *S* filed a financing statement in the Secretary of State's office on the same day. On February 1, *D* sold one of the washing machines from its inventory to *B* who owned a coin operated washing machine establishment. *B* agreed to pay *D* in installments over the following year, and gave to *D* a note promising to pay and a security interest in the washing machine. *S* has a security interest in the promise to pay and the security interest given by *B* to *D*, which are characterized as chattel paper.

TRUE   FALSE

27. On January 15, *D* gave a security interest to *S* in all of his equipment. *S* has never filed a financing statement. On March 1, *D* defaulted, and on March 15, *S* took possession of the equipment. *S* has given *D* notice that she intends to keep the equipment in satisfaction of the debt. Assuming *D* does not object, *S* can keep the equipment, but *S* will not be entitled to a deficiency judgment in the event that the value of the equipment is less than the amount of the debt, and will not have to account to *D* for any amount by which the value of the equipment exceeds the amount of the debt.

TRUE   FALSE

28. On January 15, *D* purchased a new TV from *S,* giving to *S* a security interest in the TV to secure payment of the purchase price. *D* used the TV as consumer goods. *S* has not filed a financing statement. On March 1, *D* sold the TV to B, who was in the business of buying and selling used TVs. *B* sold the TV to *P* on April 1. *P* used the TV in her home as consumer goods. *D* has defaulted on his obligation to *S*. *S* can repossess the TV from *P*.

TRUE   FALSE

29. On January 15, *D* borrowed $100,000 from *S,* and gave a security interest in his equipment. *S* filed immediately in the proper office. The security agreement did not contain a future advances clause. On February 15, *D* repaid $10,000 of the loan. On March 15, *D* borrowed an additional $50,000 from *S,* and signed a new security agreement giving *S* a security interest in the same collateral to secure the new loan. *S* did not file a new financing statement. On May 1, *D* borrowed $25,000 from *C,* giving to *C* a security interest in the same collateral. *C* filed a financing statement immediately. On August 1, *D* was in default as to both *S* and *C*. If the equipment is sold for $140,000, *S* will get the entire $140,000.

TRUE   FALSE

30. During the first two weeks of January, *D* was negotiating for a loan from *S*. By January 15, the negotiations were almost completed, and *S* asked *D* to sign a security interest describing the collateral as "all of *D*'s presently existing and after-acquired equipment." *D* signed the financing statement and *S* immediately filed it. During the next few days, the negotiations broke down. On February 1, *S* borrowed $100,000 from *C*, giving *C* a security interest in all of her "present and after-acquired equipment." *C* filed immediately. On March 1, *D* borrowed $50,000 from *S*. *S* did not file a new financing statement. As between *C* and *S*, *S* has priority in the equipment.

TRUE   FALSE

31. On January 15, *D* gave *S* a security interest in her equipment to secure a $50,000 loan from *S*. *S* filed a financing statement immediately in the proper office. On March 1, *D* borrowed $10,000 from *C*, giving *C* a security interest in the same collateral. *C* immediately perfected by filing. On August 1, *D* defaulted on her obligation to *C*. *C* has a right to repossess the equipment and sell it, and if she does, *S* has no right to the proceeds from the sale.

TRUE   FALSE

32. On January 15, *D* borrowed $10,000 from *S*. To secure the loan, *D* signed a security agreement giving *S* a security interest in his diamond ring worth $10,000. *D* also signed a financing statement describing the ring. *S* took possession of the ring until she could file the financing statement. On January 20, *D* approached *C* asking *C* to loan him $5,000. *C* had *D* sign a security agreement giving him a security interest in the same ring and a financing statement describing the ring. *C* filed the financing statement on January 20 and advanced the money to *D* on the same day. On January 25, *D* was going to a party and *S* gave the ring back to *D* so that he could wear it. On January 28, *S* filed the financing statement that *D* had signed. As between *S* and *C*, *S* has priority.

TRUE   FALSE

33. On January 15, *D* gave a security interest to *S* in his "present and after-acquired equipment" to secure a loan that *S* made to *D*. *S* immediately filed a financing statement in the office of the Secretary of State. On February 15, *D* purchased a new machine for his business from *C*, giving to *C* a security interest in it to secure the purchase price which was to be paid in installments over the next year. When *C* sold the machine to *D* and took the security interest in it, she was aware of the security interest of *S* and that it had been properly filed. *C* gave no notice to *S* that she was taking a new security interest in the same collateral, and filed a financing statement with the Secretary of State on February 20. As between *S* and *C*, *S* has priority in the machine sold to *D* by *C*.

TRUE   FALSE

34. On January 15, *S* loaned *D* $100,000 and took a security interest in *D*'s existing inventory. The agreement provided that whenever any cash resulted from a sale of inventory, the cash was to be deposited in a special account set up at First Bank. *S* filed a financing statement on January 27. On February 1, *D* borrowed $50,000 from *C*, giving to *C* a security interest in all of his present and after-acquired accounts. *C* filed a financing statement on the same day. On March 1, *D* sold some of its inventory to *B* for $10,000, *B* promising to pay on April 1. On April 1, *B* paid *D* the $10,000 by check and *D* deposited the check in the special account. Both *S* and *C* have a security interest in the $10,000 in the account and, as between them, *S* has priority.

TRUE   FALSE

35. On January 15, *S* sold a computer to *D* for use in *D*'s store. *S* took a security interest in the computer to secure payment, which was to be made on March 1. *S* did not file a financing statement. On March 1, *D* failed to pay *S* upon *S*'s demand. On March 5, *D* gave the computer to his brother *B* as a birthday present. *S* filed a financing statement on March 10. *S* has a right to repossess the computer from *B*.

   TRUE   FALSE

36. On January 15, *S* took a security interest in all of *D*'s "present and after-acquired inventory." *S* filed a financing statement on the same day with the Secretary of State. On February 1, *D* purchased new inventory from *C,* giving to *C* a security interest in the inventory that *C* sold it. *C* filed a financing statement before *C* gave possession to *D* and notified *S* that he was taking the security interest in the new inventory. On March 1, *D* sold $10,000 of the new inventory to *P* in return for *P*'s promise to pay for it on April 1. On March 15, *D* was in default as to both *S* and C. On that date, both *S* and *C* have a security interest in the promise of *P* to pay on April 1, and as between the two, *C* has priority.

   TRUE   FALSE

37. On January 15, *D* gave *S* a security interest in its existing equipment worth $1,000 to secure a $1,000 loan made on that day. On January 20, *C* lent *D* $1,000. *C* checked the filing records before making the loan and found no financing statement. *C* did not take a security interest in any of *D*'s property. *S* perfected by filing on January 30. On April 15, *C* obtained a default judgment against *D* on the $1,000 debt, and *C* had the sheriff seize the property under a writ of execution. *C* can order the sheriff to sell the property but the purchaser at the sale will take the property subject to the security interest of *S*.

   TRUE   FALSE

38. On January 15, *D* borrowed $10,000 from *S* to purchase new equipment, giving to *S* a security interest in her present and after-acquired equipment. On February 1, *D* bought new equipment from *C* for $20,000. *D* used the $10,000 loaned to her by *S* for a down payment and gave a security interest to *C* to secure his agreement to pay *C* the rest in installments over the next year. The equipment was delivered on February 15. *S* filed a financing statement on February 27, and *C* filed a financing statement on February 17. As between *S* and *C, S* has priority.

   TRUE   FALSE

39. On January 15, *D* gave a security interest in its inventory to *S* to secure a loan made by *S* to *D* in the amount of $50,000. On March 1, *D* defaulted on the loan, and *S* repossessed the inventory on March 15. *D* gave notice to *S* of a public sale to be held on April 15. On April 1, *D* filed a petition in bankruptcy seeking relief under Chapter 7 of the Bankruptcy Code. If the inventory is worth less than $50,000, *S* may proceed with the sale without petitioning the Bankruptcy Court.

   TRUE   FALSE

40. On January 2, Dan borrowed $10,000 from Susie giving her a security interest to secure the debt. The security agreement described the collateral as "all of Dan's present and after-acquired inventory." On January 3, Susie filed in the Secretary of State's office a financing statement describing the collateral as "all of the debtor's inventory and equipment." On February 7, Susie purchased new inventory from Supplier. Susie has a perfected security interest in the inventory purchased by Dan from Supplier.

   TRUE   FALSE

41. Assume the same facts as in Question 40. Susie also has a security interest in Dan's equipment.

    TRUE   FALSE

42. Dan operates a real estate business as a sole proprietor under the name "A-1 Realty Company." On January 2, Susie sold and delivered a desk and chair to the business and Dan used the desk and chair in his office. The price was to be paid in installments over the next six months, and Susie was given a security interest signed "A-1 Realty Co., by Dan." Susie filed a financing statement in the office of the Secretary of State listing "A-1 Realty Company" as the debtor on the statement. The filing would be effective to perfect Susie's security interest.

    TRUE   FALSE

43. On February 1, David purchased a new stereo from Sandy, promising to pay for it on March 1 and giving her a security interest in it. David put the stereo in his restaurant on February 2 to provide music for his customers. He found, however, that most diners did not like music while they ate, so on February 7 he sold the stereo to his neighbor George, who put it in his den so that he could listen to music while reading. Sandy filed a financing statement with the Secretary of State on February 9. If David defaults, Sandy may repossess the stereo from George.

    TRUE   FALSE

44. Dave gave a security interest in his equipment to Sally to secure a loan of $50,000. Six months later, Dave defaulted. Assume that Sally properly repossesses the collateral and that she gives proper notice to Dave that she intends to conduct a private sale of the collateral. If Sally decides to sell the goods at an auction sale she must give Dave a new notice of the auction sale.

    TRUE   FALSE

45. Seller sold and delivered a widget to Buyer for $10,000. The purchase price was to be paid in 30 days. The agreement between Seller and Buyer was in writing, signed by the Buyer, described the widget in some detail, and provided that "title to the widget is not to pass to Buyer until Buyer pays the $10,000 purchase price." When the goods are delivered, Buyer has title to the widget and Seller has only a security interest in it.

    TRUE   FALSE

46. On June 1, 2001, Dave borrowed $10,000 from Sally and gave Sally a security interest in all of his present and after-acquired equipment. Sally filed a financing statement in the proper office on the same day. On June 1, 2004, Paul purchased some of Dave's equipment. On August 1, 2006, Sally first filed a continuation statement. If Dave defaults on his obligations to Sally, Sally may repossess the equipment that Paul has purchased.

    TRUE   FALSE

47. On October 1, Brigid purchased a new automobile from Capricious Cars, Inc. She borrowed $22,000 from Big Bank, giving the bank a security interest in the auto. She was obligated to pay the Bank $500 on the first of each month. The contract contained an acceleration clause. Brigid made the payments in November, December, and January, but she missed the payment due in February. Big Bank peacefully repossessed the car on February 25. On February 26, Brigid sent Big Bank a check for $1,000, representing the missed payment in February and the payment due on March 1. Big Bank must return the automobile to Brigid.

    TRUE   FALSE

48. On January 2, Dan purchased a Model 100 Red computer from Susie for use in his business. He paid $500 down and agreed to pay the remaining $1,500 in installments. Dan gave Susie a security interest in the computer and she filed a financing statement in the proper office on the same day describing the collateral as "One Red Computer, Model 100." On February 1, Dan sold the computer to Betty who also used it as equipment. He took the $1,700 he received from Betty and purchased a Blue computer from Sally. In the event that Dan is in default in his obligation to pay Susie, Susie can repossess the Red computer from Betty and the Blue computer from Dan.

TRUE   FALSE

49. On January 2, Dan purchased a cash register from Susie for use in his appliance store, agreeing to pay for it in 30 days, giving to Susie a security interest in the register. On January 3, while he was using it in his store, Bob, who owned a shoe store next to Dan's appliance store, asked if he could buy it because his had just broken. Since Bob was willing to pay a premium price, and Dan still had his old cash register, he sold and delivered it to Bob on that day. On January 15, Susie filed a financing statement with the Secretary of State. If Dan defaults in his obligation to pay Susie, she may repossess the cash register from Bob.

TRUE   FALSE

50. On June 1, Susan lent Dan $50,000 and took a security interest in all of his inventory and accounts. Susan has never filed a financing statement. On August 1, Dan called Susan and told her that his business had lost $5,000 during July and that he was "giving up the ghost." He invited her to come and take possession of the store, which she did. The store contained all of the inventory in which Susan had her security interest. It also contained all of the documentation of credit sales that Dan had made. By taking possession, Susan perfected her security interest as to the inventory and the accounts.

TRUE   FALSE

ANSWERS TO THE TRUE/FALSE EXAM:

1. FALSE. The collateral is raw material, which is classified as inventory. § 9-102(a)(48).

2. FALSE. It need not be a record if the secured party is in possession of the collateral. § 9-203(b)(3)(B).

3. FALSE. The secured party need not authenticate the security agreement. § 9-203(3)(A).

4. FALSE. Section 9-602(10) prohibits a waiver of the right to notice except when it is made given default.

5. FALSE. Redemption requires that all of the then-due debt be tendered. Because of the acceleration clause, all of the future payments become immediately due and the full amount owed must be tendered to redeem the collateral. § 9-623(b).

6. FALSE. Sally is entitled to notice only if she gave notice to Happy of her security interest. § 9-611. Section 9-611(c)(B) does not apply because the collateral was a motor vehicle and the filing did not constitute perfection.

7. TRUE. The sale to Patricia discharges only security interests that are subordinate to those of the repossessing secured party. § 9-617(a)(3). Sally did not perfect because she did not record her security interest on the certificate of title, but neither did Happy. As between two secured parties, neither of whom has perfected, the first security interest to attach has priority. § 9-333(a)(3). Hence, Sally had priority, and her security interest was not discharged by the repossession sale.

8. FALSE. Only the holder of a security interest subordinate to that of the repossessing secured party has a right to any excess proceeds, § 9-608(a), and, as discussed in the answer to question 7, Sally had priority over Happy. § 9-608(a).

9. TRUE. Before the February 15 withdrawal of $15,000 the account contained $18,000, at least $10,000 of which was proceeds. After the withdrawal, the account had $3,000. Under the lowest intermediate balance test, the $10,000 of proceeds is considered to be the last money to be withdrawn. Because $3,000 was left after the withdrawal, this amount is traceable to the money that was deposited as proceeds. See § 9-315(b).

10. TRUE. A corporation is located in the state of registration. § 9-307(e).

11. TRUE. Sally has a PMSI in consumer goods, which is perfected automatically. § 9-309(1).

12. FALSE. Although Peter is a BIOC, he takes free only of security interests created by his seller, Rosy. § 9-320(1).

13. FALSE. Peter is not a casual or consumer buyer because the person from whom he purchased the computer was not holding it as consumer goods. § 9-320(2).

14. FALSE. Peter is a P/V w/o K (§ 9-317(b)), but that status does not help him because Sally had a perfected security interest.

15. TRUE. The Orange computer is proceeds. Sally's security interest was automatically perfected for 21 days, but that time has passed. The same office rule doesn't apply because Sally never filed. § 9-315(d).

16. TRUE. Sally has a PMSI, in something other than inventory. Hence, she prevails over other secured parties so long as she perfects within 20 days of the debtor's receipt of the collateral. § 9-324(a).

17. TRUE. Big Bank has a security interest in the accounts because they are proceeds. The Bank's perfection is effective as of April 1, the date on which it filed. §§ 9-315(d), 9-322(b).

18. TRUE. Sally has a PMSI, which was perfected automatically. Thus, she prevails over all other secured parties. § 9-324(a).

19. TRUE. Peter is a casual (consumer) buyer, but he takes subject to filed security interests. § 9-320(b).

20. TRUE. Peter is a casual (consumer) buyer, and thus, he takes free of unfiled security interests. § 9-320(b).

21. FALSE. Because Paula's promise to pay is itself secured, it is chattel paper, not accounts. § 9-102(a)(11).

22. TRUE. Under both § 544(a) of the Bankruptcy Code and § 9-102(a)(52) of the UCC, the trustee has a lien as of the date of the filing of the petition, and under § 9-317(a), a lien creditor takes free of an unperfected security interest.

23. TRUE. First in time–first in right rule applies. § 9-317(a). Time of perfection versus time that the lien attached. Sally perfected on October 6. Carla cannot get a lien until sometime after October 10.

24. FALSE. There is no attachment until the debtor has rights in the collateral, § 9-203, and there can be no perfection until there is attachment. § 9-308(a). Therefore, perfection did not occur until February 15. Remember, however, that in some cases, a secured party gets the earlier of the time of filing or the time of perfection. See § 9-322(a)(1): "Conflicting perfected security interests and agricultural liens rank according to priority in time of filing or perfection . . ."

25. TRUE. Checks are defined as cash proceeds. UCC § 9-102(a)(9).

26. TRUE. The note and security interest given by *B* to *D* is chattel paper. UCC § 9-102(a)(11). *S* obtains a security interest in the chattel paper because it is proceeds of the inventory. UCC § 9-315.

27. TRUE. If the secured party keeps the inventory in satisfaction of the debt, there is no obligation to account to the debtor nor is there any right to a deficiency judgment. § 9-620.

28. TRUE. *S*'s security interest will be good against *P* unless some provision of the Code gives *P* better rights. UCC §§ 9-201(a), 9-315(a)(1). *S*'s security interest was perfected automatically. UCC § 9-302(1). The primary exceptions are found in UCC § 9-320. Although *P* was a buyer in ordinary course of business, UCC § 9-320(a) does not afford *P* protection because it only allows her to take free of security interests created by the seller. *P* was not a casual buyer, UCC § 9-320(a), because he did not purchase from one holding the goods as consumer goods. *P* is a P\V w\o K, but that does not help her because *S*'s security interest was perfected before she attained that status. § 9-317(b).

29. TRUE. *S* had two security interests flowing from the two separate security agreements. There is no need to file again as to the second, as the filing would say nothing more than did the first filing. See UCC § 9-502. Thus, the one filing served to perfect the second security interest as well as the first, and S prevails under UCC § 9-322 because *S* perfected before *C*.

30. TRUE. The fact that *S* did not extend credit until after *C* loaned the money and perfected is irrelevant. The rule is first in time, with the earlier of perfection or filing being the critical time for each party. *S* filed before *C* either perfected or filed. UCC § 9-322(a).

31. TRUE. There is no restriction on the subordinate secured party's right to repossess, UCC § 9-609, or right to sell, UCC § 9-610. Nor does the Code provide that any of the proceeds must be given to the secured party with the prior security interest. See UCC § 9-608. The superior secured party is protected because the sale by the junior secured party is subject to the prior secured party's security interest, i.e., the purchaser at the repossession sale takes subject to the prior secured party's security interest.

32. FALSE. Although *S* perfected by taking possession before *C* either perfected or filed, *S*'s perfection was not continuous because there was a gap between the time that *S* returned the ring and filed. UCC § 9-308(c). Therefore, the critical time for *S* is when the financing statement was filed, January 28. Under the first to file or perfect rule, § 9-322(a), *C* prevails.

33. FALSE. The conflict here is between a PMSI and a non-PMSI in collateral that is equipment. *C* has priority because *C* has the PMSI, which prevails over all other security interests under UCC § 9-324(a), so long as the PMSI holder files within 20 days of the debtor obtaining possession of the collateral. Because the collateral is not inventory, *C* did not have to give notice to *S*. Knowledge of the prior security interest does not prevent the purchase-money secured party from taking priority.

34. TRUE. The cash is proceeds of the account in which *C* had a security interest, and proceeds on proceeds of the inventory in which *S* had a security interest. UCC § 9-315(a). The security interests of both *S* and *C* in the cash are perfected automatically. UCC § 9-315(c), (d). The first to file or perfect rule determines the priority between *S* and *C*. UCC § 9-322(a). *S* and *C* get the time of perfection or filing as to the original collateral for the purpose of determining who has priority. As between them, *S* filed first. UCC § 9-322(b).

35. TRUE. Although *S* has a PMSI, it is unperfected because the collateral is not consumer goods. See UCC § 9-302(1)(d). However, *S*'s security interest is good as against purchasers unless some section of the Code subordinates it. UCC § 9-201, 9-315(a)(1). Here, because *B* did not give value, *B* does not get better rights against *S* under UCC §§ 9-317(b) or 9-320.

36. FALSE. Both *C* and *S* have a security interest in the promise of *P* to pay (an account) as proceeds. UCC § 9-315(a)(2). Both are perfected under the "same office rule," § 9-315(b)(c), and the date of filing or perfection as to the original collateral controls as to the proceeds. UCC § 9-322(b). Because *S* filed before *C* filed or perfected, *S* prevails. Note: UCC § 9-322(b) does not give *C* preference as a purchase-money secured party because the preference only runs proceeds that are chattel paper, instruments, and certain cash proceeds.

37. TRUE. Although *S* did not perfect until after *C* made the loan, it is the time that *C* obtained a lien that is important. UCC § 9-301(1)(b), and *C*'s lien did not attach until after *S* perfected.

38. FALSE. Both *S* and *C* met the requirements for a PMSI under UCC § 9-103. When there are two parties who have this preference and one is a seller of the collateral, § 9-324(g) provides that the seller has priority.

39. FALSE. The bankruptcy stay prohibits a creditor from taking any action to collect a debt, including sale of property that has already been repossessed. 11 U.S.C § 362. *S* must petition to have the stay lifted.

40. TRUE. The financing statement is sufficient to perfect a security interest in after-acquired property even though it not refer to after-acquired property. Official Comment 1 to § 9-502.

41. FALSE. The security agreement did not describe the collateral to include equipment and the financing statement cannot expand the description in the security agreement.

42. FALSE. Because the debtor is a sole proprietorship, the financing statement must be filed under the name of the individual, not the business name. § 9-503.

43. TRUE. Sandy has a PMSI in the stereo. Sandy did not get automatic perfection because it was equipment, but she did file on February 9, less than ten days after David obtained possession. George is not a casual (consumer) buyer because his seller was not holding it as consumer goods, so he does not take free of the security interest which was unfilled at the time he bought it. George is not a BIOC because he did not purchase it from one selling goods of that kind. George is a purchaser for value without notice (P/V w/o K) and a P/V w/o K normally takes free of security interests that are unperfected at the time of the sale. However, because Sandy had a PMSI, Sandy had 20 days in which to perfect.

44. TRUE. In order to give a debtor an opportunity to bid at the auction, or get others to bid, the debtor is entitled to new notice of the new type of sale. See §§ 9-613, 9-614.

45. TRUE. Although the document reads as though title does not pass until the price is paid, Article 9 treats this as a secured transaction and title passes immediately. All that the seller has is a security interest in the goods. §§ 9-201(a)(35), 9-109(a)(1).

46. FALSE. A financing statement is valid for five years. It can be renewed by filing a continuation statement during the six months prior to the time it expires. In this problem, the continuation statement would have to be filed during the six months preceding June 1, 2006. Sally filed it too late. When a filing expires, it is as though there never was any filing; hence, there was no filing at the time that Paul purchased. § 9-515.

47. FALSE. A debtor party has the right to redeem the collateral after default, but redemption requires the debtor to pay the entire indebtedness in order to redeem. § 9-623. Because of the acceleration clause, the entire amount became due when Brigid defaulted.

48. TRUE. As to the Red computer, we have a priority problem: a secured party versus a transferee. Susie has a PMSI in the computer that was perfected by filing. (No automatic perfection because the computer was equipment, not consumer goods.) Betty is not a casual (consumer) buyer because she neither purchased it from one holding it as consumer goods nor did she buy it as consumer goods. She is not a BIOC because Dan was not in the business of selling computers. Her only status is that of a purchaser for value without knowledge, but that doesn't help her because a P/V w/o K takes subject to perfected security interest. The Blue computer can be repossessed because it is proceeds. The cash that Dan received was proceeds and when he used it to buy the new computer, the new computer became proceeds.

49. TRUE. Susie has a PMSI in the computer, perfected by filing on January 15, less than 20 days after the debtor obtained possession of the collateral. Hence, it cuts off the rights of purchasers for value who bought during the intervening days as purchasers for value without knowledge. Because that is the only status Bob has, he took subject to the security interest.

50. FALSE. True as to the inventory, but false as to the accounts because you cannot perfect by taking possession when the collateral is accounts. §§ 9-310, 9-313.

SHORT-ANSWER EXAM[1]:   (Two & one-half hours)

The questions must be answered in the space indicated. The answers cannot be longer. This places a premium on succinct, clear responses. Exams like this one test raw knowledge more than writing skills. Again, exams like this are very inclusive. There is a tremendous amount of information to impart, so sometimes you may need to use shorthand rather than full sentences. We try to demonstrate this in the sample answer, although we sometimes go ahead and explain in full sentences to make sure you can actually tell what the answer is.

This exam consists of 16 short-answer questions, as well as a few extra-credit questions. Students receive extra points for citing the relevant portions of the UCC or Bankruptcy Code (or other relevant applicable law). The suggested time for each question is noted. The suggested time for the exam is 130 minutes, with an extra 20 minutes to read the exam. The suggested time for each question reflects the relative weight that is assigned to that question.

THE TEST:

1. (5 minutes) Jeff lives next door to Lisa. Jeff loaned Lisa $1,000 and received a security interest in Lisa's very cool volleyball set, but did nothing else. Lisa hasn't paid as agreed, and Jeff wants to jump the fence and take the set. Describe Jeff's rights and obligations.

_____

_____

_____

_____

---

1. We thank Stewart Paley for allowing us to use this exam, which he gave in the fall of 2005.

2. (5 minutes) In one or two sentences, describe the two most significant benefits to debtors under New Mexico Exemption law. Or, feel free to answer this under your own state law.

_____

_____

_____

_____

3. (10 minutes) Fred has substantial assets, but recently got into some trouble. It seems that he has a tractor worth approximately $100,000, with a perfected first-priority security interest against it of $80,000. The secured party has repossessed the tractor, and after completing reasonable advertising, is holding a secured-party sale. As often happens, the expected proceeds from the sale will be approximately $70,000 (after costs).

A. If Fred knows of a place where he can buy a replacement tractor for $60,000, what should he do and why?

_____

_____

_____

_____

B. If Fred can only buy a replacement tractor for $75,000, what should he do and why?

_____

_____

_____

_____

4. (15 minutes) Dawn's Disco filed a Chapter 7 case three months ago. The company's assets have been liquidated and you've been asked to characterize and calculate the following claims, their order of priority, and the amount of proceeds each will receive. Unless otherwise noted, all claims arose six months before to the bankruptcy filing and no payments have been made.

Rapster is owed $100,000 from the sale of a "Newwave" sound system it sold to Dawn's. The $100,000 principal debt is still outstanding. Under the sale contract, interest accrues at 10 percent per annum.

Big Bank loaned Dawn's $200,000 in principal, also at 10 percent interest per annum. The $200,000 is still outstanding. Big Bank received a security interest in Dawn's existing and future equipment and, on the same day, filed a financing statement.

Ralph's sold and delivered an "Oldwave" sound system to Dawn's for $50,000. The $50,000 is still outstanding. Ralph's financed the sale, taking back a security interest in the sound system and filed a financing statement two weeks later. While not specified in the documents, Ralph's typically charges 6 percent interest on delinquent debts (which this debt has been since two months before the bankruptcy filing).

Dawn's other general creditors are owed a total of $120,000.

After costs, Dawn's assets generated the following proceeds:

Newwave sound system = $50,000

Oldwave sound system = $100,000 (The old stuff appreciates!)

All of the debtor's other equipment = $105,000

All of the debtor's inventory, accounts, and goodwill = $115,000

_____

_____

_____

_____

_____

_____

_____

_____

_____

_____

5. (5 minutes) Bobby Sue and Billy Joe own their home jointly and are jointly obligated for the following debts: a $100,000 first mortgage against their home; a $110,000 second mortgage against their home; and a $50,000 debt owed to a third creditor who just received judgment and recorded the judgment in the Recorder of Deeds Office for the county in which the home is located. The couple claim New Mexico exemptions, which allow $30,000 in equity per person.

Assume that the second mortgage holder takes the home to foreclosure sale and, after all costs, there are $200,000 of proceeds. How will the proceeds be distributed and what rights will the creditors have?

_____

_____

_____

_____

_____

_____

6. (5 minutes) This morning, an old high school friend, Danny the Debtor, rushed into your office and pleaded for help. It seems that Danny got a $20,000 loan to purchase a new computer system. Danny gave the lender a security interest in the computer system. Danny fell behind in his monthly payments, the lender repossessed the computer, and after giving proper notice and advertising, just this morning sold the computer at private sale for $10,000. While Danny's glad he doesn't have to deal with the lender anymore, he now wants his computer back because it brings him "good luck." Danny has now

come up with cash for the full debt owed to the lender (which was $15,000 before the sale) and wants your help. Advise Danny on his rights and obligations.

_____

_____

_____

_____

7. (10 minutes) Bank One wants to get a perfected security interest in all monies owed to the debtor from its customers and in all of the debtor's various bank accounts. The debtor is a car dealership that sells cars on a secured and unsecured basis. Explain what your client should do to best protect itself and draft the granting provision for the security agreement and the collateral description for the financing statement.

_____

_____

_____

_____

_____

_____

_____

_____

_____

_____

8. (10 minutes) Debtor Darla's Landscaping Business owns a number of large riding lawnmowers. Recently, Darla's needed some cash, so it obtained a $4,000 loan from Larry's Lenders and, in return, granted Larry's a perfected security interest in one of the mowers, a 2005 model XJMs Kitty. Three months later, Darla's again needed cash, so it sold the XJMs Kitty mower to Zeke (for his personal use) at an "informal yard sale" for $3,000. Darla's deposited the $3,000 in its bank account, which already had a balance of $9,500. Darla's then received a payment of $2,000 for another job, and deposited that money in the same account. Darla's then wrote business expense checks from that account for $1,000 (accounts payable), $4,000 (rent), and $2,000 (wages). Darla's then received another job payment of $4,500, which was deposited in the same account. No other deposits or withdrawals have been made. Larry's hasn't been paid in months, hears about all of this, and goes ballistic! What rights does Larry's have?

_____

_____

_____

_____

_____

9. (5 minutes) Recently, you heard about a secured party sale by a first-priority secured creditor owed $90,000 who, although they forgot to give a second-priority secured party notice of the sale or the proceeds therefrom (the second being owed $100,000), otherwise completed a commercially reasonable sale. After costs, the sale of the collateral (a bulldozer) brought $200,000 and proceeds were distributed. The second-priority secured party now wants to exercise all available rights. Advise the second-priority secured party.

10. (5 minutes) Danny has an earth-moving business, which owes its lender $90,000, secured by a first priority security interest against the company's bulldozer (which is also worth $90,000). Although the company is still operating, it has just filed a Chapter 11 bankruptcy case. Interest owed to the secured party is paid current and the company proposes to continue doing so. However, the entire debt, by its original terms, came due last week just before the bankruptcy filing. The company needs to use the bulldozer, but you've heard the judge is likely to grant the creditor's motion for relief. What are two facts you probably don't know about that would justify this result and under what law would this result be justified?

11. (5 minutes) Fred Hart and Ted O. are out having lunch. Fred needs $200 and doesn't have time to hit the bank. Ted happens to have the cash on him, so he loans it to Fred. Fred promises to pay it back next week. While talking, Ted also mentions that he's doing a big CLE in a few days, and admires Fred's sharp-looking watch. Fred hands it to Ted and says, "Go ahead and hold onto it. You'll look great, and I know you'll keep it safe." Ted says thanks and proudly wears the watch. One week later, Fred fails to pay as agreed, but says, "I'll definitely pay you next week. In the meantime, I need my watch back." Ted replies, "Sorry Fred, but you taught me well; the watch is 'goods' and I'm perfected. The watch stays with me until I've been paid." Fred huffs and blurts out: "That's just SO wrong, dude!"

Who's right and why?

12. (15 minutes) On December 1, Big Bank made a $100,000 loan to the debtor to be secured by the debtor's equipment. Big Bank's security agreement and financing statement (which was filed on December 20) read: "Debtor hereby grants secured party a security interest in all of the Debtor's equipment."

Previously, on November 5, debtor signed a security agreement in favor of Little Bank and authorized the filing of a financing statement, both of which read: "Debtor hereby grants secured party a security interest in all of the Debtor's property and assets of every kind and nature whatsoever, including all of Debtor's presently owned and hereafter acquired property and assets and all replacements, substitutions, and accessions thereto and thereof." Little Bank filed the financing statement on November 5. On December 30, Little Bank made a $200,000 loan to the debtor.

On December 25, BankEast made a $150,000 loan to the debtor also to be secured by the debtor's equipment. BankEast's security agreement and financing statement (which was filed the same day) read: "Debtor hereby grants secured party a security interest in all of the Debtor's present and future equipment." The BankEast security agreement has no future advance provisions.

On January 5, debtor's equipment vendor delivered a bulldozer to the debtor. The equipment vendor provided $200,000 of financing for the bulldozer, and the debtor signed a security agreement. The vendor's security agreement and Financing statement (which was filed on January 20) read: "Debtor hereby grants secured party a security interest in a 2005 CAT 1000HP bulldozer, serial #1000MsKitty." The vendor's description of the bulldozer has the correct make, model, and serial number.

On February 1, BankEast made an additional $100,000 loan to the debtor. The debtor signed a new security agreement for the loan, with the same granting provision as before, but BankEast did not ask for or file a new financing statement.

Six months later, the debtor went out of business and creditors began to fight. Assume the debtor was current on all of its interest payments to creditors. Also assume that except for the bulldozer, all of the debtor's other equipment was purchased before November 1. All of the debtor's equipment is worth $575,000 (with the majority of that value being the CAT bulldozer worth $400,000).

In what order of priority, and for what amounts, will the creditors be paid and why?

13. (10 minutes) Long, long, ago, in a faraway land (but still governed by the UCC), three creditors made three loans to a debtor secured by one piece of the debtor's business equipment. Without the creditors' approval, the debtor recently sold the equipment to Jenny for $10,000. The debtor, as often happens in fairy tales of this kind, has disappeared with the cash. It's now December 15, 2005, and the creditors disagree about legal rights and priority issues, and Jenny maintains that she's not involved in this dispute ("I didn't know about these guys, so it's not my problem, man."). The creditors and Jenny have sought your sage advice to sort out this mess. Please advise.

Creditor One made a loan, got a signed security agreement, and filed a Financing Statement on January 1, 1996. On March 1, 2001, Creditor One filed a new financing statement.

Creditor Two made a loan, got a signed security agreement, and filed a financing statement on March 1, 2000.

Creditor Three made a loan, got a signed security agreement, and filed a financing statement on February 1, 1999. On November 1, 2003, Creditor Three filed a continuation statement.

All financing statements and security agreements were complete, filed, and accurately described the equipment.

_____

_____

_____

_____

_____

_____

14. (10 minutes) You represent a client that made loans to two different debtors. Each loan was secured by all of the debtor's inventory, accounts, and equipment. You prepared a financing statement for each loan with all required information and did so correctly. Your paralegal then brought them to the filing office with the required filing fees. Unfortunately, the filing officer was having a "bad hair day." As to the first financing statement, the filing officer accepted it for filing and filed it, but indexed it under the wrong (and very different) debtor name. As to the second financing statement, the filing officer just apparently hit his breaking point and tossed it back to your paralegal saying, simply, "I'm just not accepting this!"

It's now six months later and you've just learned about these events. For each financing statement, assume two different scenarios and advise why the financing statement is or isn't effective.

Scenario I: A subsequent secured party lent against the same collateral after conducting a UCC-1 search and found no filings.

Scenario II: A subsequent lien creditor challenges the priority of your security interest after they also conducted a UCC-1 search and found no filings.

_____

_____

_____

_____

_____

_____

_____

_____

15. (10 minutes) Debtor borrows $100,000 from Big Bank. Big Bank's security agreement allows but does not require future advances, and grants a security interest in all of debtor's present and future equipment. Big Bank perfects by filing a financing statement on January 1.

On July 1, Debtor purchases a new printing press from Seller. Seller finances $150,000, being a portion of the purchase price for the machine, and receives a security interest in the printing press. The printing press is delivered to the Debtor on July 10, and Seller files its financing statement against the press on July 30.

On June 30, one of the Debtor's general creditors obtains a judgment for $75,000 against the Debtor. On July 20, the creditor has a writ of execution issued and causes the sheriff to levy against all of the Debtor's equipment.

Big Bank knows about the levy, but still makes two additional loans to the Debtor to be secured by the Debtor's equipment. One loan made on August 25 is for $25,000, and the other loan made on September 30 is for $30,000.

If the Debtor's only assets were the printing press and other assorted equipment, and the Debtor was liquidated today, explain how the proceeds would be distributed.

_____

_____

_____

_____

_____

_____

_____

_____

_____

_____

16. (5 minutes) Your client, Francis Factor, wishes to purchase all of the accounts of Dave's Shoe Store. Francis consults you. You check the filing records and find that a financing statement has been filed by Big Bank claiming a security interest in all of Dave's inventory. What will you advise Francis?

_____

_____

_____

Extra time? Extra credit—Classify, in Article 9 language, each of the following items of collateral:

Wrapping paper used for free gift wrapping at Borders Bookstore: _____

The three-story slide into the pool at the Tamaya Resort: _____

A lottery ticket you just bought at 7-Eleven: _____

The customer lists of Microsoft: _____

Unpasteurized milk in the hands of a dairy farmer: _____

Those big, fluffy, luxurious towels at the Tamaya Resort & Gift Shop: _____

A bulldozer in the hands of _____

[How many can you justify?] _____

ANSWERS TO THE SHORT-ANSWER EXAM:

1. A security interest can be enforced once it has attached (§ 9-203), and this has. Jeff can use "self-help" and jump the fence (§ 9-609) so long as he doesn't breach the peace, with no potential for immediate violence and reasonable timing and manner. It does not matter whether Jeff ever perfected his security interest, a fact left silent here.

2. There is an unlimited exception in New Mexico for annuities (retirement and pension funds), all insurance policies and products, and all clothing, furniture, books, and medical-health equipment. Where there is a bankruptcy, the state homestead exemption is much larger than the Federal too ($30,000 per person, doubled for married couples). NMSA 42-11-1.

3. (A) A debtor can redeem the collateral (§ 9-623) by paying the amount due. In this case, the debt has been accelerated, so it will cost Fred $80,000 to cure. If he lets the sale happen and buys the replacement tractor instead, he will only be out $70,000 ($60,000 for tractor and $10,000 for deficiency). He should buy the replacement.

    (B) Now it costs $80,000 to cure. If he lets the sale happen and buys the replacement tractor, he will be out $85,000 ($75,000 for the tractor and $10,000 for deficiency, assuming no anti-deficiency statute and valid sale), so he should cure the default instead.

4. Ralph's has a PMSI on Oldwave for the first $50,000 (without interest, not in k) (§ 9-324(a)), and will have priority over a conflicting security interest in the same collateral if the PSMI is perfected not more than 20 days after debtor receives possession. Because it was filed two weeks later, Ralph's has priority. Big Bank is a secured creditor with a total claim of $210,000, $5,000 of which is unsecured ($50,000 Oldwave + $50,000 Newwave + $105,000 other equip = $205,000). The unsecured creditors are Big Bank for $5,000, Rapster for $105,000 ($5,000 pre-petition interest), and others for $120,000, so the total unsecured creditor claims are $230,000. Free assets are $115,000, so there is a 50 percent distribution to unsecured creditors. Secured distributions are Ralph's $50,000 and Big Bank $205,000; unsecured distributions are $2,500 Big Bank, $52,500 Rapster, and $60,000 others.

5. The senior mortgage will continue to encumber the house. From the proceeds, the second mortgage will be deducted (consensual liens before exemptions) ($200,000 − $110,000 = $90,000), then the exemptions will be deducted ($60,000 for joint owners), leaving $30,000 for the judgment lien creditor, who

won't get paid the full $50,000 owed and will have to try to collect elsewhere through the execution process. The senior mortgage will still be able to foreclose after the sale, provided the debt is not paid.

6. Under § 9-623, a debtor can redeem by paying the full amount of the debt, including the secured creditor's attorneys' fees and expenses of sale. But there is no right to redeem after the sale, so Danny is out of luck. He is stuck with a $5,000 deficiency unless the sale can be challenged as not commercially reasonable.

7. Granting language: The debtor hereby grants to Bank One a security interest in all accounts, deposit accounts, chattel paper, and instruments, whether now owned or hereafter acquired, to secure all obligations owed by the debtor to Bank One of any kind, now owed or owed in the future by debtor to Bank One. Financing statement language: all accounts, deposit accounts, chattel paper, and instruments. Perfection: Bank One can perfect in accounts by filing a financing statement. For deposit accounts (bank accounts), Bank One needs control (§ 9-104), so it has three options (§ 9-314): have the deposit accounts at their bank, create a blocked account agreement with another bank, or put the account in Bank One's name, along with the debtor's. For instruments and chattel paper, Bank One is best off possessing the collateral.

8. *Darla's* loan is in default, so Larry can repossess. Larry's lien is still on the mower in the hands of Zeke because Zeke does not fit the "garage sale exception" (§ 9-320(b))—Darla is a business, not a consumer. Under § 9-315(a)(2), because Darla is not in the business of selling goods of this kind, Zeke is also not a buyer in ordinary course. Larry can repossess the mower and sell it. The balance in the account is $12,000. This is proceeds (§ 9-203(f)), commingling (§ 9-315(b)); the "lowest intermediate balance rule" says there is still enough in the account to pay his $3,000. He should go levy before the balance changes too much.

9. § 9-611 requires that the secured party send notice to the debtor, guarantors, and some lienors before sale. However, the failure to give notice does not invalidate the sale. The second lienholder now has a lien on the proceeds of the sale and can claim the right to those proceeds from the debtor who holds them, or get damages from the secured party if the funds cannot be obtained from the debtor any more.

10. This would be justified under Bankruptcy Code § 362(d)(1) if (1) no insurance on bulldozer (lack of adequate protection under (d)(1)), or (2) no maintenance of bulldozer (also a lack of adequate protection, now because of depreciation), and apparently no money to make adequate protection payments. Sounds like the bulldozer is needed in effective reorganization, but that does not matter as the secured party can prove a lack of adequate protection under § 362(d)(1).

11. A party can create a security interest and perfect it by possession instead of filing, providing there is value given, an oral agreement to grant a security interest, and the debtor has rights in the collateral. Although Ted O. is in possession of the watch, there was never any agreement (oral or otherwise) to grant a security interest in the watch. Thus, the A in VAR is missing. Fred is right. Ted O. has to give the watch back, as it was never intended as collateral. § 9-203.

12. § 9-615 determines who gets paid and in what order. The vendor of CAT gets paid first. It has a PMSI that beats all others, even though it filed afterward. (§ 9-324) Vendor gets $200,000 from CAT, leaving $200,000 in value in CAT. BankEast gets paid next. BankEast has secured debt of $250,000, and the $100,000 advance is perfected as of December 25 because its security interest relates back to when it perfected in equipment. (§ 9-322(a)(1)) So BankEast gets the remaining $200,000 from CAT. Big Bank gets $0 from CAT because it does not have an after-acquired property clause in its security agreement for equipment. The other equipment creates $175,000. Big Bank was the first to file or

perfect on this, so it has priority for $100,000. (§ 9-322(a)(1)). Little Bank has a generic and thus insufficient collateral description in its security agreement, so no security interest under § 9-108. After vendor and BankEast recover from CAT, from what's left: (1) Big Bank gets $100,000; (2) BankEast gets $50,000; (3) Little Bank gets the leftover $25,000, assuming there are no other unsecured creditors.

13. Jenny took subject to perfected security interests of Creditors 3 and 1. Creditor 3 is in first priority because it filed in February of 1999 and continued its financing statement within six months prior to expiration. Creditor 1 is in second position. Its financing statement lapsed, but Creditor 1 filed again in March of 2001. Creditor 2 has a lapsed financing statement as of the sale to Jenny so Jenny takes free of this security interest, which is unperfected.

14. The first financing statement under the first scenario was misindexed. This one is effective against both the secured party and the lien creditor under § 9-517. The second financing statement was a wrongful rejection by the filing office. This one is effective as to the lien creditor (§ 9-516 (d)) (we assume they do not search anyway), but not effective as to the secured party (§ 9-516(d) and comment 3).

15. Printing press: (1) Seller has first priority—PMSI (§ 9-324) for $150,000. Perfected on date of delivery (July 10). (2) Big Bank has second priority for $100,000, perfected on January 1, with earlier levy on July 20 (§ 9-317). (3) Big Bank also has second priority for $25,000 for the advance on August 25. This was made within 45 days of the levy on July 20, so the perfection date relates back to January 1 (§ 9-323). (4) Judgment lien creditor has third priority for $75,000 amount of levy. Perfected as of date of levy, July 20 (unless state statute says that perfection date is date of writ) (§ 9-317). (5) Big Bank has fourth priority for $30,000 amount of second advance on September 30 (§ 9-322(a)(1)). This second advance is last because it is outside the 45-day window from the time of levy, and Big Bank knew of levy. Now, if the local rules says date of writ = date of perfection, Big Bank's first advance would also take priority after the lien creditor because it is outside of 45 days. For the other equipment, Big Bank is first for $100,000 and $25,000, the judgment lien creditor is second for $75,000, and Big Bank is third for $30,000 in equipment. The seller does not have a lien on the equipment.

16. Francis, I wouldn't do that. Proceeds (defined at § 9-102 (a)(64)) are automatically covered by a security agreement per § 9-203(f). The accounts of the shoe store represent proceeds of Dave's inventory. Big Bank has first priority if Dave defaults, leaving you with nothing. The best Francis could do is ask for a subordination or standstill agreement.

EXTRA CREDIT:

A. Inventory	§ 9-102(a)(48)
B. Fixture or Equipment	§ 9-102(a)(41) or (33)
C. Account	§ 9-102(a)(2)
D. General Intangible	§ 9-102(a)(42)
E. Farm Product	§ 9-102(a)(34)

F. Equipment or Inventory	§ 9-102(a)(33) or (48)
G. Consumer Goods (personal use)	§ 9-102(a)(23)
Equipment (construct. co., etc.)	§ 9-102(a)(33)
Inventory (equipment dealer/sales)	§ 9-102(a)(48)

Table of Cases

Table of Statutes

Table of Statutes

Table of Statutes

UCC § 1-201(3) ... 77
UCC § 1-201(9) ... 157
UCC § 1-201(29) ... 20
UCC § 1-201(30) ... 20
UCC § 1-201(37) ... 22, 77
UCC § 1-201(44) ... 92
UCC § 1-201(a)(35) ... 5, 6
UCC § 1-202 ... 157
UCC § 1-203 ... 44
UCC § 1-204 ... 50
UCC § 1-208 ... 43
UCC § 1-201(b)(3) (revised Article 1) ... 77
UCC § 1-201(b)(16) (revised Article 1) ... 127
UCC § 1-201(b)(25) (revised Article 1) ... 105
UCC § 1-201(b)(35) (revised Article 1) ... 77
UCC § 1-204 (revised Article 1) ... 92
UCC § 1-205 (revised Article 1) ... 50
UCC § 1-304 (revised Article 1) ... 44
UCC § 1-309 (revised Article 1) ... 43
UCC § 2-102 ... 21
UCC § 2-202 ... 88
UCC § 2-501 ... 93
UCC § 3-302 ... 104
UCC § 7-104 ... 127
UCC § 9-102(a)(1) ... 28, 89, 173
UCC § 9-102(a)(2) ... 29
UCC § 9-102(a)(3) ... 55
UCC § 9-102(a)(5) ... 162
UCC § 9-102(a)(7) ... 85
UCC § 9-102(a)(11) ... 29
UCC § 9-102(a)(12) ... 6, 26
UCC § 9-102(a)(13) ... 31
UCC § 9-102(a)(14) ... 31
UCC § 9-102(a)(15) ... 31
UCC § 9-102(a)(20) ... 43, 153
UCC § 9-102(a)(23) ... 26
UCC § 9-102(a)(28) ... 6, 93
UCC § 9-102(a)(29) ... 30
UCC § 9-102(a)(30) ... 31
UCC § 9-102(a)(31) ... 30
UCC § 9-102(a)(33) ... 26
UCC § 9-102(a)(34) ... 27
UCC § 9-102(a)(34)(A) ... 172
UCC § 9-102(a)(41) ... 27, 132, 169
UCC § 9-102(a)(42) ... 30
UCC § 9-102(a)(43) ... 43

UCC § 9-102(a)(44) ... 26
UCC § 9-102(a)(44)(ii) ... 28
UCC § 9-102(a)(46) ... 29
UCC § 9-102(a)(47) ... 30
UCC § 9-102(a)(48) ... 27
UCC § 9-102(a)(51) ... 31
UCC § 9-102(a)(52) ... 4, 162
UCC § 9-102(a)(52)(C) ... 4
UCC § 9-102(a)(53) ... 28
UCC § 9-102(a)(56) ... 119
UCC § 9-103(a)(57) ... 175
UCC § 9-102(a)(59) ... 6, 93
UCC § 9-102(a)(65) ... 30
UCC § 9-102(a)(68) ... 164
UCC § 9-102(a)(69) ... 81
UCC § 9-102(a)(72) ... 6
UCC § 9-102(a)(73) ... 6, 20, 77
UCC § 9-102(a)(78) ... 30
UCC § 9-103(d) ... 153
UCC § 9-103A ... 172
UCC § 9-104 ... 77, 130
UCC § 9-105 ... 77, 130
UCC § 9-106 ... 77, 130
UCC § 9-107 ... 77, 130
UCC § 9-108(a) ... 85
UCC § 9-108(b) ... 86
UCC § 9-108(b)(1) ... 86
UCC § 9-108(b)(3) ... 86, 87
UCC § 9-108(b)(4) ... 87
UCC § 9-108(b)(5) ... 87
UCC § 9-108(b)(6) ... 85
UCC § 9-108(e) ... 87
UCC § 9-109(a) ... 20
UCC § 9-109(a)(1) ... 78
UCC § 9-109(a)(2) ... 22, 44
UCC § 9-109(a)(3) ... 21, 78
UCC § 9-109(a)(4) ... 21, 78, 153
UCC § 9-109(a)(5) ... 22
UCC § 9-109(c) ... 87
UCC § 9-109(d)(1) ... 23
UCC § 9-109(d)(3) ... 23
UCC § 9-109(d)(4) ... 23
UCC § 9-109(d)(5) ... 23
UCC § 9-109(d)(6) ... 23
UCC § 9-109(d)(7) ... 23
UCC § 9-109(d)(8) ... 24

Index